Unless re

Cornell International Industrial and Labor Relations Report
Number 27

Industrialization & Labor Relations

Contemporary Research in Seven Countries

Edited by Stephen Frenkel and Jeffrey Harrod

ILR Press
Ithaca, New York

Library of Congress Cataloging-in-Publication Data
Industrialization and labor relations : contemporary research in seven
countries / Stephen Frenkel and Jeffrey Harrod, editors.
    p.   cm.—(Cornell international industrial and labor
relations report ; number 27)
Includes bibliographical references and index.
ISBN 0-87546-338-X (alk. paper).—ISBN 0-87546-339-8
(pbk. : alk. paper)
1. Industrial relations—East Asia—Case studies.   2. Industrial
relations—Asia, Southeastern—Case studies.   3. Industrial
relations—South Africa.   4. Textile workers—Hong Kong.   5. Textile
workers—South Africa.   6. Industrialization—Case studies.
7. Comparative industrial relations.   I. Frenkel, Stephen.
II. Harrod, Jeffrey.   III. Series: Cornell international industrial
and labor relations reports ; no. 27.
        HD8720.5.I53   1995
        331—dc20   94-45946

Copies of this book may be ordered through bookstores or directly from

ILR Press
School of Industrial and Labor Relations
Cornell University
Ithaca, NY 14853-3901
Telephone: 607/255-2264

Printed on recycled acid-free paper in the United States of America
5   4   3   2   1

Contents

Tables

v

Figures

Abbreviations

ACD	Advisory Committee on Diversification (Hong Kong)
ACTWUSA	Amalgamated Clothing and Textile Workers' Union of South Africa
ADB	Asian Development Bank
AFTA	ASEAN Free Trade Agreement
ANC	African National Congress
ASEAN	Association of South East Asian Nations
BIE	Bureau of Industry Economics (Australia)
BTI	Board of Trade and Industry (South Africa)
CIGU	Cotton Industry Workers' General Union (Hong Kong)
CIWGU	Clothing Industry Workers' General Union (Hong Kong)
CLA	Council of Labor Affairs (Taiwan)
COSATU	Congress of South African Trade Unions
CPF	Central Provident Fund (Singapore)
CUEPACS	Congress of Unions of Employees in the Public and Civil Services (Malaysia)
EIWU	Electrical Industry Workers' Union (Malaysia)
EOI	Export-oriented industrialization
EPZ	Export processing zone
FTU	Federation of Trade Unions (Hong Kong)
GATT	General Agreement on Tariffs and Trade
GDP	Gross domestic product
GEIS	General Export Incentive Scheme
GMP	Good manufacturing practice
GNP	Gross national product
GSP	General system of preferences
HIC	Heavy Industries Corporation (Malaysia)
HIP	Heavy Industries Policy (Malaysia)
HR	Human resources
HRM	Human resource management
ICA	Industrial Coordination Act (Malaysia)

IDC	Industrial Development Corporation (South Africa)
ILO	International Labour Organisation
IR	Industrial relations
ISI	Import-substitution industrialization
LFPR	Labor force participation rate
LRA	Labour Relations Amendment (South Africa)
LTA	Long Term Arrangement regarding International Trade in Cotton Textiles (Hong Kong)
MAEI	Malaysian American Electronics Industry
MAS	Malaysian Airlines
MNC	Multinational corporation
MTBF	Mean time between failures
MTUC	Malaysian Trade Union Congress
NACTU	National Council of Trade Unions (South Africa)
NCF	National Clothing Federation (South Africa)
NEF	National Economic Forum (South Africa)
NICs	Newly industrialized countries
NICTEX	National Industrial Council for the Textile Industry (South Africa)
NPB	National Productivity Board (Singapore)
NTUC	National Trade Union Congress (Singapore)
NUM	National Union of Mineworkers (South Africa)
NUTW	National Union of Textile Workers (South Africa)
QC	Quality circles
QCC	Quality control circles
SACCOLA	South African Consultative Committee on Labour Affairs
SACOB	South African Chamber of Business
SACTU	South African Congress of Trade Unions
SACTWU	South African Clothing and Textile Workers' Union
SNEF	Singapore National Employers' Federation
SWDGU	Spinning, Weaving and Dyeing Trade Workers' General Union (Hong Kong)
Texfed	Textile Federation (South Africa)
TQM	Total quality management
TUC	Trades Union Council (Hong Kong and Kowloon)
TWIU	Textile Workers' Industrial Union (South Africa)
UMNO	United Malay National Organization
UWUSA	United Workers' Union of South Africa

Preface

The past decade has been marked by significant economic changes as many advanced and developing countries have registered very low growth rates while some countries in East Asia have continued an upward momentum. Several leading commentators have suggested that the management of human resources, or the quality of labor relations broadly defined, has been critical in limiting higher productivity in Western countries; hence, the need to implement "high-performance" or "mutual-commitment" models.

At the same time, labor relations has received much less attention as an explanatory variable in accounting for the rapid growth in productivity of the Asian "dragons" and "tigers." This partly reflects the dominance of conventional economics, whose practitioners treat worker commitment as unproblematic, either because the firms they are studying simply allocate resources according to relative prices or because employee cooperation has been secured by labor repression orchestrated mainly by strong states. Although repression is a continuing problem in some countries, in many industrializing nations, political democratization, penetration by multinational corporations, tight labor markets, and state support for (restricted) collective bargaining have opened opportunities for workers and unions. These developments raise two questions: how are employers responding to these changes, and what patterns of labor relations are emerging at the national, industry, and workplace levels?

In view of these developments and emerging issues, the editors of this volume decided to organize a conference on the theme of labor, management, and industrialization. The conference, which was held in Sydney, Australia, in September 1992, brought together scholars with a common interest in labor relations and human resources in industrializing countries.

Included in this volume is a selection of the papers, revised and updated, that were presented by the leading researchers at that conference. The papers were selected largely on the basis of the light they shed on the connection between structural factors and labor relations processes and consequences at the macro (national), meso (industry), or micro (workplace) level.

The volume complements an earlier study of trade unionism (*Organized Labor in the Asia-Pacific Region: A Comparative Analysis of Trade Unionism in Nine Countries*, ILR Press, 1993) edited by Stephen Frenkel. This volume is particularly suitable for courses in comparative international industrial relations and international human resource management. More generally, the book is intended to stimulate debate and promote further research on industrialization and labor relations so that sometime in the near future it will be possible to make systematic international comparisons and develop testable theories. These theories would relate forms or aspects of industrialization to labor relations arrangements and account for similarities and differences in industrial relations patterns and trends.

The chapters in this volume benefited from discussion at the conference and were revised in response to comments by the editors. We would like to thank the contributors for their cooperation and patience in the process of producing this volume.

Finally, the editors would like to thank Annette Mitchell for editorial and research assistance and Faith Short at ILR Press for improving the overall quality of the manuscript and guiding it through the various stages toward final publication.

Stephen Frenkel
Sydney, Australia

Jeffrey Harrod
The Hague, Netherlands

January 1995

Introduction

1

Labor, Management, and Industrial Relations: Themes and Issues in International Perspective

Stephen Frenkel and Jeffrey Harrod

The past decade has been notable for major political changes centered around the demise of communism, the rise of nationalism, and the gradual liberalization of foreign trade, highlighted by the Uruguay round of General Agreement on Tariffs and Trade (GATT) meetings, concluded toward the end of 1993. The past decade has also been a period of contrasting economic fortunes. For most developing countries outside East Asia, poverty and rising debt remain major problems. For the advanced countries, although more recently for Japan, strong economic growth has proved elusive. By contrast, economic and social progress have been most evident in the four "Asian dragons"—Hong Kong, Singapore, Taiwan, and the Republic of Korea—and the three "Asian tigers"—Malaysia, Thailand, and China. Further change is occurring as the East European countries wrestle with economic and industrial restructuring and previously war-torn "recovering countries," such as Vietnam and Kampuchea, begin to industrialize.

Economic stagnation and development are related phenomena: the concern over "deindustrialization," unemployment, and the proliferation of low-wage service sector jobs in advanced countries partly reflects the success of newly industrialized countries (NICs) in relatively labor-intensive manufacturing markets and the export of semiskilled jobs to lower-wage countries by multinational companies (MNCs). These cross-national production links appear to be extending into regional and global networks. Markets are expanding, and MNCs are pursuing interfirm ties into the NICs, whose well-educated citizens welcome employment in higher-skilled jobs.

The context of employment and work described briefly above highlights new concerns. In the advanced countries, providing employment, preferably in high-wage, high-skill jobs, figures prominently on the public policy agenda. More generally, ensuring that business and labor relations structures are conducive to innovation, high standards of quality, equity, and customer responsiveness is an increasing concern. The connection between business strategy, technology, and human resource policies, particularly vis-à-vis manufacturing workers, is attracting significant attention (Appelbaum and Batt 1993; Jürgens, Malsch, and Dohse 1993; Kochan, Katz, and McKersie 1986; MacDuffie and Krafcik 1992). Despite their growing importance, so-called knowledge workers (Drucker 1993; Quinn 1992) have been neglected by researchers. The same is true of the employment and labor practices of MNCs, whose expanding international subcontracting webs and interfirm alliances are subjects awaiting detailed scrutiny (Reich 1991:110–53).[1]

For the high-growth countries and those likely to develop rapidly in the near future, the issues center on the changes in direction that will ensure continuing economic growth. Public policy makers and senior managers must decide which markets merit the most attention and what kinds of industry intervention are feasible. Should foreign direct investment in selected sectors be encouraged under conditions that might undermine acceptable standards of protection for employees? If labor flexibility and high productivity are to support capital and knowledge-intensive activities, what labor market and industrial relations strategies should governments pursue? At the industry level, what should employer associations and unions be doing to mobilize their members in support of policies that encourage innovation, competitive success in export markets, and favorable employment opportunities? At the firm and workplace levels, the capacity of flexible technology to produce customized items efficiently at lower volumes and higher quality means that neo-Taylorist work arrangements can no longer be taken for granted.[2] Decisions must be made regarding new forms of job design and work organization and the extent to which information and consultation are shared among managers and employees. With the spread of education and accompanying demands for participation, mechanisms for ensuring equitable treatment in the workplace are also on management's agenda.

A distinguishing feature of this collection is that the contributors focus on these issues in countries that are not advanced societies. These include both newly industrialized countries—Hong Kong, Singapore, South Korea, and Taiwan—and developing countries—Malaysia, South Africa, and Thailand. Change is a central feature of industrialization, and the industrial relations consequences of change are evident at national, industry, and enterprise/workplace levels. Accordingly, the volume is organized into three parts, each focusing on changes in labor relations policies, structures, and practices at these different levels. More will be said about the book's organization and content later. Here only two points need highlighting.

First, the volume complements rather than duplicates recent research on labor subjugation (Deyo 1989; Southall 1988), trade unionism (Frenkel, ed., 1993), and labor relations systems (Deery and Mitchell 1993) in industrializing countries. This is in part because of the variety of theoretical frameworks used by the contributors. This relates to our second point: issue-oriented research conducted at different levels of analysis necessitates theoretical pluralism based on ideas from several disciplines. As we will argue, however, each of the original papers included in this volume is informed by, or engages with, at least one of three perspectives on industrialization described below.

Our aims in publishing this collection are threefold: first, to provide information and analysis not readily available elsewhere; second, to stimulate thinking and discussion about the relationship between industrialization and labor relations in the contemporary international economy; and third, to present an array of issues and perspectives that may encourage further research on the NICs and developing countries.

The remainder of this chapter is organized into two sections. In the first section, we outline, in turn, the independent nation, dependency, and multiple path perspectives on industrialization. These frames of reference generate research issues that connect labor relations and the process of industrialization. Key studies in these three traditions are briefly reviewed, and readers are briefly referred to subsequent chapters. The features and content of the remaining nine chapters are highlighted in the second section.

Theoretical Perspectives on Industrialization and Labor Relations Research Issues

The unifying theme of this volume is the impact of industrialization on labor relations, broadly defined.[3] Industrialization is a term normally applied to countries or regions. It is indicated by long-term economic growth rates and trends in industrial and occupational structures and human capital endowments. Industrialization is based on a variety of external (international) and internal economic relationships, typically involving various state institutions, business, representatives of labor, and other interest groups.

Theories of industrialization are typically based on one of three views on a country's external relationships. The first view is the *independent nation perspective*. Proponents of this perspective assume that national leaders are able to devise and implement development strategies that are relatively independent of those followed in other countries. An example of this perspective is the theory of industrialization advanced by C. Kerr and his colleagues (1960), in which the strategy of industrialization and its institutional conditions are assumed to depend on the type of domestic elite that secures power when the industrial sector is rapidly beginning to grow.

Another example of this perspective is B. Sharma's (1991) stage model of industrialization, which suggests that countries go through three stages: a beginning phase, which signals the start of industrialization; a rapid-growth phase, when the elites attempt to mobilize emerging interest groups, including unions, to pursue the primary goal of national development; and a third phase, when industrialization has achieved momentum and compromises are reached between the state and the major interest groups. Sharma's model allows for "reverse transformation," that is, a return to an earlier phase.

A major problem with the independent nation perspective is that its adherents underestimate the impact of international relationships in sustaining elites and influencing their policies. Although this impact varies over time and by nation, such a view clearly is untenable for most of the postwar period, dominated as it was by the Cold War. Either the United States or the Soviet Union exerted considerable influence on the economic and political affairs of industrializing nations, or the competition between superpowers provided a critical contextual explanation for the role of the state and work force responses to authoritarian rule (Haggard 1990).

The second frame of reference is the *dependency perspective,* which grew out of the preceding critique but focused on the influence of the West, particularly the United States. Industrialization was seen as being dependent on international relationships in two ways. First, followers of this view assumed that the configuration of power in an industrializing country, including the nature of industrialization, was dependent on foreign economic organizations (MNCs), supported by powerful states. Second, the assumption was that this dependence benefited the core advanced countries but led to the underdevelopment of less developed, peripheral countries (Frank 1967; Gereffi 1983, chap. 1). This perspective was unable to account, however, for the rapid and apparently relatively egalitarian nature of industrialization in Japan and the East Asian NICs. Hence, the third perspective on industrialization.

Proponents of the *multiple path perspective* make no assumptions about the relative importance of international relations except to note that it is one among several sets of factors that are likely to explain similarities and differences in national patterns of industrialization (Ellison and Gereffi 1990; Harrod 1987).[4] According to this view, and notwithstanding some similarities and differences between countries in the same region, East Asian and Latin American countries have tended to follow different paths. The former countries have tended to emulate Japan, while the latter have been more influenced by the American experience (Fajnzylber 1990). In short, the East Asian NICs industrialized more recently, mainly on the basis of export-oriented industrialization (EOI), emphasizing light manufacturing products. In several Latin American countries, exploitation of natural resources and import-substitution industrialization (ISI) formed the basis for economic growth (Gereffi 1990:3–4; Haggard 1990, chap. 7). Although the question of identifying the key agents of economic development is an empirical issue, proponents of this perspective tend to emphasize the state's role in forging and implementing specific development strategies. As we shall see, they claim this role has major implications for the patterns of industrial relations that emerge.

We turn now to a discussion of the implications for industrial relations of the independent nation, dependency, and multiple path perspectives of industrialization outlined above. Although references are made to several chapters in this volume, some of the contributions attempt to combine and indeed transcend these perspectives. For example, S. Chiu and D. A. Levin's (chap. 7) explanation for the different labor relations outcomes arising from the restructuring of the Hong Kong textile and garment industries emphasizes sectoral organization rather than the changing division of world labor or the role of the state.

Independent Nation Perspective. Leading proponents of the independent nation perspective argued that, in spite of differences in resources, history, and culture, over time, industrializing countries would tend to develop similar institutions and norms. This convergence thesis, as it came to be known, was based on the functionalist proposition that modern technology required so-called modern institutions and attitudes and that these were broadly typified by the leading industrial country, the United States (Kerr et al. 1960). In industrial relations, this meant a tendency for the state in industrializing countries to establish a bargaining framework that would facilitate collective bargaining between professional managers (or their representatives) and mature trade unions. Faced with the persistence of major societal differences, particularly between state socialist and advanced capitalist countries, Kerr (1983:86) subsequently argued that it was the determination of elites to perpetuate themselves and "inertia, inefficiencies, resource constraints, and the holding power of any antagonistic preindustrial beliefs" that prevented convergence. He nevertheless maintained that when convergence did occur it was most noticeable in workplace relations.[5]

Sharma's (1991) theory also suggests that, assuming there is no reversion to a previous stage of industrialization, convergence will occur in the industrial relations patterns of industrializing countries. This argument also focuses on the development strategies of elites, especially the probable political and industrial relations consequences at different stages of economic development. In brief, in the beginning stage, the industrializing elite's primary interest is in seeking alliances to maintain its authority in the newly independent country. This means forging close ties between unions and government. In the second stage, this alliance becomes strained as union demands grow in the wake of increasing prosperity. The state is committed to achieving sustainable economic growth, however, so that conflict and the state repression of unions ensue. In time, this conflictual pattern gives way to a cooperative pattern, characteristic of the third stage of industrialization.

Further growth makes a country less dependent on holding down domestic consumption, thereby generating internal savings, and appear more attractive to foreign capital, thus sustaining investment and maintaining prosperity. In other words, the state can afford to grant concessions to the union movement and so induce employee cooperation. According to Sharma (1991:94), in granting these concessions, the state holds out the possibility of guided collective bargaining along state corporatist lines; Singapore is an exemplar in this regard (Deyo 1989). The stage theory of convergence implies that countries at the same stage of industrialization will tend to have similar industrial relations patterns.

A third convergence thesis has been advanced by R. Dore (1973, 1989), who argues that Japan, as a relatively successful late developer, is the most appropriate model for industrializing countries. He asserts that technological change, large corporations, an increase in the relative importance of human capital, and reasonably powerful trade unions form the basis of a prosperous, modern society. With this context in mind, Dore suggests that early and late developers are converging on what he calls an "organization-oriented enterprise," characterized by their adoption of key elements of large Japanese manufacturing firms. These include a sharp distinction between "core" and "peripheral" workers; internal labor markets for core employees; enterprise-specific training; single rather than multiemployer bargaining with a single, enterprise-oriented union; and employee involvement in decision making, as well as other measures to increase employee commitment to the organization (Dore 1989). Hence, we can expect convergence on the Japanese model of employment relations.

The convergence issue is explicitly addressed in chapter 3 by S. Kuruvilla in an analysis of industrialization and labor relations in Malaysia and in chapter 4 by J. Begin, whose focus is on Singapore. In addition, chapter 5, by A. Joffe, J. Maller, and E. Webster, examines South Africa's recent history of industrialization with particular reference to trends in trade unionism. In brief, the empirical evidence does not support the versions of convergence promoted by Kerr and his colleagues or by Dore.

Sharma's thesis is refuted by Kuruvilla in discussing Malaysia. Similarly, Sharma's thesis does not appear to explain trade union trends or wider changes in South African labor relations. His thesis may be applicable to Singapore, but Begin's analysis, which concentrates on recent government policy and labor relations practices, is unsuitable for appraising this particular version of the convergence argument.

Before summarizing our position on convergence theory, mention should be made of an influential variant of the convergence on Japan thesis that focuses on the workplace rather than the national level. Although restricted to the world auto industry, the argument can be generalized to manufacturing. J. P. Womack, D. T. Jones, and D. Roos (1990) interpret their research findings as demonstrating the superiority of lean production systems (used more by Japanese firms) over mass (i.e., neo-Taylorist) and craft manufacturing arrangements.[6] Japanese human resource practices, as described by Dore (1973, 1989), complement just in time (JIT) and total quality manufacturing (TQM) systems. This points to a convergence on Japanese manufacturing and human resource systems, a proposition Frenkel challenges in chapter 9 in his analysis of workplace relations in two subsidiaries of a U.S. MNC.

To conclude, we believe that convergence on a particular model of industrial relations is problematic on both theoretical and empirical grounds. First, technology permits a variety of forms of work organization and labor relations. Second, sustained economic growth has not required large enterprises or strong unions. Third, because countries at a similar stage of development are likely to differ in resources, size, history, and geopolitical position, their development patterns are likely to vary and hence we can expect different forms and trends in industrial relations. Fourth, few countries conform to the simple stage model Sharma (1991) outlined. Some sectors may be more advanced than others so that at earlier stages of industrialization it may be difficult to identify a national industrial relations system. Moreover, even if various stages of development are distinguishable, countries may become frozen at a particular stage without this necessarily impeding changes in industrial relations. This is because, as noted earlier, labor relations may be strongly influenced by political dynamics, which are likely to be triggered by a variety of factors, not simply major economic change.

Fifth, and finally, as noted above and according to previous research (Frenkel, ed., 1993; Poole 1986), there is little evidence at the national level that unions or industrial relations systems in developing and newly industrializing countries are converging on any single pattern. Research informed by the independent nation perspective and the idea of convergence should not be totally discounted, however. The extent of national independence varies: some states have been able to pursue relatively independent paths, as in the cases of Myanmar (Burma) and China, while others, for example, Taiwan and the Republic of Korea (hereafter Korea), have been highly dependent on the United States. Where states have become dependent on a larger nation or international alliance for security and economic viability, or where national governments have ceded authority to supranational institutions (such as the European Union), institutional convergence, including convergence in industrial relations structures and processes, can be anticipated. This varies, however, according to the extent of dependence and may take considerable time. It is likely to be most evident where dependence is multifaceted and points toward increasing political integration. This being so, convergence might be expected to occur between countries moving toward supranational, regional integration. Such convergence will coexist, however, with divergent trends between countries outside or in other regional blocs.

Dependency Perspective. The dependency perspective tends to inform studies of the changing world division of labor. Industrialization of previously underdeveloped countries (the periphery) is viewed mainly as a consequence of substantial foreign direct investment and/or networks linking Third World factories with production centers and markets in advanced countries (the core). Some authors claim that manufacturing in the developing countries and the NICs is displacing rather than simply complementing this activity in the advanced countries (Fröbel, Heinrichs, and Kreye 1980).

Capital is said to be attracted to peripheral countries for a variety of reasons, including low labor costs, flexible and acquiescent workers, emerging market demand, limited taxation, freedom to repatriate profits, and political stability. Dependence on foreign direct investment implies that governments vigilantly uphold the interests of capital against labor by such measures as the repression of independent unionism (Munck 1988). Control at the workplace is said to depend mainly on "primitive Taylorization" and/or "peripheral fordism" (Lipietz 1987:74–81). The former arrangement is characterized by the employment of young female workers in low-skilled, hierarchically organized, labor-intensive, export-oriented work, while "peripheral fordism" combines mechanization of production with neo-Taylorist work organization. There are limited but growing proportions of skilled workers, high levels of accumulation, and rising consumption demands fueled by domestic expansion.

The dependency perspective also suggests questions regarding the diffusion of new management practices. Japanese or other forms of "high-performance" human resource management practices (Kenney and Florida 1993; Lawler 1992), including "lean production" systems (Womack, Jones, and Roos 1990) more generally, compete with one another for attention by managers and policy makers in developing and newly industrializing countries. Is choice between these workplace systems a necessary requirement for competing in world markets?

The superiority of any particular human resource system or manufacturing arrangement has yet to be proved universally both across industries and across countries. Nevertheless, the matter of the extent of such technology transfer and its impact is important. Deyo, in chapter 2, addresses this issue in his analysis of contemporary labor practices in Thailand, with particular reference to the auto and textile industries. Frenkel, in chapter 8, as mentioned earlier, and A. Hiramoto, in chapter

10, examine the labor relations patterns of U.S. and Japanese MNC subsidiaries respectively. They show considerable transfer of home-country practices to subsidiaries in Malaysia and Taiwan, but implementation and outcomes are mediated by the local context. These case studies do not lend themselves to evaluating the impact of MNC labor relations policies on local labor markets and labor practices. Kuruvilla (chap. 3) and Begin (chap. 4) explore this issue, however, in their discussions of MNC influence in Malaysia and Singapore respectively.

The dependency perspective suffers from four major misconceptions. First, it exaggerates the role of MNCs as direct investors or as production and marketing nodes of local firm networks in industrializing countries. Thus, over the 1980–89 period, foreign direct investment in developing countries constituted less than a third of aggregate international, long-term net resource flows, considerably less than official loans and grants. More attention therefore needs to be paid to the conditions attached by donors to these forms of capital inflows and to their implications for labor relations policies.

Second, foreign direct investment outside the advanced countries has been highly concentrated. According to the World Bank (1991:24), "Just twenty developing economies, mainly in Asia and Latin America, accounted for 90 percent of the net flows between 1981 and 1990."

Third, this perspective understates the complexity of the sources and composition of foreign direct investment, which complicates any picture of supposed MNC economic domination. Thus, although most foreign direct investment emanated from the United States, Japan, and the United Kingdom, investment by firms based in the four Asian NICs (Hong Kong, Korea, Singapore, and Taiwan) overtook Japanese firms in the 1980s as the largest investor in Southeast Asia (Lim and Pang 1991; Renshaw 1993:308–9). In addition, the implications of the mix of foreign and local investment in developing countries and hence the impact of the foreign control of companies is complex and difficult to evaluate, a point highlighted by H. Hill (1993) in relation to Indonesia. Fourth, the state's role in harmonizing the national interest with MNC objectives and practices is underplayed, a process clearly evident in Singapore, which is highly dependent on foreign direct investment (Rodan 1989).

These comments nevertheless raise the issue of dependence on exports to world markets and appropriate human resource and labor relations policies in the context of flexible technology and intensified competition between NICs, developing countries, and emerging, "recovering" countries. Deyo, in chapter 2, considers the case of Thailand from this perspective, while Chiu and Levin, in chapter 7, illustrate how Hong Kong's textile and clothing firms have restructured in quite different ways to remain competitive.

A significant limitation of the dependency perspective is that it fails to distinguish different countries adequately according to their patterns of economic development and so cannot explain these variations. For example, Malaysia and South Africa have roughly similar average standards of living (see table 1.1) but have had quite different development paths. Malaysia has relied far more on foreign direct investment in export-oriented manufacturing (chap. 3) compared with South Africa, where import substitution, mainly on the basis of domestic capital, has been more the norm (chap. 5). Related to the above, the dependency perspective underestimates the often critical role of the state in steering and controlling capital in the interests of national development (Amsden 1989; Wade 1990).

Multiple Path Perspective. The multiple path perspective, which tends to be state-centered, has been most consistently pursued by Deyo (1987, 1989) in analyzing labor in Hong Kong, Singapore, Korea, and Taiwan. He has, however, mainly sought to explain labor weakness, a supposedly common denominator, rather than differences in labor relations patterns in these countries. The essence of Deyo's argument is that the state's role prior to industrialization is important.

In the case of the four Asian NICs, the state consolidated its power and was thus in a position to preempt emerging union opposition and shape its future course. Economic growth conferred legitimacy on an authoritarian, interventionist state, although Hong Kong was something of an exception in this regard. State functionaries were able to insulate themselves from influence by interest groups, including independent unions, which were repressed and later replaced by official unions or marginalized, as in Hong Kong.

Workers, according to Deyo (1989, chap. 6), were divided: many unmarried, young females were employed in insecure jobs in light industry. They worked for low wages doing low-skilled work. The only workers who developed an organized opposition, most evident in Korea, were the more skilled male workers in heavy industry. Other employees had to contend with various forms of management control based on the cultural characteristics of the four societies. These included patriarchy (small family firms in Hong Kong and Taiwan), communal paternalism (large firms in Hong Kong and Taiwan), bureaucratic paternalism (MNCs employing higher-level personnel), and patrimonialism (large firms in Korea) (Deyo 1989, chaps. 5 and 6).

Although Deyo convincingly argues that the state played a strong role in limiting worker opposition in the four Asian NICs, it does not necessarily follow that the state is the critical factor in explaining patterns of labor relations in these societies. Indeed, as Deyo makes plain, apart from limited collective protest, there is considerable diversity in the labor control systems in the four Asian NICs, so it is reasonable to anticipate diverse patterns of management-employee relations. This point is supported by evidence on trade unionism in these countries (see Frenkel, ed., 1993).

Apart from the state's role, what factors might account for the differences in the four Asian NICs? Clearly, industrial structure, local social structure and culture, and management organization and style are prime candidates. Deyo (1989:196–208 and chap. 3) does not provide a detailed empirical analysis of these conditions. T. Kim (chap. 9) goes some way toward redressing this issue by describing human resource management (HRM) in large Korean manufacturing firms. It is useful to compare countries where the state has recently pursued different development strategies—for example, Hong Kong, where the state has strongly supported market mechanisms, and Singapore, where the state has a guided, high-technology strategy (Haggard 1990, chap. 5).

Exploring changes in development strategy in the same country is also illuminating, for such reorientations can be expected to lead to changes in labor relations policies and patterns (see chap. 3). More generally, some states may pursue contradictory policies, such as Korea (chap. 9), or be too weak (Kampuchea), unstable (Nigeria), or bureaucratically incapable (Thailand) of implementing consistent development strategies. Consequently, industrial relations may reflect economic and industry-related factors, and political crises, rather than the hand of a strong state.

There is another emerging area of research that focuses on the impact of political change. The role of political change as a major influence on labor relations has been explored in a recent comparative historical study of eight Latin American labor movements (Collier and Collier 1991). R. B. Collier and D. Collier use what they refer to as a critical junctures framework to explain such relatively enduring aspects of politics as the extent of political polarity or cohesion among parties; state or party incorporation of labor; patterns of sectoral and class coalitions; and the extent of stability and conflict. Critical historical junctures or periods of substantial change are said to differ from one country to another, leading to distinct institutional legacies (Collier and Collier 1991, chap. 1).

The notion of historical turning points has also prompted explanations of major changes in the industrial relations frameworks of several advanced societies (Cox 1987; Frenkel 1986; Korpi 1978:80–86). In their analysis of U.S. labor relations, D. M. Gordon, R. Edwards, and M. Reich (1982) have argued that the emergence of crisis and the subsequent institutional restructuring are closely associated with long-term swings in the pace of capital accumulation.

The critical juncture, or crisis, explanation has a number of limitations, including identifying these historical turning points and establishing their relative importance compared with other factors that operate subsequently. More important, because critical junctures occur infrequently, they are not geared to explaining variations in labor relations patterns in the intervening period. Nonetheless, the political change perspective is valuable in directing our attention to countries where major political change has occurred recently or is currently taking place so that the processes and consequences for industrial relations can be studied. Examples of such countries that are examined in this volume include Korea, Thailand, Taiwan, and South Africa, which are in the process of transformation from state authoritarianism to more democratic regimes. The role of politics is particularly pertinent to the dynamics of labor relations at national (chap. 5) and industry levels in South Africa (chap. 6) and in meeting the requirements of militant workers employed in large manufacturing enterprises in Korea (chap. 9).

In summary, taken together, the three perspectives discussed above serve four useful purposes. First, they provoke debate by providing contrary interpretations of key processes, for example, the characteristics and effects of industrialization. Second, they emphasize different explanatory factors. For example, as noted earlier, the dependency approach focuses on the international economy, particularly the role of MNCs, while the multiple path perspective is state-centered. Closer scrutiny of key variables and theoretical synthesis are clearly needed. Third, the limitations of these perspectives and their attendant implications for industrial relations in a changing world underscore the need for theories more closely related to emerging features of the world political economy. These include the fragmentation of nation-states; the growth of supranational trading and political entities; the increase in the flow of capital, labor, and knowledge internationally; and the trend from cost to quality and service-based competition in global markets based on advances in information technology.

Features and Content of the Volume

The nine chapters that follow address a variety of issues in selected developing and newly industrializing countries. Key characteristics of these countries are shown in table 1.1, together with comparable data for two leading advanced countries, Japan and the United States.

Several points are worth noting. First, six of the seven countries addressed in this volume are located in East Asia: the NICs, at a higher average standard of living, in Northeast Asia, and the developing countries in Southeast Asia. In broad terms, these countries have recently experienced rapid and sustained economic growth based mainly on the export of low-cost manufacturing goods (World Bank 1993).[7] The NICs' higher labor costs have, however, led to an emphasis on advanced-technology products—for example, semiconductors in Korea and computers in Taiwan—based on substantial postwar investment in education and vocational

Table 1.1. Economic and Educational Data for Nine Countries, 1991

	GNP in U.S. $, per capita	Percentage of GDP		Average annual GDP growth, in percent (1980–91)	Real manufacturing earnings growth per employee (1980–90)	Foreign trade as percentage of GDP	Percentage of youth in secondary schools (1990)
		Industry	Services, etc.[a]				
Developing Countries							
Malaysia	2,520	41.7	38.9	5.7[b]	2.6	90.5	56
South Africa	2,560	44	51	1.3	0.2	24.8	67[c]
Thailand	1,570	39[b]	49[b]	7.9[b]	5.9	43.7	32
Newly Industrialized Countries							
Hong Kong	13,430[d]	25	75	6.9	4.9	144.1	74.1[e]
Singapore	14,210	38[b]	62[b]	6.6[b]	5.0	196.7	69
South Korea	6,330	45[b]	47[b]	9.6[b]	7.4	31.6	87
Taiwan	8,788	42.5	53.8	7.6	7.3[f]	46.8	86.2
Advanced Countries							
Japan	26,930	42[b]	56[b]	4.2[b]	2.0	13.5	96
United States	22,240	29[b,g]	69[b,g]	2.6[b]	0.7	12.5	92

Sources: Bamber and Lansbury, eds., 1993; Census and Statistics Department, Hong Kong, 1992a; Directorate-General of Budget Accounting and Statistics 1989; FEER 1994; Kuruvilla, chap. 3, table 3.1; International Institute for Management Development 1993; World Bank 1993.

[a]Excludes construction, electricity, water, and gas, which together with mining and manufacturing are included in the industry category. Includes unallocated items not included in agriculture or industry.

[b]GDP and its components are at purchaser values.

[c]Data are for 1991.

[d]Data refer to GDP.

[e]Data are for 1991.

[f]Data are for 1980–89.

[g]Data are for 1990.

training (Vogel 1991; World Bank 1993:43–46). This is only roughly indicated by the data on secondary schooling in table 1.1 (which probably underestimate the proportion of Singapore's youth in secondary education), but they nevertheless point to the high proportion of youth receiving secondary schooling.

An alternative but important response by the NICs to their higher labor costs is the networking that is occurring across borders by firms in search of lower manufacturing costs. This process of restructuring is highlighted by a shift in manufacturing facilities from Hong Kong and Taiwan to the southern provinces of China (see chap. 7; Frenkel 1993b:n16, 349).

The impressive records of the Asian NICs and of such developing countries as Malaysia and Thailand stand in contrast to those of most African and Latin American countries, where the connection between industrialization and labor relations has understandably attracted less attention. South Africa—the most industrialized nation in Africa—is addressed in this volume, partly in the context of "stalled industrialization" and for three additional theoretical reasons. First, in contrast to the other countries referred to above but like many South American countries, South Africa has relied mainly on exports of primary commodities (particularly minerals) and the import substitution of manufacturing goods to maintain economic growth. Second, as noted earlier, its politics at the time of writing are at a critical juncture and so are likely to stimulate further major changes in labor relations.[8] Third, the strength of the union movement, coupled with the transition to majority rule, holds out the possibility of some form of societal corporatism, in contrast to the many NICs and developing countries that have embraced a variant of authoritarian corporatism.[9]

As mentioned at the outset, change is a central theme of this volume. In some cases the focus is on analyzing the relationship between economic and industrial developments on the one hand and union or broader labor relations changes on the other (chaps. 3 and 5). In other cases, the authors examine various factors contributing to stability and change in management strategy and organization and hence having employment and labor relations consequences (chaps. 7 and 8).

Another common theme of the volume is that the contributors rely more on qualitative than on quantitative analysis. This is largely for three reasons. First, much of this work is exploratory: the field is being mapped, variables are being identified and clarified, and preliminary investigations of relationships between variables are still being conducted. Second, many of the issues being studied are more appropriately analyzed using qualitative methods. The nature and impact of complex institutions cannot easily be transformed into numbers. Third, in some countries, official data are often unreliable and therefore unsuitable for quantitative analysis. In addition, primary data are difficult to collect without a sound knowledge of the local language, strong contacts with gatekeepers in high positions, and considerable time to negotiate access to research sites.

The final common denominator of this volume is that many of the contributors include comparative analysis. Deyo (chap. 2) and Begin (chap. 4), for example, make explicit international comparisons; Chiu and Levin (chap. 7) focus on an interindustry comparison; and Frenkel (chap. 8) and Hiramoto (chap. 10) compare plants owned by American and Japanese MNCs respectively. Other contributors highlight historical differences in patterns of labor relations. Kuruvilla (chap. 3), for example, contrasts labor relations in Malaysia under varying development strategies, while Joffe, Maller, and Webster (chap. 5) and J. Maree and S. Godfrey (chap. 6) analyze the transformation of labor organization in South Africa. Finally, Kim (chap. 9) explores HRM in large South Korean firms, contrasting the traditional approach with a new system geared to the needs of high-technology production and the expectations of more assertive, educated employees.

Although the contributors are careful not to restrict their analyses to factors operating at a single level, the chapters are grouped according to whether the studies are focused mainly at the macro (national), meso (industry), or micro (enterprise/workplace) level.

Part I contains four chapters that analyze changing labor relations at the national level. In the first of these chapters, Deyo (chap. 2) focuses on the major features of contemporary export-oriented industrialization in Thailand with reference to developments in two key industries, automobile manufacturing and clothing. He concludes that in a period when industry is caught in a "sandwich trap" between competition from below (from "recovering" and other less developed countries) and from above (the NICs), the state could be expected to play a major role in facilitating skill formation and innovation-oriented human resource practices. Instead, the Thai state—influenced in part by international funding bodies and arguably by political instability—has relied increasingly on market forces, resulting in firms that tend to adopt cost-cutting approaches to human resources. This, according to Deyo, has led to increasing inequality, both within advanced branches of the economy and more generally. Deyo remains skeptical about whether this approach will be sufficient to ensure rapid economic growth over the longer term.[10]

In chapter 3, Kuruvilla suggests that "it is not the logic of industrialism or the level of industrialization per se but the choice of an industrialization strategy and the shifts between such strategies that influence changes in industrial relations policies." He focuses on the shifts in state industrialization strategy in Malaysia, or what he terms the "moments of transition," to explain changes in labor relations policies and practices. An earlier ISI period, between 1957 and 1977, is characterized by its relative union autonomy and restricted pluralism. This differs from the subsequent EOI period (1980 onward), when labor repression, marginalization of unions, and an emphasis on cost containment, in part influenced by pressure from MNCs, constitute the key elements of government policy. Many of these policies were apparently initiated during the period of transition from ISI to EOI in the years 1977–80. In chapter 4, Begin evaluates the success of Singapore's contemporary industrial relations practices in the context of a strongly articulated state development strategy that emphasizes skill formation and flexibility associated with the transition to a society based on advanced technology. A systematic comparison of industrial relations along several dimensions relating to system effectiveness is made between Singapore, Japan, Germany, the United States, and the United Kingdom. Begin argues that Singapore's industrial relations practices remain less effective than anticipated, resulting in a hybrid system influenced not only by state development policy but by emerging technology, MNC practices, and local culture. The preliminary evidence therefore does not support a convergence argument.

Industrialization in South Africa and the emergence of a new type of unionism is the subject of chapter 5. Joffe, Maller, and Webster describe how the postwar period, dominated by a "racial Fordist" system of production and white craft unionism, gave way in the 1970s to a broader-based, militant social movement unionism that linked struggles in the townships with those in the factories. Toward the end of the 1980s, major changes in labor legislation and the legalization of black political parties, and, in 1990, freedom for black leaders, led to the dismantling of apartheid and the beginning of a political transition to majority rule. These changes, together with the lifting of sanctions, provided an opportunity for a new democratic partnership between a relatively strong union movement and the state. Notwithstanding the difficulties of creating and sustaining "strategic unionism," Joffe, Maller, and Webster are optimistic about its prospects in the new South Africa.

Part II contains two industry-level studies. In chapter 6, Maree and Godfrey provide a historical overview of the South African textile industry, setting it in the wider context of the manufacturing sector and thereby complementing Joffe, Maller, and Webster's analysis in chapter 5. Four phases of growth are identified. Following the second and crisis phase, in the 1980s, the third phase is characterized by efforts at restructuring in order to move from import substitution to export promotion. Government assistance to employers without any substantial union involvement had limited impact. Meanwhile, unions in the textile industry had merged and leaders of the large textile industrial union began to pursue a strategy intended to improve industrial competitiveness and maintain employment and earnings opportunities for union members. Maree and Godfrey explain the switch from militant abstentionism to proactive engagement and show how, in the early 1990s, this emergent "strategic unionism" has encouraged a tripartite approach to the industry's problems. Strategic unionism, they argue, is a possible precursor to democratic corporatism at the meso level and thereby complements, and at the same time is supported by, a trend toward democratic corporatism at the macro level, suggested in the preceding chapter.

Chiu and Levin's analysis in chapter 7 of industrial restructuring and labor relations in Hong Kong's textile and garment sectors provides both a useful comparison with changes in the South African textile industry and highlights differences between the two sectors in Hong Kong. First, contemporary restructuring was undertaken earlier than in South Africa. According to the authors, restructuring arose mainly from pressure by the advanced countries to limit Hong Kong's exports and competition from other East Asian countries, particularly China. Second, in contrast to South Africa, in Hong Kong, unions and the state continue to play a limited role in the textile industry, although more so than in the clothing sector.[11] The authors highlight substantial differences in the processes and industrial relations outcomes regarding restructuring in Hong Kong's clothing and textile industries. Their analysis emphasizes the concept of sectoral organization. This notion refers to a combination of technical, economic, and institutional features of particular industries that over time result in distinctive industrial relations contexts. These contexts in turn explain variations in the form and consequences of industrial restructuring.

Part III of the volume focuses on the enterprise, particularly human resource policies and labor relations at the workplace level. In chapter 8, Frenkel investigates patterns of workplace relations in two subsidiaries of the same U.S. MNC, located in Malaysia and Taiwan respectively. Despite differences, the institutions share a common feature in encouraging management to regard "labor as a tradable commodity, subject to limited protective rights, rather than as a resource necessitating continuous investment." This factor, together with features of the product market and several intraorganizational variables, are advanced to explain the persistence of neo-Taylorist workplace relations patterns at the two plants, including a slight tendency toward lean production at the Taiwan establishment. Frenkel finds the impact of such characteristics of MNCs as their corporate nationality and management ideology, strategy, style, and organization to be important. He concludes that there is little evidence for convergence on the Japanese system of manufacturing or human resource management.

The problematic of Kim's analysis in chapter 9 is similar to that of Begin's in his discussion of Singapore in chapter 4, namely, the need for a more efficient, flexible, and commitment-enhancing system of HRM appropriate for manual employees of Korean *Chaebol*s (large, diversified enterprise groups). Kim highlights the unique characteristics of Korea's variant of neo-Taylorist patterns of work relations. These include intermittent hiring based on personal contacts, a legal restriction on redundancies, the employment of workers with higher-than-neccesary educational levels to execute low-skilled work, unsystematic worker training, limited opportunities for promotion, and ineffective communications systems. It is noteworthy that the traditional work system in Korea has several features in common with large Japanese enterprises. These include a tendency to hire employees with limited qualifications and to have seniority-based payment systems and quality circles. According to Kim, in their current context, these practices are not conducive to organizational efficiency. Hence, he proposes a transformation of HRM in the *Chaebols*.

A concern with the relationship between human resource practices and performance is reflected in the final chapter, by Hiramoto. He shows that, although the major subsidiaries of two Japanese electronics MNCs in Malaysia and Taiwan have both adopted Japanese human resource practices, there is less evidence of the Japanese practices in the Malaysian firm. The plant in Malaysia does not regularly recruit high school graduates or have a qualification-based wage system or an enterprise union. Hiramoto shows that the transfer of Japanese human resource practices is limited by two main factors: the companies' global strategies, which affect the structure and politics of the subsidiaries, and the hiring of local personnel, who do not share Japanese norms and are unfamiliar with Japanese management practices. He ascribes importance to the tight local labor markets, which in conjunction with management strategy result in high labor turnover and limited employee commitment. Hiramoto remains skeptical about whether a more complete transfer of Japanese practices would improve the subsidiaries' performance.

Part I
Changing Labor Relations at the National Level

2

Human Resource Strategies and Industrial Restructuring in Thailand

Frederic C. Deyo

The economic ascent of East Asia's newly industrialized countries over the past twenty-five years has spawned significant academic and journalistic efforts to explain the remarkable performance of these economies and to extrapolate from their experiences lessons for other developing countries. More recent attention has been directed to a second tier of rapid Asian industrializers: China, Thailand, and Malaysia.

Both old and new NICs confront what might best be termed a "sandwich trap." In both cases, there is growing pressure from below from countries whose lower labor costs give their exports a competitive edge in world markets. Similarly, both old and new NICs face the problem of exclusion from above, as industrially more advanced countries continue through political and economic means to preempt higher-value-added market niches. This chapter assesses the likely consequences of current labor and human resource practices in Thailand for that country's future economic advancement.

There are numerous grounds for pessimism regarding future economic restructuring among emergent NICs such as Thailand, in part because the possibilities for their continued upward mobility in the world economy are in some ways less favorable than they were when the established NICs were undergoing their periods of industrial ascent. First, during the 1970s and 1980s, the NICs moved upward into something of a market vacuum, resulting from the rapidly escalating labor costs in the core economies, increased efforts by multinational corporations to relocate production to

I gratefully acknowledge helpful comments by Stephen Frenkel and Jeffrey Harrod on previous drafts of this chapter. The research was supported by grants from the Thailand-U.S. Educational Foundation (The Fulbright Program) and from the Social Science Research Council.

developing countries (Fröbel, Heinrichs, and Kreye 1980), and continuing, dramatic expansion in world markets for the products of many "mature," mass-production industries. Second, with the arguable exception of Hong Kong (but see Castells 1984), industrial restructuring in the earlier period was accompanied and supported by interventionist, developmental states through such means as industrial targeting and subsidies; state enterprise, tariff, and other protections for sunrise industries; state-brokered technology transfers; industrial rationalization schemes; and high-technology industrial parks. Global economic liberalization has greatly diminished the possibilities for governments to play such roles today.

A third difference between earlier and current efforts at industrial restructuring relates to the new global hegemony of the innovative-flexible manufacturing systems pioneered by Japanese industry (Kenney and Florida 1993). If the earlier ascent of the East Asian NICs centered on the global diffusion of standardized production for mass markets, industries must now compete in higher-value-added product niches by means of continued quality improvements, product diversification, and process and product innovation. The competitive need to adopt more flexible, quality-enhancing production systems is heightened by fundamental changes in the nature of markets, including growing instability and fragmentation alongside the increasing interpenetration of national markets, such that virtually all major industrial companies must now compete more vigorously in all major markets, including their own.

What are the implications for developing countries of the globalization of post-Fordist innovative flexibility in industrial manufacturing? One possibility is that many developing countries will be increasingly locked into stagnant, standardized production niches in the global division of labor, precluding continued movement toward advanced economic status. This would follow as a result of the efforts of core industrial firms that are destandardizing production processes, enhancing manufacturing flexibility, and innovating through more tightly integrated supplier production chains, the development of high-quality, innovative suppliers, and the employment of more highly skilled workers. It would follow, as well, from the more stringent requirements of innovative-flexible production for infrastructure that facilitate rapid transportation and communication, advanced research and development institutions, and high levels of education. J. P. Womack, D. T. Jones, and D. Roos (1990), K. Hoffman and R. Kaplinsky (1988), and others argue that such changes work strongly to the disadvantage of developing countries. Suppliers are disfavored inasmuch as labor cost considerations now weigh less heavily and physical and functional proximity to core corporate customers more so. Final-product manufacturers are disfavored where they continue to rely on standardized, Fordist production systems with their lower standards of quality, limited ability to serve niche markets and respond to market turbulence efficiently, and weaker capacity for continued process and product improvements.

The fourth and final basis for a pessimistic prognosis for the continued industrial advance of developing countries in a post-Fordist world stems from the more stringent human resource requirements of flexible production, including, at a minimum, deeper and broader employee training, employment stability to capture the returns from such training, and greater involvement of employees, including production workers, in problem solving to improve efficiency and quality. Such human resource systems, it is often additionally argued, may also necessitate employment practices and industrial relations supportive of heightened worker involvement and commitment to organizational goals and success (Kochan and Katz 1988; Streeck 1991). Such requirements may include job security, improved employment benefits, information sharing, and an equitable sharing of profits and productivity gains, all of which encourage trust, involvement, cooperation, and work force stability. These conditions, typically associated with strong unionism and democratic polities in advanced countries, are less often found in developing countries, thus inhibiting the development of human resource systems adequate to the needs of innovative flexibility.

Countering this rather gloomy prognosis, however, are accounts of industries in developing countries that have continued to prosper and expand, in some cases by adopting flexible production systems in response to new competitive challenges (e.g., Shaiken 1991 on Mexico; Rasiah 1992 on Malaysia; Amsden 1989 on South Korea). And, contrary to expectations, industries have generally adopted these flexible production systems in the absence of many of the supposed human resource and industrial relations preconditions for flexibility. In particular, industries in developing countries have typically adopted flexible production systems in the context of autocratic management, harsh employment practices, low-trust industrial relations, the absence of effective employee representation, and authoritarian or repressive political regimes.

Continued industrial advance in some developing countries in the absence of the widespread adoption of flexible production systems suggests that standardized mass production still affords considerable latitude for growth across many industries and production processes. In other words, we may be overgeneralizing the requirements for flexible production across all production and market niches. Based on this assumption, continued efforts to cut costs and increase efficiency and productivity through reduced labor requirements, increased scale of production, increased technological innovation, and improved marketing may suffice for the foreseeable future.

Alternatively, the pessimists may be overemphasizing the difficulties of instituting high-skill flexible production systems in the seemingly inhospitable sociopolitical environments of developing countries. It will be suggested here that in circumstances of technological dependency auto-cratic hybrids of flexible production do in fact provide an adequate foundation for developing countries such as Thailand to advance into the ranks of the industrialized semiperiphery. It is primarily in the NICs such as South Korea and Singapore that these autocratic hybrids impede further development.

Flexible Production and the Role of the State

Left to their own devices, and in the absence of union or state intrusion, managers often respond to growing competitive pressure largely through short-term cost-cutting measures rather than through longer-term invest-ments in organizational, technological, and human resource upgrading. In the area of human resource management, this choice favors casualization, cost-driven outsourcing, antiunionism, and wage and benefit restrictions over investments in training and work reorganization.

Short-term, cost-cutting, competitive strategies follow in part from the free-rider dilemma of collective action: firms are unlikely to invest heavily in activities that may provide subsequent benefits to competitor firms as well. The costs incurred in employee training, for example, are wasted if other firms subsequently hire the trained workers. In addition, short-term competitive pressures discourage long-term investments in technological, human resource, and organizational upgrading when these put a firm at an immediate disadvantage vis-à-vis other firms that are not making such investments.

Such considerations suggest the importance of government in encourag-ing actions that would not otherwise be taken but that are important for national industrial restructuring and long-term competitiveness (Piore and Sabel 1984; Scott 1992; Hirst and Zeitlin 1991). The government role, of course, includes expanded education, especially vocational and technical. Equally important are direct inducements, subsidies, and mandates for firms to adopt long-term upgrading strategies relating to research and development, employee training, quality circles, and so on.

Where firms seek to move into product niches requiring more participa-tive, innovation-intensive forms of flexibility, state labor policy becomes a key determinant of success. Legislative mandating of fair labor practices, employee representation, job security, and adequate pay and benefits strongly encourages firms to adopt labor policies that promote trust and cooperation in labor-management relations. As in the case of employee training and research and development, such mandating, by imposing a similar obligation on all firms, also solves the free-rider problem facing firms otherwise hesitant to provide benefits above those offered by their competitors. Finally, government support for strong democratic unions and cooperative labor-management relations reduces the possibility that firms can freely adopt cost-cutting strategies at the enterprise level.

The remaining discussion traces the responses of management in Thailand to new competitive pressures by exploring the implications of these responses for industrial restructuring and further advance. It then assesses the role of government in influencing these strategies, especially through labor and human resource policies. Finally, comparisons are made with Malaysia, Singapore, and South Korea.

The Thai economy has grown rapidly in recent years, averaging about 10 percent during the late 1980s and then slowing to 7 to 8 percent during the early 1990s. Much of this growth derived from dramatic gains in manufacturing output, which expanded at roughly 15 percent during this period. Pursuant to a strategy of export-oriented industrialization, light manufacturing has been the pace setter for economic growth. This sector, led by textiles, clothing, jewelry, toys, and electronics assembly, has until now competed successfully in world markets on the basis of low domestic production costs (*Bank of Thailand Quarterly Bulletin,* March 1992, 23). Increasingly, however, these industries have been subject to growing competitive pressures, particularly from China and Indonesia.

These competitive pressures have been heightened by the ongoing liberalization of trade and domestic economic policy (Laothamatas 1992). Indeed, the very choice of an export-oriented industrialization development strategy encourages trade liberalization, both to increase competitiveness in local industry and to gain access to foreign markets. Liberalization has, in turn, had two important consequences. First, it has dramatically boosted Thailand's trade dependency and competitive vulnerability. Between 1986 and 1991, trade as a percentage of gross domestic product (GDP) rose from 60 to 80 percent (*Nation,* 29 Sept. 1992). Second, economic liberalization has reduced the capacity of the state to buffer local industries from such pressures or actively to promote and subsidize industries and firms. In response to these heightened competitive pressures, employers have adopted cost-reduction measures, on the one hand, and, to a far lesser degree, have pursued longer-term efforts to enhance quality, flexibility, and productivity through technology innovation, work reorganization, and the introduction of more effective human resource practices, on the other. By and large, short-term considerations have encouraged cost-cutting measures, which themselves often impede broader enterprise reforms.

The textile industry, the leading sector in recent export-led industrialization, illustrates this trend. In 1992, the fabric and clothing branches of the textile industry employed about 800,000 workers, 85 percent of whom were women, and accounted for about 15 percent of total 1992 exports, including agricultural commodities. Like other labor-intensive, export-oriented industries, textile manufacturing has been especially vulnerable to competition from low-cost foreign producers. Indeed, the industry faces the dual threats of reduced protection at home and continuing trade barriers in such major export markets as the United States and Europe. In part, this vulnerability stems from the fact that Thailand has provided exceptionally strong import protection to its textile industry, giving it the highest tariffs on textiles and garments (30–100 percent) in the ASEAN region. Under the "fast-track" provisions of the ASEAN Free Trade Agreement (AFTA), the textile industry will very quickly lose this trade protection and will thus face growing pressure from Indonesia, China, Vietnam, Pakistan, and other low-cost producers in both domestic and export markets (*Nation*, 17 Feb. 1993 [special section, "AFTA Outlook"]; *Far Eastern Economic Review* [*FEER*], 22 July 1993, 18).

Major Thai textile companies have sought to meet these new pressures in part through diversifying and investing in upstream higher-value-added activities, especially petrochemicals and fiber production. Within Thai textile/clothing plants themselves, the relatively high percentage contribution of labor to total production costs (Satitniramai 1992) has encouraged employers to give special priority to mechanization and other measures to reduce labor costs (*FEER*, 22 July 1993, 18; 5 Aug. 1993, 42). The competitive nature of the Thai textile industry and a corresponding inability on the part of employers to pass increased labor costs on to consumers through price increases further encourage this response. Many employers have sought to relocate production to cheaper labor sites. Several firms in the garment industry plan to establish training centers and new plants in northeast Thailand, where the official minimum wage (102 baht per day as of April 1993) is well below the Bangkok level (125 baht) (*Bangkok Post*, 22 Feb. 1993, B26). Saha Union, a major textile manufacturing firm in Thailand, has announced plans to extend its textile operations to China, in large measure because of the lower labor costs there (*Nation*, 17 Feb. 1993, B3).

As a related response, employers have refused to comply with minimum wage and labor welfare laws (*Nation*, 30 Sept. 1992; 19 Oct. 1992). A 1992 survey of companies in a large industrial park found that fully half were in violation of wage, holiday, overtime, or safety laws (*Bangkok Post*, 21 Aug. 1992, II-20). And of 36,941 factories inspected by the labor department in 1990, 25,757 were found to be in violation of minimum wage or other labor legislation (Labour Department 1991). A more recent survey found that only 30 percent of all firms were paying at least the minimum wage in urban areas, thus indicating a worsening of this problem (*FEER*, 22 July 1993, 18). Similarly, employers often challenge or delay workers' compensation claims ("ASEAN Outlook," *Bangkok Post,* 30 Sept. 1992, 1). Most of the cases referred by workers to the National Labour Court related to breaches of labor contracts by employers or violations of labor legislation (Labour Department 1991). Larger employers, which are more often unionized and less able to evade the provisions of labor legislation, have adopted a strategy of casualization: replacing permanent employees with temporary and short-term workers (Zuesongham and Charoenloet 1993). In 1992, S. Piriyarangsan and K. Poonpanich reported that in many garment establishments that they surveyed in the late 1980s, some 40 to 60 percent of employees were temporary, a finding confirmed in other studies. A 1988 survey of six textile mills in the Bangkok area found that 35 percent of all workers were short-term workers, hired on either a temporary or contract basis.

A further cost-cutting strategy used in Thailand is to subcontract production to households and cottage industries. This practice, which substantially reduces labor costs, is prevalent in garment, handicraft, and other light export industries (Zuesongham and Charoenloet 1993). In small-scale and cottage industries, compliance with minimum wage and other labor legislation is especially weak (Labour Department 1991). A. Yosamornsunton (1986) reports that less than half the small firms in his survey of garment factories in the Bangkok region were in compliance with legislation regarding sick leave and holidays. Many more failed to comply with legislation governing minimum wage, overtime, and holiday pay.

Piriyarangsan reports that for the clothing industry as a whole about 35 percent of total employment is in factories, with the remainder in small subcontract establishments and households where simple cutting and sewing are consigned by brokers. In the latter, workers are paid on a piece-work basis and rarely reach minimum wage. Although this arrangement encourages fast work, any resultant problems in quality reduce workers' pay. Lack of a formal work contract eliminates the employer's legal obligations under existing labor law. As a consequence of these practices, working conditions in the textile and clothing industry, as in other light industries, have improved little during the recent industrial boom.

Unions have generally been unable to challenge employers' cost-cutting strategies. In larger firms in the formal sector, employers have used a variety of means to prevent or weaken unions, including casualization policies (Arom Pongpa-ngan Foundation 1988), dismissal of union organizers, temporary plant closure followed by selective reemployment of former workers, and even physical violence (Brown and Frenkel 1993). Partly as a result of these measures, only about 1 percent of all garment plants are unionized (Satitniramai 1992). In firms that are unionized, such as some large textile factories, the male union leaders are not likely to address themselves to the issues of particular interest to the female employees, a problem compounded by the fact that few females rise to positions of leadership in the unions.

Interviews by B. Mabry (1987) in Bangkok firms suggest that unions have had moderate success in influencing government policy. There is some question, however, whether this influence has resulted in significant changes in employment conditions, in part because these policies have been so inadequately enforced. Further, deregistration of state enterprise unions, the vanguard sector in the Thai labor movement, following the February 1991 military coup d'état, more generally undercut the strength of the union movement nationwide through its negative consequences on the financial resources, leadership, and bargaining and political power of the national union federations to which private sector unions also belong.

Lacking community or union-based organizational resources available to state enterprise workers, the only viable options for most workers in light industry are to quit their jobs and search for better work, to try to become self-employed in hairdressing, dressmaking, or similar activities, or, more typically, to maintain close links with their family of origin through seasonal migration and eventually secure a better livelihood through marriage. A result of such individual or household-based strategies, of course, is a further reduction in the likelihood of benefiting from union organization and participation. In addition, the high annual turnover rates among casual laborers—22 percent in Bangkok-area textile factories in 1990 (Labour Department 1991)—further reduce the incentives for employers to sponsor training programs.

In smaller firms, where unionization is less feasible, quasi-paternalistic practices lock employees into bonds of dependency and obligation to employers, who often provide food and accommodation, along with wages and benefits, determined in part by personal relationships (Mabry 1987). In such a context, leverage in informal bargaining is determined primarily by particularistic considerations.

There are indications that extensive reliance on casualization and subcontracting has increased throughout Thai industry in recent years (Arom Pongpa-ngan Foundation 1991; Zuesongham and Charoenloet 1993). Survey data collected for the Thai Development Research Institute (Sussangkarn 1990) show that the percentage of temporary and contract workers outside the Bangkok area increased significantly during the 1980s (Charsombut 1990:19). A 1988 labor survey in the Bangkok area found that about 19 percent of factory workers were employed on a temporary basis (Samakkhitham 1990:32). As noted earlier, this percentage is far higher in light industries.

A more focused survey of four industrial areas near Bangkok showed a rapid increase between 1983 and 1988 in the number of firms employing at least 20 percent of their work force on a temporary basis. In one industrial area, more than 60 percent of all workers in thirty-one factories were temporary employees. In many cases, the decision to make increased use of temporary workers has followed labor disputes or worker efforts to establish labor unions. Whether or not the processes of informalization and casualization have actually deepened in recent years (see Brown and Frenkel 1993 regarding earlier years), such strategies clearly remain the predominant response to growing competitive pressures.

Thai Automobile Industry: Exception to the Rule?

There are, to be sure, important exceptions to this pattern of cost-cutting competition. Large, resourceful firms in product and market niches characterized by continuing rapid change have in some cases adopted longer-term competitive strategies. Foremost among these are the locally owned Siam Cement Group and several large foreign companies, such as Toyota, Yamaha, Hitachi, and Mitsubishi (e.g., Siengthai 1988). The larger Japanese auto assemblers illustrate this divergent pattern.

Under liberalization, the Thai auto industry has faced growing international competition in both export and domestic markets. Beginning in 1991, import tariffs on autos were substantially reduced. Similar tariff reductions were effected for imported kits for local assembly. Further, a decision to increase incrementally the required domestic content of locally assembled cars was rescinded, although suppliers of auto parts continue to enjoy moderate protection under an existing 54 percent domestic content rule. As a result, both auto assemblers and suppliers have faced increased trade pressures during recent years as seen in the rising level of imports and declining exports (*Nation,* 31 Oct. 1992, B8). By late 1992, vehicle-related exports were valued at only one-tenth the value of imports (*Asia Week,* 24 Feb. 1993, 58). It has become ever clearer that local assemblers and suppliers must improve their efficiency, quality, and flexibility to maintain even domestic market share, not to mention their level of exports.

Even before trade liberalization, the Thai auto industry faced a highly fragmented market in which many import-sheltered assemblers produced several vehicle models each for a small market, thus boosting relative production costs (for discussion, see Doner 1991, chap. 8; also *Nation,* 5 April 1993, B1). Despite rapid expansion in the domestic auto market, this problem may increase as a result of recent proposals to permit the entry of additional assemblers to Thailand (*Bangkok Post,* 5 April 1993, B1).

Production runs in assembly tend to be small and economies of scale minimal. These competitive disadvantages of import liberalization are somewhat eased, however, by new opportunities for increased economies of scale through greater concentration on a few product models and a reliance on imports of other models to fill out local sales offerings. In addition, Thailand's rapidly expanding domestic auto market, which grew by 36 percent during 1991–92, along with increasing possibilities for exports, create further potential for longer production runs, although even here, the exploitation of these new opportunities will itself require industrial upgrading.

Parts suppliers are more directly affected by the trade liberalization. First, the increase in imports reduces the potential for rapid growth in local assembly operations, the primary source of demand for original equipment. Second, the freezing and probable future relaxation of domestic content requirements enable and encourage assemblers to purchase parts for original equipment regionally, thus increasing quality and delivery pressures on local suppliers. Indeed, under ASEAN industry complementation plans, ASEAN firms will be forced into head-on competition to become regional suppliers. Third, a proliferation of vehicle models, both imported and domestic, has further fragmented the market for replacement parts, thus reducing economies of scale among parts manufacturers.

Market fragmentation alongside increased quality requirements demands improved flexibility, quality, and efficiency. Enhanced production flexibility, in turn, requires greater investment in multiskill training and increased involvement and problem solving by shop-floor employees. Unlike the textile and garment industries, where training requirements for production workers are less stringent (a few months versus several years in the auto industry) and interdependence among workers on the shop floor is less pronounced, auto companies have not had the option of adopting simple cost-cutting measures.

How well have auto assemblers and suppliers done in the face of these new challenges? Major assemblers such as Toyota and Mitsubishi have sought to introduce core elements of flexible production. In the area of human resource management, for example, they have instituted quality circles on the shop floor, multiskilling of workers, *kaizen* continual improvement programs, suggestion systems, in-process worker inspections, job rotation, and flexible labor deployment (see Deyo, forthcoming). It is clear that such organizational innovations have sometimes enabled firms to attain high levels of quality and efficiency. Mitsubishi has a successful export program that sells Thai-produced Lancers (as Colts) in North America. And in 1992, Toyota Japan designated Toyota Thailand the second highest quality international affiliate.

How, in Thailand's low-trust, adversarial industrial relations environment, have companies succeeded in instituting flexible production systems? A. Amsden (1989), in her account of South Korean industrialization, distinguishes between "innovation-based" and "learning-based" industrialization: the former centering on the capacity continually to create and implement new products and production processes; the latter based on the ability to introduce and improve on innovations achieved elsewhere. It may be suggested that the emergent NICs (e.g., Thailand and Malaysia) are now pursuing learning-based industrial paths, while the established NICs (South Korea, Singapore, Taiwan) must increasingly improve their innovative industrial capabilities if they are to enter upper-tier industrial niches now dominated by firms in core countries.

This distinction helps explain documented successes in introducing flexible production systems in developing countries that seem to lack several of the human resource, industrial relations, and other prerequisites of flexibility commonly noted in the literature. In other words, learning-based industrialization greatly reduces the requirements for shop-floor participation and innovation and privileges and instead shifts the focus to the production engineers and managers, who act as gatekeepers and implementors of products and processes developed elsewhere. In such a context, more autocratic, top-down forms of flexibility may entirely suffice to improve competitiveness, thus greatly reducing the importance of cooperative labor relations and progressive employment practices. Such a possibility is given further credence by the patterns of group interaction observed during factory quality circle meetings, which more resemble supervisor-directed question-and-answer sessions than collaborative problem solving. Conversely, innovation-based industrialization in countries such as South Korea and Singapore will increasingly require trust and cooperation-enhancing labor practices at both national and company levels.

It is important to keep in mind that high-quality flexible organization is confined in Thailand to a few large firms. Even in these firms, continued use of temporary and contract labor for a significant portion of the production work, along with extensive reliance on outsourcing to lower-tier suppliers to cut production costs, suggests that cost-cutting strategies are important even in advanced industries. The resulting problems of labor turnover, lack of motivation to participate in quality circles, and conflictual labor relations, in turn, have partially undercut the effectiveness of attempts to institute flexible work reforms. Morale problems, for example, recently resulted in the temporary abandonment of quality circles at a Mitsubishi plant near Bangkok. Likewise, high levels of employee turnover have discouraged training efforts at the enterprise level. A recent industrial survey found widespread reluctance on the part of employers and employees to invest in job training under conditions of high levels of worker turnover (19 percent in the Bangkok area during 1990) (Labour Department 1991). Conversely, employee turnover was closely associated with a perceived lack of opportunity for skill and career advancement (Charsombut 1990).

The State's Role in Industrial Restructuring

Recent research suggests that except in a few advanced core production sectors where autocratic forms of flexible production have been introduced (Rasiah 1994), industry in Malaysia, like that in Thailand, remains strongly committed to short-term cost-cutting strategies (Standing 1989). At the same time, both Thailand and Malaysia have achieved moderate success in moving into industrial and market segments dominated until recently by the established NICs. Such success may be attributed in part to the continued viability of standardized production in many industry segments and in part to the viability of truncated forms of autocratic flexibility in other industrial sectors. The prospects for continued advance depend in part on a deepening of work reforms and industrial restructuring across a broader industrial spectrum. Whether such reforms will occur depends importantly on changes in government policy.

The Thai government has been slow to provide support for industrial restructuring. In response to repeated calls from the Thai Garment Manufacturers' Association (TGMA) (*Nation*, 22 Feb. 1993, B1), the Ministry of Industry is considering establishing an institute that would provide technology and human resource development assistance to the textile industry (*Bangkok Post*, 2 Feb. 1993, B26). In addition, the government will offer modest support to the TGMA, enabling it to provide research and training activities for member firms, and assist in the creation of four textile training institutes outside Bangkok to accommodate firms wishing to locate in up-country provinces. Tax incentives and infrastructural support have also been provided for the development of high-tech industrial parks.

Beyond these limited initiatives, however, support to upgrade industry more generally has been minimal. In 1990, 42 percent of Thai production workers lacked more than an elementary education (Labour Department 1991), thus substantially reducing the ranks of middle-school graduates, the backbone of productivity and skill-enhancement programs in the NICs. Indeed, the percentage of youth enrolled in secondary schools is the lowest in the region, lower even than in China or Indonesia (*Economist*, 16 Nov. 1991, 18). A new proposal to extend mandatory education from the current six years to nine will be helpful, although the proposal does not include a provision for increased attention to vocational education. In 1990, only twenty-four thousand workers received vocational training, much of it in nontechnical areas, through the Institute for Skill Development, the major national vocational training program operated by the government (Labour Department 1991). Research and development expenditures in Thailand are substantially lower than in such countries as South Korea and Taiwan (*Nation*, 28 Nov. 1992, B1).

One result of the lack of state support for industrial restructuring is that workplace reforms and flexible production systems have been confined to a few large, resourceful firms, most of them Japanese, that are capable of creating their own supportive human resource environments in the absence of government assistance. In only a few rare cases have domestic firms achieved these successes. Cost-cutting strategies, it is clear, only exacerbate the underlying causes of noncompetitiveness in the long run, especially in such industrial sectors as electronics, chemicals, petroleum, machinery, and transport equipment, where survival requires ever-greater attention to workers' skills, initiative, and participation in problem solving (Charsombut 1990). The lack of substantial state human resource efforts further discourages longer-view managerial policies. The general lack of investment in human resources has prompted increasing official recognition that such investment must be viewed not only as welfare-enhancing but as essential for continued economic growth under economic liberalization (*Nation*, 28 Nov. 1992, B1). The lack of progress in this area has led to growing pessimism among academics regarding the possibilities of a high-tech industrial future for Thailand. Ironically, the decline in the state's economic role is occurring precisely when decisive state leadership may be required, as it was earlier in South Korea and Singapore, to initiate industrial restructuring.

Comparative Note on the Asian NICs

What of South Korea, Singapore, and the other NICs as they seek to challenge core industries in more innovation-intensive sectors? South Korean industry has achieved remarkable success in restructuring out of light, labor-intensive production niches into higher-value-added niches characterized by greater capital, skill, and technology (Amsden 1989; Rodgers, forthcoming). Singapore, while relying more extensively on foreign investment than South Korea, has achieved similar success in restructuring into upscale production and market niches. Such restructuring, the basis for the achievement of NIC status, was in turn associated with the instituting of more bottom-up, participatory decision making among managerial and professional ranks (*FEER* 1993:62–63). But although more flexibility was introduced in shop-floor production, it clearly took a more traditional autocratic form (see Rodgers, forthcoming). In both these cases, the state has played and continues to play a critical role in ongoing restructuring.

In South Korea and Singapore, economic restructuring during the 1970s relied strongly on state-based or legislatively mandated human capital investments in education, training, housing, and public health. In Korea, companies were required to establish joint labor-management councils and worker training programs. In Singapore, the government urged dramatic wage increases in 1979–81 precisely to discourage further investment in labor-intensive production in favor of investment in higher-value-added, high-skill activities (Deyo 1989:140–42). At the same time, the Singapore government provided effective incentives for company training programs, vigorously supported quality circles, works councils, and worker-involvement programs, encouraged loyalty-enhancing personnel policies, and instituted a wide range of state-supported technical education and training activities. In addition, Singapore has systematically controlled trade unions by involving them in campaigns to improve productivity and product quality.

Finally, in both Singapore and South Korea, tight government controls over trade unions and more generally authoritarian political regimes have encouraged and supported autocratic management. Despite recent democratic reforms in South Korea, there are indications the government is reverting once again to repressive measures to contain a rising swell of union militancy and independent organizational efforts. Such controls, along with the distrust and latent confrontation they engender, may well hinder the instituting of more innovative forms of workplace flexibility. In this sense, continued industrial restructuring may require rather fundamental political changes to foster innovation-supportive human resource systems.

Conclusion

Three concluding observations help to place the Thai experience of industrial restructuring in broader perspective. First, short-term cost-cutting strategies have been the predominant response among Thai employers to new competitive pressures. Such a response will likely compromise continued industrial advancement in the future.

Second, successful long-term strategies of flexibility and quality enhancement, even in such advanced, engineering-based industries as automobile manufacturing, are confined to a few large companies that are using them in their core production processes. Without substantial state support, these innovations are unlikely to be generalized to other industrial sectors.

Third, where flexibility-enhancing work reforms have been introduced, they have generally not entailed substantial worker participation in decision making on the shop floor. Rather, they have drawn workers into problem solving within narrow parameters laid down by managers and supervisors. In large measure, the limited extent and autocratic nature of the work reforms reflect the lack of state support for anything more.

Competitive success under autocratic forms of flexibility, as is found in Mexico, Malaysia, and Thailand, represents an exception to and provides support for the notion that flexible production systems require progressive, trust-engendering employment and industrial relations practices. These cases refute this notion, insofar as the reforms have been instituted in the absence of such putative requirements. They support this view, however, in that autocratic flexibility is far less efficacious in fully mobilizing human resources on the shop floor to the extent necessary for innovation-based flexible production systems. In this sense, although dynamic companies in Thailand and other emergent NICs may continue their successful ascent into more advanced semiperipheral industrial niches, continued reliance on truncated, autocratic forms of flexible production may define the upper limit for long-term industrial advancement there as in the older established NICs.

3

Industrialization Strategy and Industrial Relations Policy in Malaysia

Sarosh Kuruvilla

The notion that the logic of industrialism (Kerr et al. 1960) would lead to a convergence of industrial relations systems has been swept aside by history. Nonetheless, in addition to political regimes and market pressures, industrialization is still regarded as a central variable in explaining industrial relations policies or transformations in industrial relations systems. The argument that stages or levels of industrialization are correlated with certain patterns of industrial relations and trade union influence has received particular attention. For instance, Frenkel (ed., 1993) suggests that, in the most general terms, it appears that a country's level of industrialization is related to the influence trade unions have in shaping workplace industrialization. In Frenkel's nine-country study, the least industrialized countries—Malaysia, Thailand, and China—show less trade union influence in workplace industrial relations than the more developed countries, such as Singapore. Frenkel contends, however, that it is simplistic to assume that industrial relations systems in countries at similar levels of industrialization ought to be similar, given the variation in patterns of industrialization across the four "Asian tigers," which are at similar levels of industrialization.

M. Bjorkman, L. Lauridsen, and H. Marcussen (1988) hypothesize that different patterns of industrialization are associated with different kinds of capital-labor relations. Their theoretical work suggests little or no relationship between capital-labor relations and two levels of import-substitution industrialization (simple and advanced). They argue that simple export-oriented industrialization, based on labor-intensive production, is associ-

My thanks to Pan Shih-Wei and Lee Byoung-Hoon for assistance with the research and to Stephen Frenkel and Jeffrey Harrod for their helpful comments. Errors, if any, are mine.

ated with a highly repressive labor system, while more advanced forms of
export-oriented industrialization, based on capital-intensive production
systems and that rely on highly skilled labor, are likely to result in more
inclusive and less repressive industrial relations systems. In their scheme,
different forms of industrialization reflect the nature of different forms of
capital accumulation, which translate into different kinds of capital-labor
relations, an argument Sharma (1985) also advanced.[1] Empirical tests of
their propositions have yet to be conducted, however. Deyo (1989) also
finds policies of labor suppression by East Asian states consequent to
export-oriented industrialization.[2]

Somewhat related to this argument is the suggestion of the new
international division of labor (NIDL) theorists that industrialization has
been thrust upon peripheral societies by core economic powers and that
this industrialization, through the transmission belt of global multinationals and condoning local governments, has led to union repression and
marginalization in peripheral societies. Frenkel (ed., 1993) does not find
this hypothesis to be supported in his study, although he suggests that
further research is necessary in this regard.

What is missing from this literature is a closely reasoned argument
about how industrialization strategies affect the actions of management,
labor, and government in the labor relations sphere. More specifically,
what factors lead governments to decide on a specific industrialization
strategy? What implications does the choice of such a strategy have for
the industrial relations (IR) system and, specifically, the institutional
arrangements governing labor relations? The institutional arrangements in
particular are central to the way in which the industrial relations policies
of the state and the industrial relations practices of the actors develop and
change. A focus on rules and laws is not enough. Previous literature has,
by and large, ignored these arrangements. Instead, they have concentrated
on broader typologies of IR systems, such as "collaborative-repressive."

In this chapter, a different view is taken of the relationship between
industrialization strategies and industrial relations policy and practice. I
argue that it is not the logic of industrialism or the levels of industrialization per se but the choice of an industrialization strategy and the shifts
between such strategies that influence changes in industrial relations
policies. Different industrialization strategies exist, such as import-substitution, export-oriented, basic industries, and small-scale strategies, each
with its attendant implications for industrial relations policies. The argument developed here is that it is the shift from one strategy to another
that is important in understanding transformations in industrial relations
systems (i.e., these shifts provide a window through which to assess the
dynamics of change in industrial relations systems).

It is not my intent to suggest that the changes in industrial relations
policies are solely determined by shifts in the industrialization strategy.

Other factors, such as changes in political regimes, are often critical reasons industrial relations systems change, as demonstrated by Collier and Collier (1991) for Latin America and suggested by various others (e.g., Frenkel, ed., 1993; Bjorkman, Lauridsen, and Marcussen 1988). It is important to note, however, that the relative importance of various factors differs from country to country. In the countries of East Asia and Southeast Asia, whose industrialization experiences are relatively recent and largely successful and whose political regimes, with the exception of Thailand, have been relatively stable, the variables related to industrialization may have stronger explanatory power than those related to politics.

Nor do I argue that the type of industrialization strategy that a country pursues is deterministic (i.e., a change from strategy X will lead to industrial relations systems type Y). Rather, I argue that the shift from one strategy to another provides a rare "moment in the transition" of economies that enables researchers to view the dynamics of industrial relations transformation. The particular pressures and the direction of change in an IR system are necessarily specific to each country, but in the context of the NICs of Southeast Asia, the shifts in industrialization strategies could provide a general framework for the analysis of IR system change. Implicit in this argument is the notion that certain industrialization strategies tend to be associated with, and to sustain, certain industrial relations policies and practices.

In this chapter, Malaysia is used as an example to examine this "moment in transition" in an industrial relations system. In Malaysia, industrialization strategies were largely a function of the ethnic tensions and the economic results of policies introduced to manage these tensions. I argue that the shift from an import-substitution policy to an export-oriented policy resulted in an increasingly inflexible and government-dominated industrial relations system. In assessing the dynamics of change in the industrial relations system, three factors appear important. These include the demands of the industrialization strategy itself (EOI, based on low-cost, labor-intensive manufacturing), the state's dependence on foreign investment to sustain this strategy, and the state's need to increase the economic efficiency of state-run plants, all of which constituted pressures for change in industrial relations.

Although the focus is on Malaysia, the argument is equally applicable to the Philippines, Indonesia, and Thailand (Kuruvilla 1992), as well as to other Third World countries that are under pressure to restructure their economies (Katz, Kuruvilla, and Turner forthcoming; Singh 1992). The next section briefly describes the Malaysian economy, including previous and current state industrialization strategies. I then discuss industrial relations strategies. This is followed by an analysis of the outcomes of Malaysia's industrial relations policy. The final section provides some concluding observations and notes several implications for further research.

Malaysia's Economy Today

Malaysia is one of the fastest growing economies in the world and in many ways a Third World success story. Twenty years of sustained growth and diversification have reduced the economy's reliance on primary products, such as tin and rubber. Malaysia is still the world's largest exporter of tin and rubber, however, the largest exporter of palm oil, and a significant producer of oil, natural gas, and timber. More recently, it has become one of the largest manufacturers of semiconductors and a sizable manufacturer of electronics, electrical products, and textiles. Exports account for about 61 percent of gross national product (GNP), which makes the economy very dependent on the external economic climate.

Although growth was slowed during 1982 and 1985–86 as a result of falling prices in commodities, Malaysia has sustained high economic growth since then through its booming export trade in manufacturing, which is driven primarily by foreign investment. Industry has supplanted agriculture as the major contributor to gross domestic product, accounting for 42 percent of GDP, and low-cost, labor-intensive manufacturing accounts for about 48 percent of export earnings. In the last few years, Malaysia's GDP has grown at an average annual rate of 8.7 percent, making it among the highest in the world, and manufacturing has grown at about 15 percent annually. National and per capita incomes are increasing at a rate of 7 percent annually, and the per capita income—about U.S.\$2,000—is higher than the per capita incomes of most Third World countries.

Foreign investment in Malaysia continues to increase, attracted by the favorable investment policies, the cheap, docile, and skilled labor, and the well-developed infrastructure (Malaysia has 30,000 kilometers of paved roads, reliable and efficient telecommunications, cheap and abundant electricity, and efficient transportation systems). Foreign investment is still dominated by low-cost, labor-intensive industries, although a small shift to more higher-technology production is apparent and the country has begun attracting more larger companies. Japan is the largest investor, closely followed by Taiwan, which alone accounts for 25 percent of the total foreign direct investment and the largest number of projects. Industrial relations in Malaysia have recently been characterized as becoming highly repressive and trade unions as weak, excluded by the government in decision making at national levels, and having very little influence at the workplace level (Arudsothy and Littler 1993). Table 3.1 provides basic economic statistics.

Industrialization Strategy in Malaysia

Malaysia's industrialization strategy has been determined largely by tensions between the three dominant ethnic groups: the Malays, who form

Table 3.1. Summary of the Malaysian Economy, 1990

Population (in millions)	16.92
Per capita income (in U.S.$)	2,000
Civilian employment	
Agriculture	30.8%
Industry	23.1%
Services	43.6%
Sectoral share of GDP	
Manufacturing	41.7%
Agriculture	19.4%
Services	38.9%
Unemployment rate	8.1%
Unionization rate	10.1%
Exports as percentage of GDP	61
Share of labor-intensive sector involved in producing	
manufactured goods for export	
1980	29%
1988	51%
Contribution of EPZs to total exports	
1988	33%
Contribution of MNCs to total exports	
1971	28%
1980	54%
1986	58%

Sources: Lim and Pang Eng Fong 1991; Ministry of Finance 1991; author's calculations.

54 percent of the population, and the Chinese and Indians, who represent 37 and 16 percent respectively (Bowie 1991). The following discussion draws heavily on A. Bowie's analysis.

Before its independence from Great Britain in 1957, Malaysia was dependent on exports of primary commodities, and tin and rubber production accounted for 85 percent of export earnings and 48 percent of GDP. Agriculture, mining, banking, and external trade were controlled by foreign interests (mostly British), while small-scale industry was owned largely by ethnic Chinese and Indians.[3] Ethnic Malays were concentrated largely in the rural agricultural sectors. Although they accounted for 50 percent of the population, they owned less than 10 percent of the registered businesses and less than 1.5 percent of the share capital and paid less than 4 percent of the nation's income tax. At independence, the industrial strategy relied primarily on the processing of raw materials for export.

Import-Substitution Industrialization

Market-Led ISI. Economic policy in 1957–70 focused on the state's involvement in the development of an infrastructure and the rural sector (which accounted for 30 percent of planned expenditures), while industrialization was left to the private sector. The state restricted itself to the creation of a favorable climate to attract foreign investment in import-substitution industries. Among the state initiatives during this period was the enactment of the Pioneer Industries Relief from Income Tax Ordinance of 1958 and the creation of the Malaysian Industrial Development Finance Corporation, which was responsible for providing investment capital and for the development of industrial estates. After the 1968 withdrawal of Singapore from the Federation of Malaya, the Investment Incentives Act was introduced, aimed at stimulating industrial growth by attracting foreign investment with a plethora of tax concessions, enhancing the Pioneer status conditions, and creating free trade zones. (For a detailed description of specific policies, see Spinanger 1986.)

The decision to leave industrial investment to the private sector was largely a political compromise reached between the parties making up the ruling alliance (Bowie 1991). The United Malay National Organization (UMNO) realized that Chinese and Indian acceptance of the UMNO's political role was to some extent dependent on the state's not interfering in private commerce and industry (which they dominated) beyond its regulatory role. The UMNO therefore accepted (temporarily) the Chinese and Indian dominance of business and commerce, in exchange for their acceptance of UMNO political domination and UMNO efforts to increase Malay participation in the rural sector and in transportation, mining, construction, and timber industries. World Bank recommendations favoring industrialization under private sector auspices also influenced this policy (Spinanger 1986; Bowie 1991).

The strategy had mixed results. On the one hand, by 1969, Malaysia's economy had grown by more than 5 percent per year, manufacturing growth rates were high, at 10.2 percent annually, and private investment had increased by 7.3 percent annually. The fastest growing industries were textiles, electrical machinery, and motor vehicle assembly. On the other hand, the participation of the ethnic Malays in this economic growth was limited. Ownership among Malays still remained static, at 1.5 to 2 percent, while the share among the Chinese and Indians grew somewhat.[4] Malay participation in manufacturing employment had increased only marginally and was much lower in skilled and managerial jobs.

It became clear that the market-led approach succeeded in strengthening the economic position of the Chinese and Indians, relative to the Malays, and anger over this outcome was responsible for the communal violence after the 1969 parliamentary elections (Bowie 1991; Lim and Pang Eng Fong 1991). The relative economic stagnation of the Malays resulted in Malaysian politics becoming increasingly polarized on ethnic lines during this period (Bowie 1991).

New Economic Policy (NEP) and State-Led ISI. The NEP, promulgated in response to Malay nationalism, was designed to increase the ethnic distribution of the work force in proportion to the ethnic distribution of the population and to increase the *bhumiputras'* ("sons of the soil")—that is, the Malays'—share of corporate ownership from 2.4 percent, in 1970, to 30 percent by 1990. The strategy emphasized redistribution via growth in output and employment. In operational terms, employment quotas of 30 percent for Malays were a prerequisite for firms to qualify for import protection and tax concessions. Government contracts were reserved for Malay-owned firms, and all firms had to keep aside 30 percent of their shares for Malays.

Arguing that economic growth would "increase the size of the pie," the UMNO was able to convince its Chinese and Indian counterparts in the ruling alliance that the empowerment of the Malays would not detrimentally affect Chinese and Indian interests. To ensure the levels of growth required, the state, for the first time, became a significant actor in ISI investment. State intervention was justified on the grounds that Malays did not currently possess the wealth or the entrepreneurial ability to start new businesses. The UMNO's investments in the private sector were therefore to be made on behalf of Malay interests and would ultimately pass to Malay hands.

Although these policies resulted in increasing the economic participation of Malays (their share of total manufacturing employment increased to 32 percent, while the percentage of Malays in managerial positions rose to 17 percent and their ownership share to about 8 percent [Bowie 1991]), they were still short of Malay nationalists' expectations. There were not enough qualified Malays to meet the 30 percent employment target in *each firm*, and the policies did not result in the development of entrepreneurship. Industry continued to be dominated by ethnic Chinese. Bowie (1991) notes an increase in "Ali-Baba"–type ventures in which Malay businessmen acted as "fronts" for Chinese capital.

Citing the failure of the policies to increase the Malays' participation significantly, and under pressure from Malay nationalists, the state intensified its investment in ISI by enacting the Industrial Coordination Act (ICA) of 1976, which gave the Ministry of Trade and Industry complete powers to direct and control the development of industry, including the power to issue licenses to industries based on their compliance with NEP goals. The Bhumiputra Investment Fund was created with state funds for the purpose of investing in shares on behalf of Malays, and the ICA mandated majority share ownership by Malays in all joint ventures and foreign projects. Also during this phase, the Petroleum Development Act of 1976 was enacted, which enabled the government to acquire control over the petroleum and petrochemical industries without compensation (Bowie 1991; Lim and Pang Eng Fong 1991).

The economic implications of state intervention were far-reaching. For the first time since independence, the Malaysian state exerted increasing control over the private sector via *regulation* and *direct investment* in the furtherance of NEP goals. Government revenues poured into NEP and ICA policies, assuming that private sector investment would continue as before. Private and foreign investment balked at investing, however, given the NEP and ICA policies and fears of nationalization. Consequently, levels of private sector investment fell dramatically, from expected levels of 12 to 14 percent to about 3 percent of GDP in 1976. This shortfall, and the utilization of government funds to buy shares (undersubscribed by the Malay business community for which they were reserved) resulted in a major resource crunch, which led to increased borrowing from international banks. Foreign debt as a percentage of GNP increased from 8.45 percent in 1975 to almost 11 percent by 1976–77.

Transition to Export-Oriented Industrialization

The resource crunch drove the government to articulate a mixed policy. On the one hand, the government launched a massive campaign to encourage private and foreign investment during the 1977–80 period. Policies emphasized investment incentives, the development of infrastructural facilities, and numerous tax, labor, and other incentives. (Spinanger 1986 and Lim and Pang Eng Fong 1991 discuss these in greater detail.) Electronics and textile industries were specifically targeted. Foreign companies manufacturing for export were exempted from the ICA policies on Malay share ownership, and labor laws that might have discouraged foreign investment were relaxed or went unenforced. Unions were excluded from key industries and the export sector. This new phase saw the beginnings of massive foreign investment in the electronics sector by U.S. and Japanese companies.

On the other hand, the state increased its involvement in the development of heavy import-substituting industries. The continued failure of state-led NEP and ICA policies to achieve economic power for Malays commensurate with their distribution in the population (Malays owned only 12.4 percent of corporate wealth in 1978, and the target of 30 percent ownership by 1990 appeared out of reach) led to further pressures from Malay nationalists to increase ownership by Malays (Bowie 1991).

In response, in 1980, Dr. Mahathir Mohammed, the then–industries minister, announced a heavy industries policy (HIP) geared to achieving the twin objectives of accelerating industrial growth and improving the economic position of Malays. Through the Heavy Industries Corporation (HIC), the state now had a leading role in establishing large-scale, capital-intensive, import-substituting industries to provide industrial goods and consumer durables for the domestic market and a foundation to support a range of private sector and consumer goods industries. The HIC invested in a series of large-scale joint ventures, including PROTON (Malaysian Small Car Project), iron and steel works at Trengganu, and plants for cement, motorcycles, aluminum, and gas, of which were Japanese private sector firms with about 30 percent investment from the government.[5]

The outpouring of government revenues to sustain the NEP and ICA policies, combined with the recessions of 1982 and 1985 and the draining of revenues by the heavy industries program, drove Malaysia's external debt to unprecedented levels (Lim and Pang Eng Fong 1991). By 1986, debt as a percentage of GNP had tripled, bringing it to 30 percent, over 1976 levels. Foreign borrowing became the primary source of foreign capital inflow in the first half of the 1980s. The poor performance of the HIC contributed further to the revenue crunch. Thus, by 1987, the HIC had reported losses exceeding U.S.$100 million, total state liabilities exceeded U.S.$2.24 billion, and 37 percent of the public debt was the result of government-backed foreign loans.

Given this second "resource" crunch, and under pressure from the World Bank and other lending agencies, Malaysia announced a series of austerity measures. In addition to cutbacks in public spending, these included the privatization of various state-owned public sector industries. Further, Malay managers in the state-owned heavy industries program were replaced by more "professional" Japanese and private sector managers.

To meet its interest payments on foreign debts, the state also encouraged export-oriented industries, simplifying bureaucratic controls, increasing investment allowances and incentives, and reducing corporate and development taxes. Clearly, the economic situation of the 1980s showed that the state could not reconcile its heavy industries program and its NEP and ICA programs with rapid industrial growth. The state came to be dependent on foreign investment for the growth of its manufacturing sector and exports. As a result, development priorities once again shifted to EOI from a policy of heavy industrialization for an increasingly protected domestic market. Since 1989, favorable external factors, dramatic increases in foreign investment, and growth in exports of manufactured goods have stimulated economic growth.

Outcomes of Export-Oriented Strategy

The description above suggests that during 1977 and then during 1988 it was the shortage of revenues brought about by the government's involvement in NEP, ICA, and the HIP, and the consequent increases in international debt, that brought about the shift to EOI policies. The shift from an import-substitution strategy to a more export-oriented strategy transformed the Malaysian economy in several ways.

First, foreign direct investment in Malaysia has grown dramatically since 1987. In 1989, total direct foreign investment in Malaysia exceeded

U.S.$1.86 billion, representing a 157 percent increase over the previous year (investment increased by 127 percent between 1987 and 1988) and accounting for roughly 12 percent of GDP. In the first half of 1989, foreign enterprises accounted for 80 percent of the proposed equity investment in the country. Eighty-five percent of these investments were in export-oriented industries.

Second, the origins of investment have changed substantially over the 1980–90 period. Although the United States was the largest investor, its position was rapidly supplanted by Japan and then by the Asian NICs. The majority of these investments are in 100-percent-foreign-owned firms.

Third, the locus of investment (and particularly investment from the NICs) is primarily in the low-cost, labor-intensive, export-oriented manufacturing sector, although recently there has been an increase in the number of small and medium-sized firms from Japan oriented toward more high-skill-based manufacture. Nearly 85 percent of approved manufacturing investors for 1988 were committed to export at least half their production, compared with 25 percent for the 1982–86 period. The three industries now receiving the largest amount of foreign investment funds are electronics and electrical products, textiles, and chemicals, which export 98 percent of their production.

Fourth, the total manufacturing sector now accounts for 32 percent of employment, 42 percent of GDP, and 40 percent of export earnings. Manufacturing exports have grown by an average of 15 percent annually since 1988 and account for more than half of export earnings. Within this sector, the contribution of low-cost, labor-intensive manufacturers increased from 29 percent of production and export earnings in 1980 to 51 percent in 1988 (Ariff and Hill 1985; Tyers, Phillips, and Findlay 1987). The contribution of export processing zones (characterized by labor-intensive production, which contributes to employment creation but little to government revenues) to total exports exceeded 33 percent in 1988 (Ariff and Hill 1985; Tyers, Phillips, and Findlay 1987). Finally, the contribution of transnational corporations to exports has increased from 28 percent of exports in 1971 to 58 percent in 1988 (Tyers, Phillips, and Findlay 1987).

Fifth, the electronics industry has been the centerpiece of this dramatic economic performance. The importance of semiconductors to Malaysia's economy is well known. The electronics industry, specifically manufacturers of semiconductors, employs 16.7 percent of the manufacturing work force (Onn 1989). Total exports of semiconductors exceeded M$4 billion, accounting for 24.8 percent of total manufacturing exports in 1989 (Grace 1990). A 1987 United Nations report (United Nations Centre on Transnational Corporations 1987) shows that the majority of foreign (mostly American- and Japanese-owned) plants in the electronics industry concentrate on low-skilled assembly and testing, although two higher-skill wafer fabrication plants have been established since 1992.

In sum, although Malaysia's economic transformation has resulted in impressive growth rates, the EOI strategy has made the country dependent on low-cost, labor-intensive, foreign-dominated manufacturing for export to meet interest payments and sustain industrial growth. The dependence on this form of EOI has forced the Malaysian government to continue to enact policies geared toward attracting and retaining foreign capital to its low-cost export sector. As the next sections will indicate, this transformation has affected labor relations policy significantly.

Government Industrial Relations Policies

Industrial Relations Policy under ISI: Restricted Pluralism

This section briefly describes industrial relations policy during the import-substitution period, from the 1950s to about 1977. The central pieces of legislation in the industrial relations sphere included the Employment Act of 1955, the Trade Unions Ordinance of 1959, and the Industrial Relations Act of 1967. The principle that the government followed was essentially one of pluralism, based on the belief that workers required some degree of fair and humane treatment but also reflecting the view that economic development goals had supremacy over unfettered trade union rights (Bot 1988). The Employment Act focused on legislating fair conditions of work. Although collective bargaining was the primary form for resolving industrial problems, unions were controlled through the union registration process.

Any seven persons could form a union, but the registrar of trade unions had wide discretionary powers in according registration, canceling registration if two or more unions catered to any sector of the work force, or for any other reason and in determining the nature of the bargaining unit. The registrar also had the power to exclude particular individuals from union activity. Although the principle of one union per occupation within an industry should have strengthened the power of unions, P. Arudsothy (1990) suggests that it was used primarily to weed out those unions that were most militant. Unions were allowed to affiliate themselves with peak federations; however, the registrar had the power to withhold permission to do so. In general, the principle followed was that permission to affiliate would be granted if the registrar was convinced that the purpose of affiliation was not for trade union purposes. Peak federations, such as the Malaysian Trade Union Congress (MTUC), were incorporated as societies. This policy was selectively used to ensure that the state exercised control over the growth and character of the labor movement.

Consistent with the notion of the supremacy of economic development goals, the subjects of collective bargaining were restricted. Unions were not permitted to bargain on issues relating to management decisions with respect to recruitment, promotions, transfers, job assignments, or termination of employment on account of dismissals or retrenchment.

To encourage foreign investment, under the Pioneer Industries ordinance, the state guaranteed that the terms and conditions negotiated with unions were not more favorable than the provisions of the Employment Act of 1955. Strikes were allowed, subject to various restrictions: notice had to be given, a strike ballot had to be taken, and the ballot results had to be registered with the registrar within seven days. The registrar then had ninety days to check the validity of the ballot results. In addition, under the Industrial Relations Act of 1967, strikes were prohibited once the dispute had been referred to arbitration by the minister of labor.

Conciliation was invariably the first option available to the parties to settle a dispute (Khan 1989). If conciliation was not reached, the dispute could be referred to binding arbitration by the minister of labor in the Industrial Court, after a joint application was submitted from the parties or on the minister's own initiative. The court, in making its award, was required to "have regard for the public interest, the financial implications, and the effect of the award on the country, the industry concerned and also to the probable effect on similar industries" (Ayadurai 1990). Furthermore, all collective bargaining agreements had to be "cognized" (certified) by the Industrial Court. The court had the power to refuse to cognize if the agreement contained provisions that were deemed not to be in the national interest.

Even under an import-substitution industrialization strategy, one could argue that the Malaysian system of industrial relations in the private sector was closely controlled by the state, the freedom of unions to organize and to bargain was severely restricted, and the industrial relations rules and regulations clearly reflected the state's efforts to contain industrial conflict in the interests of economic development. The prohibition on political strikes and the restrictions on the ability of peak bodies to carry out trade union functions also ensured that unions would not constitute a significant opposition to the government.

The nature of IR policy reflects a "controlled pluralism" during this period. Despite the considerable powers given to the state in industrial relations matters (Arudsothy and Littler 1993), the state's intervention, in terms of administrative practice, was relatively minimal.

Industrial Relations Policy under EOI: Repression, Exclusion, and Cost Containment

As we shall see, the shift in industrial relations policies arising from the adoption of EOI reflected the common strategic interests of the state and foreign investors. First, the dependence on low-cost, labor-intensive manufacturing for export forced the government to enact policies that kept costs low, so as to preserve Malaysia's competitive advantage in having cheap and disciplined labor and thereby continue to attract foreign investment.[6] Naturally, the manufacturing and export sectors were the target of these policies. Second, the state increased its involvement in the industrial relations sphere to a considerable extent, moving from controlled pluralism to repression. The increase in repression reflected the state's need to increase the economic efficiency and productivity of state-owned enterprises and to sustain the EOI strategy. The specific mechanisms through which this shift was accomplished are described below.

Several rules and regulations directly affecting the competitive position of Malaysian exports were introduced. First, the minister of labor extended the tax and labor-exempt policies for Pioneer industries and industries in export processing zones (EPZs). Collective bargaining in this sector is circumscribed to the extent that the terms and conditions of employment may not be better than those defined under Part XII of the Employment Ordinance of 1955. Since there is no minimum wage legislation in Malaysia (except for certain classes of employees determined regionally), the Employment Act is concerned mainly with rates of pay for overtime, leave, and holidays. Second, the government has repeatedly refused to enact comprehensive minimum wage legislation, despite repeated demands by trade unions.

Third, in 1988, the definition of wages for the calculation of overtime was changed to reduce costs. Previously, wages for overtime included all allowances and bonuses; it now excludes them (Pi'i and Kumaraguru 1989). In addition, the rate of overtime pay for working on days of rest was reduced from three to two times hourly pay, and pay for working on holidays was reduced from 4.5 to 3.5 times hourly pay. Although these reductions may appear reasonable, because of the shortage of unskilled and semiskilled labor in Malaysia (Arensman 1990), these reductions have significant cost implications. Union leaders argue that this change was the result of pressure from foreign electronics manufacturers located in Malaysia who were concerned about maintaining their competitive cost advantage (Grace 1990).

Fourth, the refusal of the government to enact equal pay for equal work is another example of its efforts to keep costs low to meet the demands of foreign companies (Grace 1990). Although females represent only 40 percent of the manufacturing work force, they account for more than 78.6 percent of the work force in the electronics industry. Arguably, this explains why the electronics industry has been exempted from the provisions of the Employment Act (1955), which forbade the employment of women between the hours of 10 P.M. and 5 A.M. Support for the exemption is evidenced by a 1988 amendment to the Employment Act, whereby the definition of days for maternity leave was changed to include holidays, rather than excluding them (Grace 1990).

Fifth, the government has been willing to grant exemptions from labor laws to foreign companies; for instance, in 1981, the government exempted the INTEL Corporation from the provisions of the Employment Act of 1955 and allowed INTEL to work its employees continuously for sixteen hours. More recently, the 1988 amendment to the Employment Act allows the director general of industrial relations to permit employers to work their employees for more hours than stipulated by the act, up to a maximum of forty-eight hours a week, giving considerably more flexibility to employers.

Sixth, the state continued its exclusionary policy with regard to the general banning of trade unions in the export sector. After intense pressure was brought to bear by the International Labour Organisation (ILO), the International Metal Workers' Federation, and leaders of the American labor movement (who unsuccessfully petitioned the U.S. government to revoke Malaysia's General System of Preferences [GSP] status for noncompliance with ILO conventions), the general ban was lifted in 1988.[7] A partial ban continues, however, in the form of a decision by the registrar that unions in the electronics sector can operate only on an "in-house" basis. This policy has circumscribed considerably the power of unions to organize.[8] E. Grace (1990) finds that the ban was put into effect so as to appease U.S.-based electronics manufacturers that threatened to move production outside the country.

Although in-house unions can now be organized in the electronics sector, recent outcomes in cases involving two factories that were subsidiaries of multinational companies, Harris Semiconductors (United States) and the Hitachi Group (Japan) (see Duthie 1990, Arensman 1990, and Barnard 1992 for details), make it abundantly clear that the right to organize exists in theory but not in practice. For example, after the workers in the Harris subsidiary won official recognition for their union in January 1990, the company shifted most of its operations and workers to a nonunion subsidiary. By April 1990, most of the workers had become nonunion, and Malaysia's high court ruled against the workers' petition that the shift was illegal. Currently, despite the existence of more than 140 companies in the electronics sector, only two electronics unions exist.

The outcomes at Harris and Hitachi are examples of how foreign corporations manipulate Malaysian trade union regulations to their advantage. The MTUC alleges, for example, that the Malaysian American Electronics Industry (MAEI), a trade group representing American employers in Malaysia, has pressured the Malaysian government into restricting workers' rights by threatening to close plants in Malaysia (Arensman 1990). The MTUC cites a letter written in 1986 to Malaysia's labor ministry by an official at General Instrument Corporation stating that "if there is a union of any kind, it is quite likely that GI corporate will sell this optoelectronic business, and it may mean closing an off-shore plant in Malaysia" (Arensman 1990:47). Although MAEI executives have denied the allegations, it is clear that Malaysian workers in the electronics industry face numerous obstacles to their right of freedom of association.

Although the evidence cited above supports the idea that foreign manufacturers demanded a policy of union suppression, it must also be remembered that the state has had a substantial interest in maintaining the low-cost advantage that Malaysian exports enjoyed. Every change in policy mentioned above reflects this objective.

Increased Government Control and Involvement in Industrial Relations

In addition to enacting various "cost-containment measures" for the export sector, the government has systematically tightened labor rules and regulations in general. Here the changes reflect an increased "activism" on the part of the government, beginning with the onset of EOI in 1979–80 and continuing after EOI in 1988. Although I place more emphasis on EOI as the primary reason for the increase in government intervention, another significant factor has been the government's increased role as an employer, given its involvement in the NEP, ICA, and heavy industries program. One could argue that, given the poor performance of state-owned industries, the government's desire to promote economic efficiency has contributed to its increased involvement in regulating unions. Support for this argument can be seen in the changes in the government's policy consequent to the Malaysian Airlines (MAS) strike of 1979.

Following that strike, the Industrial Relations Act was amended, first, to give the minister of labor wide-ranging powers beyond the extensive ones already available to him with respect to industrial relations issues, including, most significantly, the power to declare any industry or service "essential." This implied that unions could be disallowed in essential services. Second, the minister was given the power to suspend a trade union for six months if he felt that it was acting against the national interest. Although the public sector MAS strike was the prime motivation for this change in legislation, it cannot be overlooked that, with increasing government intervention in industry as part of the NEP, ICA, and heavy industries policy, the government itself has become a significant shareholder in the private sector, with a direct interest in labor suppression beyond its purely regulatory role. "Essential," therefore, has broad connotations and can include airlines, food processing, electricals, road transportation, and any other industry deemed to be in the national interest. The following examples are illustrative of the government's increased intervention in the industrial relations sphere.

Table 3.2. Union Recognition Claims in Malaysia, 1980–86

	1980	1981	1982	1983	1984	1985	1986
All Industries							
Total claims	125	149	119	112	169	224	224
Voluntary recognition	54	74	59	38	51	3	7
Recognition accorded by minister	5	16	8	6	8	2	6
Recognition rejected by minister		29	23	15	39	80	131
(Percent)	—	(19.4)	(19.3)	(13.3)	(23.0)	(35.7)	(58.4)
Manufacturing							
Total claims		78	55	66	105	136	172
Voluntary recognition		44	26	25	30	26	20
Recognition accorded by minister		4	5	5	5	1	2
Recognition rejected by minister		12	13	7	26	62	98
(Percent)		(15.3)	(23.6)	(10.6)	(16.7)	(45.5)	(56.7)
Rejections in manufacturing as percentage of total rejections		41.3	56.5	46.6	66.6	77.5	74.8

Sources: Department of Industrial Relations. Kuala Lumpur, and Pehie, Mansour, and Chen 1988.

Trade Union Recognition Claims. Consistent with the more activist stance of the government, the minister of labor's involvement in union recognition claims has been increasing. As table 3.2 indicates, his rate of rejection of claims for recognition has increased, and the proportion of rejections to total rejections in manufacturing has increased substantially. Under normal circumstances, once a union is registered after meeting the stringent requirements of the registrar of trade unions, it requests recognition by the employer. If the employer does not voluntarily recognize the union (and invariably the employer does not, as table 3.2 shows), the claim is sent to the director general of industrial relations for investigation. The minister of labor makes a final and binding decision on recognition. At least half the recognition claims have been in the low-cost, labor-intensive manufacturing areas of textiles and light electricals. This is where the greatest number of recognition claims have been rejected by the minister, although data are available only until 1986.

Government Intervention in Dispute Settlements. The activist stance of the government is reflected in dispute settlements in two ways. First, the labor minister has been far more willing to refer disputes on his own initiative for binding arbitration to the Industrial Court. This effectively curtails the operation of free collective bargaining. This practice has increased

Table 3.3. Number of Dispute Settlements in Malaysia in Which Labor Minister Was Involved, 1981–86

	1981	1982	1983	1984	1985	1986
No. of disputes	498	606	836	757	827	956
No. settled by conciliation	398	538	741	602	666	675
No. referred to industrial court (total)	89	60	54	107	113	158
No. referred by joint application of the parties	35	32	15	20	34	44
No. referred by minister on own initiative	54	28	39	87	79	114
No. settled by minister	11	8	39	48	48	121
Percentage settled by minister	2	1	4.6	6.34	5.80	12.68

Source: Compiled by the author from Bot 1988.

dramatically and at a much greater rate than the rate of industrial disputes. Second, as table 3.3 shows, in many cases, the minister has used the power of his office to effectuate settlements, in some cases by convincing one party to modify its demands, in the interest of keeping the peace. Since manufacturing accounts for 41 percent of all disputes (see table 3.6), it follows that the minister becomes involved in dispute settlements much more in this sector.

Amendments to Collective Agreements. Malaysian labor law requires that once an agreement is reached, it must be cognized—that is, submitted to the Industrial Court—which then provides legal status to the agreement by converting it to an award of the court. The Industrial Court has the power either to reject a collective bargaining agreement or to suggest modifications before cognizance, if the court determines that provisions of the award are against the national interest. This provision limits good-faith bargaining, since employers can agree to "excessive" wage demands made by unions, knowing that "high wage costs" are likely to be deemed as against the national interest and modified by the court.

Although this system existed under ISI, as noted earlier, since EOI, as table 3.4 shows, there has been a steady increase in the number of agreements that have been sent back to the parties for amendment before cognizance was granted. In 1985, more than 50 percent of the agreements were accepted only after amendments were added. Clearly, the Industrial Court has been acting under the directions of the labor ministry. As Arudsothy (1990) suggests, the Industrial Court has been operated virtually as an instrumentality of the Ministry of Labour. Any semblance of

Table 3.4. Number of Collective Agreements in Malaysia Accepted by Industrial Court with and without Amendments, 1978–85

Year	Total agreements deposited	No. accepted without amendments	No. accepted with amendments
1978	186	186	0
1979	204	204	0
1980	207	114	93 (44%)
1981	262	221	41 (15.5%)
1982	266	140	125 (46.4%)
1983	268	123	136 (50.7%)
1984	234	110	117 (50%)
1985	330	145	185 (56%)

Source: Sivagnanam 1988.

Table 3.5. In-house Unions in Malaysia, 1984–88

	1984	1985	1986	1987	1988
Total	177	189	199	210	224
Percentage of total unions	49.3	51.2	52.5	51.3	54.5
Percentage of private sector unions	28.2	32.5	36.1	36.7	38.2
Percentage of statutory authority unions	94.8	95.1	95.1	95.1	96.6
Percentage of government service unions	45.8	47.2	47.6	47.2	46.7

Source: Arudsothy and Littler 1993.

independence was further removed in 1986, when the government decided that the appointment of officers of the court would be left largely to the discretion of the minister.

Enterprise or "In-House" Unions. Under the Trade Unions Ordinance of 1959, unions could be organized on an occupation-within-industry basis and could affiliate themselves with national unions but could not have national unions represent them for trade union purposes. Although this policy was designed to keep unions small and responsive to the particular conditions of their industries, it was also a system by which the labor movement could be kept fragmented in ways that would threaten the government politically (Arudsothy and Littler 1993).

Under Dr. Mahathir Mohammed's "Look East" policy, the successful example of Japanese enterprise unions was introduced to Malaysian legislation, although in-house unions were in existence even before by means of the registrar's decisions.[9] Table 3.5 shows the rapid growth in the number of enterprise unions since the 1980s.

In 1985–86, out of twenty-eight new unions registered, twenty-seven were enterprise unions. In theory, enterprise unions organized on Japanese lines produce more integrative labor-management relations since the goals of the enterprise and the unions coalesce. It must be remembered, however, that enterprise unions are only one feature of various interrelated polices in Japan that make the industrial relations system successful. For instance, long-term employment contracts, seniority-based pay systems, firm-specific training systems, and considerable labor-management consultation reinforce the enterprise union system. In Malaysia, the concept of enterprise unions alone is unlikely to result in the kind of stable and flexible labor-management relations that the Japanese have and the Malaysian government seems to want. The other ingredients, notably the acceptance of unions as a partner in the business, are noticeably absent.

There are other contradictions in promoting enterprise unions. For instance, if an enterprise union is to be successful, all employees in the enterprise must become members. Under Malaysian law, however, various classes of employees, including supervisors, secretaries, and security personnel, are not allowed to become members of a union. Further, there are considerable restrictions on unions concerning the subject matter of bargaining, and little or no participation in workplace decision making exists. Given these conditions, the criticism that the legislation requiring enterprise unions was enacted to keep the labor movement fragmented is certainly plausible.

Policy on Labor Federations. The latter criticism is supported by the government's unwillingness to consider forming one major labor federation. Attempts in 1985 to unify the two major federations, the Malaysian Trade Union Congress and the Congress of Unions of Employees in the Public and Civil Services (Malaysia) (CUEPACS), failed since the registrar of trade unions requested numerous changes in the proposed constitution that the unions felt were impossible. Although this reflects the government's desire to discourage the formation of a national union federation, recent restrictions on trade union rights in the public sector have forced some public sector unions to affiliate with the MTUC. Increased disillusionment with its traditional leadership has prompted the promotion of a rival national federation by the National Union of Newspaper Workers, which is still unrecognized by the government. The government's determination to keep the labor movement fragmented is also evidenced by its "behind-the-scenes" support of a rival labor federation—the Malaysian Labour Organization (MLO)—sponsored by the Bank Employees' Union, which currently has fifteen affiliated unions with 142,000 members (Arudsothy and Littler 1993).

The general tightening of labor relations laws and the suppression of unionization and collective bargaining rights noted in the private sector have had some spillover effects in the public sector. Arudsothy (1990) suggests that all sections of the public sector have progressively been excluded from the provisions of parts of industrial relations legislation. The right to strike in the public sector is largely illusionary, given the inapplicability of Parts II–VI of the Industrial Relations Act and the elaborate rules that effectively circumscribe the right to strike. There has, in fact, been a shift to a more unitary and paternalistic system of industrial relations in the public sector (Arudsothy and Littler 1993).

In sum, as these examples demonstrate, the state's role as an employer and its dependence on foreign investment for its manufacturing base, particularly in the electronics industry, has created a labor relations system that is repressive and dominated by the government. The shift from ISI to EOI was the primary catalyst for the tightening of labor relations policies. The specific cost-containment policies were determined by the government in response to pressure from foreign companies on which it was so dependent. The involvement of the government in industrialization also appears to have been important. The federal government is now involved in industrial relations in many different ways: as a sponsor of IR legislation; as an administrator of IR legislation; as a third party in dispute settlements; as an employer in the public sector; and as a stakeholder in various private corporations (Ayadurai 1990).

Consequences of Industrial Relations Policies

The changes in state industrial relations policy in Malaysia have led to several important outcomes. These are discussed below. It is worth noting that the impact of these changes tends to be reflected primarily in the industrial sector. Other sectors of the economy, such as the plantation sector, where there has been a longer history of bargaining and there have been well-entrenched unions, remain relatively unaffected. Nevertheless, in the context of a rapidly industrializing economy, it is the manufacturing sector that sets industrial relations trends; hence, the focus on this sector.

Structural and Institutional Consequences

State labor policies have left Malaysian unions weak and fragmented at the national level. Union density, defined as the percentage of the total work force that is unionized, declined from 11.2 percent in 1985 to about 9.4 percent in 1990. Measured as a percentage of the nonagricultural work force, union density is about 17 percent. Much of this decline can be attributed to state policy and employer opposition (Arudsothy and Littler 1993). In the manufacturing sector, the largest and fastest-growing sector of the economy in terms of employment and contribution to GDP, union density is less than 11 percent. In the plantation sector, where there has been relatively less government intervention, the figure is 46 percent (Arudsothy 1991).

Unions remain fragmented and small, resulting in organizational and financial weaknesses that limit their ability to organize effectively and to represent their members (Arudsothy and Littler 1993). Although central union federations exist, such as the MTUC, CUEPACS, and the government-supported MLO, their effectiveness is limited, given that they cannot involve themselves in collective bargaining or unionlike activities since they are incorporated as societies. Moreover, there is little unity among these organizations, thus limiting their ability to mobilize the work force. The wide-ranging powers given to the registrar of trade unions and to the labor minister further serve to contain union action.

Bargaining in the private sector tends to be decentralized, so that there are a variety of different bargaining structures (Arudsothy and Littler 1993) and little evidence of pattern bargaining. By and large, bargaining power rests with the employers, given the limitations on the ability of unions to strike. Collective bargaining agreements are in force for a legislatively mandated period of three years, thus limiting the ability of firms to respond quickly to changes in the economic environment (Ayadurai 1990). The wage system also exhibits a number of institutional rigidities, such as predetermined automatic annual adjustments and nonadjustable contractual bonuses, and wages are linked to seniority (Salih 1988).

Although dispute settlement is effective in terms of the success of conciliation, the limitation on the subjects that can be raised as disputes (by virtue of the restricted scope of bargaining) makes the effectiveness of conciliation less certain. The number of strikes in Malaysia has been steadily declining, as can be seen from table 3.6.

Although administrative procedures limit the freedom to strike, this does not mean that there is little conflict in the system. Rather, the limitations on strikes tend to increase the dependence on third-party dispute resolution, having a so-called narcotic effect. The number of strikes has declined, but the number of disputes has been increasing steadily, indicating substantial conflict in the system. Relevant data are provided in tables 3.6 and 3.7.

The rise in disputes has been mostly in manufacturing. This sector accounted for the majority of disputes—41 percent—in 1986. The correlation between the number of strikes and the number of disputes is negative at .45 (p < .05), suggesting that the restrictions on striking do result in increased conflict through more disputes and thereby control the level of unionism. Although unionization increased by only 1 or 2 percentage points over the period 1981–86, the number of disputes doubled. The increase in the number of disputes, therefore, is evidence of the weakness of Malaysian unions and the consequent reliance on third-party dispute resolution mechanisms.

Table 3.6. Number of Unions, Strikes, and Disputes in Malaysia, 1981–89

	Unions	Disputes	Strikes
1981	—	498	24
1982	383	606	26
1983	386	834	24
1984	386	757	17
1985	392	827	22
1986	401	1123	23
1987	409	1001	20
1988	398	989	9
1989	322	—	7

Table 3.7. Distribution of Disputes in Malaysia, by Industry, 1983–86

Industry	1983	1984	1985	1986
Manufacturing	296	270	388	468
(Percent)	(35.8)	(37.3)	(45.0)	(41.67)
Plantation	276	212	191	232
Transport	128	127	147	218
Services	65	66	65	104
Commerce	36	26	40	43
Other	25	21	31	58

Limitations on the subject matter of bargaining, state intervention to prevent or contain strikes, and the weakness of trade unions result in an industrial relations system in which the unions are extremely dependent on third-party intervention. Such involvement by the government inhibits the development of a pluralistic system characterized by free collective bargaining. It can be argued that the system does not create the climate under which unions and managements can develop collaborative relationships, based on their bargaining strength, necessary for mutual problem solving.

Industrial Relations Practices of Firms

The antiunion stance of the Malaysian government complements the antiunion stance of Malaysian employers. Employer opposition to unions is widespread. P. Arudsothy and C. Littler (1993) note that union busting and other antiunion activities increased during the 1980s relative to the 1970s. Indigenous companies appear far more inclined to be antiunion than foreign-owned concerns, although union avoidance appears to be the dominant strategy in export-oriented manufacturing and electronics.

Despite the government's announcement that unions could be formed in the electronics industry, only one enterprise union has been established. E. Grace (1990) suggests three reasons for this phenomenon. The first reason is that the workers view enterprise unions with skepticism and mistrust; the second is that they fear employer reprisals if they join a union; and the third is that it has become clear to workers that examples of unionization drives in other companies result in increases in wages and benefits in their own (i.e., a union substitution effect).

Employers clearly use both union suppression and union substitution strategies in dealing with workers. Motorola, for example, increased its workers' pay and benefits one month after the government's announcement that unions could be formed in the electronics industry (Grace 1990). The owner of one U.S. electronics factory offered a box of Kentucky Fried Chicken to any worker willing to disclose the name of persons signing a union membership application. Another U.S. corporation invited a Muslim religious instructor to speak during working hours about why it was against the Islamic faith for women to become members of a union.

Motorola, Matsushita, and many other companies have threatened to move operations to Thailand and China if a union was formed. Workers in these companies who have exhibited pro-union sentiments have routinely been transferred to other plants and intimidated.

In June 1990, Hitachi's Malaysian subsidiary fired 1,003 striking workers after they walked out in protest of the government's refusal to allow their in-house union to be represented by a national electrical workers union. Although most of the workers were hired back after they apologized, workers who were considered activists were not reinstated. Although Hitachi clearly was within the law in this case, its unwillingness to reinstate the activists suggests the company's antagonism toward unions, a view shared by many American and Japanese employers. Clearly, although unions are weak as a result of government policy, they are further weakened by employer policies and by the interaction of government and employer policies.

Evidence of New Industrial Relations and Human Resource Practices

Despite the intense avoidance of unions in Malaysia, leaders of plant-level industrial relations, particularly in the modern bellwether electronics sector, are gradually moving toward practices followed in similar industries in more advanced countries, such as Germany, Japan, and the United States. Changes in the production processes in the electronics industry, for example, have brought about changes in industrial relations practices. In the early 1980s, by and large, the production system was driven by "Fordist" methods, characterized by assembly-line systems in which workers did highly specialized and repetitive tasks requiring minimal skill and training. Wages above the daily base rate were based on a variety of piece rates and production incentive systems (Rasiah 1988; Grace 1990).

Given the effect of two recessions, however, there has been considerable restructuring of the production processes in an effort to increase efficiency. The industry is being increasingly automated, and new manufacturing systems, such as just in time, total quality management, and materials requisition planning (MRP), have been introduced in many plants. These new systems have brought with them new methods of training and remuneration systems. Increasingly, wages are tied to learning new skills. R. Rasiah (1988) notes that in many companies a production worker needs to know at least three processes to become a super-operator with a salary of almost M$750 a month (approximately U.S.$300). The team concept in production has been introduced in many U.S.-owned plants, giving workers more and more input into the manufacturing process and in many cases resulting in more efficient production and lower employee turnover. Texas Instruments, for example, has had exemplary success with the introduction of self-managed teams for production and quality control (Arensman 1991). Turnover rates have declined to 3 percent, and 85 percent of the employees have been in their jobs for more than five years. This contrasts with the electronics industry more generally, where labor turnover reached about 35 percent in 1985–86. There is still no job security, however, even for regular production staff.

In other parts of the economy, there are isolated examples of the emergence of new industrial relations practices, based on the acceptance of trade unions and employee involvement. For instance, since the 1979 strike at Malaysian Airlines, industrial relations have become stable and unions have become somewhat involved in decision making. Joint consultative committees, composed of union-management representatives, decide on grievances and quality issues, and turnover has declined to less than 3 percent. In a manufacturing organization (Seng and Hashim 1987), management meets once a month with the area union committee to resolve issues, and the managing director meets with union representatives on a regular basis. Employee involvement has been increasing since the introduction of self-managed teams for quality control and production improvement, and employee suggestions have increased dramatically, to an average of 17.2 per employee in 1988. The banking sector has also undergone changes, including increased employee participation, and an "interrelations" committee, composed of union and management representatives, meets periodically to resolve industrial relations issues and to plan production (Arul, Saidin, and Abu 1987).

There are several motivations for these new practices. In the state-owned enterprises, there is a gradual realization that productivity enhancements require the active participation of the workers. In other companies, the shift to more employee participation may be driven by competition, changes in technology, and the need for increased flexibility. At the same time, it is also possible that this shift to the institution of more human resource management techniques reflects a desire for more sophisticated forms of labor control.

It is difficult to conclude that these changes represent a clear trend, however. To reach such a conclusion would require a comprehensive survey of industrial relations practices. A key question here is the extent to which these new forms of human resource management will be successful in the absence of other policies that appear essential to the creation of stable and flexible industrial relations systems, such as increased job security, increased training to prepare workers to participate more actively in decision making, and more cooperative labor-management relations (Katz, Kuruvilla, and Turner forthcoming).

Future Issues

Assuming that the process of export-oriented industrialization follows the standard pattern in the region (i.e., simple EOI to more advanced EOI) (Bjorkman, Lauridsen, and Marcussen 1988), the current labor policy articulated by the Malaysian government may result in some future dysfunction. First, Malaysia's competitive advantage, based on its low labor costs, is likely to be eroded given the competition from the Philippines, Thailand, China, and Vietnam. A key issue is whether Malaysia can make the investments necessary to increase its workers' skills through education, training, and labor market policies and thereby upgrade its industries and attract more high-technology investment.

Second, the rapid technological changes occurring in the electronics sector require changes in the method of labor utilization. Rapid technological change to more high-cost, high-skill, capital-intensive methods of production may induce foreign investors to relocate to their own "high-skill/high-cost" countries or to Malaysia's competitors (e.g., Singapore) unless Malaysia can provide the kind of work force the foreign investors need.

These changes have several implications for industrial relations practice. First, they require the creation of a well-educated and highly trained work force that is capable of participating in production decisions characteristic of the new post-Fordist production methods. Second, to develop such a work force requires personnel policies, such as increased job security, training, wage systems, joint problem solving, and cooperative labor-management relationships, that enhance participation and knowledge acquisition, Third, these changes are not possible unless state and employer labor policy become less repressive and more collaborative. More fundamental changes, therefore, appear necessary.

Current evidence suggests that such changes are indeed occurring

(Kuruvilla 1994). Already, investment incentives have been restructured to attract higher technology-based investments, and the Malaysian education system has been deregulated, resulting in a mushrooming of private colleges with exchange arrangements with universities in Australia and Canada. This should lead to an increase in the supply of qualified workers for higher-technology industries. In addition, the government enacted the Human Resources Development Act of 1992, which instituted the Skills Development Fund. The law forces larger enterprises to pay a certain percentage of their payroll costs into the fund, to which the government contributes a matching sum. The funds are used to subsidize the training costs of all firms that apply for funds. Immigration policies have also been restructured to permit the import of both skilled and unskilled guest workers to meet the demands of industry.

Clearly, the focus of government policy has shifted from cost containment and involvement toward skills development. In addition, in the heavy industries sector, there is an increased focus on labor-management cooperation. Policies oriented toward skills development at the national level are complemented by employer approaches emphasizing increased worker involvement. The movement in the electronics industry is toward increasingly positive human resource management in a nonunion environment.

Conclusion

It would appear that the ISI strategy was associated with an industrial relations policy that was, in some sense, pluralistic. With the shift to EOI, however, the government labor policy essentially became repressive and exclusionary. The motivation for this repressive policy stemmed from the demands of the EOI strategy (for a low-cost, labor-intensive strategy) to attract foreign investment. There is some evidence that foreign manufacturers did exert some pressure on the Malaysian government to contain costs. The mechanisms by which repressive state policies were enacted included various changes in the industrial relations rules and increased government involvement in the industrial relations sphere.

This chapter has a number of limitations that deserve mention. First, it is implicitly assumed that the restrictions on trade union rights in Malaysia favor employers in all sectors in the same way. This may not be true, particularly with respect to the plantation sector.

Second, this chapter did not address variations in the abilities and strategies trade unions have used to counter and mobilize against government and employer policies. The focus has been on the export-oriented manufacturing sector, where unions are exceptionally weak, because this focus helps illustrate the underlying theoretical argument that is being proposed.

Third, it would be useful to disentangle further employers' motivations to change their industrial relations practices. On the one hand, employers following an antiunion strategy may be motivated entirely by cost considerations. On the other hand, the recent move toward cooperation and worker involvement may represent a movement toward more sophisticated forms of worker control through "corporatist" practices. It is also possible that the movement toward cooperation may be due to changes in production technologies that require greater levels of worker involvement.

From a comparative industrial relations research standpoint, this chapter raises several questions regarding the explanatory role of industrialization policies in affecting industrial relations policy. Are certain types of industrialization strategies associated with certain types of IR systems? Are there variations within an industrialization strategy that have implications for different IR policies? What is clear from the evidence is that a shift in industrialization strategy has an effect on an industrial relations system. (This conclusion appears supported by more recent comparative investigations in Singapore and the Philippines [Kuruvilla 1994, 1995]). Future researchers may wish to consider these issues in more detail.

Implicit in this case is the notion that the shift from one industrial strategy to another represents a discrete moment in the transition of economies and industrial relations systems. History shows that there are key moments of transition in industrial relations systems, after which they get set and are hard to modify. Often these key moments are a result of legislative changes (e.g., the National Labor Relations Act in the United States) or other economic junctures (e.g., postwar reconstruction in Germany and Japan) or historical factors (e.g., independence movements in the Third World). Recent policy prescriptions forcing Third World countries to liberalize their economies to integrate into the world market (e.g., India) require changes in industrialization strategies that provide yet another moment in transition for industrial relations systems. For those interested in the transformation of industrial relations systems in Third World countries, focusing on the shifts in industrialization strategy may be a particularly useful starting point for study.

4

Singapore's Industrial Relations System: Is It Congruent with Its Second Phase of Industrialization?

James P. Begin

The development of the economic miracle in Singapore over the past twenty-five years has been well documented. Under the successful first phase of the industrialization process, labor-intensive industries were brought in to take advantage of low-cost but low-skilled labor. The results were an almost unprecedented economic expansion and improvement in the standard of living for the 2.6 million people living on the 240-square-mile island.[1] As Pang Eng Fong has noted (1988a:1), "In less than two decades after independence in 1965, the island state has been transformed by an activist state and the influx of foreign multinational companies from a stagnating entrepot into a modern manufacturing-service economy."

These economic achievements were accomplished with substantial government planning; indeed, it would be difficult to envision an industrial structure and a derivative industrial relations system that were more coordinated during their transition. To attract the foreign investment required to fuel its economic growth, Singapore, at an early point in its evolution as a former British colony, placed a heavy emphasis on the development of a stable IR system, a strategy that included integrating the union movement into government decision making as a substitute for disruptive communist unions (Anantaraman 1990; Chew Soon Beng 1991; Pang Eng Fong 1988b; Foo, Chan, and Ong 1991).

Leaders of the People's Action Party (PAP), the dominant party for all of Singapore's history as an independent country, founded the National Trade Union Congress (NTUC) as a substitute for communist-influenced union organizations in 1961 and integrated the union movement into

The author appreciates the insights provided by numerous Singaporean government, union, and employer officials who met with him and provided materials.

government decision making; in 1990, the top official of the NTUC, its secretary-general, was the second deputy prime minister of the country, and nine of the eighty-one members of Parliament were union officials (U.S. Department of Labor 1990:5). Union officials hold other important government positions and serve on many tripartite councils established by the government to regulate IR issues (NTUC 1990:6, 7). As we shall see, one of the most influential of these councils, the National Wages Council (NWC), has had a key influence on IR policies.

The government, with the support of the NTUC, also passed a substantial body of legislation to regulate the IR system. The Industrial Relations Act and the Employment Act, both enacted in 1968, were among the most important. The effect of these laws was to restrict the scope of collective bargaining and to limit strikes and encourage peaceful resolution of disputes. The results for employers were substantial flexibility over organization-level IR decisions and peaceful labor-management relations.

The state corporatist IR structure, which developed very early in Singapore, as it did in other Asian NICs (Deyo 1989), was believed to be an important determinant of the nation's economic progress. As the first development phase was ending, however, Singapore began to lose its competitive advantage to other developing countries that had lower wages (Pang Eng Fong 1988a:196). Like other developing Asian countries, Singapore had begun the process of industrialization more than twenty-five years earlier with an economy based on the utilization of simple knowledge. Like Hong Kong, however, Singapore had an entrepot economy, which possibly gave it some advantage over countries whose economies were primarily agrarian.

As Singapore proceeded through the first phase of development, it acquired substantial investment from foreign multinational firms. By 1979, the proportion of the GNP accounted for by manufacturing had risen to 29 percent from 12 percent in 1960 (Lim 1984:19), and it remains at approximately that level today. By the mid-1980s, three thousand foreign MNCs, mainly from the United Kingdom, the United States, Japan, Hong Kong, Australia, Switzerland, Germany, and the Netherlands (Department of Statistics 1990:96), owned about 25 percent of the manufacturing enterprises in Singapore, employed half the employees in manufacturing, and accounted for 70 percent of the manufacturing output (Deyo 1989:23). This investment is high even compared with the other Asian NICs. In South Korea, for example, only 10 percent of the labor force is employed in foreign-owned manufacturing firms (Deyo 1989:158).

The first technologies that Singapore, and other undeveloped countries, borrowed were from the simple end of the knowledge continuum, often involving low-value-added assembly operations, where they competed on the basis of their low cost of labor. The organizations and derivative IR systems that evolved to support this industrial structure, at least in Singapore and most English-speaking countries, were bureaucratic and inflexible (Begin 1991; Mintzberg 1983). Jobs required simple knowledge because they involved simple functions with little authority; pay was low and employment was insecure (Deyo 1989).

It is this phase that Singapore is now in the process of ending as it attempts to evolve a high-technology industrial structure. It became apparent to the government that labor-intensive industry was not going to maintain or improve the standard of living, in part because of labor shortages (Hilowitz 1987:61). Thus, since 1979, the government has been aggressively guiding the second phase of industrialization with the aim of achieving high-value-added production and product technologies. A recent indication of the substantial planning that has been undertaken to support Singapore's second phase of economic development is the Strategic Economic Plan, issued by the Ministry of Trade and Industry in December 1991.

The purpose of this chapter is to examine whether the IR system that has been evolving in Singapore since its independence in the mid-1960s is congruent with the second phase of economic development, for which planning began in the late 1970s. The relevance of the Singapore experience to the industrialization process of other developing nations, including whether there has been a convergence of economic, political, and social systems under industrialization, as posited by Kerr and his colleagues (1960), will also be discussed. Of particular interest will be the circumstances affecting IR system congruence that are unique to developing countries. The Singapore experience can provide important insights into these circumstances, including the following: (1) the problem of moving away from the Fordist job designs used in the first phase of development because of the dominant presence of low-skill workers; (2) the problem of developing worker commitment to particular work organizations in the tight labor markets of rapidly expanding economies; (3) the contribution of strong government control, which is characteristic of the most successful developing countries in Asia (Deyo 1989); (4) the influence of multinational corporations on developing IR systems, particularly the British, Japanese, and U.S. MNCs, which account for almost half the foreign investment in Singapore (Department of Statistics 1990:96); and (5) the relative influence of local versus external culture on the IR system. The Chinese culture is dominant in Singapore—the Chinese represent 76 percent of the population—but the influence of British social, political, and economic systems on the IR system is also important.

Structure and Methodology

An IR systems effects framework will be used to compare Singapore with other nations, rather than the "network of rules" framework employed

Table 4.1. Definitions of Terms Used in Evaluating Singapore's IR System

Term	Definition
Competence	Supply of qualified employees
Commitment	Employee loyalty/attitude to organization
Integration	Level of conflict and ease of decision making
Cost effectiveness	Efficiency/productivity
Financial flexibility	Ability to adjust wage bill to reflect performance
Functional flexibility	Freedom to deploy workers across tasks
External numerical flexibility	Freedom to adjust size of work force
Internal numerical flexibility	Freedom to adjust employees' working hours

Sources: Adapted from Beer et al. 1984 and Brunhes 1989.

by J. Dunlop (1958) or the "conflict" framework employed by M. Shalev (1981), among others. It is argued here that what is important with respect to the operation of a nation's IR system over time is whether it contributes to the achievement of an acceptable balance between the standard of living of the workers and the economic performance of the organizations comprising the industrial structure (see Begin 1992 for a full development of the framework). Accordingly, the work, participation, training, staffing, and reward systems of the Singapore IR system will be evaluated based on the extent to which they build a competent and committed work force and integrated, cost-effective organizations that have balanced financial, functional, internal numerical, and external numerical flexibilities.[2] Table 4.1 defines these terms.

The IR effects categories were derived from the substantial recent literature on the possible effects on organizational and societal performance of IR reforms that produce flexible job designs and IR policies (e.g., Beer et al. 1984; Boyer, ed. 1988; Brunhes 1989; Mathews 1989; Piore and Sabel 1984). These effects are intended to provide a holistic, qualitative assessment of the effects of IR institutions. The categories are not independent, quantitative measures of IR outcomes, as indicated by the fact that competence is important for functional flexibility, and are directly related to cost effectiveness. When comparing national IR systems, examining the effects of the web of rules and conflict inherent in an industrial relations system, rather than the system itself, has the advantage of controlling for the fact that national IR systems, once in place, change very slowly (e.g., Poole 1986). For this reason, a simple comparison of IR systems is of limited value in testing issues related to convergence.

Since IR system effects can vary substantially by business sector within a nation, the comparison across nations will be limited primarily to natural resources and manufacturing organizations. Although these sectors do not dominate the employment and GNP output in the nations that will be compared here, a case can be made that national IR systems evolve initially in the context of the first industrialization phase of a nation, a phase that focuses on natural resources extraction and low-value-added manufacturing. In addition, international competition more often takes place in the natural resources and manufacturing sectors than in the service sector (Porter 1990).

Determining when there is, or is not, congruence between an industrialization strategy and the IR system effects needed to implement that strategy is not an easy undertaking since the current state of our understanding of the industrialization process, and the relationship of IR systems to that process, does not permit a comparison of Singapore with an "ideal" model to assess relative progress. Consequently, the development of Singapore's IR system in relation to its industrialization process will be assessed against several benchmarks. First, the IR system will be assessed in terms of the comprehensive goals set for it by the dominant actors in the system, which in the case of Singapore is mainly the government. Second, since Singapore has attempted to develop a flexible IR system, along the lines of the Japanese IR system, Japan and Germany will be used as benchmarks representing flexible systems. Third, the IR systems of the United States and the United Kingdom as of two decades ago or so will be used as benchmarks representing inflexible systems. Since the multinational corporations of these four nations—Japan, Germany, the United States, and the United Kingdom—are among the largest investors in Singapore, it will be possible to see if Singapore's IR system converges one way or the other under the influence of the MNCs from these countries. The United Kingdom is additionally important because many of Singapore's institutions reflect the fact that the country was once a possession of the United Kingdom. It is not suggested here that any of the benchmark IR systems should represent an "ideal" model for Singapore's development. Rather, these benchmarks establish a territory within which an effort will be made to place the Singapore experience.

Information on the Singapore IR system and its effects was obtained from discussions with approximately fifty labor, management, and government officials during three visits to Singapore over the past four years and a review of relevant literature, particularly recent surveys of IR practices of Singapore organizations.

The next section reviews the IR institutions in Singapore. It is followed by a section identifying the "effects" of these institutions. A final section reviews the lessons to be learned from Singapore with respect to the industrialization process.

Singapore's Industrial Relations System

Despite extensive government efforts to introduce a wide range of flexible IR practices at the organization level through legislation and tripartite government bodies, and despite experimentation with some or all of these techniques in many organizations, the analysis below of the organization-level work, training, staffing, rewards, and governance systems indicates that these systems have not taken on the characteristics of the integrated, flexible IR systems of some of the most successful advanced nations, namely Japan and Germany. The operational effects of the IR system at the organization level are more like those evident in the recent past in manufacturing sectors of the United States and the United Kingdom, although there are important differences to be sure, particularly in the area of compensation.[3]

Work Systems

One of the major reasons Singapore's IR system has taken on many of the characteristics of Western, English-speaking countries is that, like firms in those countries, Singapore's businesses relied on Fordist principles for organizing work, thereby creating nonintegrated work systems (Hilowitz 1987). Building on the low skills among workers available during the first phase of industrialization, jobs were designed with a narrow range of tasks and little authority. A few hours of on-the-job training was sufficient to bring workers up to speed.

There is evidence that changes are beginning to take place through substantial government efforts to make the work force more flexible. A recent survey by the Singapore Institute of Personnel Management (SIPM) of 408 firms indicated that multitasking to provide flexibility was being employed by 41 percent of the firms, while job restructuring (enlargement, redesign) was being used by 33 percent (1991:42). Unlike the United States, however, this work system is not underpinned with the use of job evaluation; indeed, the SIPM survey reported that job evaluation was one of the least performed HR functions (13).

Singapore's pattern of work organization is probably the result of the influence of Western, particularly British, institutions, coupled with the fact that sophisticated work design was not required to drive the first phase of Singapore's economic development, in which labor-intensive technologies were employed (Hilowitz 1987). In Japan, Japanese firms, at a much later stage of development than firms in Singapore, expect more from their workers. Job descriptions are vague and wide-ranging because jobs tend to require a broader range of tasks conducted with more authority. Further, Japanese employees receive substantial in-house training, empowering them to carry out these more complex tasks, and participate in a system of job rotation that enhances their flexibility. In Singapore, Japanese MNCs do not practice these policies to the same extent (Putti and Toh 1990:320).

Staffing Systems

Staff planning is a highly centralized function in Singapore, and the government takes the major role in ensuring that Singapore has sufficient quantities of qualified employees to fuel its economic development. The SIPM survey indicated that 70 percent of the firms engaged in manpower planning; the major reason the other firms did not do so was their small size (1991:43).

One of the planning strategies the government follows is that it gives employers substantial freedom to develop certain important staffing policies. According to the Industrial Relations Act, promotions, transfers, recruitment, retrenchment, dismissal, and the allocation of duties to workers have been removed from the scope of negotiations with unions, although many employers consult with their unions over these policies. Accordingly, Singapore's managers have a great deal of opportunity through external staffing policies to develop the Japanese core-peripheral staffing model to underpin worker job security. Employment security programs are not a common characteristic of Singapore's organizations, however, even in foreign-owned multinational firms that commonly provide them at home.

Employers are free to adjust employment levels through subcontracting or layoffs. A survey by the Singapore National Employers' Federation (SNEF) of thirty-four companies in four industries indicated that subcontracting is practiced widely (1990a:1). Layoffs are also used when necessary and were used commonly during the economic downturn of the mid-1980s and are being used again during the current downturn.

Selection from the external labor market is not restricted by equal employment opportunity policies; some newspaper advertisements openly state race, age, sex, or religion as a qualification. Employers also have flexibility with respect to their internal staffing policies. Overtime is freely used, up to a maximum of seventy-two hours each month.[4] Employers also have flexibility with respect to juggling work schedules without incurring overtime.[5]

A policy of promoting from within is widespread in Singapore. The SIPM survey indicated that 70 percent of all firms had such a policy (1991:24), but high job turnover at all levels negates the degree to which this policy fosters commitment. Many employers also deemphasize seniority as a basis for allocating jobs, particularly promotions and transfers (Wilkinson 1988:205).

Staffing inflexibilities are evident in the low numbers of rank-and-file workers who are promoted to supervisory, management, and technical positions and are largely the result of the limited training rank-and file workers are provided (Putti and Toh 1990:320). In addition, job rotation is not commonly practiced as a development tool to build flexibility in employee reassignment (Jain, Jain, and Ratnam 1992), although, as noted above, employers are beginning to use multitasking as a means of developing this flexibility.

Finally, with labor at a premium, the government has been active in trying to expand the labor supply through policies to make part-time work more attractive to women, to relax policies on the use of foreign guest workers, and to encourage workers to retire later.[6]

Education and Training

Planning for the development of an adequately trained work force to fuel the second phase of development has been a major priority of Singapore's government. Through a highly centralized system of education, the government has invested heavily in preentry and postentry education, which accounts for about a fifth of all public expenditures. The British-derived primary and secondary educational system tracks students early. Although this system has helped produce a literacy rate of more than 90 percent (compared with more than 99 percent in Japan), the recent Strategic Economic Plan indicated that "61 percent of the non-student population has an education level of primary six or below, compared with the better developed countries, where 90 percent or more of their population have completed 10 years of education" (Ministry of Trade and Industry 1991:30). Neither vocational education nor certifying the acquisition of skills through exams is emphasized in high school (Hilowitz 1987).

Singapore's public higher education system enrolled a total of more than fifty-five thousand students in 1990 (Department of Statistics 1990:286), approximately two and a half times the enrollment in 1980.[7] Only 12 percent of Singapore's students in the eligible age group obtain higher degrees, compared with 30 percent in Japan, 32 percent in South Korea, 13 percent in Taiwan, and 60 percent in the United States (Balakrishnan 1989). Since planning efforts indicated that a shortage of skilled and professional employees was one of the greatest impediments to technology absorption (reported in Ministry of Trade and Industry 1991), additional investments have been made in polytechnics and an open university.[8] The plan also calls for encouraging individuals with needed skills to immigrate (48).

Although the government has established several technical education programs to prepare the work force for more sophisticated employment, in general, government investment in vocational and technical education is small compared with expenditures for general education; in 1990–91, for example, only 4 percent of all government expenditures was for vocational and technical education (Department of Statistics 1990:305).[9]

There are also indications that company-sponsored training is lagging, although the country wishes to emulate the Japanese training model and the government has made significant efforts to encourage training in organizations.[10] One source pegged the average annual expenditure for training in organizations at U.S.$100 per person per year, compared with U.S.$2,000–3,000 in Japan and about U.S.$800 in the United States (Lee 1985:14). One cause of this difference appears to be that foreign multinational firms in Singapore, Japanese firms, for example, do not invest in training as much as they do at home (Putti and Toh 1990:318–21).

Disparities in expenditures to train managers and professionals, on the one hand, and to train workers in the operating core, on the other, are also evident, according to J. M. Putti and Toh Thian Ser (1990:320). This finding was confirmed by the interviews. In contrast to Japan and Germany, Singapore has followed the style of Western, English-speaking countries of training professional managers by sending them to business schools.

Reward Systems

The Singapore government has attempted to influence the rewards system through incomes policies that encourage, among other goals, a better work ethic,[11] the development of flexible pay practices, and investments in higher-value-added activities.[12] A major player in these policies has been the NWC, which annually since 1972 has recommended wage policies to the government that usually were adopted. Statutory amendments have also been employed as a strategy to improve the work ethic.[13]

In recent years, the government, principally through the NWC, has attempted to build wage flexibility; indeed, the government has attempted to affect all aspects of wage setting by, among other measures, strongly encouraging employers to adopt performance appraisal systems to underpin flexible pay programs.[14] The government's goal was to make 20 percent of the wage bill flexible.[15] Currently, incentive systems are in widespread use; three-quarters of the companies the SIPM surveyed have some incentive system (1991:29). Individual incentives are used the most, followed by productivity incentives for supervisors and rank-and-file workers and profit sharing for managers. A 1989 Ministry of Labour survey (32) confirms that variable payments are used extensively; 74.8 percent of the firms used a variable payment beyond the basic wage (15.7 percent) or both a variable and an annual wage supplement (59.5 percent). Seventy percent of the flexible wage systems were initiated very recently (SNEF 1990d:13).

Benefits are comprehensive and paid for by employers and constitute 30 to 40 percent of payroll.[16] Contributions by employees and employers into the Central Provident Fund (CPF) provide for the retirement and medical needs of workers. The fund can also be used for other needs, such as education and housing; indeed, the high rate of home ownership in Singapore has been aided by the availability of CPF funds.

Since job-hopping has been identified as one of the two important factors impeding the absorption of technology (the other is the absence of sufficient numbers of skilled and professional workers), the government has also encouraged employers to shape their benefit programs so as to promote stronger identification among employees with their work organizations. [17]

Although systematic survey data are not available, the interviews indicated that status differentials between managers and workers tend to be high. For example, wage differentials between managers and workers are wide, closer to the 25:1 ratio found in the United States than the 11:1 ratio found in Japan. There are also differences between managers and workers in the availability of certain fringe benefits, such as housing, chauffeured, company automobiles, and training (Putti and Toh 1990:320).

On the other side of the wage-effort bargain, working hours in Singapore are comparable to those in other Asian nations but are long compared with those in Western industrialized countries; a standard workweek is forty-four hours, and overtime is paid at one and one-half times after forty-four hours. Almost half the firms in the SIPM survey indicated that moving to a five-day workweek was an important QWL (quality of working life) goal. Only a fifth had flexible working hours (1991:42).

Worker Participation

Employees in Singapore participate in the industrial relations system through means of collective bargaining as well as other mechanisms for employee involvement at the organization level. As noted above, because of the importance of such tripartite bodies as the NWC in policy determination, and because of the substantial legislative limitations on the scope of collective bargaining, strikes, and the arbitration of grievances, [18] the primary involvement of unions in Singapore is at the macro policy level, where the union movement's symbiotic relationship with the government provides it with substantial involvement in the formation of the government's comprehensive industrial relations programs. One result has been peaceful labor-management relations; from 1978 to 1994, there has been only a single work stoppage, a three-day strike that occurred in 1986 (Department of Statistics 1990:77). Limitations on strikes, compulsory interest arbitration, and the aggressive efforts of the Ministry of Labour to encourage win-win bargaining and to enter disputes early help account for this outcome. The encouragement of enterprise unions following the Japanese model, starting in 1980, also contributed to this outcome (NWC 1977), although by 1990 enthusiasm waned as concerns about the need to maintain these unions' independence from the NTUC grew. Nonetheless, the incidence of enterprise unions is very high—45 percent fall into this category (Frenkel 1993b:311).

Another consequence of having the locus of union power at the macro level, and the government substitution to which the unions thereby contribute, is that employee support for unions at the enterprise level has been declining. As of 1990, there were eighty-three employee unions with a membership of 212,204—14.4 percent of the labor force (Department of Statistics 1990:16, 76), down from a high of 25.5 percent in 1976 (Deyo 1989:72). The high standard of living also probably contributes to this outcome.

The government has also made a substantial effort to expand employee participation in other ways. One such effort, started in the early 1970s, has been promoted by the National Productivity Board, established in 1972. Initially, the NPB encouraged the formation of workers' councils based on the German model, but this effort failed and energies were later refocused on productivity (Lee 1985:147).

Momentum picked up in 1981 with a campaign by the Committee on Productivity to encourage organizations to emulate the Japanese model of industrial relations, including employee participation at the organization level. Work excellence committees (WECs) were proposed for departmental or higher levels of participation in the private sector (they were called work improvement teams [WITs] in the public sector), while quality control circles (QCCs) were proposed for work-level involvement. The first QCCs were begun in 1973 (Lee 1985:149), and from 1983 to 1990, the number of registered circles increased from 1,460 in 90 organizations to 10,363 in 212 organizations. The 76,228 members of quality circles in 1990 represented about 5 percent of the labor force (Department of Statistics 1990:16, 75).

Despite the government's substantial encouragement of worker participation systems in Singapore and their substantial growth in recent years, they do not begin to have the extent and level of authority provided workers in many firms in Japan, where a cooperative, bottom-up, information-sharing method of achieving consensus for organizational decisions is in widespread use.[19] Nor, given the continuing problems with turnover and declining productivity, have Singapore's participation systems been successful in building worker commitment. Lack of employer and employee commitment to the concept of participation was identified in the mid-1980s as an important reason for the lack of success of worker participation programs (Lee 1985; Wilkinson and Leggett 1985).

Societal and Organizational Effects of Singapore's Industrial Relations System

Table 4.2 summarizes the analysis that follows of the societal and organizational effects of the Singapore IR system and provides a comparison

Table 4.2. Singapore's Industrial Relations System and the Systems in Mature Market Economies

Variables	Singapore	Japan	Germany	U.S./U.K.[a]
Competence	Moderate	High	High	Low
Commitment	Low	High	High	Low
Integration	Low[b] High[c]	High	High	Low
Cost effectiveness	Moderate	High	Low/Moderate	Low
Flexibility				
Financial	Moderate/High	Low/Moderate	Low/Moderate	Moderate
Functional	Low	High	High	Low
External numerical	High	Low/Moderate	Low	High
Internal numerical	High	High	Low/Moderate	High

Source: Literature review of each country.

[a]These patterns are now less dominant because of recent efforts to restructure the IR systems.

[b]Organizational integration.

[c]Labor-management accommodation.

of the Singapore system with the systems in developed countries. The IR system that has evolved in Singapore is a hybrid of the inflexible U.S. and U.K. systems of two decades ago and the flexible Japanese and German systems.

Competence

While economists argue that economic development is heavily influenced by the quality of a country's human capital endowment, their work has not been very helpful in pinpointing how much or what kind of training is needed, or whether investments in training have been effective (Behrman 1990). Accordingly, judging whether any country's human capital endowment is appropriate to its needs is a difficult undertaking. A comparison of Singapore's stock of human capital to that of developed countries is the process that will be primarily relied upon here, as well as Singapore's own assessment of its needs.

Singapore's public and private educational systems appear to be congruent with its existing technological base, as indicated by the fact that "a large proportion of fresh graduates tend to be absorbed in productive employment relatively quickly" (Islam 1987:146). Further, Singapore's work force has been favorably compared with the work forces of other NICs and even with those of the most advanced nations (Lim 1990:78, 84). Indeed, some observers believe that Singaporeans are overtrained for the existing industrial structure (Hilowitz 1987; Pang Eng Fong 1982). The competence of Singapore's workers can be rated only as moderate, however, in light of the country's goal of supporting a new phase of technological development.

Although Singapore stands out compared with other developing countries in regard to its investment in an educational infrastructure and the resulting quality of its work force, compared with developed countries whose knowledge-creation activities it wishes to emulate, and in accordance with its own assessments, Singapore's workers are undertrained at almost all levels in regard to both their general and technical educations. Singapore continues to develop a substantial system of general education, and over the past decade it has made great progress in setting up government-sponsored vocational training. But it still appears to lack the emphasis on vocational education provided by corporations in Japan and the government of Germany and that has proved so important in those countries in underpinning career mobility, flexible work assignments, employee governance, and employee commitment.

Given Singapore's continuing attention to the training of its labor force and the redesign of work, the chances are good that its human capital will soon support technological development, particularly if employers can be encouraged to invest more in training; however, convincing the foreign multinationals that dominate the manufacturing industry to support such development may be difficult. For example, a survey of Japanese training practices in Singapore found many differences; the Japanese firms in Singapore did less in-house training, had less job rotation, and offered less continuous training than Japanese firms at home (Putti and Toh 1990:320–21).

With respect to the size of the labor force, declining birth rates and the low labor force participation rates of females and older workers have reinforced the tightness of the labor market and promoted turnover. The demand for foreign guest workers to fill low-skilled positions has also increased. The creation of policies by the government to increase the participation of females and older workers and to increase the birth rate will alleviate the tight labor market to some extent. The call to encourage the immigration of skilled and professional workers underlines the country's concern that it has insufficient human capital to drive the second phase of economic development.

Commitment

Workers' commitment to their employing organizations and to their society and the extent to which this commitment contributes to organizational efficiency are complex subjects to sort out because many factors contribute to commitment. But if the high-commitment Japanese and German IR systems have any validity, then the low commitment Singapore workers have to their organizations is one of the nation's larger IR problems, although other developing countries with tight labor markets have similar problems. Absenteeism, abuse of sick leave, tardiness, and high turnover have all been identified by one report or another as problems of concern to employers and the government. As an indication of this concern, the National Productivity Board appointed a task force on job-hopping to study and make recommendations on the issue. Its 1988 report confirmed that labor turnover was widespread; in 1987, the average annual resignation rate was reported to be 23.3 percent, compared with 16.7 percent in 1986 and 19.8 percent in 1985 (12), and 6.1 percent of employees surveyed indicated that they had held three or more jobs within the past twelve months (16). A subcommittee report on fringe benefits by the Singapore National Employers' Federation (SNEF) (1990b) also indicated that absenteeism and abuse of sick leave were employer concerns.

One cause of the high turnover, of course, has been the tight labor market created by Singapore's economic prosperity. Labor economists would argue that a certain level of turnover provides for the efficient allocation of employees to the most productive employment. But the parties in Singapore are in common agreement that the lack of commitment is undermining organizational efficiency. The Strategic Economic Plan (Ministry of Trade and Industry 1991) identified the poor bond between workers and their employers as one of the country's major problems in absorbing new technologies. Further, 31 percent of the 318 firms surveyed for the Task Force on Job-Hopping considered their resignation rates to be high, and many felt that the loss of productivity, work disruption, and high training, recruiting, and hiring costs were critical consequences of the lack of commitment. Low-quality products and low worker morale were considered related problems (NPB 1988:9).

In 1977, the National Wages Council attempted to address the commitment problem by recommending that the NWC wage adjustment not be given to employees with less than twelve months' service or to employees who exhibited absenteeism or tardiness. It also recommended that employees leaving too soon after expensive training should have to pay employers back for the training (NWC 1977). The government rejected a 1980 NWC recommendation that an employee's CPF contribution from an employer for which he or she worked fewer than twelve months be forfeited. Instead, in 1981, the NWC implemented a CPF job record program in which an employer could check on job-hopping behaviors by contacting the CPF, but the program was ended in 1983 because of disuse. Also during this period, the NPB recommended that employers be required to issue cards showing employees' job histories as a way to limit job-hopping, to contribute a portion of an employee's salary to a special fund from which the employee would be paid if he or she stayed with the employer for a minimum period, and to make the work environment safer for and more appealing to workers (NPB 1988).

The Task Force on Job-Hopping made a comprehensive series of recommendations based on its findings on the causes of job turnover. The problems that both employees and employers identified were all related to IR system parameters: salaries were low; there was little concern for employees' welfare; opportunities for job advancement were limited; job content was narrow; supervisor-worker and peer relationships were poor; the physical work environment was unsatisfactory; work schedules (shift work) created problems; there was no job security; and jobs had no status. Included were recommendations to improve worker participation through the development of quality circles and to expand job security, indicating that these features of Singapore's IR system needed to be expanded more generally to encourage worker commitment, even in foreign multinational firms that commonly employed these policies at home. A recommendation to expand the labor supply by encouraging more women to work part time was also made. The task force rejected the NWC's recommendations that employers withhold their CPF contributions for workers who were not committed to their organizations, that new employees be given bonuses in an effort to retain them, that a program be set up to recover training costs from workers who left after training, and that employees be issued national employment cards.

Several of the features of Singapore's IR system—namely, the work system design, training systems, reward systems, employment security systems, and participation systems—contribute to the high turnover and the related labor problems, as indicated by the government's significant efforts to remedy them. As a result of the Fordist work systems that emerged in the first development phase, on average, the investment in training by organizations is still very low and consists primarily of on-the-job training. Although technological requirements drive this outcome to some extent—that is, the early phase of the development cycle does not require sophisticated skills—the absence of training interferes with the development of workers' commitment to their organizations. It also interferes with employees' abilities to take on more demanding jobs or to participate in decision making.

Worker participation systems have been widely encouraged in Singapore, but they have been less than successful in building employee commitment and productivity, and they do not begin to provide the level of authority granted workers in many Japanese and German companies. Nor have stock ownership plans been widely used to build commitment.

The rewards and staffing systems also contribute to the lack of worker commitment. Overall, the rewards system has led to a reasonably balanced distribution of income (Lim 1990:86), and in most recent years increases in the earnings of production workers have exceeded that of professional workers (86–87). Interview data indicate, however, that status differentials between managers and workers still tend to be high, probably because of the strong presence of U.S. and U.K. MNCs, coupled with the historical effects of U.K. social systems. For example, wage and benefit differentials between managers and workers are perceived to be higher than in Japanese and German firms in their home countries. Further, differences in the training given managers and workers tend to stifle rank-and-file workers' chances of career advancement, rendering promotion difficult and undercutting workers' commitment. Wide disparities in wages, benefits, and training between managers and workers are not common characteristics of German and Japanese firms. Finally, unlike Germany and Japan, Singapore does not have an employment security system, although it is not clear that employment security would help build commitment in a tight labor market.[20]

Cost Effectiveness

As a result of Singapore's incomes policies, labor costs have increased significantly. Unit labor costs increased by 27 percent from 1980 to 1988, for example (Lim 1990:76), and next to Japan, Singapore has had the highest wage rates in Asia for some time (Deyo 1989:91). Consequently, Singapore has, to a degree, lost its comparative advantage in labor-intensive industries, and some companies have moved operations to other developing countries. But this was part of the nation's purposeful strategy to move upscale with respect to technological competence.

Since 1984, salary and wage increases have exceeded productivity rates (output per worker) in every year but 1986, when there was a recession (NWC 1990), and annual increases in worker productivity in the service sector have exceeded those in manufacturing in every year but one since 1984. These results have been of concern to the government, and it is recommending a wage policy that will prevent real wage increases from exceeding increases in productivity. Further, the substantial investments being made in training and work reform are intended to shore up the declining rate of productivity. Singapore's compound annual growth in productivity from 1970 to 1987 was 4.8 percent, compared with 5.9 percent for Japan, 5.8 percent for Korea, 1.4 percent for the United States, 2.2 percent for the United Kingdom, and 3.8 percent for Germany (Porter 1990:22, 23). In recent years, the growth has been at or below that figure; 3.4 percent in 1990, for example (Ministry of Labour 1990:63).

Foreign investment in Singapore has remained strong despite fears that rising costs have been undermining the nation's appeal as a production center. In 1992, foreign investment jumped 13 percent, and its largest trading partner, the United States, increased its investment by 24 percent (Holman 1993, A10).

It is a remarkable economic achievement that despite a tight labor market, low unemployment, and declining productivity, Singapore has not had a problem with inflation (Department of Statistics 1990:12–13). Further, competitiveness in the global marketplace has remained strong, as indicated by the fact that exports and imports more than doubled from 1980 to 1990 (4).

Financial Flexibility

The government, through the NWC and other organizations, has successfully been encouraging the development of flexible payment systems, as indicated by the SIPM and SNEF surveys. If the surveys indicate actual implementation, then a good share of Singaporean workers have their pay tied to individual, group, or organizational performance. The use of layoffs also permits employers to adjust their wage bills in response to economic change, and the strategy of the NWC since 1981 of permitting flexible application of its wage recommendations makes wages more sensitive to market conditions. Clearly, Singapore is moving to a high level of financial flexibility.

Functional Flexibility

Functional flexibility in manufacturing concerns in Singapore is generally very low, but not because of restrictive government or union "job-control" policies that allocate employees to jobs by seniority. Indeed, as noted earlier, the Industrial Relations Act removed from collective bargaining policies related to transfers, promotions, and work assignments, which have impeded the ability of employers in nations such as the United States and the United Kingdom to allocate workers based on merit rather than seniority. Therefore, Singaporean employers have a great deal of flexibility in how they use employees, even though many employers still consult with unions on these policies. Rather, the low degree of functional flexibility results primarily from the narrow job designs, which give workers little authority and require only a few hours of on-the-job training to bring workers up to speed. Accordingly, workers in Singapore are not as flexible as workers in Germany and Japan in taking on a broad range of tasks in times of change or as capable of participating in complex business decisions.

Workers in Japanese firms in Japan, by comparison, tend to perform a broader range of tasks, with more authority. Further, Japanese workers are trained during downturns, rather than laid off, which results in a more flexible work force that is adaptable to change. As substantial ongoing efforts to redesign work to make it more meaningful, to expand training, and to broaden employee authority are successful, functional flexibility in Singapore will no doubt improve.

External and Internal Numerical Flexibility

The freedom to subcontract and use part-time and foreign guest workers, the absence of employment security systems, and the common use of layoffs during downturns create a high degree of external numerical flexibility for Singapore's employers. But if the Japanese IR system has any validity, the impact on employee competence and commitment and organizational integration undermines productivity. Employers also have a great deal of internal numerical flexibility, so that they can adjust workers' schedules to expand or contract their hours. Overtime and flexible scheduling are widely used. The longer workweek also provides employers with greater flexibility, although there is a trend toward shortening the workweek.

Integration

Labor-management relations in Singaporean organizations are peaceful, as indicated by the fact that there has been only one strike since 1978 (Department of Statistics 1990:77). Similarly, the 1991 SIPM survey indicated that only 3 percent of the respondents believed that the labor-management relations at their firms were either adversarial or antagonistic (35). Nonetheless, the flexibility afforded Singaporean employers in many aspects of human resources decision making has not produced integrated organizations.

The high degree of worker turnover and the absence of job security systems hinder the development of continuity and the efficiency of decision making, to be sure. But the ease of organizational decision making is also hindered by the narrow job designs, by disparities in the training and rewards afforded managers and employees, and by the incomplete development of programs that encourage employee involvement and information exchange, all of which interfere with the communications needed in an integrated organization. Finally, the absence of job rotation as a staffing strategy inhibits broad understanding of organizational functioning.

In 1981, the Committee on Productivity recommended the implementation of the Japanese IR system in Singapore (Lee 1985:147–48). Integration in many Japanese firms begins with work designs that require and challenge workers' competence and branch out to include extensive development systems that employ job rotation, to staffing systems that build commitment through job security and promotion from within, to egalitarian rewards systems, and to governance systems that include the open sharing of information. Japanese firms, in essence, exchange low external numerical flexibility for the development of more competent, committed workers and more integrated, cost-effective organizations that are the most productive in the developed world. The Task Force Report on

Job-Hopping discussed above indicated that little progress had been made in implementing the Japanese IR system called for by the Committee on Productivity, and many of the causes of job turnover that the task force identified (listed under "Commitment" above) confirm the lack of integration in Singapore's organizations.

In sum, if the integrated IR systems of Germany and Japan contain any lessons for Singapore, it is that Singapore is not currently in an ideal position to support the development of the flexible, competent, committed, integrated, productive work force required to perform complex work. Although there are major institutional differences between Singapore and other advanced English-speaking countries with respect to their IR systems, Singapore's IR system is more like the ones these nations are attempting to move away from as they, like Singapore, try to emulate the integrated, flexible IR systems of more economically successful nations such as Japan and Germany. As is clear from table 4.2, however, as Singapore develops a higher-tech industrial structure, it has a substantial headstart on countries such as the United Kingdom and the United States in developing a flexible, integrated IR system. In the conclusion are important lessons for other developing countries.

Developing Congruent Industrial Relations Systems in NICs

Singapore's well-planned economic transition has relevance for other developing countries willing to engage in a similar degree of government coordination of labor-management interests with the goal of attracting the foreign investment required to fuel the phases of the industrialization process. Furthermore, the Singaporean experience has relevance for researchers examining the life cycle of the industrial structures of developing countries in that it illustrates the instability of the low-value-added phase of industrialization in the context of international competition and the need to plan well for the transition to more complex technologies. The substantial presence of foreign MNCs also has had implications for Singapore's IR system design, although the effects are moderated in some areas by the government's extensive IR policies. Finally, the convergence of Singapore's political, social, and economic institutions toward mature market economies has affected and is affected by cultural traditions.

Role of Government

Like other developing countries, Singapore began the process of industrialization more than twenty-five years ago with an economy that was based on the utilization of simple knowledge. As Singapore proceeded through the first phase of development, its businesses borrowed technologies and organizational designs and acquired investment from foreign multinational firms. Indeed, the extremely high level of foreign investment in Singapore, and the IR policies developed to attract this investment under the strong government control that characterizes the most successful developing countries (Deyo 1989), are major determinants of the IR system effects in Singapore.

At a very early stage in Singapore's development, the government made a strategic decision to place a dual emphasis on improving the living standards of its citizens and on developing IR policies that were attractive to foreign investors. As a result, by most indexes, the standard of living in Singapore is higher than in the other Asian NICs, Hong Kong, South Korea, and Taiwan and second only to Japan in Asia. The high productivity, high standard of living, reasonably balanced distribution of income, and rapid economic growth that took place in the context of the government's extensive labor control lend weight to the proposition that extensive labor standards, when properly meshed with development policies, contribute to the development process by creating productive workers. This result is in conflict with the argument of neoclassical economists that expensive labor standards create uncompetitive labor costs and undermine international competitiveness (Herzenberg, Perez-Lopez, and Tucker 1990:3–4).

There is little question that the stability introduced into Singapore's society by corporatist policies, particularly the development of a union movement that was incorporated into the government decision-making structure, was instrumental in attracting the foreign capital that fueled the development of the country. As Deyo (1989:213) suggests, whether the degree of corporatist control in Singapore can be maintained over the life cycle of the nation depends on how well its social needs are anticipated and on how long Singapore can maintain the economic growth required to sustain the materialistic needs of a corporatist society. At the present, it would be difficult to argue that the economic development strategy has been anything but effective.

Life Cycle of Development

In the early phase of the economic development of Singapore and other industrially advanced countries, the first technologies they borrowed were from the simple end of the knowledge continuum, often involving low-value-added assembly operations where they competed on the basis of cost and benefited from their low cost of labor. The organizations and derivative IR systems that evolved to support these industrial structures tended to be bureaucratic and inflexible (Begin 1991; Mintzberg 1983). Singapore has been leaving this phase for well over a decade as it has attempted to evolve a high-technology industrial structure. Nonetheless, despite substantial efforts to move from the Fordist job designs and inflexible IR practices of the first phase to flexible IR practices by borrowing heavily from the Japanese and German IR models, Singapore, as indicated in table 4.2, has been only partially successful. A major reason is that Singapore is at a much earlier phase of development than Japan; many of its manufacturing operations are small by comparison.

Japan's current IR system serves an industrial structure that is already composed of many large, high-value-added, home-based, internationally competitive industries. As M. Porter (1990) points out, although Singapore has made important progress, it still relies heavily on factor-driven technologies provided by foreign MNCs. If Singapore stays on course in developing flexible work practices as it evolves an industrial structure composed of larger organizations using more complex technologies, its IR system will probably converge to a greater extent toward the Japanese IR model, as Singapore learns from the mistakes and successes of such mature, advanced societies as the United Kingdom and the United States, which are also attempting to converge toward the Japanese lean production model.

Because Singapore is so small, and consequently limited land is available to support commerce and population growth, it is unlikely that Singaporean manufacturing organizations will ever approach the average employment size of advanced nations. At the same time, Singapore's size should be an advantage in implementing and maintaining flexible IR practices, since its smaller organizations will be less affected by the bureaucratizing effects of size. As will be discussed below, cultural factors may also help produce a unique, hybrid IR system in Singapore.

Moving to the next stage of development is not an easy undertaking; Porter points out that only a handful of nations (he identifies nine) have moved to an investment-driven, innovation-driven, or wealth-driven stage of development (1990:566). Major countries, including Australia and Canada, have never moved beyond the factor-driven stage of development and, accordingly, have not evolved an internationally competitive, high-technology industrial structure that not only uses advanced technology but creates new knowledge. Technological innovation requires an appropriate business strategy, advanced factors (such as a sophisticated educational system), a sophisticated home market, and internal competitive forces that are extremely difficult to create (Porter 1990). Singapore has used Porter's ideas in its recent Strategic Economic Plan, in which the development of high-tech, home-based corporations was one of the major long-term goals (Ministry of Trade and Industry 1991:86).

A major difference between Singapore and Japan and between Singapore and other advanced nations but not between Singapore and other small developing countries is that its small size makes it difficult for it to develop a very large home market, sophisticated though the country may be. Singapore must always rely on substantial exports, as indicated by the fact that it exported 43.9 percent of its GNP in 1987 (Porter 1990:23), more than any other developing or developed country. By way of comparison, Japan exported 10.7 percent of its GNP; Korea, 39 percent; and the United States, 5.5 percent. As a result of its reliance on exports, Singapore is subject to a much greater extent than other developing countries to the dynamic vagaries of international competition. In addition, a factor-driven economy is inherently unstable, since other developing nations can undercut its rising standard of living. These forces probably will continue to drive the development of a flexible IR system in Singapore.

Role of Multinational Corporations

Another important factor that distinguishes Singapore from Japan but not necessarily other developing countries is Singapore's substantial reliance on foreign investment. The success of Singapore in attracting investments and jobs has created a very tight labor market that has impeded the transfer of Japanese training policies in Japanese MNCs (Putti and Toh 1990). The tight labor market also has made it difficult to develop employee commitment, an important component of a congruent Japanese IR system.

Although data are not available to assess this point, worker commitment could be expected to be more difficult to develop in foreign firms than in indigenous firms because such commitment requires being loyal to foreign managers and foreign organizations whose policies have been developed at the companies' home bases. Further, these policies may not involve bringing the latest technologies to Singapore and therefore may slow down the restructuring of production in the capital-intensive manner sought by the government (Islam 1989). Indeed, one study found that one explanation for the stagnant total-factor productivity in Singapore in the 1970s was the predominance of foreign MNCs in the manufacturing sector (Tsao 1982).

The lack of long-term commitment to the development of Singapore by foreign MNCs is also indicated by the fact that some MNCs have already moved production to other lower-cost developing countries, although, as noted, foreign investment in Singapore to this point is still increasing. To help build commitment by MNCs to Singapore and to help cement employee commitment to these MNCs, Singapore's Strategic Economic Plan sets the goal of encouraging foreign MNCs to set up home bases and to conduct basic research and development functions in Singapore, and, as noted previously, the government has encouraged organizations to adopt policies that reinforce employee loyalty to firms.

The dominance of foreign MNCs in the manufacturing arena in Singapore has no doubt affected the direction that the Singapore IR system has taken. Research on the transfer of Japanese IR practices to the United Kingdom and the United States, for example, indicates that industries in these countries have successfully adopted such practices, particularly those such as the automobile industry in which labor is a significant cost of operating (Galbraith 1989). But in neither the United Kingdom nor the United States has government influence on labor standards been as extensive as in Singapore, with the result that the effects of the MNCs have been moderated.

The government of Singapore has shown through its policy mandates a strong preference for many features of the Japanese IR system. That Singapore's mandates have been partially successful in converging toward that model is indicated by the results of a study that compared Singapore with Malaysia and India and found that the policies of locally owned firms in Singapore were more like those of the Japanese MNCs operating in Singapore than the policies of locally owned firms in Malaysia and India were like the policies of Japanese MNCs operating there (Jain, Jain, and Ratnam 1992:361). Neither the Malaysian nor the Indian government has followed the same corporatist route with regard to industrial relations policies. As another indication of the government's success, government encouragement and direct government policy have led many MNCs to implement IR policies in Singapore that are less commonly practiced at home, for example, flexible compensation practices.

Role of Culture

Cultural differences between Japan and Singapore have also been pinpointed as hindering the transfer of Japanese practices, and probably those of other countries as well. Research by P. S. Kirkbride and S. F. Y. Tang (1992) on cultural barriers to the transference of quality circles from Japan to Hong Kong concluded that G. Hofstede (1980) correctly identified cultural differences between the countries that accounted for the lower utility of QCCs in Hong Kong, such as the greater need for power centralization in Hong Kong organizations, the lower levels of employee loyalty and work orientation in Hong Kong, and, unlike the situation in Japan, the workers' orientation to their families rather than their organizations. Since Singapore and Hong Kong are much closer on Hofstede's cultural measures (Shaw et al. 1992), similar cultural impediments to the transfer of Japanese IR practices to Singapore were predicted.

Although these studies suggest that the Chinese culture has impeded the transference of some foreign IR practices, according to W. McCord (1991), under the advance of industrialism (and also perhaps because of Singapore's long association with British traditions), " 'Western' attributes such as materialism, hedonism, and individualism" developed to the point that the government felt it necessary to announce that "Confucianism would be taught as moral instruction in secondary schools" (1991:58). This seemingly contradictory evidence on the effects of culture suggests that, as industrialization proceeds through phases related to a nation's industrial structure, the process of industrialization, when coupled with the substantial dependence of an emerging nation on the global marketplace and the investments of foreign multinationals, diminishes but does not eliminate the impact of national culture on the design and impact of the society's institutions, including its IR system, and thus opens the path to convergence.

Conclusion

The most that can be concluded at this point about the nature of the convergence issue in Singapore is that the country's unique IR system is a complex hybrid, reflecting neither the inflexible models from which the United Kingdom and the United States are moving nor the flexible models currently operating in Japan and Germany. This outcome results from outright government influence in some areas (for example, flexible wage policies); government-provided flexibility to employers in other areas (for example, the removal by statute of most staffing areas from collective bargaining); the influence of the MNC, through the application of home policies; the relatively small size of Singapore's manufacturing organizations; and market- and culture-driven influences in other areas (for example, Putti and Toh [1990] pointed to Singapore's high turnover rate and individualistic culture to explain the imperfect transfer of Japanese training policies).

This study is only a preliminary effort to sort out the relative influence of these factors, in part because most published surveys on Singapore's IR practices did not break the data down by foreign or local ownership or by business sector. More systematic analysis of the IR system along these dimensions would probably provide additional insights into the convergence issue.

5

South Africa's Industrialization: The Challenge Facing Labor

Avril Joffe, Judy Maller, and Eddie Webster

I n their classic study of industrialization, C. Kerr and his colleagues (1960) proposed that in industrializing nations, industrial relations practices will vary systematically with the nature of the elite directing the industrialization process. This elite, they argued, consists of "the political leaders, industrial organization builders, top military officers, associated intellectuals and sometimes leaders of labor organizations" (Kerr et al. 1960:8). "Labor," they claim, "seldom really leads society into the future." In fact, management is not central either. Rather, it is the political leaders who are generally dominant. An examination of strategies that promote industrialization tends to confirm Kerr and his colleagues' conclusion that it is the state, rather than management or labor, that is central to the industrialization process (Deyo 1987). This was certainly the case in apartheid South Africa, where the state was central in changing the economy from one that was primarily extractive and agricultural to one that was primarily industrialized (Seidman 1990a:124–25).

The discovery of gold and diamonds in the late nineteenth century transformed South Africa's agrarian economy into one based on extractive industry. It also entrenched racial divisions in the workplace, creating two distinct labor markets: one for whites, the other for blacks. European immigrants monopolized early craft production, having learned the value of union protection in the period of deskilling in their home countries. Craft workers became a privileged stratum, organized into craft unions that used the techniques of entry restriction, apprenticeship, and the closed shop to protect their monopoly of control. Craft unionism was prominent among foundry, railway, and engineering workers at the turn of the century

We would like to thank Stephen Frenkel for his extensive comments on an earlier draft.

and remained powerful throughout the early decades. Black workers, by contrast, entered wage labor on a weak and unorganized basis, mainly as unskilled migrant laborers. This division of labor markets and the allocation of rights to white workers and their denial to black employees was institutionalized by the Industrial Conciliation Act of 1924.

With the emergence of manufacturing in South Africa in the 1930s and 1940s, job opportunities were opened up for black workers, thereby eroding craft-based control. The exclusion of blacks from the industrial relations system, compounded by their lack of political rights, fueled a political trade union tradition that has a trajectory into the present.

After World War II, South Africa underwent rapid state-assisted industrial growth. This involved a transformation of the labor process, a despotic system of labor control, a lack of social infrastructure in communities, and restricted access to political power. This is the pattern of industrialization that creates the conditions for the rise and strong growth of social movement unionism, whereby the scope of unionism is broadened to include union involvement in new urban social movements (Seidman 1990b; Munck 1989). In South Africa, these movements include the civic associations and the organizations struggling for democracy, such as the African National Congress (ANC). A central characteristic of South Africa's social movement unionism is militant abstentionism: the refusal by black workers to identify with any of the goals of the enterprise or the concerns of management.

The prospect of a new democratic order, especially since February 1990, when political movements were no longer banned, has led to a shift in union leaders' thinking and practice away from abstentionism toward the assumption of a central role and responsibility in shaping a new industrial strategy. The idea that trade unions can shape national economic policy necessitates a different form of unionism—what has been called strategic unionism. This form of unionism has emerged in certain countries, such as the Nordic nations and arguably Australia, where the unions have become the "bearers of industrial regeneration" (Higgins 1987:213). In the 1980s, manufacturing unions in Australia launched a comprehensive campaign to rescue and modernize the country's crumbling manufacturing sector. Among the strategies they used was targeting industrial policy and intervening directly at the enterprise level. This new unionism, writes W. Higgins (1987), confounds the pessimism of industrial relations theorists that trade unions are unable to go beyond their craft origins to address managerial issues directly.

Strategic unionism calls for conscious intervention at the macroeconomic level and the setting of goals such as low unemployment, low inflation, and social development. It requires a commitment to growth and wealth creation, as well as to equitable distribution. It requires democratization of the workplace, participation in tripartite bodies, and a strong research and educational capacity inside the union movement. With strategic unionism, in essence, instead of merely reacting to events, unions become proactive, take the initiative, and seek to set the agenda (Ogden 1992:21). The potential exists in South Africa for labor to adopt strategic unionism, but it will have to overcome the strong tradition of abstentionism. If any industrial, labor-led restructuring is to occur, it will also require the active cooperation of capital and an alliance with a strong developmental and democratic state.

This chapter is an investigation into whether the South African labor movement could play a central role in a new industrialization strategy.[1] In the first section, we examine the pattern of industrialization under "racial Fordism," its subsequent crisis in the 1970s, and its decline in the 1980s. The second section describes the growth of the labor movement in the 1980s and its emergence as a leading force in the process of transition to a new democratic order. In the third section, we look at the possibilities for a new industrialization strategy and the role of labor within it. We show how the Congress of South African Trade Unions (COSATU) has begun to challenge the unilateral restructuring of the economy by the state and capital. With its allies in the ANC, COSATU is formulating a reconstruction strategy that attempts to combine economic growth with social justice. By bringing together the themes of economic growth and social justice in policy making, this strategy questions the pessimistic conclusion of Kerr and his coauthors (1960) that "labor seldom really leads society into the future." Whether labor has the capacity to meet this challenge, and what implications such a role might have for the industrial relations system as a whole, remains to be seen.

Earlier studies have explored the relationship between extractive industrialization and craft unionism (J. Lewis 1984; Webster 1985). The focus of this chapter is the form of unionism that emerges under racial Fordism and the possibility that a new form of unionism could emerge in the future. The premise of our argument is that the form of unionism that emerges is essentially a response to the pattern of industrialization and that changes in trade union strategies take place within the limits set by this pattern. This is not to suggest that the form of unionism is determined by the pattern of industrialization alone or that the form of trade unionism could be identified based on an investigation of the pattern of industrialization. At the center of our argument is the idea that leaders of trade unions face strategic choices and that these choices must be understood in the context of past traditions and the organizational capacity of the labor movement. The logical structure of our argument is captured in figure 5.1.

Social movement unionism in South Africa was a response to racial Fordism. Now that a new industrialization pattern is emerging, it is possible for the form of unionism to shift from that of social movement

Figure 5.1. Patterns of Industrialization and Forms of Unionism in South Africa

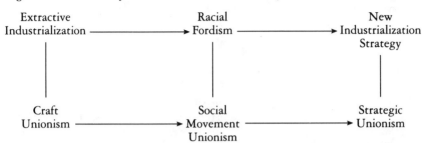

unionism to strategic unionism. This shift is by no means a necessary outcome, however.

Racial Fordism and Industrialization

The basis for South Africa's postwar economic development was import-substitution industrialization featuring three sets of policies: tariff walls were raised to protect domestically produced goods against competition from industrial imports; basic inputs required for industrial expansion were provided by state companies; and public works programs constructed a transportation network that employed and trained "poor whites," creating a highly stratified market. This state-sponsored industrialization changed South Africa from a primarily extractive and agricultural society into an industrialized one (Seidman 1990a:124–25).

This process saw the growth of large firms and the introduction of semiautomatic technology. Mass production, coupled with a limited domestic market, led to periodic overproduction, and so various export drives were initiated. Finally, the international relocation of industry enabled South African manufacturing to develop an indigenous and autocentric form of capital accumulation firmly bonded to overseas capital (Sitas 1983).

The growth of secondary industry depended crucially on the development of heavy industry by both the public and private sectors. Import substitution was pursued in selected industries, such as consumer durables. The manufacturing sector as a whole was relatively capital-intensive and relied heavily on imported intermediary products, capital equipment, and technology. This history underlines the importance of foreign capital derived from the sale of minerals, especially gold.

The postwar period saw the deepening of industrial concentration and centralization, especially in the iron and steel and the engineering sectors. By the late 1970s, the economy already exhibited a high degree of cartelization (Innes 1983:174; Lewis 1991a:32–35). Many manufacturing concerns also developed close ties with foreign companies in order to secure access to advanced technology and, increasingly, new sources of capital. These ties took the form of licensing and patent agreements, as well as joint ventures. Foreign assets in 1983 totaled U.S.$7,555 million; by 1988, they totaled U.S.$15,737 million (Industrial Development Corporation 1992:72).

A form of "racial Fordism" characterized the postwar industrialization process, in which consumption was geared to the higher-income, mainly white market and production was based on principles of mass production.[2] The manufacturing sector developed primarily to serve the needs of this small, high-income elite. Because of the demand for variety, this process involved the manufacture of nonstandardized products, resulting, for example, in a vast array of automobile models and features.

Although light consumer goods, such as boots, saddles, blankets, and soap, were produced by the emergent manufacturing sector, most manufactured goods, even those for mass markets, continued to be imported from Britain, and later from the United States. Postwar dumping of foreign goods, as well as a shortage of capital, prevented local industries from developing rapidly (Callinicos 1985:118).

As evidenced by the production of luxury commodities to the production and pricing structures of industries ranging from building materials to pharmaceuticals, the already skewed distribution of income has worsened (Joffe and Lewis 1992). The rapid expansion of manufacturing in the 1960s saw a decline in South Africans' share of total personal income from 21.4 percent to 19.3 percent (Lipton 1986). In the following decade, 83 percent of the population classified as African, colored, or Indian received approximately 25 percent of total personal income.[3] By the 1980s, South Africa had the highest Gini coefficient (that is, the most extreme disparity in income distribution when compared with complete income equality) in the world (McGrath 1984).[4]

The organization of work has been shaped by the peculiarities of South Africa's industrialization path. The racially skewed nature of consumption in the country has prevented the emergence of the mass consumption of products other than those related to basic subsistence. This in turn has meant that mass production in manufacturing has never been dominant.

The manufacturing industry boomed in the 1960s, with output growing by 8.6 percent, but in the following decade signs of a severe crisis in production began to emerge, and in the 1980s, output grew by a paltry 0.1 percent. The manufacturing industry also declined in relative employment terms: in 1980, it accounted for 28.8 percent of total employment, but by 1989 this figure had fallen to 26.6 percent (Lipton 1986). Import-substitution industrialization, combined with manufacturing along the lines of "racial Fordism," survived into the early 1970s, when market saturation compelled the government, employers, and labor to reevaluate this path.

Crisis in South Africa's Industrialization Path

The early 1970s were a turning point in South Africa's industrial development. Some semi-industrialized economies were able to begin exporting an increasing proportion of their industrial production, both to reap scale economies and to benefit from the process of "learning through exporting" (Kaplinsky 1992:4). For a variety of reasons, including the introduction of sanctions, South Africa was excluded from such development.

The multifaceted reasons for the crisis in South Africa's growth have been documented extensively elsewhere (Gelb 1990). They include the "freed" gold price, which put an end to the stable export earnings that had financed the foreign purchase of capital equipment and entrenched South Africa's technological backwardness. The growth of industrial unions during the 1970s generated rising real wages for black industrial workers and, as a result, unit labor costs were pushed up, further slowing rates of productivity. The oil shocks negatively affected the economy, as did capital flight after political upheavals such as the 1976 Soweto uprising. Capital flight continues to be a problem, with net capital outflow in 1990 being set at U.S.$1.12 billion, compared with U.S.$1.64 billion in 1989 (South African Institute of Race Relations [SAIRR] 1992:405). The uncompetitive nature of industry produced meager export markets, which were further curtailed by the progressive imposition of sanctions internationally. Industry has also been hamstrung by the South African foreign debt, estimated at U.S.$19.4 billion by the South African Reserve Bank at the end of 1990 (Kahn 1992:504).

During the 1960s, the South African GDP per capita increased steadily, but it slowed dramatically in the 1970s. This decline continued throughout the 1980s, until the South African standard of living was 7 percent lower in 1989 than it had been in 1979 (South African Chamber of Business [SACOB] 1991:13–14). Just how sharply living standards have fallen is apparent from the latest World Bank report (1992), which shows that South Africa has slumped from being the world's twenty-fifth richest economy in the 1970s to being thirty-ninth in 1992.[5]

Real growth in South Africa in 1991 was estimated at between zero and 0.5 percent, compared with 4.1 percent in 1988, 2.1 percent in 1989, and −0.9 percent in 1990 (SAIRR 1992:406). The Central Statistical Service attributed the drop to declines in the agricultural, mining, and manufacturing sectors (SAIRR 1992:406). According to the Development Bank of South Africa, the South African growth rate from 1980 to 1988 averaged 2.6 percent—slower than all the other southern African countries except Angola (1991:4).

The manufacturing industry's reliance on foreign exchange earned from gold continues to be significant, and, paradoxically, "although South Africa has the technological and financial capacity for minerals beneficiation, it continues to sell huge quantities of unprocessed ores, concentrates and ferro-alloys" (Jourdan 1992:3). South Africa's reliance on gold and other primary commodities for foreign exchange has been compromised by a severe and systematic decline in their prices.[6]

Problems within manufacturing constitute a key element in the country's economic crisis. Manufacturing provided the key stimulus for the country's postwar expansion and accounts for a major share of employment and output (Black 1992). In 1988, the sector contributed 24 percent to the GDP, while mining and quarrying contributed 13 percent and agriculture 6 percent. For the same year, manufacturing employed 1.3 million people, mining 0.7 million people, and agriculture 1.1 million (Ngoasheng 1991). Since the mid-1970s, however, manufacturing employment has been declining in absolute terms and relative to total nonagricultural employment. The sector's share of total fixed investment declined from 26 percent in 1960 to 18 percent in 1989 (SACOB 1991).

Manufacturing faces the exhaustion of its import-substitution heritage while it continues to depend on imports, to perform badly in exports, and to have a high capital intensity, all of which seriously constrain growth (Black 1992). While import substitution substantially reduced the importation of consumer goods such as clothing, fabricated metal products (except machinery), and food, this was achieved at the expense of increased imports of capital equipment and materials. As a result, South African industry is still import-intensive and the economy dependent on foreign technology (Kaplan 1991). This suggests that further import replacement will have to be directed mainly at capital equipment, intermediate goods, and high-technology subsectors. Although replacement could be achieved with state support and tariff protection, this would be extremely expensive unless sufficient economies of scale could be attained (Black 1992).

South Africa's manufacturing sector remains a poor earner of foreign exchange. In 1989, manufacturing exports constituted 29.1 percent of total exports, compared with mining, which represented 65.6 percent. This suggests that South Africa's particular form of import-substituting industrialization has worked against competitiveness on international markets. As long as locally produced intermediate goods or imported items are subject to stringent import tariffs, it will be difficult for local manufacturers to break into international markets.

Rise of Social Movement Unionism

The crisis of racial Fordism was not simply a structural problem of "import substitution"; it also represented a crisis of control in the workplace, and indeed in the broader political system. A strong shop floor-based union movement began to develop in the early 1970s among African workers, following the momentous Durban strikes of 1973, in which more than 100,000 workers downed tools in support of higher wages. This emergent trade union movement would soon eclipse the white craft unions both numerically and in organizational strength in the workplace. The craft unions, located primarily within the South African Confederation of Labour and clinging to their racial privileges, remained intact, however.

The 1973 strikes were followed by the 1976 Soweto uprising, in which students took the lead in protesting against an unequal and inadequate education system; their parents—members of the industrial working class—were also galvanized into political action. The Wiehahn Commission, established in 1977 to restructure the state's industrial relations system, introduced unitary arrangements that ended racial divisions with respect to mechanisms for regulating industrial conflict.

Thus, the origins of social movement unionism lie in the history of South Africa's industrialization and system of political domination, which reached a turning point in the late 1970s as black workers began to assert their economic and political power through the emerging trade union movement. This trend became more evident during the periods of state repression and civil war in the 1980s, when popular political organizations remained suppressed and the labor movement emerged as a significant political actor. COSATU, in particular, formed alliances with the exiled ANC and internal political organizations, such as the United Democratic Front, with the common program of achieving democracy in South Africa.

The development of a powerful labor movement challenged the alliance between the apartheid state, employers, and white labor. The growth in membership of the new, nonracial industrial unions outstripped that of most countries in the world. The membership of registered unions increased at an average of nearly 22 percent per year between 1980 (808,053 members) and the end of 1991 (2,750,400 members). Membership in unregistered unions at the end of 1991 stood at 300,000, bringing the total membership in unions to more than 3 million. This means that approximately 45 percent of the labor force covered by the Labour Relations Act (approximately 3 million) is currently unionized (Levy 1992).[7]

Although there are six trade union federations, COSATU is unquestionably the major force in the union movement. With a total membership of more than 1.25 million, COSATU has more members than all the other federations combined.[8]

An important feature of the democratic labor movement affiliated under COSATU is its organization into nationwide industrial unions in all the major sectors of the economy (Webster 1984). Union penetration in the different sectors nevertheless remains uneven, as is evident from table 5.1.

The negotiation of recognition agreements, which set out the rights and duties of shop stewards and trade unions in the workplace, was an important step in establishing "the rule of law" on the shop floor (Webster 1985). Trade unions did not win these rights without a fight, however. In

Table 5.1. Union Density in South Africa, by Industry Sector, 1990

Industry sector	Percentage of work force unionized
Leather production	80
Clothing and textiles	80
Metals, motors, and tires	74
Mining	72
Chemicals	68
Food	32
Building and construction	31
Retail, wholesale, hotels, restaurants, and financial services	14
Forestry	14
Paper, printing, packaging, and furniture	27
Domestic	10
Agriculture	5

Source: Survey conducted by E. Webster in Jan. 1990 and admitted as evidence by the ILO Fact-Finding and Conciliation Commission concerning Freedom of Association, Johannesburg, Feb. 1991.

the late 1970s and early 1980s, there were hundreds of strikes in support of the demands for recognition.

During the 1970s and early 1980s, the democratic unions concentrated on building their strength on the shop floor and bargaining at the plant level with management. Their core demands were for recognition and negotiation for improved wages, leave, hours of work, health and safety, and pensions.

Although the unions were becoming a formidable force on the shop floor, by the early 1980s they were unable to coordinate strike waves, which erupted in isolated struggles in different factories (Webster 1985). Consequently, several unions reevaluated their strategy and began to adopt a more centralized approach to bargaining, mainly by seeking membership in statutory industrial councils that regulated labor relations on an industry basis. This signaled a major strategic shift.

By the end of the 1980s, many unionists were arguing strongly for centralized bargaining in industrial councils. They argued that it allowed for more efficient use of union resources, that it established minimum conditions and wages in the industry and extended these conditions to small and nonunionized factories, and that it made possible benefit funds and training schemes as a result of the economies of scale. Finally, industrial councils provided a forum where unions could engage in industrywide negotiations, which could potentially be extended to include issues concerning industrial restructuring. Significantly, the unions are now making new demands involving industrial training, retrenchment, and industrial strategy (Allie 1991).

The democratic internal structures of the emergent unions enabled them to articulate the demands of their constituencies effectively, and in so doing they have been able to sustain and consolidate their membership over time. At the core of these democratic structures is the shop steward system. There are now more than twenty-five thousand shop stewards in COSATU spread across nine regions and thirteen affiliates. In a recent survey of shop stewards, it was found that the vast majority had formal recognition from management (97 percent) (Pityana and Orkin 1992). Furthermore, they were subject to regular elections, either through a show of hands (52 percent) or through secret ballot (48 percent). A strong democratic political culture has thus been built up inside the union movement.

The involvement of shop stewards in issues beyond the shop floor distinguishes South African shop stewards from their contemporary European counterparts. It also distinguishes South Africa from the rest of Africa, where the struggle against colonial rule did not involve the mobilization of a grassroots worker movement with its own tradition of politics. Instead, independence was won either by peasant-based guerrilla movements or by nationalist movements led largely by the professional middle class. The participation of the labor movement in a large number of general strikes, called "stayaways," from 1984 until the present has promoted its intervention in the political realm, consolidated its alliance with the ANC, and confirmed its ongoing role in the process of social transformation.

Unions and Politics in the 1980s

Conflict between the state and labor escalated during the mid-1980s. In response to growing township militancy, the government imposed a state of emergency in 1985. Some 440 trade unionists were detained between 1985 and 1989. In December 1986, the first direct attacks on trade unionists began. Since the mid-1980s, there have been approximately sixty-five attacks on the premises of trade unions and on individual trade unionists associated with COSATU, and several people have been killed (International Labour Office 1992). Very few prosecutions have followed.

Open conflict between the state and COSATU reached a climax in 1987. In April of that year, police shot four striking railway workers during a protest march in Johannesburg. A week later, four scabs were murdered after being interrogated at COSATU House, the organization's headquarters. On 5 and 6 May, a successful nationwide stayaway against the white general election was held. Early the following morning, COSATU House was bombed (Fine and Webster 1989).

During 1987, the year of the strike action, 340,000 miners went out on a three-week strike over wages. The strike was characterized by a management offensive to try and break the power of the National Union of

Mineworkers (NUM), which had been built up over the previous five years. This offensive was mirrored in the response of the state when public sector employees in the railways and post offices staged a protracted strike action that year (*South African Labour Bulletin* 1990, special issue on the public sector, 4, 8). During this period, there was a broad shift in management attitudes toward the trade union movement. Employers clearly felt that the unions had made unacceptably deep inroads into management power and that it was time to roll back trade union gains.

In 1988, after extensive consultation with employers, the government tabled new labor legislation in the form of the Labour Relations Amendment (LRA) Bill. The purpose of the LRA was to curb union power and rights won through industrial courts (Baskin 1991).

The threat posed by the LRA galvanized the unions. Over the next two years the labor movement held worker summits and launched a campaign of protests, stayaways, and bans on overtime in protest of the bill (which became law in September 1988).

Struggles over the LRA deepened the crisis of control on the shop floor under apartheid. Concomitantly, alienation and resistance to institutionalized racial privilege contributed to South Africa's productivity crisis. This is illustrated by the comments of a local Mercedes Benz manager:

> The workers have been radicalized to such an extent that they don't feel part of the company. Supervisors used to clock in and then lock themselves in their offices for the whole day. They did not dare go out on the assembly lines. Since 1987 we have never achieved our weekly production target. Five years ago the plant built seventy cars a day. Then workers said they were working too hard and since then we have only built forty a day. . . .
> Sometimes workers even stood at the assembly lines with mock AK47s or bazookas strapped to their backs. This was a symbol of defiance and rejection of the company, which many workers believed was merely an extension of the repressive apartheid structures. (Von Holdt 1991b:38)

The union campaigns, protests, wildcat industrial actions, and disruption on the shop floor were taking their toll on employers. But in late 1989 the winds of political change were also being felt. The reformist F. W. de Klerk replaced P. W. Botha as president of South Africa. As de Klerk signaled his intention to reform apartheid, the democratic movement launched a defiance campaign across the country. In October, de Klerk released the veteran leaders of the ANC, who had been jailed on Robben Island since the 1960s. In February the next year, de Klerk announced the unbanning of the ANC, the Pan African Congress, and the South African Communist party and released Nelson Mandela, who had been imprisoned for twenty-eight years as de facto leader of the ANC.

There was a noticeable shift in the attitudes of major employers during this period as it became clear that South Africa was moving toward democracy. In May 1990, the historic accord between labor (COSATU and the National Council of Trade Unions) and employers (the South African Consultative Committee on Labour Affairs [SACCOLA]) led to the signing of the Laboria Minute between employers, trade unions, and the Department of Manpower. In essence, the Laboria Minute repealed the objectionable amendments to the labor laws made in the Labour Relations Amendment Bill of 1988 and signaled the extension of basic trade union rights to all workers, including farmworkers, domestic workers, and public sector workers. In the future, all labor laws would be considered by SACCOLA (representing employers) and the trade union movement before being put before Parliament. The trade unions would participate in the National Manpower Commission, a statutory consultative body established under the 1981 Labour Relations Act.

For the first time, both the state and employers accepted that an industrial relations order could not be imposed on the labor movement. In addition, the trade union movement was no longer confined simply to resisting state and employer action over which it had no control and very little influence. The trade union movement now faced the challenge of participating in shaping labor law and collective bargaining and tripartite institutions.

The anti-LRA campaign had raised a debate within the trade unions on what kind of labor law should replace the LRA. Participation in the National Manpower Commission raised the same questions at a concrete and practical level, as the labor movement entered into negotiations with employers and the state over the future of industrial relations in South Africa.[9] Thus, the anti-LRA campaign, which was the high point of the politics of resistance, ushered in a new era characterized by the politics of reconstruction. The emergence of a powerful labor movement in South Africa had opened up the possibility of a distinct role for the trade union movement in the process of transition to a new democratic order (Adler, Maller, and Webster 1992).

The Emerging Industrialization Strategy and Labor's New Path

There is widespread agreement in South Africa that the country's economic future depends on an economic transformation from dependence on minerals to an economy based on a strong manufacturing sector. The apartheid government and the ANC (ANC 1990:6) agreed that the performance of the manufacturing sector would have a significant effect on future economic development. There is also a growing consensus among the state, business, the ANC, and COSATU on the current status of the manufacturing sector and some strategies for resuscitating economic growth (see Maree and Godfrey, chap. 6). These strategies contain concrete proposals regarding the restructuring of the manufacturing sector to meet the demands of the population *and* become a significant earner of foreign exchange.

The apartheid state's industrial policy revolved around four central themes: the continuation of privatization/deregulation; inward industrialization; export promotion; and, closely related to this, a proposal to open up markets previously inaccessible as a result of political isolation. Of particular importance was the government's export promotion policy. The principal reasons for export promotion are the need for foreign exchange in order to purchase intermediate inputs and machinery from abroad and the desire to reduce South Africa's dependence on gold and other primary products.

The apartheid state's promotion of exports was not particularly successful: in 1989, merchandise exports (as distinguished from gold, which is the bulk of South Africa's exports) made up 16.8 percent of the GDP. This is only slightly higher than the figure for 1961 (16.5 percent), while the figures for the interim years have generally been lower (the low was 10.8 percent in 1983) (SACOB 1991:45). Exports in 1989 totaled U.S.$22.088 billion, compared with U.S.$20.984 billion in 1987. This seemingly encouraging increase in recent years needs to be balanced against the increase in imports over the same period, from U.S.$14.116 billion to U.S.$16.978 billion (Industrial Development Corporation 1992:70). The challenge then is to create new production and employment as well as expand domestic markets. This may involve combining duties on imports while encouraging exports (Bell 1990:12). The dismantling of the economic model of racial Fordism and the need to formulate a new growth path have had a profound impact on business, the labor movement, and industrial relations.

A New Corporate Industrial Strategy

Employers are seeking to develop their own set of proposals aimed at increasing industrial competitiveness and stimulating economic growth. This is taking place in a relatively uncoordinated, ad hoc way, given the fragmentation of employer associations in South Africa (Bendix 1992). One of the major stumbling blocks to business development has been identified as the unfavorable investment environment, which has hindered the inflow of foreign investments, local investment in productive enterprises, and the availability of capital for small business, informal sector, and low-cost housing initiatives.

The lack of competitiveness of South African manufacturing is also a key concern. The South African Chamber of Business, which coordinates a number of employer organizations in a loose affiliation, has called for a "new industrial policy" (1991). Such a policy would focus on promoting a dynamic manufacturing sector that would be internationally competitive. SACOB is particularly concerned about export performance. Key factors that inhibit the promotion of exports are the cost of capital, the cost of imported intermediate inputs, the cost of labor, the taxation and tax rates, the real interest rates, and the inflation. Accordingly, a new industrial policy would have to incorporate tax holidays and exemptions for manufacturers as well as subsidized loans to purchase facilities and equipment. Lowering the levels of corporate tax, lowering the import tariffs for imported inputs, and charging no levy on imported production facilities and equipment are all seen as essential if the investment necessary for the growth of the manufacturing sector is to take place. There has been positive support for the state's latest proposal to establish "export processing zones" to provide "competitive" firms with relief from taxation and regulation.

Unlike the ANC and COSATU, big business advocates the withdrawal of the state from the economic sphere. This proposal ignores the lessons of the newly industrialized East Asian countries and Japan, where state interventions have benefited the manufacturing sector (Best 1990). SACOB, for example, has called for further privatization and deregulation of the economy and also proposes the "privatization or devolution of activities [by large companies] to small businesses" (i.e., subcontracting) (SACOB 1991:7).

There is widespread support in the business community for a wage freeze, for reduced industrial relations conflict, and for higher levels of productivity. In particular, arguments for improved labor productivity cite the need for a substantial skills training program (SACOB 1990) and for national wage and productivity policies that will give due regard to the need to maintain a relationship between wages and productivity. Employers are also changing their strategies with regard to the management of the work force to boost labor productivity, reduce manufacturing costs, and achieve competitive advantage. In many cases this has prompted a range of initiatives to restructure work, as outlined below.

Restructuring Work and Industrial Relations on the Shop Floor

The macroeconomic proposals put forth by management in South Africa must be understood in the context of restructuring efforts that are taking place in manufacturing firms. The reorganization of work currently under way is a product of the lack of competitiveness and the restricted nature of the market and is focused particularly on labor in the absence of significant technological innovation. These efforts have had a very significant impact on industrial relations, forcing both management and unions to reconsider traditional structures of bargaining and shop floor relations. Recent research shows that the influence of Japanese manufacturing strategies is becoming pervasive among management, although the implementation of such strategies is both limited and piecemeal.[10]

The tentative restructuring of work taking place in manufacturing is paralleled by a shift in the politics of control on the shop floor. Adversarial industrial relations excluded South African unions from decision making related to corporate policy. In turn, the militant abstentionism of the unions led them to label participation in management as co-optive. This is slowly beginning to change as management introduces communication structures that are widespread on shop floors in Japan and as labor seeks to influence macroeconomic policy.

Management has introduced a variety of communication and suggestion schemes that incorporate workers into a system of information sharing but that do not extend their participation to decision making. Many of these schemes are designed to solicit workers' ideas about improving throughput, quality, and productivity, on the assumption that workers can contribute to problem solving and innovation in response to Japanese-style management initiatives.

The most common schemes used in South African firms are shop-floor communication structures, which include quality circles, green areas, and other channels for workers to contribute their ideas and problem-solving skills. Workers are consulted on production schedules, work allocation, and product runs, and their suggestions are elicited about productivity and quality improvements. These structures represent a direct form of participation, unmediated by union involvement. In the vast majority of cases, the structures of participation have not been negotiated with the union and they do not provide much opportunity for workers to influence decisions. Instead, they are a recognition by management that shop-floor workers have a wealth of experience and "tacit skill" that need to be harnessed to ensure more productive and innovative working practices.

Few companies have developed cooperative forms of decision making in which unions are represented, but the new structures, nevertheless, mark the beginning of a trend in shop-floor politics that puts joint decision making on the agenda. Approximately 10 percent of the companies in the metal and motor sectors have established joint committees of union and management representatives. These committees meet to discuss corporate decisions, and unionists are actively included in decision making about appointments, production organization, job grading, and technology upgrading.

There is ample evidence of the ad hoc nature of management production strategies, which do not conform to the models associated with either mass production or flexible production. The particular strategies used by South Africa's management must be seen as responses to the particular conditions of accumulation that prevail, including the restricted and specialized markets, the outdated technology, and a work force that is unskilled because of the legacy of apartheid's education system and the conflictual industrial relations system.

Labor's New Growth Path

The rapid changes on the shop floor and in the political and economic arenas confronted the trade union movement with the question of what role it should play in economic development.[11] A strong view emerged in COSATU that the trade unions should not only seek to stop the government's unilateral restructuring of the economy—in the form of privatization and deregulation—but actively intervene in the development and implementation of economic policy. Debate on these issues has been led by COSATU's metal, mining, and textile and clothing affiliates—the National Union of Metalworkers of South Africa, the National Union of Mineworkers, and the South African Clothing and Textile Workers' Union. COSATU argues that South Africa needs to develop a new growth path for the economy. To establish this path, restructuring needs to take place at all levels—macroeconomic, industrial, corporate, and workplace.

COSATU's proposed growth path is based on a two-pronged strategy of "growth through redistribution." The first aim is to bring about a massive increase in production to meet the black population's needs for housing and basic consumer goods. The expansion of these industries may provide a great boost to job creation. The second aim is to increase the export capacity of South African manufacturing industry. This requires an input of new technology, a comprehensive training program to improve the skills of the work force, and a commitment to increasing productivity (Joffe 1991).

COSATU believes economic and industrial restructuring will require comprehensive and integrated planning. Business does not have a strategic vision of restructuring, and the process will have to be labor-driven. Unions find that neither employers nor the apartheid state has a global vision of how to increase competitiveness, create jobs, or restore growth to the economy. Most affiliates report that employers respond to problems with wage cuts, threats of massive job losses, and unilateral attempts to raise productivity. Employers are motivated by a short-term view of profitability, rather than by any long-term perspective of development.

Although COSATU sees productivity as being linked to increasing workers' participation and control in decision making, its proposals for a union-driven policy on restructuring are not uncontroversial among the federation's affiliates. The most developed thinking along participatory lines has emerged within the National Union of Metalworkers of South Africa. Many of the more grassroots activists and some of the other affiliates in COSATU are suspicious of such proposals.[12] They suspect that they mark an abandoning of revolutionary socialism and a shift toward social democracy. Many unionists also fear that the trade union movement lacks the capacity to develop and implement a union-driven policy.

At the core of the concept of a labor-driven restructuring of the South African economy is the idea that it would rest on the powerful organization of labor and that it would serve to increase and deepen that power. Central to such an idea is the existence of a layer of skilled workers able to use new technology and help increase productivity. These are the workers who would benefit most from restructuring and the new opportunities it offers. They are also the most articulate, confident workers, who could easily rise to leadership positions in the unions. Indeed, the leadership of most COSATU affiliates already consists of such workers (Pityana and Orkin 1992).

There is a danger, then, that if the unions lead a program that introduces new technology and participative management techniques, they could increasingly reflect the interests and aspirations of the most skilled and articulate workers and neglect the interests of the semiskilled and un-skilled. Such a development could become the basis for the establishment of an organized labor elite. Underpaid and less skilled workers could be pushed to the margins of society together with the vast masses of unemployed.

Although labor and employers have tentatively engaged in national negotiations over economic issues, more concrete developments have taken place in specific sectors—in mining, in clothing and textiles, and in metal and engineering. In 1992, the NUM and the Chamber of Mines convened a historic summit of unions, employers, and the state in response to the crisis in the gold mining industry. International gold prices have declined, and more than 100,000 black miners have been laid off in the past three years. Another 200,000 more may face retrenchments as marginal mines begin to close (Leger and Nicol 1993).

Marcel Golding, assistant general secretary of the NUM, revealed the thinking behind the summit: "The problems facing the industry have to be managed and more efficiently planned, and for that reason we've called for a permanent mining commission that will try to co-ordinate the down-scaling of the industry. Resource-based industries do decline. . . . We are arguing that there has got to be more efficient management for South Africa's mining resources and the only way that can be done is through better co-ordination and planning" (Von Holdt 1991a:19, 23).

The union proposed a joint union, employer, and state program to coordinate restructuring of the mining industry, with the aim of making it more modern and highly productive. Proposals included joint initiatives on health and safety and on industrywide training, as well as on retraining for retrenched mineworkers through the development of a social plan ("Miners Want Deal on Social Plan" 1993). The summit agreed to set up a steering committee to coordinate working groups on these issues and to lobby the state to withdraw taxes on workers' retrenchment packages. But employers refused point-blank to agree to a permanent union-employer mining commission, which the union had proposed. "It's seen as an intolerable intrusion in the autonomy of the mining houses," one source said ("Summit on the Mining Conference" 1991).

The NUM also negotiated a national framework for productivity agreements in the gold mines, involving information disclosure and workers' participation in industrial restructuring. Golding explained that the productivity agreement was part of a far-reaching strategy to increase worker control: "For us a greater control over the production process is starting with participation. It is the first stage. To achieve greater control requires training and skills development. . . . We have already challenged managerial prerogative on dismissals and other abuses, but I think through this we are beginning to challenge management prerogative in decision-making over what they believed was their exclusive right—setting targets, setting the production plan" (Von Holdt 1991a:20, 21).

Golding's reasoning is clear: either the union remains a spectator of the process or it becomes a central player in the management of transition. COSATU's decision to participate in government and tripartite institutions is not without its contradictions, as illustrated by its continued participation in the National Training Board while simultaneously withdrawing from the National Manpower Commission. The National Manpower Commission was targeted for national-level engagement provided it was restructured into an effective negotiating forum. COSATU insisted that participation did not constrain its independence and retained the option to withdraw and take mass action in support of its demands should the restructuring not proceed. COSATU did withdraw, but it subsequently reentered the commission after certain changes had been effected. This combination of engagement, agreement, withdrawal, mass action, and popular pressure is one COSATU exercised during the anti-LRA campaign and one it will probably use during the negotiations around macroeconomic policy in the newly established National Economic Forum (NEF).

Launched in November 1992, the NEF is a permanent tripartite forum to negotiate economic policy. The original proposals for such a forum were put forward by the labor movement in the wake of the massive stayaway protesting the unilateral introduction of a value-added tax in November 1991. The labor movement aims to extend the negotiation process to include economic restructuring.

COSATU sees the NEF as a negotiating body where formal, binding agreements can be reached between representatives of the state, business, and labor. This view is not generally accepted within the NEF, insofar as the state upholds the sovereignty of Parliament in determining state (economic) policy. During its deliberations, the amount of influence that the NEF will exert over economic policy formulation will emerge; it is bound to be significant. The NEF has already formulated proposals concerning job creation, and, in all likelihood, it will negotiate agreements concerning an incomes policy and strategies for economic growth.

The labor movement faces several problems in its quest to renew and restructure South Africa's economy. First, there is increasing stratification in the employed working class between the more highly skilled and highly paid workers with job security and wide-ranging benefits, on the one hand, and the less skilled, insecure, poorly paid workers with minimal benefits, on the other. Employers are making increasing use of casual and contract labor.

This stratification is beginning to be reflected within COSATU itself. The stalwarts of many of the new unions, as they engaged in militant struggles for recognition and negotiating rights during the 1970s and early 1980s, were the migrant workers who live in hostels. During the 1980s, however, the leadership of the trade unions passed to a more articulate, sophisticated, urban-based, and educated group of workers. The use of English in national union meetings and the complexity of the issues debated exclude the less educated migrant workers and hostel dwellers. This holds obvious dangers for the labor movement. The failure of unions to address the hostel dwellers' grievances has contributed to the feeling of alienation among many and has helped make the hostel dwellers an ethnic constituency that could easily be mobilized by Inkatha (Webster 1991).[13]

The second problem confronting COSATU is the uneven development of union structures. COSATU policy is in many ways dominated by the three biggest affiliates—the National Union of Mineworkers (NUM), the National Union of Metalworkers of South Africa, and the South African Clothing and Textile Workers Union—which have relatively large head offices with specialized departments, access to experts, officials, relatively well-developed structures, and centralized bargaining in industry forums. There are, however, a number of smaller affiliates that are struggling to be efficient and develop policy and strategy. These affiliates struggle to keep up with the rapid development of COSATU policy and negotiations on a range of fronts with employers and the state.

The third and related problem is whether the labor movement has sufficient research and educational capacity to drive a strategy of industrial restructuring. At the moment the unions do not have the necessary capacity (Keet 1992). COSATU's economic research team, known as the Industrial Strategy Project, consists of fifteen researchers based in South Africa's universities and is funded from abroad. The team is examining key components of macroeconomic policy, such as trade, technology, ownership and competition policy, industrial relations systems, and regional and local development (Joffe et al. 1993).

Conclusion

The trade unions face enormous challenges as they strive to play a leading role in developing a new industrial strategy for South Africa. The changing pattern of industrialization raises the key question of whether the union movement will be able to shift from a political culture of resistance to one of reconstruction, from social movement unionism to strategic unionism. Although we have distinguished between social movement unionism and strategic unionism, these are ideal types. Reality is more complex, and there is continuity between unions that leads to blurring of the types. First, social movement unionism is not concerned simply with broad political struggles; it is also vitally concerned with the establishment of union and worker rights on the shop floor and with the institutionalization of bargaining with employers. During the 1970s and 1980s, formal recognition and protection from arbitrary management power were achieved, but these concerns are still relevant today (Von Holdt 1993:8). Indeed, the capacity of unions to intervene strategically in corporate policy and the process of production presupposes such institutionalization.

Second, strategic unionism in South Africa involves consolidation and the extension of alliances with political organizations in the process of political transition; however, these relationships are changing, as the labor movement promotes the interests of working people, in contrast to the broader, cross-class interests typical of political organizations such as the ANC. In the past, social movement unionism and the ANC shared a primary objective of replacing apartheid with democracy. With apartheid's demise, the alliance with the ANC is more complex, given that the future state may expect workers to limit some of their demands and activities in the interests of a broader economic development program.

The success of the shift toward a more strategic type of unionism depends crucially on whether South Africa's unions have the capacity in terms of organization, education, research, and leadership to pursue a strategy of "industrial renewal" based on labor's active participation. Despite organizational unevenness, equivocal leadership in certain unions, and limited educational and research capacity, the evidence outlined in this chapter is that the COSATU unions have begun to play a leading role in developing a new industrial strategy and a significant role in extending the experiments in limited participation in management at the shop-floor level.

Although COSATU has not developed a formal response to participative management, many of its affiliated unions are attempting to extend the parameters of collective bargaining to include negotiations over work organization, the quality of products, flexible working practices, and technology (Maller 1992; Ntshangase and Solomons 1993). These unions have demonstrated their comparative advantage over fragmented employers with a short-term view of profitability and a government that under apartheid clung to a traditional view of industrial policy and was constrained by its unrepresentativeness. Indeed, according to P. Hattie (1991), convener of the SACOB Industrial Policy Committee, union thinking is clearly more advanced than collective business thinking and demonstrates the proactive engagement of South Africa's unions in industrial restructuring issues.[14]

If the labor movement is, in fact, the primary bearer of a new industrialization strategy, there will have to be a radical shift in power to organized labor at enterprise, industry, and national levels. In other words, for a new industrialization strategy to be effective, the workplace, industry, and the economy must be democratized. This will require a training program to improve the skills of managers and employees so that new technology can be harnessed for sustained economic growth. It will also be necessary to fashion new institutional arrangements between labor, capital, and the state along the lines of a social accord.

South Africa's challenge is unique among African countries, where the struggle against colonial rule has not involved the mobilization of a grassroots working-class movement with a distinct class politics. Instead, independence was won either by nationalist movements led largely by the professional middle class or by peasant-based guerrilla movements whose interests differed from those of the industrial working class. African governments have expected unions to play a dualistic role: on the one hand, sacrificing their narrow interests to the overall demands of national development while, on the other hand, representing the job interests of their members. The argument for their primary role being developmental rather than representational has been based on the proposition that unions represent a small and allegedly privileged proportion of the labor force (Webster 1991:63).

There are, then, immense obstacles facing the labor movement in South Africa, but the real dangers are either that it will retreat into the militant abstentionism of the past or that it will fail to develop the will or the capacity to shift decisively in a "left corporatist" direction. There are those who believe that corporatism is an unrealistic strategy in South Africa, that the conditions necessary for the success of corporatism—sustained high growth and improvement in working-class conditions—will not be present. L. Harris predicts that "as a result, conflict over control of production and the distribution of resources will intensify and undermine any (corporatist) arrangements" (1992:11).

This critique of corporatism goes to the heart of the dilemma facing the labor movement in the 1990s by arguing that the options have narrowed. According to G. W. Seidman (1993:179): "In the past militant labor activists often believed they knew how to proceed once they gained control of the state: programs of nationalization and state ownership. . . . But with the collapse of East European states, a general pessimism about statist solutions was reinforced. Moreover, most Third World movements recognize that socialist experiments have proved extremely risky. . . . Monetarist ideologies, which insist that growth requires unlimited freedom for capital, seemed to have become internationally hegemonic." That is why COSATU's approach to economic restructuring appears to be one of radically reforming capitalism while strengthening the power of labor.

The crucial struggle lies in the labor movement's effort to "intervene and shape a capitalist order which is more humane and more dynamic than has been true of . . . capitalism in the past, a capitalist order which could be more favorable for socialist prospects in the long run, by enabling the working class to become considerably better off, economically and politically, than they have been" (Gelb 1991:43).

COSATU has launched itself on a political project that confronts both the legacies of apartheid and the global challenge of the future; in so doing, it is beginning to emerge as the "major bearer of the public interest in industrial renewal, and as the unified bearer of the majority interest in redistribution and social justice" (Higgins 1987:234). Whether COSATU succeeds in this project is the key question facing South Africa in the second half of the 1990s.

Part II
Changing Labor Relations at the Industry Level

6

Toward Mesocorporatism: From Labor Exclusion to Union Intervention in the South African Textile Industry

Johann Maree and Shane Godfrey

I ndustrialization has increasingly required the formulation of strategic industrial policy to encourage and manage economic growth. The state has been the key player in developing such policy but has in certain circumstances needed the support of key interest groups. Capital has historically been the state's major partner in formulating industrial policy. Indeed, capital is always implicated, because, in broad terms, industrial policy has to meet the requirements of accumulation if it is to achieve its aims.

An important aspect of industrial and wider economic policy is the way the state regulates relations between capital and labor. In fact, the state's relationship to labor, especially the role labor is given within the policy formulation process, is one of the defining features of particular paths of industrialization. Thus, the state may exclude labor entirely from policy formulation and partly base its industrial strategy on that exclusion. In other words, industrialization, in this case, is built upon union repression. Alternatively, labor may be a bargaining partner in policy development, so that in developing strategy, business takes into consideration labor's concerns with employment and distribution.

Most countries reveal a complex of forms of industrial policy somewhere between the two extremes noted above. One broad form can, however, be identified in practice, namely, the corporatist negotiation of policy by the state and organizations of capital and labor (Schmitter 1982:262). Corporatism is defined as an institutionalized process in which sectors of

We would like to acknowledge the financial assistance provided by the Center for Science Development Human Sciences Research Council and to thank Stephen Frenkel for his valuable comments and suggestions on an earlier draft. Responsibility for the chapter lies solely with the authors.

113

the state and powerful monopolistic interest organizations negotiate public policy because the cooperation of the interest organizations is essential if the agreed policies are to be implemented (Cawson 1986:35). A key factor that explains the tendency for corporatist arrangements to emerge is the need for new forms of economic management. These are aimed at resolving various kinds of market failure; that is, they represent institutional interventions in market mechanisms (Goldthorpe 1984:12).

Corporatist arrangements may emerge at the macro, meso, or micro levels. At the macro level, the peak organizations of capital and labor "aggregate interests on a broad class basis," and the negotiations are usually directed at "major socio-economic issues that affect the interests of classes as a whole." Mesocorporatism "concerns organizations which aggregate interests at a sectoral level" and which "define specific locations within broader class groupings" (Cawson 1986:72). At this level, negotiations occur between state agencies and specialized interest organizations, often around particular policy initiatives. Finally, at the micro level, negotiations are between the state and individual firms, occasionally with the participation of workers or their unions.

The presence of the state is common to all levels and has been described as "a defining characteristic of corporatism" (Cawson 1986:38). The degree of intervention by the state may, however, vary and can also take differing forms. Indeed, two types of corporatism—societal and state—can be distinguished on the basis of the state's relationship to interest organizations. Societal or democratic corporatism exists where the legitimacy and role of the state are mainly or exclusively dependent on autonomous, representative organizations (Schmitter 1979:20). By contrast, under state or authoritarian corporatism, exemplified in the recent history of South Korea, Singapore, and Taiwan, interest organizations are created and remain dependent on the state (Deyo 1989:107–45).

P. Katzenstein suggests that democratic corporatist societies, such as those in Scandinavia and in Western Europe more generally, have three key characteristics: "an ideology of social partnership expressed at the national level; a relatively centralized and concentrated system of interest groups; and voluntary and informal coordination of conflicting objectives through continuous political bargaining between interest groups, state bureaucracies, and political parties" (1985:32).

Katzenstein distinguishes between liberal and social variants of democratic corporatism. The former has "politically strong, internationally oriented, centralized business communities and relatively decentralized and weak labor movements," whereas the social variant has "strong, centralized labor unions and business communities that are politically weak, express a national orientation, and are relatively decentralized" (1985:105). The common factor, and a key to understanding the consolidation of democratic corporatism in all these countries, is "their openness to and dependence on the world economy" (81).

The concept of democratic corporatism is especially germane for understanding and explaining the arrangements that are currently emerging between the state, capital, and labor in South Africa. The political transition to majority rule and the presence of a strong, independent labor movement are key factors that contribute to a democratic form of corporatism. The new arrangements are being established at a number of levels, but the trend is particularly evident at the meso level (Schmitter 1990:12; Cawson 1986:125).

This chapter highlights the major factors influencing the fundamental shift from a symbiotic state-capital relationship to an embryonic, democratic mesocorporatist arrangement in South Africa. Our focus is the South African textile industry. We analyze the emergence of mesocorporatism by examining the historical development of the industry. This history illustrates the changing role of the state, employers, and unions in developing a policy framework in response to both domestic and international conditions in the industry and to changes in the balance of political power attendant on the demise of the apartheid regime. Special attention is paid to the way industrial relations has interacted with the wider process of industry policy formulation. This interaction provides a key to explaining why labor has become the leading proponent of mesocorporatism for resolving problems within the textile industry.

Four phases in the growth of the textile industry are outlined. In the first phase, one sees the emergence and fairly rapid growth of the industry as the state pursued a strategy of import-substituting industrialization. This period was profitable for textile companies, but the industry developed inefficiently behind tariffs and quota protections, thereby entrenching its incapacity to face up to international competition. This phase is also characterized by the effective exclusion of workers from decision making with regard to both policy and production at all levels of industry. By the 1970s, however, an independent, shop floor-based trade union, imbued with a militant and adversarial disposition to management, emerged and grew rapidly.

The second phase is distinguished by the growing economic crisis in the textile industry, marked by a decline in output, employment, and plant utilization. This crisis, although part of a wider crisis in the South African manufacturing sector and economy as a whole, reflected important changes in the international textile industry, especially the competitive challenge from several Asian countries. The need for restructuring in the industry became increasingly apparent.

The third phase is characterized by preliminary attempts to restructure the industry as the need for a shift from import substitution toward export promotion became more pronounced. The government introduced a limited structural adjustment program and an export incentive scheme for manufacturing. Some companies responded by improving their performance, but in the absence of a more comprehensive restructuring policy, the schemes had limited impact. Meanwhile, the South African Clothing and Textile Workers' Union (SACTWU) had emerged as a major force; its leaders were beginning to turn their attention to industry strategy.

The fourth phase is characterized by an expansion of the catalytic role played by the union in intervening to manage the process of industry restructuring. Indeed, SACTWU exemplifies the tendency toward strategic unionism identified in chapter 5 by Joffe, Maller, and Webster as a more general trend within the South African union movement. The information on this phase draws heavily on an extended interview with the assistant general secretary of the textile union in which he explored the union's approach to industry restructuring and associated key issues.

Finally, in the concluding section, we return to the concept of mesocorporatism. We argue that, although the emerging institutions and processes in South Africa's textile industry do not yet meet the requirements that would define them as mesocorporatist, they do appear to be prototypical of such institutions and processes under mesocorporatism. Whether these arrangements consolidate will depend on the outcomes reached through tripartite cooperation and bargaining.

Phase One: Import Substitution and Labor Exclusion

Industrialization in South Africa began toward the end of the nineteenth century, when a limited range of industries emerged to service the mining sector. This development remained limited, however, until 1924, when a nationalist government came to power and created a developmental state that actively fostered industrialization. The state promoted a policy of import-substituting industrialization and the incorporation and subordination of labor. As early as 1925, the government passed the Customs Tariff and Excise Duty Act, which provided protection for a number of consumer goods industries, including textiles (Houghton 1973:116–22).

On the labor front, the government followed a dual strategy that was informed by racial considerations. The foundation was laid by the Industrial Conciliation Act of 1924, which provided a framework for the regulation of collective bargaining and industrial conflict between registered trade unions and employers' associations. A key feature of this framework was a provision that allowed the above parties to establish industrial councils that could negotiate agreements on wages and other conditions of employment for all employers and employees within their jurisdictions.[1] African male workers were, however, excluded from the definition of "employee" in the act.[2] They were thus denied membership in registered trade unions and hence representation on industrial councils. Other laws, together with naked repression, further restricted and undermined the ability of most African workers to organize and defend their interests in the workplace. Their exclusion from participation in the industrial relations system meant that they were subject to the arbitrary control of employers at the level of the enterprise.

Following the devaluation of the South African currency in 1933, manufacturing industry grew rapidly until World War II, which gave further impetus to its development. This growth was sustained throughout the 1950s and 1960s, and by 1969 manufacturing had become the largest sector in the economy, accounting for no less than 30 percent of national income (Houghton 1973:122–24). The pattern of industrialization entrenched a structural imbalance between exports and imports, however, in that manufacturing exports remained low compared with imports.[3] This imbalance was sustained by the foreign exchange that the gold mining industry was earning and continued into the 1970s and beyond (Black 1991a:160–62; Board of Trade and Industry [BTI] 1988a:154).

South Africa's rapid industrial development was matched by the expansion of a dual system of industrial relations. Large numbers of industrial councils were set up between 1924 and the 1970s, but because of the low levels of trade union organization, most were limited to providing subsectoral and regional coverage rather than becoming national bodies. Despite this limitation, the councils provided virtually the sole locus for industrial relations activity by white, colored, and Indian workers. The introduction of the councils ushered in an unprecedented period of labor stability and compliance by participating trade unions (Godfrey 1992:11–26).

The results for registered trade unions of participation in the councils were contradictory. The privileged position of white workers gave them the ability to secure wage increases and additional benefits at the expense of unorganized African workers. Unionized workers thus came to rely on their politically privileged position on industrial councils for bargaining strength at the expense of organization on the shop floor. As a result, industrial action by these workers at both the level of the enterprise and at the level of the industrial council became almost nonexistent.

Development of the South African Textile Industry

Although the textile industry developed in distinct stages, its trajectory fits the broader pattern of change in manufacturing outlined above. A common feature of each stage was the use of protective tariffs and quotas to promote the growth of particular subsectors.

Blanket manufacturing signaled the beginning of the textile industry (Hirsch 1979:13). The first weaving factory was built in 1891, but it was not until 1925, when the customs duties on blankets, rugs, shawls, and heavy sheeting were increased, that the blanket industry really took off. The duties were very high, ranging from 197.5 percent to 312 percent (Steenkamp Report 1983:7).

After World War II, the textile industry became more substantial. During this period the clothing, household, and industrial textile sectors were firmly established. Government support contributed considerably to this development. One form of support was financial and was provided through the Industrial Development Corporation (IDC), a public sector institution that played an active entrepreneurial and financial role in setting up textile plants. The other form of support came through protection. This was based on a report published by the Board of Trade and Industry in 1950. The report was aimed at determining the conditions, including the level of protection, necessary to develop the local textile industry to a stage where it could obtain a substantially larger share of the local market on the basis of economic competitiveness (BTI 1950:2).

Although the report recommended only moderate tariff protection, quantitative import control subsequently played an important role in preserving the local market for the domestic textile industry (Steenkamp Report 1983:11 and 64–65). From the time the BTI report was published until 1960–61, "the expansion of the textile industry proceeded rapidly, especially in the spinning, weaving and finishing of cotton and wool products and in the knitting section" (Barker 1963:292).

H. A. F. Barker, a renowned economist in the textile industry, was sharply critical of the BTI and the modus operandi of textile industrialists. The thrust of his criticism was that the board too readily extended tariff protection at the request of these industrialists, who also frequently applied for amendments to the rates of protection for textiles (Barker 1963:290). This led textile industrialists to rely entirely on protection to sustain the textile industry: "Once an implied pledge of protection had been given and received, there was understandably little disposition on the part of textile manufacturers to consider anything that might tend to limit or regulate the operation of their mills, even temporarily or only tacitly. . . . In any event when an industry has been conceived, born and brought up in the expectation that its well-being will be ensured by tariffs, it is likely to have a built-in mistrust of its own ability to compete on any other basis" (Barker 1963:291–92).

The final stage of development was notable because the synthetic fibers subsector emerged in the 1960s and consolidated itself in the 1970s. It also relied on protection for its growth and survival. According to a 1983 report of a committee of inquiry appointed by the government to investigate the textile and clothing industries: "The synthetic fibers industry would not have been able to exist, let alone to expand as it has done, without the assistance of tariff protection and, in particular, of quantitative import control" (Steenkamp Report 1983:14).

The textile industry in South Africa was therefore built behind a wall of protection that included both tariffs and quantitative restrictions. As a consequence, although it grew rapidly up to the end of the 1960s, it was not an economically efficient or internationally competitive industry.

Industrial Relations in the Textile Industry

Industrial relations in the textile industry were conditioned by the dual system introduced in 1924, but the major trade union operating in the industry distinguished itself by its long opposition to the government's racial segregation of worker organization. The Textile Workers' Industrial Union (TWIU) was formed in the mid-1930s and had a history of militancy, including persistent attempts to organize African workers alongside its "official" members (Hirsch 1979:16–22).

The TWIU also distinguished itself from many other registered trade unions by focusing its activity for many years at the level of the enterprise, rather than opting for centralized bargaining at an industrial council. It was not until 1950 that the first industrial council, the National Industrial Council for the Textile Industry (NICTEX), was set up in the textile sector. And even after the formation of NICTEX, there was still a focus on the enterprise level in large parts of the industry because the national council covered only a narrow subsector. It was only in the late 1950s and early 1960s, when two more regional industrial councils were formed to cover the cotton and worsted sectors of the industry, that the union's collective bargaining focus shifted firmly away from the enterprise level to the centralized forums.

The militancy of the TWIU had always resulted in state repression. This increased in the 1950s, and initially the union responded by becoming part of a trend that saw some trade unions forming closer relationships with the growing African nationalist movement. The union became a founding member of the South African Congress of Trade Unions (SACTU), which allied itself with the African National Congress (Friedman 1987:27). The alliance collapsed in 1960, however, when the ANC was banned, and many SACTU activists and officials fled into exile. Thereafter, the TWIU moved in a more conservative direction. It joined the compliant Trade Union Council of South Africa and confined its organization to colored and Asian workers. African workers were therefore left largely to their own devices.[4]

The demise of SACTU signaled the start of more than a decade of dormancy by labor that was ended by the eruption of largely spontaneous strikes by African workers in Natal in 1973. The textile industry was at the center of these strikes. It was also the only industry in which a registered trade union—that is, the TWIU—intervened to assist strikers

(Institute for Industrial Education 1974:16–22). In fact, the Natal branch of the union had begun organizing some African workers before 1973.

These tentative attempts at organization bore fruit under difficult conditions after the strikes. By the end of 1973, organization had already advanced to the extent that a new union, the National Union of Textile Workers (NUTW), had been formed for African workers and begun to operate alongside the registered TWIU (Hirsch 1979:36). The NUTW was one of a number of so-called independent trade unions for African workers that grew rapidly during the 1970s and 1980s in the face of tremendous hostility from employers and the state.

Within a few months of its formation, the NUTW achieved a major victory when it was formally recognized by the Smith & Nephew textile firm. The victory was significant for two reasons. It was the first time that an unregistered African trade union was granted recognition by an employer, which showed these unions that the legal framework created by the Industrial Conciliation Act was not necessary to establish bargaining rights at individual factories. Second, it laid the foundations for a particular organizational strategy that the NUTW and other independent trade unions pioneered—namely, the development of strong plant-level organization—and the signing of recognition agreements with employers to secure bargaining rights and shop steward structures (Maree 1986:156–65).

This strategy proved extremely successful in attracting workers to the trade union over the next decade, because plant-level bargaining pushed wages for African workers well above the minimums set through industrial council negotiations. The strategy was, however, not an easy one for the NUTW to pursue. Besides taxing the union's resources, the strategy met with strong resistance from many textile manufacturers, who refused to bargain at any level other than the industrial council (NUTW 1982:95–101). Recognition was usually granted only after the victimization of union members, followed by industrial action and painstaking negotiations.

Despite the resistance from employers, and to a certain extent because of it, the union continued to grow and successfully pursue its strategy to erect plant-level organizational structures (NUTW 1982:98). At the same time, the union strongly resisted participation in industrial councils. Councils were seen as historically tainted bargaining institutions that had tended to lead to the bureaucratization of trade unions. Furthermore, the independent trade unions saw plant-level bargaining as best suited to their own structural requirements and democratic goals, as well as a way to optimize their organized strength (Godfrey 1992:27–31). This focus on struggle at the level of the plant, together with the hostility displayed by employers, resulted in an extremely adversarial industrial relations scenario throughout this period.

Phase Two: Economic Crisis and the Impetus toward Industrial Restructuring

The South African economy was in a crisis from the 1980s onward. From a growth rate of 4.1 percent in the 1950s, which peaked at 5.8 percent per year on average in the 1960s, the GDP slowed to an annual average of 3.9 percent in the 1970s. It plunged to a mere 0.7 percent per year on average in the 1980s and became negative in the 1990s (Moll 1990:76; South African Reserve Bank 1988, 1991). In 1990 and 1991, the rate of growth was almost −0.5 percent, and it fell to an alarming −2.1 percent in 1992 ("SA's GDP Takes 5.1% Tumble" 1993).

The manufacturing industry was in a crisis in the 1980s as well. From a peak in the first half of the 1960s, the rate of growth of both manufacturing output and employment became negative in the first half of the 1980s (Black 1991a:157). This decline continued into the 1990s. In the period from 1985 to the end of 1992, manufacturing employment fell in absolute terms from 1,428,988 to 1,388,116 jobs, and the physical volume of manufacturing output rose by only 1 percent over the same period (Central Statistical Service [CSS] 1992a:7.11, 1993a:4, 1993b:4).

Crisis in the Textile Industry

Output and employment in the textile industry from the 1970s onward display two distinct trends: one of growth up to 1981 and one of decline from 1982 onward (see fig. 6.1). During the first period, from 1972 to 1981, textile output grew soundly: the average annual compound growth rate over this period was 5.7 percent. Employment also grew during this period, but it displayed a cyclical trend with two peaks, one in 1976 and the other in 1981. At the time of the second peak, the textile industry employed a total labor force of 113,700 (IDC 1992a).

The second phase, from 1981 to 1992, was one of decline. Output decreased by 26 percent up to 1990, and employment fell drastically over the period, especially from 1981 to 1985, when it decreased by 16 percent (i.e., by 18,580 employees). In 1986, the downward cycle bottomed out and production and employment increased until 1989, but thereafter production and capacity utilization declined once again. The latter fell to 79 percent in 1990. In May 1992, it was down to 74 percent, reaching the lowest capacity utilization yet (CSS 1992b; van Coller 1992:4). Once again, employment plummeted, from 97,500 at the end of 1990 to 86,800 by October 1992 (CSS 1993c; National Clothing Federation [NCF] 1993:40).

The decline of the textile industry has had a detrimental effect not only

122 *Johann Maree and Shane Godfrey*

Figure 6.1. *Production and Employment in South Africa, 1972–90 (at constant 1990 prices)*

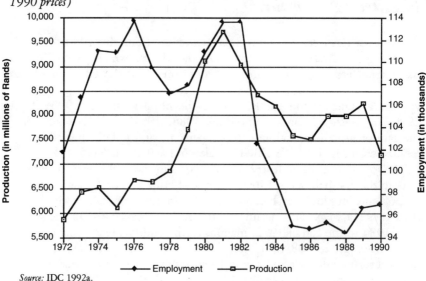

Source: IDC 1992a.

on employment but on the technological development of the industry. Over the two decades up to the early 1990s, capital investment in the textile industry lagged behind that for manufacturing as a whole, in that the proportion of the capital stock from the textile industry within the manufacturing sector went from 4.8 percent in 1972 to 2.4 percent by 1990.

The low level of investment in the textile industry over the past twenty years means that much of the technology has become dated, as indicated in table 6.1. Table 6.1 shows that, with the exception of open-end spindles, which were an average of eight years old at the start of 1992, the average age of the textile machinery used in spinning, weaving, and knitting ranged from thirteen to twenty years. The table also shows that, again with the exception of open-end spindles, 59 to 100 percent of the installed machinery was more than ten years old. All the shuttle looms were more than ten years old, whereas 93 percent of the flat knitting machines and two-thirds to three-quarters of the remaining machinery was more than ten years of age.

The two major technological advances in spinning and weaving over the past four decades have been the development of open-end spindles and shuttleless looms. They are considerably faster than conventional ring-spinning spindles and shuttle looms, thereby increasing productivity significantly (United Nations Industrial Development Organization [UNIDO] 1990:198–205). H. Strolz has estimated that the spindles installed since 1980 are 60 percent more productive than those in place at

Table 6.1. Ages of Textile Machinery in South Africa, 1992

	Number of machines[a]						
Type of machinery	0–5 years	6–10 years	11–15 years	16–20 years	20 years	Average age	% >10 years old
Median age	2.5	8	13	18	25		
Spindles	112,502	70,155	64,752	106,298	213,799	15.8	67.8
Conventional	87,654	65,931	57,328	100,346	210,631	16.4	70.6
Open-end	24,848	4,224	7,424	5,952	3,168	8.3	36.3
Looms	500	348	724	692	667	14.5	71.1
Ordinary	—	—	178	—	21	14.3	100.0
Automatic	—	—	7	180	60	19.6	100.0
Shuttleless	500	348	539	512	586	14.1	65.9
Knitting machines	63	186	173	99	161	14.2	63.5
Circular	60	151	132	64	109	13.5	59.1
Warp	1	35	41	22	40	15.9	74.1
Flat	2	—	—	13	12	20.0	92.6

Source: Textile Federation 1992.

[a]Most of the large companies in the spinning, weaving, and knitting industries were included in the survey sample.

the end of 1979 (1991:34). Table 6.2 shows the extent of investment in new spindles and looms over the ten-year period ending in 1988 for South Africa compared with other countries.

Table 6.2 shows that South Africa has fallen behind internationally regarding investment in open-end spindles. Of the eleven countries listed, only Australia has a larger proportion of open-end spindles that are more than ten years old. No less than five of the countries completely (or almost completely) replaced all their open-end spindles over the period. South Africa falls in the median position with regard to the replacement of shuttleless looms, but it lags considerably behind West Germany, Australia, and Italy. The significance of the age of textile machinery is that by 1988 the world's four top textile exporters—West Germany, Italy, China, and Hong Kong (in that order)—had invested extensively in new open-end spindles and shuttleless looms over the preceding ten-year period. China is an exception, in that it has a low replacement rate of shuttleless looms. The relatively low level of investment in new technology in the South African textile industry therefore serves to undermine its ability to face up to international competition.

Trade Protection in the Textile Industry

The tariff structure in South Africa has been described as "one of the most complex in the world" (Belli, Finger, and Ballivian 1993:3). The

Table 6.2. Ages of Textile Machinery in Eleven Countries, 1988

| | Percentage of machinery > 10 Years Old | | | | |
| | Spindles | | Looms | | |
Country	Short-staple	Long-staple	Open-end rotors	Shuttle	Shuttleless
West Germany	79.5	64.7	0.0	98.7	38.5
Italy	50.7	79.4	0.0	99.5	44.5
Turkey	82.2	69.5	19.9	96.4	88.1
Taiwan	63.5	18.2	16.2	88.9	63.5
South Korea	68.0	81.7	8.4	67.0	88.7
Hong Kong	69.2	n.a.	0.0	97.4	54.9
Indonesia	74.8	33.8	14.6	87.2	92.8
Thailand	75.3	22.6	0.0	96.8	96.5
China	98.6	89.5	1.5	99.9	98.1
Australia	n.a.	83.8	34.5	98.8	40.0
South Africa[a]	78.2	71.0	32.2	100.0	65.9

Source: UNIDO 1990, tables IV.50, IV.54, IV.56, IV.62, and IV.64.
[a]Based on ten-year period ending in 1992.
n.a. = not available.

Table 6.3. Nominal Rates of Protection on Manufacturing and Textile Goods in South Africa, 1990

Sector	Weighted mean	Unweighted mean	Minimum rate	Maximum rate	Coefficient of variation
Manufacturing	28%	30%	0%	1389%	158.4
Textiles	69%	60%	0%	1389%	140.6

Source: Belli, Finger, and Ballivian 1993: 13–15, tables 3 and 5.

tariff structure on textile goods is no exception and displays three main features. First, the tariff rates on textiles are among the highest in the manufacturing sector. This is partly because of the extensive lobbying of the BTI by the textile industry over many years. Table 6.3 indicates that the weighted mean of the nominal rate of protection on textile products is more than twice the rate for the manufacturing sector as a whole (69 percent as opposed to 28 percent).

Second, the tariff rates are very fluid and have been changed frequently. Third, the rates are highly dispersed and very specific. Tariffs are imposed on more than twenty-three hundred lines of textile goods, on which the rates vary from 0 percent to no less than 1,389 percent (Belli, Finger, and Ballivian 1993:2 and 12).[5]

The high level of protection accorded textile goods has not prevented

Figure 6.2. Textile Imports and Exports, to and from South Africa, 1974–92 (at constant 1990 prices)

Source: IDC 1993.

imports from generally exceeding exports in South Africa's textile trade, as shown in figure 6.2. It was only for the three-year period from 1984 to 1986 that exports exceeded imports. In the 1990s, the gap between imports and exports widened to the extent that imports outstripped exports by R800 million in 1992 ("13,000 Jobs Lost But Exports Help" 1993).

There is also a structural imbalance in the composition of the South African textile trade. This becomes clear when one studies the export and import rates for the thirteen textile product groups.[6] These are indicated for the year 1991 in figure 6.3.

The most striking feature of South Africa's textile imports and exports is that they are overwhelmingly dominated by the export of wool-related products (chapter 51) and the import of products related to chemical staple fibers and chemical filaments (chapters 54 and 55).[7] The importance of this distinction is that of the wool-related products exported in 1991, the vast proportion was unprocessed wool. About half (U.S.$161,000) was not carded or combed and consisted mainly of shorn wool, while the other half (U.S.$163,000) was carded or combed wool and was mainly wool tops. Only a very small proportion (0.7 percent) consisted of woven fabrics of wool and other fine animal hair.

A similar picture emerges in the import and export of yarns and fabric

Figure 6.3. Imports and Exports of Wool and Chemical Staple Fibers, by Chapter, under the Harmonized System in South Africa, 1991

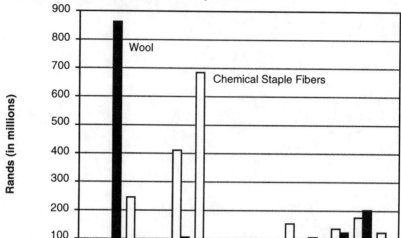

Source: IDC 1992b.

in the chemical filaments and chemical fibers product groups or chapters. Almost two-thirds of the imports under these product groups consisted of higher-value-added woven fabrics. But the picture is reversed for chemical filament and fibers exports. Only 11 percent of the exports in both chapters consisted of woven fabrics, the remainder being staple fibers and yarn. Although a considerable degree of technological know-how is required to produce export-quality filament yarn, what emerges from the trade pattern of goods in chemical fibers and filaments is that South Africa imports a substantial proportion of higher-value-added woven fabric and exports mostly lower-value-added filament yarn (IDC 1992b).

International Developments in the Textile Industry

Dramatic changes have occurred in the global textile industry during the twentieth century. Most of it happened in the second half of the century, as countries in the Far East challenged the dominance of America and advanced industrialized countries in Europe. Even before World War II, Japan had made heavy inroads into Britain's dominance in world trade in textiles, and by 1939, Japan was exporting 22 percent of the world's

Table 6.4. South Africa's Exports and Imports of Textile Fibers, Yarn and Fabric, and Clothing (in U.S.$, in millions FOB), 1970–87

	Exports			Imports		
	1970	1980	1987	1970	1980	1987
World	115	628	562	320	703	601
Developed market economies	n.a.	530	413	287	569	315
EC	n.a.	345	295	151	273	194
Developing market economies	n.a.	98	127	33	134	286
Asian market economies	n.a.	19	71	21	84	239
Africa	n.a.	72	51	n.a.	42	42

Source: United Nations Conference on Trade and Development 1990 A.11; A.44–47.
n.a. = not available.

exports of textiles. In the late 1950s and early 1960s, however, a fresh generation of export-oriented, newly industrializing countries emerged in the Far East, most notably Hong Kong, South Korea, and Taiwan. These countries made significant headway in the 1970s. For example, South Korea, starting from a small output of U.S.$715 million in 1970, increased its production tenfold by the end of the decade.

During the 1980s, the textile and clothing industries of mainland China and some Southeast Asian economies (particularly Thailand, but also Malaysia, Indonesia, and the Philippines) grew very rapidly. These countries had considerably lower wages than Hong Kong, South Korea, and Taiwan, which, in turn, had significantly lower labor costs than the advanced European countries and the United States (GATT 1990a:24; "World Textiles" 1991).

The response of the textile industries in the more advanced industrialized countries was to move to higher-value-added production requiring more sophisticated technology. Some sectors of the textile industry, notably spinning and weaving, were turned into capital-intensive industries, thereby undermining the Asian countries' advantage of low labor costs. The more advanced countries thus concentrated on the value-added areas of production where cost was less of a criterion (Dertouzos et al. 1989:17; "World Textiles" 1991). In so doing, they restored their international competitiveness and managed to remain among the world's top textile exporters. In 1989, of the world's top ten textile exporting countries, six were advanced industrialized countries (GATT 1990b:62).

These changes have made the South African textile industry particularly vulnerable to foreign competition, as an examination of the countries South Africa traded with in textiles and clothing during the 1970s and 1980s reveals.

Table 6.4 shows that between 1970 and 1987, textile and clothing imports to South Africa from Asian market economies increased more than elevenfold, although they started from a low base of U.S.$21 million in 1970. Exports to these Asian countries also increased, but the export level (U.S.$71 million) in 1987 was considerably below the import level (U.S.$239 million) in the same year. These trade figures show that, even with protection, the South African textile industry has not been able to compete effectively with Asian textile and clothing imports.

The South African textile industry therefore became caught between the low-cost challenge from the East and the technological advances of the West. The industry was thus being squeezed from opposing ends on a global scale. In conjunction with the decline in output and employment in the industry, as well as its lag behind the rest of the world in technology and labor productivity, the need for a new industrial policy to rescue the industry became imperative.

Phase Three: Emergence of International Competitiveness as a Basis for Industrial Policy

Although government and economic commentators were aware for a long time of the structural imbalances in the manufacturing industry, there was no agreement on how to resolve the problem. It was only in 1972 that a government-appointed commission of inquiry, the Reynders Commission, argued for a shift in state policy toward greater emphasis on manufactured exports. The government took little effective action, however. Export incentives were introduced in 1978, but because of continued differences of opinion within the government and the international sanctions against South Africa for its position on apartheid, implementation of an outward-oriented industrial policy remained half-hearted up to the mid-1980s. As a result, the government's policy was one of strategic self-sufficiency (Black 1991b:4). In 1988, however, the BTI published a major report entitled *A Policy and Strategy for Structural Adjustment of Industry in the Republic of South Africa* that recommended that "a high priority be granted to measures to bring about structural changes in the real economy in order to achieve growth of the required quantity and quality by means of greater output of final manufactured goods for export and the local market" (BTI 1988a:a).

The report argued for the support of industries on a selective basis and introduced notions such as dynamic comparative advantage and performance criteria as bases for granting incentives. It argued that the central objective was to reorient the manufacturing sector to enable it to compete effectively in export markets. It also came out in favor of a series of sectorally based structural adjustment programs aimed at improving the competitive capability of local industry (Black 1991b:5–6). One of the industries it selected for investigation was textiles.

Export Incentive Schemes: The Structural Adjustment Program and the General Export Incentive Scheme

The report on the Structural Adjustment Program (SAP) for the textile and clothing industries was finalized by the BTI in October 1988 (BTI 1988b). The BTI's objective was to improve the export performance of both industries, and to do so it realized it had to give exporters access to inputs at world prices and assistance to improve their own productivity. The SAP was introduced in April 1989, but it was poorly conceived and was implemented in such a way that it undermined not only its own objectives but the performance of the textile industry.

The first problem was that the export incentives were structured so that they offered the producers an incentive to export up to only 2.5 percent of their turnover. Second, the SAP undermined the demand for material produced by the domestic textile industry by making the duty-free import permits obtained from exporting the 2.5 percent of turnover very valuable compared with the return on the exports.[8] The SAP therefore encouraged exports at the expense of local textile production.

Not surprisingly, textile manufacturers strongly opposed the implementation of the SAP on the grounds that it undermined the industry. After the Textile Federation made frequent appeals to the BTI on behalf of textile employers, the government phased out the SAP in March 1994.

In addition to the SAP, the government also introduced an export incentive scheme for the manufacturing industry as a whole. Known as the General Export Incentive Scheme (GEIS), it was implemented in April 1990. It was designed to offset the price disadvantage that South African exporters face in international markets. It provides a tax-free financial subsidy to exporters based on the value of exports, the degree of processing, and the local content of the exported product. The subsidy increases with the level of beneficiation (processing), the level of local content, and the value of the Rand against a basket of currencies.

GEIS has played an important role in improving exports in manufacturing by making a large proportion of exports profitable. It is estimated to have increased the value added in manufacturing exports by about 83.9 percent in 1991, and it is doubtful whether South Africa could sustain the current level of manufactured exports without GEIS (Belli, Finger, and Ballivian 1993:27–28). It is, however, equally doubtful whether the government can afford to retain GEIS. In 1991, R900 million was paid out under GEIS; of this, R100 million went to the clothing and textile industries. In 1992, it is estimated that GEIS paid out R1.5 billion (U.S.$526 million) (*Trade Monitor* 1993, no. 1, 8). The state's policy of coming to the aid of the textile industry is therefore not proving sustainable. It is also doubtful whether the state is contributing to the international competitiveness of the industry.

Response from Textile Manufacturers

The general response of the textile industry to the growing international challenge and the emerging crisis was the same as its response had been for sixty years: it turned to the government in an effort to secure more effective protection for the industry. The Textile Federation (Texfed), the only body representing manufacturers in the textile industry as a whole, actively lobbied the BTI to secure what it deemed to be effective protection.

This was, however, not the response in the industry as a whole. Several individual companies had perceived the need to adopt strategies that would make them more competitive, either locally or in international markets. To ascertain the manner in which these firms were becoming more competitive, seven were selected for case study research. All were known to be profitable, and all but one were vertically integrated mills engaged in spinning, weaving, and finishing of fabric. The remaining one manufactured synthetic filament. The mills varied in size from small to large and included a couple of South Africa's largest and best-known textile companies.[9]

A common feature of all seven companies was that they based their strategies on the production of higher-value-added, differentiated products. Not one sought to base its strategy on those textile products called "commodities" in the industry (i.e., basic, undifferentiated, relatively straightforward products that are low in added value). The primary basis for competition in "commodities" is price, and the companies could not compete with the Far East in this way.

The ways in which the companies added greater value or differentiated their products did vary considerably, however. Three of the companies distinguished themselves on the basis of their design of either clothing or household goods or both. Two companies added more value by means of product specialization in which either the technology or the process of production or both were highly specialized. In this way the companies created specialty niches for themselves and were able to export to countries around the world. One company based its strategy on providing consistently high quality (it supplied Woolworths, the top-quality retail chain store in South Africa); another company added value to its fabric by having it made up into jeans through subcontracting and then selling the jeans. Further value was added by obtaining the franchise to make brand names. In all the companies, there was also a drive to improve quality, although companies placed the emphasis on different aspects.

Of the seven companies, four deliberately sought and increased their exports. Two exported only sufficient amounts to qualify for the duty-free import permits, whereas one company concentrated only on the South African market, where it had a record of reliability, consistency, and closeness to the customer that ensured its continued success.

All seven companies had invested extensively in new technology over the past ten years. In most of the plants, new state-of-the-art equipment made up a considerable proportion of the existing technology. In one mill, 100 percent of the looms were new, but in most mills there was a mixture of old and new technology. Similarly, there was a general drive to improve production processes, although specific systems were not usually being adopted. The exceptions were one company in which total quality management (TQM) was being implemented and another in which manufacturing resource planning (MRP2) had been installed. Usually a mixture of systems, adapted to suit the needs and circumstances of the company, were being pursued.

Using a mixture of systems did not always work well, however. For instance, almost all the companies still had high stock levels. In the case of raw materials, this was sometimes because of external factors and uncertainty about the country's political and social stability, and large stocks were being held "just in case." Two of the companies, however, had turned their large stocks of finished goods into marketing assets by implementing quick delivery times for "out-of-range" fabrics.

Thus, the companies investigated had mostly gone only part of the way in adopting the organizational strategies that tend to make firms internationally competitive. With two exceptions, they still had a long way to go to become world class and to implement properly more sophisticated production and organizational techniques, such as computer-aided production management, a just-in-time approach, and TQM.[10] Significantly, the two companies that had implemented some of these techniques were performing well in selling their exports in market niches. The company that had installed MRP2 was exporting 20 percent of its output of designed household fabrics, while the one that was implementing TQM was selling no less than 40 percent of its output outside the country.

Overall, however, the response of the textile industry to the international challenge and crisis in its industry was either traditional or sporadic. No clear policy or plan for the restructuring of the industry had emerged from within the ranks of textile manufacturers. Such a policy had to await union consolidation and the creation of a strong force on the labor side.

Emergence of Union Dominance in Setting the Development Agenda

The South African Clothing and Textile Workers' Union developed out of the NUTW, which, through vigorous organization and a series of mergers, grew very rapidly from a small, weak union for African workers in the Durban area to a giant, nonracial, national trade union with a membership of about 185,000 in 1989.[11] In the process, the NUTW swallowed up every other union of any size or significance in the textile and clothing sectors. This was done by a series of mergers, the first of which was with its main rival in the textile industry, the TWIU, and another union, the National Union of Garment Workers (SA), in 1987. The new union, the Amalgamated Clothing and Textile Workers' Union of South Africa (ACTWUSA), completed the process in 1989 when it finalized protracted merger negotiations with the Garment and Allied Workers' Union to form SACTWU (Godfrey 1992:134).

The rapid growth of the NUTW and the strain it placed on the union's organizational resources was a major factor leading to its decision to participate in industrial councils. Thereafter, it applied for membership on regional councils in the clothing (Natal) and knitting sectors (Transvaal), the cotton textile subsector (Cape), as well as NICTEX (Graduate School of Business 1989:23–27). This was, however, done on the basis of a continued focus on plant-level organization.

The formation of SACTWU took this trend toward centralization of bargaining a step further. The series of mergers that created the new union resulted in its becoming the sole trade union party on all the industrial councils in the clothing and textile industries (i.e., the three industrial councils in the textile industry, the five councils in the clothing industry, and the knitting council in the Transvaal). SACTWU's focus therefore turned more and more to centralized, industrial council bargaining while it tried to build up shop steward structures and democratic practices among certain of its newer members.

A second impetus toward centralization of bargaining came from the different wages and conditions of employment the various industrial council agreements laid down for SACTWU members. It was imperative that the union consolidate the mergers by building a national consciousness among its members, and regional and subsectoral wage differences hampered this process. The solution was to unite members behind a common set of demands at a national, industrywide bargaining forum. To do this would involve consolidating the existing subsectoral and regional industrial councils into national bodies. The demand for national, industrywide industrial councils in the clothing and textile industries was therefore included on the agenda for negotiations at the existing councils a couple of years after SACTWU's formation.

Initially, the demand for industrywide councils was met by strong resistance from employers, many of whom favored maintaining the status quo (as in the clothing industry) or decentralizing bargaining to the enterprise and plant level (as in the cotton textile industry). Employers were aided in their resistance by the voluntary nature of industrial council participation (Godfrey 1992:136–39, 142–44, 277–78).[12]

Developments in both the clothing and textile sectors indicate, however, that employer resistance to national collective bargaining has been overcome to a large extent. In the clothing sector, employers have recently agreed to the establishment of a national industrial council, and a blueprint for a national bargaining structure has been agreed to by an employer and trade union working group in the textile sector. The latter arrangement has still to be accepted by the respective constituencies, but although there have been a number of delays, it is envisaged that a national industrial council will be formed by the end of 1994. SACTWU is therefore overcoming the fragmented system of industrial councils that it inherited and is about to establish national bargaining councils in both the clothing and textile sectors. A platform has therefore been laid for moving beyond the narrow set of industrial relations issues to which unions in these sectors have traditionally been confined and starting to grapple with issues of performance.

Phase Four: Organized Labor's Thrust toward Corporatism

A complex set of factors are combining to generate the corporatist tendencies that are emerging in South Africa's textile industry. These factors underpin and arise from the strategy that SACTWU is pursuing to protect its members' long-term interests, a strategy that has seen industrial relations and industrial policy formulation become increasingly interconnected. SACTWU—a prime example of strategic unionism, as noted in the introduction—is the driving force behind the meso-level corporatist tendencies. This role contrasts with the roles played by the government and employers, who have been reluctant to take bold strategic initiatives. SACTWU's role in forging the emerging corporatist arrangements is discussed below.

The most obvious factor contributing to the corporatist tendencies is SACTWU's size and monopoly position in the textile and clothing industries.[13] This factor has led to the trend to centralize industrial relations arrangements. Another contributing factor is the crisis in the textile industry and the exposed nature of the industry, given South Africa's increasing reintegration into the world economy. Yet another factor was the political crisis facing the apartheid government and its inability to give any long-term direction to the economy and particular industrial sectors. Finally, the worldwide restructuring of industries and markets is being felt, and although the textile industry in South Africa has not undergone any major structural changes as yet, the perception is growing that it is only a matter of time. These factors explain SACTWU's involvement, and indeed its leading role, in the formulation of industrial strategy through a process of negotiation. It is a logical extension of the struggle to secure better wages, working conditions, and job security for workers in the textile industry.

E. Patel, the assistant general secretary of SACTWU, has played a critical role in the formulation and implementation of the union's policy on industrial strategy. He was interviewed by the authors on 8 March 1993, and what he said critically informs what follows in this chapter. He argued that the crisis facing the textile industry and the inability of the state and capital to provide a coherent strategy for its restructuring have left the union with no choice but to focus on industrial policy in addition to the issues of distribution and power relations on the shop floor that historically were its concerns.

Furthermore, the mobility of capital internationally vis-à-vis labor has forced the union to rethink its traditional role and to acquire a more strategic outlook to protect the long-term interests of workers. For Patel, this does not mean co-optation or incorporation but an engagement in new areas to secure benefits for SACTWU's members: "Whether capital is interested in growth or not, we are interested in growth. . . . So it's not that we are being absorbed on capital's terms, but that the real drive to have a competitive, strong industry employing the maximum number of people, paying the best possible wages, that is our mission. . . . We are doing it because that is what is needed for our membership."

According to Patel, the union is therefore engaging in the process of industrial policy formulation with a very clear vision of how the industry should be restructured to provide the maximum benefits for labor: "The union . . . is seeking to restructure in a particular direction. That direction is strongly job creation in character, but not at all costs. . . . We would want a growth strategy that systematically empowers and assists workers, empowers them through redefining shop floor relations. It's about redefining power relations on the shop floor; it's about decreasing the number of supervisors and devolving more supervisory power to the work force through having them more trained."

These aims underpin SACTWU's proposed strategy for the textile industry, namely, to create a long-term growth path for the clothing and textile sectors. For the union, the key to this strategy is that it is both long term and industrywide. SACTWU's leaders argue that these perspectives have been absent from employers' strategies, which have tended to focus on sporadic lobbying first by a small group of textile manufacturers and then by an opposing small group of clothing manufacturers (or vice versa) around the issue of tariffs.

Union Engagement in Formulating Industry Strategy

By the middle of 1990, at the same time that the call for a national industrial council was emerging as a key union demand, the textile industry was starting to feel the full brunt of recessionary conditions. These conditions were exacerbated by the early effects of the Structural

Adjustment Program, the most visible result of which had been a rapid fall in employment. Consequently, at the start of 1991, the union's leadership identified industrial policy as the critical area of intervention for the future. The issue was debated at a workshop for shop stewards in April of that year, and in the following month an economic conference was held for shop stewards, to which a few selected manufacturers from the clothing, textile, and leather industries were invited. SACTWU also invited BTI to send representatives, but it declined.

The issues raised at the workshop and the conference were then brought up at the union's national congress in June, and the union adopted a resolution on industrial restructuring. This resolution provided, as a short-term strategy, for a national protest over the retrenchments hitting the industry; as part of a longer-term strategy, it identified key areas of focus for policy, namely, establishing an export orientation to the economy, a strategy to train and retrain workers, and a wool beneficiation program.

SACTWU had acted with urgency in the face of the mounting crisis in the industry, but there was as yet no process through which it could engage in the formulation of policy. This remained the preserve of the BTI, which refused to recognize SACTWU and appeared to formulate policy by way of consultation with elites in the clothing and textile industry.[14]

Following its national congress, SACTWU therefore focused on the role of the BTI, which it criticized strongly for its tendency to be influenced by lobbying by elites and for its failure to provide constructive leadership for the industry. Patel took the attack a step further when he addressed the National Clothing Federation (NCF) conference in November 1991 on labor's role in promoting international competitiveness.

In his speech, Patel not only spelled out the way in which labor could contribute to international competitiveness, he also argued that there would have to be a return for the union (i.e., a broad contract would have to be entered into to secure its cooperation). During the question period, Patel underlined the union's intentions when he stated that SACTWU would be prepared to take the industry out on a strike if the government promulgated a new tariff regime without the union's participation in its formulation.

The threat of an industrywide strike had an immediate effect. The day after the conference, SACTWU received an invitation from the minister of trade to attend a joint meeting with Texfed and the NCF to consider the question of Texfed's application for higher tariffs for the textile industry. The union, in a calculated move, turned down the invitation and proposed that a "stakeholders' conference" be called at which each and every stakeholder in the industry could put forward strategies for the future development of the industry. To the extent that there was a difficulty with tariffs in the short term, the union agreed that a committee should be set up to look at that issue but that the fundamental thrust should be to look at the long-term growth path of the entire industry. This proposal provided the foundation for SACTWU's future thinking on the process of industrial strategy formulation. It was opposed to a strategy based on tariff policy but favored a process open to all the players in the industry, including small, domestic producers. In other words, the union emphasized that the nature of the process should give it widespread legitimacy in the industry.

The minister went ahead with the meeting, however, without SACTWU's participation but declined to make a final decision about tariffs. Instead, he proposed that a working group be established with representatives from the textile and clothing industries, including the union, to try to solve the problems facing these industries.

Creation of Tripartite Strategic Planning Groups

At the first meeting of the working group, which became known as the Hatty Committee, the union tabled a submission that the textile industry needed to restructure itself to become more efficient but that this could be done only if there were a development plan that would provide a framework to manage the process. The union's submission went on to state that a long-term solution required that there could no longer be separate sectoral representations and special pleading to government; rather, a comprehensive industry program carrying the backing of all had to be formulated. The union proposed that an industry summit be held to consider the formulation of a development plan that had an appropriate tariff policy as one of its components but that it also include a growth strategy, an investment program, a productivity training and technology policy, and an industrial relations policy.

Patel argues that from the outset the Hatty Committee was problematic because it was not launched legitimately and was dominated on the employer side by the very elites who had led the lobbying process for so long. Furthermore, over the next few months, the emphasis in the committee switched from the union's proposal for a restructuring program with a tariff policy as one component to a focus on tariffs only. What emerged from the Hatty Committee was a tariff/quota system, which, once released, was attacked vigorously by small clothing manufacturers. It collapsed within six months as a result of their protests over the lack of benefits for them as small producers for the domestic market.

After the Hatty Committee plan collapsed, the government introduced a new tariff arrangement, which set the Texfed and the NCF off on a new round of lobbying over tariffs. The union then tried hard to bring the two parties together. It not only succeeded in doing so, it also got them to agree to end the tariff "war." At the same time, the union encouraged the government to proceed rapidly with the launching of a long-term plan.

In September 1992, the Department of Trade and Industry duly established two tripartite forums—the Panel Group and the Task Group—to advise the government on long-term strategy for the textile and clothing industries. The smaller of the two forums, the Task Group, is responsible for meeting regularly and drafting a report containing recommendations. It has to consult with the Panel Group, which has broad representation from the textile and clothing sectors as well as state representatives. The main task of the two forums is to formulate a strategy with achievable recommendations, based on sound economic principles, for the restructuring required to develop clothing and textile industries that are "viable and competitive" (NCF 1992:29). The Panel and the Task Group presented their report to the minister of finance on 28 March 1994.

Union Considerations regarding Strategic Intervention

Patel argues that SACTWU's strategic intervention, coupled with its democratic organizational goals, has meant that a clear line cannot be drawn between the arenas of industrial relations and industrial strategy and between levels of engagement:

> Sometimes the debate is posed that national accords are for the union leadership and that shop floor restructuring is for the shop stewards. We think that that is the most dangerous formulation that one can have because, on the one hand, for national accords to stick requires the support of workers as a whole, and hence you have got to make the worker leadership at the factory level part of that and they have got to understand the issues. And secondly, for factory restructuring to take place on terms that will favor workers requires that the union's national leadership must take an active interest in plant issues and not only concentrate on the macro picture and leave shop stewards who have had less opportunity of thinking through the challenges and the dangers of restructuring to manage the plant ones.

Patel believes that engagement must take place at both the industry level and the plant level. He sees both as equally important but argues that the national level has to take precedence at this point in time: "We have got to reach a national agreement that sets the terms and the framework for what is permissible and what are the parameters and what are the rewards of shop floor transformation. . . . One wouldn't see it as two rigid stages that you first fix up the national and then you go to the shop floor, but in emphasis and direction the union is seeking first to reach the broad accord at the national level." Regarding the importance of plant-level engagement, Patel maintains that "an incredibly large measure of the productivity gain in our industry is going to come about through shop floor transformation, rather than only through the macro picture."

Future Challenges Facing the Union

Patel argues that the union must build on its organizational strengths as it begins the process of involving workers at the plant level in industrial policy issues. He identifies five strategic goals that will form the basis for this process. The first of these goals is that the union must continue to conduct effective campaigns, which in the past were successfully directed at distributive issues (e.g., the living wage campaigns). The second goal is that the union's shop stewards must continue to have high legitimacy on the shop floor and gain valuable skills. Patel believes the shop stewards are going to play a critical role in the transformation of the shop floor. This will mean a considerably expanded role for them beyond their existing focus on disciplinary concerns and will require a concerted training program to equip them with the necessary skills.

The third goal is to introduce industrial policy issues into the union's program of action (i.e., put these issues onto the agenda of regional congresses of the union for discussion and debate). Following from this is the fourth goal, namely, to project the issue of industrial policy as a legitimate worker concern. The union's aim, according to Patel, is to increase awareness of industrial policy issues in such a way that the "lesson that the future of our industry is also the responsibility of workers starts to become part of the daily discourse, part of the psychology of every SACTWU member."

The fifth goal is to restructure the existing collective bargaining arrangements and agreements. This process is now virtually complete, and a national centralized bargaining structure is on the verge of being put into place. Patel argues that this strategy is not an end in itself but is only one component of a union-driven industrial strategy: "There is a fallacy that says that through restructuring your collective bargaining you can get growth in your economy. That is nonsense—you can't have a growth strategy that is determined by collective bargaining. You need an industrial policy to get growth, but your collective bargaining is an element that can contribute or retard growth. So we must see all the time how do we enhance the economic growth elements of your collective bargaining agreements."

For the union, a direct link exists between these two strategies, in that it will make a commitment to productivity only if an institution for centralized bargaining is established. In fact, the blueprint for a national bargaining structure for the textile industry indicates that there will be a permanent forum for both collective bargaining and the formulation of an industrial strategy to manage the process of industrial restructuring.

The union's involvement in the formulation of an industrial strategy for the textile industry and its intention of engaging with employers at the plant level over those aspects of strategy that are pertinent to that level are clearly not going to be unproblematic. For a start, the union's proactive involvement is at times going to conflict with its historic focus on distributive issues. An even more challenging task is to "sell" the process to all its members on the shop floor, many of whom are rooted in a tradition of conflictual industrial relations. Patel indicates that the union is aware of the nature of the task facing it:

> Often the restructuring process entails particular jobs becoming redundant. . . . The challenge is to find a way of managing that process and involving workers in it. Now that is a huge debate, and it is a debate that you must have with workers because you can either do it in a top-down fashion or you can do it with a commitment by workers. . . . Depending on how the issues are introduced, the union is confident that the membership will give its strong support to all the challenges that will be identified out of restructuring. But it is not going to be an easy one; there are going to be a lot of debates and at the start a lot of reluctance by groups of workers to immediately go. We can't assume anything but a turbulent transition toward a restructured industry.

Patel believes that the next few years will be critical ones in which to involve workers on the shop floor systematically in the issues of industrial restructuring. At the same time, the union will have to arrive at suitable structures at the plant level so as to facilitate a proactive engagement by workers, without their being absorbed into the strategies of individual employers. The need to create suitable plant-level structures to manage the process of improving performance at individual enterprises is going to be critical for the union. Patel argues that when individual employers engage with workers over improved performance, they will be interested in raising efficiency in their own firms only. These individual strategies will therefore lead to a shrinking of the industry, whereas the union is concerned with creating an efficient and growing industry. The challenge for the union is to find the right structures and mode at the micro level for engaging with individual employers and articulating these structures within the meso-level framework.

Conclusion

The ending of economic sanctions and South Africa's economic reintegration into the world economy are the results of the political transition from an apartheid state to majority rule. During the era of sanctions, the government disregarded the rules of international trade in an effort to sustain the system of apartheid. Such practices are no longer feasible as the country starts to conform to the rules of GATT.

South Africa was pressured by its major trading partners to reduce tariffs to ensure that the country could qualify for most favored nation status under GATT. Tariffs on textile goods were bound to be lowered because, as indicated in table 6.3, they were among the highest in the manufacturing sector. South Africa made an offer on textiles and clothing that was accepted during the Uruguay round GATT meetings. The offer was that South Africa would more or less halve its existing nominal tariff rates over a twelve-year period. This means that the tariff on yarns will come down from 35 to 17.5 percent, on fabrics from 50 to 25 percent, and on clothing from 100 to 50 percent.

The Panel and the Task Groups, which are responsible for drafting a long-term strategic plan for the textile and clothing industries, regarded the GATT tariff reductions as too lenient and came up with stronger proposals. But the constituencies on the Panel and on the Task Groups could not reach consensus on the issue and ended up putting forward two sets of proposals. One proposal, supported by SACTWU and the textile and clothing federations, suggested only slightly lower rates, to be phased in over ten years. The other, suggested by retailers, other distributors, and a small business group, proposed more drastic cuts: tariffs on fabrics would come down to 18 percent over five years and to 30 percent on clothing over a seven-year period (Panel and Task Group for the Textile and Clothing Industries 1994:152–67).

International pressure through GATT, as well as a weak economy, necessitates a fundamental restructuring of the manufacturing sector, including the textile industry, if South Africa is to compete successfully internationally. Given the industrial relations history of the country, it is ironic that the union movement rather than the state or employers is playing the strategic role in formulating policy and pursuing corporatist arrangements at various levels.

The emerging industrial policy arrangements are at an embryonic stage, however, and there are a number of obstacles to overcome before one can speak of the birth of corporatism. Even at the meso level in the textile industry, the arrangement and processes that exist at present are temporary. At most, they can be termed a form of tripartism, that is, a weak form of corporatism characterized by macro-level discussions on economic policy, resulting in general guidelines and imposing no responsibilities for implementation and hence having a tenuous connection with developments at the meso or micro level (Grant 1985:9). By contrast, corporatism requires that "the policy agreements are implemented through the collaboration of the interest organizations and their willingness and ability to secure the compliance of their members." Furthermore, corporatism is not a top-down arrangement but builds on arrangements that have evolved between capital and labor at the base (3–4, 9). One has only to consider the three characteristics of democratic corporatism Katzenstein identified—not one of which has fully emerged in South Africa as yet—to realize that South Africa still has a long way to go.

What is clear, however, is that the growth of large, nationwide, autonomous industrial unions over the past two decades started the trend toward democratic corporatism. Aiding that development was the fact that the apartheid government no longer had the political base to either co-opt labor into, or exclude labor from, policy formulation. But the evidence that the corporatist trend is being forged primarily at the meso level at this stage, and that political change has made the national level particularly fluid and open-ended, points to the likelihood of a mixture of corporatist variants emerging in the future at the industry level, including the micro level in some sectors.

The textile industry exemplifies a trend toward the social corporatist variant at the meso level. On the one hand, SACTWU has achieved a virtual monopoly position as the representative of labor. On the other hand, textile employers have historically been relatively weakly organized and have had a domestic market orientation. Moreover, the new democratically elected government could undermine much of the political influence textile employers once had. In any case, the employers have been slow to adjust to the changing balance of domestic political forces and new international pressures, as evidenced by their attempts to rely on the traditional method of lobbying the state to secure protection.

Several requirements will have to be met for existing arrangements in the textile industry to develop into a form of mesocorporatism. First, the new government will have to endorse the corporatist paradigm and accept that, in the future, economic policy will be negotiated between itself, employers, and unions. Second, permanent structures will need to be established to institutionalize the process. Third, employers will have to strengthen and unify their organization and reorient their approach away from lobbying for preferred policies and toward bargaining and consultation with the union, so that a united front on industry policy can be achieved.

Fourth, the industrial relations system needs to be reformed so that it actively encourages industrywide bargaining and promotes strong links between industry and workplace levels (Baskin 1993:15–28). SACTWU has almost secured a national bargaining structure in the textile industry, which partly addresses this requirement. But union leaders' intentions to negotiate industrial restructuring at this forum point to the need for a fifth requirement: a separate forum must be established to formulate industrial policy. This is because the current industrial relations institutions provide for bilateral involvement while industry development requires participation by the state. In addition, these institutions tend to be dominated by distributive issues whereas industry strategy requires a more integrative approach. Thus, the proposed arrangement could place too great a burden on a single set of institutions.

The sixth and final requirement is that a strong link must be established between the micro and macro levels, capable of encouraging worker support and involvement in issues such as workplace efficiency and quality of production. These matters are quite different from the traditionally contentious industrial relations issues that have been the subject of many industrial conflicts. Workers will not find it easy moving from an adversarial to a cooperative approach, although SACTWU has acknowledged the need to change workers' attitudes. Much will depend on employers' responses at the workplace level. Managers will have to give employee participation a chance in order to cement cooperative relations at this level.

Clearly, much will also depend on developments at the macro level and how these are linked to meso-level arrangements. A forum already exists at the macro level, the National Economic Forum, but at this stage the link with the meso level is personal rather than structural. In other words, particular actors in meso-level arrangements are also participating in the NEF. It remains to be seen whether the ambit of negotiations will be extended, and procedures introduced, for coordinating macro- and meso-level policies.

Despite the embryonic state of industrial policy formulation, the drive toward corporatism in South Africa has gained momentum, particularly in the textile industry. The advent of a new labor-oriented government will almost certainly add to this momentum, as will international pressure from GATT. The proof of the pudding is going to be in the eating: if benefits flow to those involved, corporatist arrangements will be consolidated. If, however, there are no advantages, the chances of establishing mesocorporatism in the South African textile industry will be slim.

7

The World Economy, State, and Sectors in Industrial Change: Labor Relations in Hong Kong's Textile and Garment-Making Industries

Stephen Chiu and David A. Levin

T he postwar economic transformation of Hong Kong from an entrepôt trade center into a dynamic industrial economy is now a well-
known story, although the explanation for this industrial take-off
remains contentious. Some emphasize the crucial role of a laissez-faire state
policy and free markets (Friedman and Friedman 1980), others the stimulus
of the world economy and the changing international division of labor
(Henderson 1989; So 1986), and still others the influence of neo-
Confucianist values or Chinese "entrepreneurial familism" (Berger 1986;
Wong 1991). These are neither exhaustive nor necessarily mutually exclusive explanations, but in any case most of the relevant studies of Hong
Kong's economic transformation have focused largely on the problem of
explaining the expansion of manufacturing from the 1950s through the
1970s. Relatively less attention has been given to the qualitatively different
phase of development since then (exceptions are Lui and Chiu 1993 and
Sit and Wong 1989). From the late 1970s, Hong Kong manufacturing
industries have faced challenges on a number of fronts and have been
compelled to reorganize to remain competitive in world markets.

This chapter explores the nature of this restructuring process in textiles
and garment-making, two of the most important industries in Hong
Kong's postwar economic success. Our contention is that despite similar
environmental "triggers," the two industries diverged significantly in their
restructuring process. Our main aim, therefore, is to identify and explain
the sectoral differences in the restructuring strategies of textile and
garment-making firms and the labor and industrial relations effects.

The authors wish to thank Mr. Francis Ho of the Labour Department and Mr. Chow Tung-
shan of the Employee Retraining Board for assistance, and Stephen Frenkel, Jeffrey Harrod,
and Alan F. K. Siu for their helpful comments on a draft of the paper.

The first section of the chapter outlines the theoretical issues in the analysis of industrial restructuring and proposes a conceptual model for understanding the nature of industrial restructuring in Hong Kong. The second section traces the historical development of Hong Kong's textile and garment-making sectors, including relevant distinctive characteristics. The third section turns to the restructuring process in these two industries over the past decade, noting the sources, timing, and nature of change. The fourth section examines the effects of restructuring on labor, including employment insecurity, wage levels and wage structure, and industrial accidents. The fifth section discusses the impact of restructuring on industrial relations through an analysis of trends in industrial disputes, union membership, and union structure. The sixth section seeks to interpret the changes in the two industries and their industrial relations in the light of the conceptual model proposed in the first section. The final section draws out further implications, including alternative scenarios for the future of the textile and garment-making industries in Hong Kong.

International, National, and Sectoral Determinants of Restructuring

One obvious starting point for the analysis of the process of industrial restructuring in Hong Kong, given its heavy dependence on foreign trade, is the economic theory of international trade. According to the Heckscher-Ohlin model it will be most beneficial for an economy open to international exchange to specialize in the production of commodities in which it has a comparative advantage (Caves and Jones 1973, chap. 8). Thus, a small, open, agrarian economy will gain most if it specializes in the production of primary products and exports them in exchange for manufactured goods. Over time, as the stock of industrial capital grows, the economy's export specialization will gradually move away from primary products to manufacturing, normally of a more labor-intensive nature. As more countries become involved in manufacturing for export, the economies that took the lead in exporting manufactured goods will shift to the production of more capital-intensive commodities for export. According to this theory, for example, the industrial development of Japan occurred like this:

> The resource-poor, rapidly industrializing Japanese economy gradually strengthened its comparative advantage in textiles and clothing from late last century but subsequently lost it steadily during the postwar period as exports of these items dwindled and imports from newly industrializing neighbors rose. . . . The industries which use unskilled labor most intensively, namely producers of finished textiles and standard clothing, were the first to come under pressure to decline, while Japan's capital-intensive synthetic fiber and fabric producers are still competitive in

international markets (although pressure from Korea and Taiwan has been increasing rapidly during the past decade) (Park and Anderson 1991:15–16, 28).

If the theory is correct, the development of textiles and garment-making in Hong Kong should follow the trajectory traveled by Japan by "adjusting" to the changes in its comparative advantage in the world market.

The standard trade theory of industrial change fails to address two fundamental issues (Tyson and Zysman 1983:26–31). First, it does not include in its purview the human and social costs that an economy must bear as a result of changing trade patterns and the resultant "adjustment" in industries. Second, once comparative advantage is considered in dynamic rather than static terms, and the assumption of perfect competition is dropped, the theory becomes problematic. Starting from alternative assumptions of dynamic comparative advantage and market imperfections, a variety of noneconomic factors then enter the picture as significant influences on the process of industrial change. Public policies, for example, can modify comparative advantage by leading to investments in the infrastructures or human resources. The institutional make-up of an economy can also affect technological innovation or the supply of capital, which determines the path of industrial adjustment.

Several theoretical alternatives to traditional trade theory have therefore been advanced. One example is the capitalist world economy perspective (Fröbel, Heinrichs, and Kreye 1980; Henderson 1989; So 1990; Wallerstein 1979). This perspective, in taking the world economy as the relevant unit of analysis, emphasizes the ways in which the nature of structural links between the developed capitalist economies and the less developed economies condition the latter countries' capacity for economic development. In this respect, Hong Kong, along with the other three newly industrializing countries of Taiwan, Singapore, and South Korea, can be viewed as cases that fit the dependent development model (cf. Gold 1986). The growth of the NICs' export-oriented manufacturing sectors has been dependent on the economic growth and policies of the major importing countries, mainly North America and Western Europe. By the same token, the restructuring of the NICs' economies is, in this view, forced upon them by a combination of economic and political imperatives emanating from the world economy. The proposition that follows from this perspective is that the evolution of industries in the NICs of Asia—both their past development and their forms of restructuring—are determined by the economic and political opportunities and constraints set by developed capitalist economies.

An international political economy perspective is obviously important for understanding the sources of Hong Kong's industrial development and restructuring. Yet it seems to be less useful for understanding how restructuring occurs, because it has less to say about the influence of national and industry-specific factors on the process of restructuring.

This then leads to the third perspective, called the "statist perspective" or "developmentalist state" perspective (Appelbaum and Henderson 1992; Clark 1989:35–42; Deyo 1987). From this standpoint, mediating between the international political economy and the activities of local producers are states or national governments that formulate industrial policies that shape local producers' responses to the changing international economy. From this perspective, it is the state that plays the key role in determining the form, the process, and the outcomes of industrial restructuring. The state, for example, may induce or force rationalization of domestic industry, through mergers of smaller producers into larger units, to facilitate international competitiveness. From the statist perspective, the process of industrial transformation is largely a consequence of strategies deployed by developmentalist states responding to changes in the world economy. This may take various forms, including fostering production for market niches and promoting technological upgrading.

Developmentalist states in Singapore, Taiwan, and Korea have played a major role in the postwar period by shifting industrial policy from import-substitution to export-oriented industrialization in ways that fostered the development of particular manufacturing industries (Bello and Rosenfeld 1990; Deyo 1987; Haggard 1990; Rodan 1989; Wade 1990). It is doubtful, however, whether the developmentalist state concept applies to Hong Kong. Historically, the Hong Kong colonial state has not played a role in facilitating the development of particular industries or of engineering industrial restructuring. The state's strategy, sometimes labeled "positive noninterventionism," entails not playing any favorites when it comes to capital investment and restructuring, although the state does play an indirect role in providing services that support industry. Still, even under this approach toward economic management, the legal and regulatory environments are important considerations in restructuring calculations by firms. Perhaps more important, the actions and inactions of the government also condition the responses of local firms to international market pressures, as well as the impact of restructuring on labor.

The statist perspective seeks to deepen the world economy perspective by pitching its analysis at the national level in order to understand how states react to international market changes. We, by contrast, think that important factors operate below the national level. We contend that it is at the *meso level* of an industrial sector, between individual firms and the national economy, that the dynamics of industrial restructuring can be examined most fruitfully. According to P. Schmitter (1990:13), a sector is "a decision arena bounded by a subset of actually competing or potentially substitutable products." As he points out, the capitalist economy cannot be meaningfully analyzed as a whole but must be broken down into subsystems. Instead of a single unified and perfectly competitive market, as neoclassical economics would want us to believe, there is "significant, persistent and growing variation in the conditions under which resources and rewards are distributed" (Schmitter 1990:12).

We thus propose, as a fourth perspective, the sectoral organization model. Sectoral organization refers to the ways in which both the techno-economic and institutional features of particular industries—economic and technological structure, patterns of ownership and management, the character of employment systems and industrial relations—interact over time to produce distinctive industrial environments, which, in turn, influence the form and process of industrial restructuring. This perspective suggests that the strategies and process of industrial restructuring will differ among industries depending on their historically derived sectoral characteristics and that these differences will be associated with variable outcomes in terms of labor's welfare and industrial relations. In short, there will be different "recipes" for restructuring associated with various sectoral organizations.

An advantage of the sectoral organization approach is that it is not confined to the subnational level of analysis but can be used to integrate three levels of analysis: subnational, national, and international. As S. Haggard (1989:13) notes: "National trade and industrial policies are generally formulated with reference to particular sectors and both business and labor tend to be organized by industry. Taking the industry as the unit of analysis thus provides a good entry into the *domestic* politics of interdependence. At the same time, the sectoral approach necessarily places industries in their global setting, a necessity given multinationalization, international competitive pressures and the growing web of bilateral accords" (emphasis in original).

The sectoral organization model thus makes possible an analysis of what goes on within and between firms at the subnational level, the interaction between firms and the state at the national level, and how firms face up to international forces. Using this model, we will show that although the Hong Kong textile and garment-making industries faced broadly similar international and national environments, the differences in their technoeconomic and institutional characteristics shaped the labor and industrial relations outcomes of the restructuring process.

Origins, Growth, and Sectoral Organization of Textiles and Garment-Making

Textile manufacturing began in China in the 1880s in the treaty ports of Shanghai, Qingdao, and Tianjian. By the 1920s, textiles was a leading manufacturing industry in China, with 118 cotton mills operating 3.8

million spindles and 24,000 looms (Clairmonte and Cavanagh 1981:189). In 1899, Jardine, Matheson and Company started a cotton mill in Hong Kong with fifty-five thousand spindles and quarters for seven hundred workers, but in 1914 it was liquidated and the machinery moved to Shanghai to form a new company (Wong 1988:66–67). Chinese-owned knitting and weaving factories operating in Hong Kong were more successful. A 1939 survey reported that 133 knitting factories employed some 6,745 workers and 82 weaving factories employed some 6,151 (Butters 1939).

Following the end of World War II, Chinese textile industrialists who survived the war restarted their operations in Shanghai but faced growing state intervention and competition from the Nationalists (then involved in a civil war with the Communists), who took control of former Japanese-owned mills, rationed cotton, and imposed price controls. When several Shanghai capitalists were prosecuted for violating government regulations, "They began to look for a safer cover so as to preserve their industrial strength" (Wong 1988:19).

In the late 1940s, several cotton spinners from Shanghai relocated their operations in Hong Kong because of its "accessibility, stability, and relative absence of government regulations in economic life" (Wong 1988: 40). In so doing, they brought with them skills and experience in operating spinning factories, as well as machinery and capital. From an initial 6,000 spindles and about one hundred workers in 1947, the cotton-spinning industry expanded to 132,000 spindles and about 7,400 workers three years later.

The textile industry in 1950, including cotton spinning, weaving, finishing, and knitting, included 450 establishments employing twenty-five thousand workers, or about 30 percent of the manufacturing work force at that time. By contrast, the clothing industry had only about forty factories employing fewer than two thousand workers (Advisory Committee on Diversification [ACD] 1979:41).

Between 1960 and the mid-1970s, the textile sector expanded, although the rate of growth slowed in the early 1970s with the growing use of man-made fibers. Employment in spinning peaked in 1975 at 26,000, while the number of installed spindles peaked at 900,000 the following year, as did yarn production at 517 million pounds.[1] Weaving followed a similar pattern. Employment peaked in 1976 at 37,000, as did the production of piecegoods at 1,110 million square yards, while the number of looms installed continued to increase to 40,000 in 1978. In the finishing sector (bleaching, dyeing, printing, and finishing of yarns and fabrics), however, employment increased from 3,700 workers in 1960 to 18,380 in 1978.[2] The clothing sector experienced a substantial growth between 1960 and 1978, with the number of establishments increasing from 689 to 8,684 and the number employed from 42,200 to 256,200 (ACD 1979:42–43,

Table 7.1. *Indicators of Technoeconomic Organization in Hong Kong's Garment-Making and Textile Industries, 1978*

Indicators (in H.K.$ in 1,000s)	Garment-Making	Textiles
Labor cost/total cost	24.8%	17.0%
Fixed assets per worker	6.7%	24.7%
Output per worker	61.4%	101.0%
Fixed assets per establishment	184.0%	581.5%
Output per establishment	1697.9%	2381.0%
Floor space per establishment (square meters)	60.4%	149.1%

Source: Census and Statistics Department 1981, vol. 2, pt. 2:14, 18, 115, and 118.

46). Exports of textile clothing in current prices grew at 16.3 percent per year during the period 1960–78 and by 17.7 percent per year during the period 1968–78.[3] During the three decades of development, distinctive sectoral characteristics had crystallized in textiles and garment manufacturing. This was due in large measure to their differing technologies. Although both industries are sometimes regarded as labor-intensive, textiles, especially the spinning branch, involves relatively large overhead investments in spinning frames and other machinery to achieve economies of scale. For example, in the United Kingdom, annual capital investment per employee in textiles in 1968 was five times that in clothing (Hirsh and Ellis 1974:129). In garment-making, by contrast, a cottage factory with a few workers and sewing machines is capable of profitably churning out a reasonable flow of garments. Several indicators for the two industries in Hong Kong, shown in table 7.1, also testify to the more capital-intensive nature of textiles compared with garment-making.

In 1978, for example, labor costs accounted for some 25 percent of total costs in garment-making, compared with 17 percent in textiles. The value of fixed assets per worker and per establishment in textiles was three times that in garment-making. In spinning (cotton, man-made fiber, and wool), each establishment invested on average H.K.$26 million (U.S.$3.3 million) in fixed assets (Census and Statistics Department [CSD] 1981, vol. 2, pt. 2, 15).

The average floor space used by textile firms was also far greater than that used by garment-making firms. Because of their space requirements, many of the Hong Kong spinning mills established in the late 1940s and early 1950s were located in the then-rural areas of Hong Kong, where land was relatively cheap. The spinning mills were thus able to purchase large plots of land at relatively low cost.

Another technoeconomic difference between the two industries was their markets. As an intermediate industry, textiles mainly produced the inputs for garment manufacturing. The spinning branch of the industry was especially dependent on the domestic market. For example, in 1964, more than 89 percent of domestic cotton yarn production was estimated to have been used by Hong Kong weavers and knitters (Commerce and Industry Department 1965:4). Woven and knitted fabrics, in turn, supplied the needs of the local garment-making industry. In the early 1960s, about half the total woven piece goods of Hong Kong's weaving industry was for domestic consumption (6). Although there are no figures for total garment production to compare with export figures, it is reasonable to suppose that most local garment production was for export, given the limited size of the domestic market.

In addition to the differences in the technoeconomic organization of the two industries, institutional differences are apparent. One difference is in the ownership structure of the two sectors. Several large-scale textile mills were listed on the stock exchange and became public companies, whereas very few garment-making firms were listed.

Another institutional difference concerns the nature of the typical employment system in the two industries. Based on their experience in Shanghai and faced with the need to recruit, train, discipline, and retain a new work force in Hong Kong, the Shanghainese employers who dominated the Hong Kong spinning industry created a system of paternalistic employment practices that included dormitory accommodation for workers, relatively stable employment for core workers, and fringe benefits that were superior to those offered by other local manufacturers. By comparison, the employment relationships in garment-making were less stable, and recruitment (of nonfamily members) was largely through the external labor market. Employers were willing to pay only the "going rate," and the welfare benefits they provided were minimal (England and Rear 1981:83–88; Wong 1988:68–73).[4]

A third institutional difference is that unions were better established in textiles than in garments. Unions with a stable and large membership already existed in textiles from the late 1940s. The left-wing Hong Kong Spinning, Weaving and Dyeing Trade Workers' General Union (SWDGU) was formed in 1949, whereas the right-wing Cotton Industry Workers' General Union (CIGU) was formed in 1954. In 1956, the SWDGU was the third largest union in the colony, with 8,516 members (Registrar of Trade Unions 1956:24). Garment unions, by contrast, were comparatively smaller, and union membership in the industry could not keep up with the fast expansion in employment.[5] In 1961, for example, union density in textiles is estimated to have been 9.1 percent, compared with the average of 6.2 percent for all manufacturing. In garment-making, the union density rate was only 2.5 percent, even when tailoring unions were included (Chiu 1987:211–12).

For reasons of space, we cannot provide a detailed account of the origins of these differences between the two sectors. What needs to be emphasized is that although the contrasting technological requirements of the two sectors accounted for much of the interindustry differences in capital intensity and size, historical and institutional contingencies cannot be neglected. Because textiles, especially the spinning branch, was not entirely indigenous to Hong Kong but largely transplanted from Shanghai, many of the production and managerial practices instituted in Hong Kong bear the imprint of the industry in Shanghai. That these textile mills were well-established firms at the time they moved to Hong Kong also meant they could afford the expensive overhead investment required by a relatively capital-intensive production function.[6] Moreover, the larger Shanghainese spinning mills were able to obtain substantial local bank credits by using Shanghainese intermediaries with connections to the Hong Kong banking industry (Wong 1988:50–53, 117–19). Their smaller and newer counterparts in the garment industry faced serious difficulties in obtaining loans for capital investment and were forced to rely on their own savings or loans from relatives and friends (Goodstadt 1969:226; Sit, Wong, and Kiang 1979:336–37).

In contrast to the technoeconomic and institutional differences, the institutional environments of the two industries at the national and international levels have been broadly similar. First, as mentioned above, both have faced the same laissez-faire colonial state, which, historically, adopted an arm's-length approach toward domestic industries. Thus, there was no industrial policy that guided or regulated the development of either industry or sector-specific assistance. Nevertheless, the state's investment in physical infrastructure (new industrial towns, ports, roads, and so on) and education, as well as its low-tax policy, helped create a favorable business environment for private firms in general.

The state has also pursued a "voluntarist" policy in industrial relations by minimizing its direct intervention into industrial relations at the industry and enterprise levels in the private sector. At the same time, the state has set certain minimum standards of employment and has sought to regulate workplace safety. Its capacity to enforce these regulations, however, differed for these two industries. The size and visibility of firms in the textiles sector increased the probability that the factory inspectorate would monitor labor conditions in textiles more closely. The multitude of small garment factories made it much more difficult for the state to enforce labor standards and safety regulations effectively in garment-making (Levin and Chiu 1991:158–59).

Internationally, both textiles and garment-making encountered the development of a protectionist regime of foreign trade. During much of the 1950s, the Hong Kong textiles and clothing industries had benefited from relatively free access to major overseas markets. This was the result of trading arrangements that progressively relaxed import restrictions, such as the United Kingdom's preferential tariff treatment for imports from the commonwealth countries, the rights enjoyed by virtue of the United Kingdom's General Agreement on Tariffs and Trade, and the membership of the Organization for European Economic Co-operation, which progressively relaxed import restrictions through its 1958 Code of Liberalization (ACD 1979:51–52).

By the late 1950s, Hong Kong was coming under pressure from the developed capitalist countries, whose textile industries began to press for measures to minimize "disruption" caused by lower-priced imports from developing economies. In 1958, under pressure from the United Kingdom, Hong Kong agreed to restrict the export of cotton textile and apparel goods to that country (Aggarwal 1985:54–63). In 1959, the United States asked GATT members to develop a system for coping with low-cost imports, and in late 1960, GATT adopted the Decision on the Avoidance of Market Disruption, which provided that "restrictions could be applied even if actual injury had not taken place, and against individual countries responsible for the import surge rather than on a most-favored-nation basis" (Cline 1987:147).

In 1961, the first of a number of instruments for controlling international trade in textiles and apparel was introduced that incorporated the concept of "market disruption" as a basis for action by developed countries to restrict imports from developing countries. The first of these multilateral instruments was the 1961 Short Term Arrangement regarding International Trade in Cotton Textiles. This was followed in 1962 by the five-year Long Term Arrangement regarding International Trade in Cotton Textiles (LTA), involving nineteen major trading nations, which was intended to limit import growth for most cotton textiles and apparel to 5 percent annually. These arrangements, renewed in 1967 and again in 1970 for three years, "provided for bilateral consultations and automatic annual increases of 5 percent in restraint levels in the absence of agreement otherwise" (Cline 1987:147). These arrangements mark the beginning of what V. Aggarwal (1985:16–17) calls an "international regime" in the world textile and apparel industries (cf. also Friman 1990 and Haggard and Moon 1989). This set of institutional rules governing the conduct of international trade was to be a critical factor in the eventual restructuring of the two industries in Hong Kong.

Triggers and the Process of Restructuring

Textiles and garment-making were the motor of Hong Kong's postwar industrialization, and as of the late 1970s, no other industry matched their importance in the economy. In 1976, for example, garment-making and textiles employed 31.6 percent and 17.7 percent respectively of all workers engaged in manufacturing establishments. Together, they accounted for some 20 percent of the labor force in that year (Census and Statistics Department 1985:30). In 1978, textiles accounted for an estimated 3.6 percent of Hong Kong's GDP and garment-making for more than 6 percent. The combined export value of the two industries in the same year was H.K.$26 billion (U.S.$3.3 billion), some 47.2 percent of Hong Kong's total exports (19.3 percent for textiles and 27.9 percent for garment-making) (76).

By the late 1970s, however, these industries faced a cumulative set of problems associated with protectionism and competition from new lower-cost competitors. As import growth of man-made fibers not covered under the LTA continued, the U.S. government, under domestic political pressures, negotiated bilateral agreements restricting imports of man-made fibers and wool products from Hong Kong, Japan, Korea, and Taiwan (Cline 1987:148). When exports were diverted to European countries, their governments agreed to join the United States in formulating a new multilateral mechanism covering man-made fibers and woolen goods. The outcome was the Arrangement regarding International Trade in Textiles (the Multi-Fiber Arrangement or MFA-I), which went into effect in 1974 and was renewed for another four years in 1977 (MFA-II). Under MFA-II, developed countries could individually pursue bilateral agreements with developing country exporters to reduce quotas or volume growth below the 6 percent standard. Flexibility under swing and carry-over provisions was ended.

Under European Community (EC) bilateral agreements negotiated in late 1977, MFA products were divided into 114 categories and five groups. Group 1 contained the eight most sensitive categories, and Hong Kong agreed to cut back exports in this group to the EC by 8.4 percent. Over the next two years, the United States "renegotiated bilateral agreements, tightening up swing and carry-over provisions for Hong Kong, Korea, and Taiwan. . . . Total quotas from the big three suppliers were frozen in 1978 at the 1977 levels, and allowed to grow only at rates well below 6 percent thereafter" (Cline 1987:152–53). The Hong Kong government had little choice but to accept these arrangements, although it was successful in pressing for the right to administer the quota-control system for Hong Kong.

The problems created as a result of the restraints from the international regime in the textile trade were publicly acknowledged by the governor of Hong Kong in his October 1977 address to the Legislative Council when he referred to the restrictions faced by textiles and clothing industries that "add new urgency to the long term desirability of broadening our industrial base." Shortly afterward, the governor appointed the Advisory Committee on Diversification, which was required, among other things, to consider "the past, present and likely future course of the regulation of international trade in textiles and the implications for the growth of the economy" (quoted in ACD 1979:1).

Another set of problems facing Hong Kong textile and clothing industries arose from the supply side. Hong Kong's comparative cost advantage
in drawing upon cheap and abundant labor was gradually eroding as a
result of almost three decades of uninterrupted growth and the emergence
of lower-cost competitors. A comparative study reporting wage data as
of December 1976 in nine cotton-spinning factories from four Asian
countries—Hong Kong, Taiwan, Malaysia, and Thailand—found that the
highest daily pay for ring spinners in two Hong Kong factories (U.S.$4.80
and U.S.$5.00) and two Taiwan factories (U.S.$3.84 and U.S.$4.55) was
considerably higher than that for ring spinners in two Malaysian factories
(U.S.$2.00 and U.S.$1.60) or three Thai mills (ranging from U.S.$2.60
to U.S.$2.86) (Nihei, Levin, and Ohtsu 1982:163). Fröbel, Heinrichs,
and Kreye (1980:136) report average hourly earnings for 1975 of U.S.$.72
in apparel (ISIC 321) in Hong Kong, compared with U.S.$.31 in South
Korea. According to A. Mody and D. Wheeler (1987:1281), in 1982 the
average hourly wage in the Hong Kong apparel industry was U.S.$1.80,
compared with U.S.$1.50 in Taiwan, U.S.$1.00 in Korea, U.S.$.40 in
the Philippines, and U.S.$.20 in China. In the late 1980s, according to
estimates from Werner International, the "average cost per operator hour"
for Hong Kong's textile industry (U.S.$2.44) was lower than for South
Korea (U.S.$2.87) and Taiwan (U.S.$3.56) but in all three cases greatly
exceeded comparable figures for China (U.S.$.40), Indonesia (U.S.$.23),
the Philippines (U.S.$.64), and Thailand (U.S.$.68) (cited in Bello and
Rosenfeld 1990:123).

W. Cline (1987:139) describes the effects on Hong Kong since the
1960s of the growing competition from other Asian suppliers:

> In the early 1960s, India and Hong Kong dominated developing-country
> exports of textiles, while Hong Kong alone provided three-fourths of apparel
> imports from these countries into the OECD nations. Then, in the 1960s
> and early 1970s, South Korea and Taiwan achieved extraordinary export
> growth to capture, in each case, approximately one-sixth of exports of
> apparel from developing countries and 10 percent of textile exports. In a
> third distinct phase, mainland China emerged forcefully in the market to
> capture nearly 9 percent of developing-country exports of apparel and 18
> percent of their textile exports by 1984 (up from 3 percent and 12 percent
> in 1973, respectively). By 1984, Hong Kong's share of apparel imports into
> OECD countries from developing countries had declined from 74 percent in
> 1963 to 27 percent, largely as the result of a sharp rise in the shares of
> Korea, Taiwan, and China.

Lower labor costs, the pursuit of import-substitution strategies for textiles,
and the initial absence of export restraints in textiles for these countries
encouraged both local and foreign direct investment in new production

facilities in Asian countries outside the NICs (de la Torre 1984:104–6; cf. Toyne et al. 1984:22).

It was, however, the EC bilateral agreements negotiated in late 1977 and those negotiated by the United States shortly thereafter that provided the immediate "trigger" for restructuring in the Hong Kong textile industry. One journal, *Textile Asia*, commented as follows on the effects of these protectionist measures on the local textile industry: "This injustice [of protectionism] has undermined Hong Kong's confidence in the textile industry. A leading spinner was subsequently lured away into property development and closed its spinning and weaving operations, touching off a series of acts of retrenchment and closure of several other spinners. That was the darkest hour of the Hong Kong textile industry" ("Neither Bleak Nor Broad" 1979:280).

This comment points to an internal inducement to the restructuring process: the lure of the property market boom in the late 1970s. Given Hong Kong's limited supply of land, the real estate industry has generally prospered. The growing population and the recovery from the 1974–75 recession stimulated a new boom in commercial and residential property development. It affected the textile industry more acutely than other industries because most textile firms in spinning, weaving, and finishing owned and occupied large tracts of land. In the early years of industrial development, these sites lay outside urban Hong Kong, but with the creation of new towns in Kwun Tong and Tsuen Wan around these sites, by the late 1970s they had become prime sites for redevelopment. As a result, many land-rich textile firms decided to cash in on the property boom by either liquidating their textile production or moving their operations to other outlying areas of Hong Kong where land was then cheaper, such as the new town of Tuen Mun.

Process of Restructuring

This sudden confluence of push-and-pull factors in the late 1970s led to a very rapid restructuring of the spinning industry. The membership of the Hong Kong Cotton Spinners Association shrank from thirty-three companies in 1978 to twenty-one in 1982. Total spindleage began its historic slide, with the number of spindles dropping from 766,084 in 1979 to 474,100 in 1982, or by 38 percent. The number of workers employed also decreased, by 46 percent, over the same period (Hong Kong Cotton Spinners Association 1988). Changes in employment in the textile industry as a whole, however, were less dramatic; the total number of workers engaged fluctuated between 122,000 and 126,000 from 1977 to 1981. In 1982, employment plummeted to 111,871 and then stayed at more or less that level throughout the rest of the 1980s, largely because of the growth of the knitting and finishing sectors of the industry. Still, the textile industry declined relative to other sectors. Although textiles accounted for 6 percent of the labor force in 1978, it employed only 3.6 percent in 1990 (CSD 1985:25, 30; 1992a:32, 36).

As textile firms began to diversify into the real estate business by developing their factory sites into residential and commercial complexes, income from property development began to account for a large portion of their profits. Thus, although textiles remained an important source of profits for the Nan Fung Textiles Consolidated Company, one of the leading textile groups, real estate also figured prominently, especially in the early 1980s. The share of profits from real estate development accounted for an annual average of 41 percent of total profits from 1979 to 1988 (information compiled from company annual reports).

Other firms restructured by expanding their garment operations, as in the case of the South Sea Textiles Manufacturing Company Ltd., whose profits from its garment division assumed an increasing share of its total profits during the 1980s. Profits from garment operations generated 7.5 percent and 13.2 percent of total profits in 1980 and 1981 respectively, but the annual average for the rest of the 1980s was close to 40 percent (information compiled from company annual reports). Some companies relocated their production facilities to China, whose economy began opening up to outside investment in the late 1970s. But, as we shall discuss below, relocation in textiles has not been as extensive as in some other Hong Kong manufacturing industries since textile exports are bound by country-of-origin rules.

When the textile industry stabilized in the mid-1980s, it was much slimmer than in the late 1970s, although it would be erroneous to consider it a sunset industry. As a consequence of restructuring in the early 1980s, the industry was revitalized as it became more capital-intensive and efficient. Since the protectionist restrictions were quantitative in nature, textile firms invested heavily in machinery to economize on scarce labor inputs and to produce higher-quality products to increase the unit value of their exports. In real terms, additions to fixed assets in the textiles industry in the mid-1980s surpassed the level of the late 1970s (calculated from CSD 1985:47, 1992a:55). As an official report (Industry Department 1991:83) states: "The industry has made considerable investments in automation and is capable of producing high quality products efficiently. Computer-aided design (CAD), computer-aided manufacturing (CAM) and intelligent manufacturing systems (IMS), which use computer control technologies to achieve streamlined production and to increase production accuracy and product performance, are widely used."

Spinners also used more open-end rotor spinning frames and weavers used shuttleless looms, both of which increased productivity dramatically ("Productivity by OE" 1979:74; Industry Department 1991:83–84). Similar productivity gains were also observed in other branches of the industry.

As a result, although the labor force of the industry continued to shrink, real output per worker (deflated by the implicit price deflator of GDP at 1980 prices) was 73 percent higher in 1989 than in 1978 (CSD 1981, 1991b).

The increase in productivity was expected since it had been estimated that the transition from manual to semiautomatic technologies in spinning and weaving would lead to a decrease in labor requirements by a dramatic 86 and 85 percent respectively (Mody and Wheeler 1991:66). The share of textiles in total exports also increased, from about 17 percent in the late 1970s to 20 percent in the late 1980s, as a result of producing higher-end products (calculated from CSD 1985:76, 1992a:98). The more gradual contraction of the industry was due to a change in the internal structure. Although the weight of spinning and weaving in the industry dropped between 1978 and 1989, the higher-value-added knitting and finishing sectors gained in their relative share of employment.[7]

Besides the changes in the production processes and the internal structure of the textile industry in the 1980s, there were significant changes in its product markets. Locally spun yarns were still largely for domestic consumption, with less than 0.5 percent of total sales in the spinning branch generated by exports (Industry Department 1991:4). In weaving, by contrast, export sales assumed increasing importance. In the early 1980s, fabrics made of cotton and man-made fibers were largely for domestic consumption and a small portion was sold to the United States, China, and the Philippines, in that order. Between 1981 and 1990, weaving production increased by almost 41 percent in quantum terms, but export volume increased by 2.8 times (CSD 1992a:59, 103).[8] Following the development of garment manufacturing in China (often involving investment by Hong Kong entrepreneurs), China surpassed the United States as the largest market for local textile products. In 1981, China and the United States accounted for 10.8 and 13.8 percent respectively of Hong Kong's export of textile fabrics.

By 1990, Hong Kong's share of China's textile fabrics had shot up to almost 40 percent, while that of the United States had dwindled to less than 10 percent (CSD 1992a:99). Hence, restructuring in textiles also took the form of an intensification of exports, mainly to the burgeoning Chinese garment-making industry. This again indicates the resilience of the Hong Kong textile sector as a result of efforts to rejuvenate the industry. Even as Chinese textile exports have gained ground in the world market by virtue of China's low labor costs, Hong Kong has still been able to increase exports to China.

While the textile industry held up well by restructuring and modernizing production, the garment-making industry experienced restructuring of a different sort. In the early 1980s, garment-making was at its peak. Between 1973 and 1985, Hong Kong was the largest exporter of clothing

in the world by value (Industry Department 1991:35). Thus, at a time
when the textile industry was doing badly, garment-making firms were
reporting hefty profits ("Garments Hold Up" 1982:69–70). Total employment in the industry rose from 244,510 in 1976 to 255,677 in 1980 and
continued to increase until 1984, when it reached 268,938.

Employment in the industry plummeted after 1986. By 1990, the
industry employed only 80 percent of its peak number of workers in 1986.
Although garment-making establishments accounted for about 30 percent
of workers employed in all manufacturing establishments throughout the
1980s, the sector's share in the labor force as a whole declined from about
10 percent in the first half of the 1980s to less than 8 percent in 1990 as
manufacturing employment contracted relative to other sectors (CSD
1992a:32).

To what extent did garment manufacturers seek to maintain profitability
through such restructuring strategies as automating, relocating, and increasing labor and product market flexibility? A 1991 study of automation
in twelve firms (apparently chosen because of their advanced status) in the
Hong Kong garment and textile sectors reports some examples of "hard,"
"soft," and "linked" automation in use among larger garment-making
manufacturers. Hard automation includes the use of work aids on sewing
machines; automated pneumatic pick-up and presentation of small, cut
pieces; sewing machines with automated thread trimming, backtacks, and
footlifts; and printing machines with computers for repeat adjustment and
fault diagnosis. Examples of soft automation include automated pattern
grading and marker-making systems and computerized management information systems. An example of linked automation is a computerized
pattern grading and marker planning system that is integrated with an
automatic cutting system.

Automation appears to be the exception rather than the rule, however.
T. Lui and S. Chiu (1992:9) found "few signs showing that garment-
making manufacturers have reshaped the production structure of the
industry." Most of the above forms of automation are not thought to be
viable options for smaller firms, which are unable to afford the investment
(Industry Department 1992:18–20).[9] A very rough indicator of the differential capacities for automating production processes is survey findings
that 32.8 percent of clothing firms reported investing in machinery to
reduce labor needs, compared with 38.1 percent of textile companies or an
average of 37.3 percent of the fourteen industries covered (Industry
Department 1990:27).[10] The second option, restructuring by relocation,
became more widely adopted in the 1980s. This has taken the form of
relocating more labor-intensive processes to lower-cost areas, notably
China, while the finishing stages of production remain in Hong Kong
(Sung 1991:110; Anderson and Park 1991; Whalley 1991). This option is
used less frequently in clothing (and textiles) than in other Hong Kong

industries. A 1990 survey of 1,954 Hong Kong establishments in fourteen industries found that the proportion of clothing firms with production facilities outside Hong Kong (22 percent) was much lower than the proportion among firms that produced photographic goods (53.3 percent), toys (50.9 percent), household electrical appliances (49.3 percent) electronics (45.1 percent), plastics (37.4 percent), and watches and clocks (33.2 percent) (Industry Department 1990:34).[11] As in textiles, garment production has tended to remain tied to Hong Kong because of the rules of origin associated with the quota system.

The more common mode of restructuring in the garment-making industry seems to be to enhance flexibility in production. For example, local garment firms have been able to compete in the volatile international market by keeping a short production lead time between the placement of orders and delivery (Kurt Salmon Associates 1987:144). Garment firms also maintain their competitiveness by relying on the global commercial network to gather information on the latest market changes and reacting accordingly. Another basis for the survival of the local garment industry has been its flexibility in the use of labor, specifically its ability to make extensive use of outworking and subcontracting. For example, the 1990 survey of establishments in fourteen manufacturing industries found that 68.7 percent of Hong Kong's clothing firms reported having subcontracted locally in response to difficulties in filling job vacancies (Industry Department 1990:27). Other studies also show that the use of subcontracting and outwork, especially among small and medium-sized garment factories, increased in the 1980s.[12]

Consistent with the continuity in methods of production, the market mix of Hong Kong's garment exports remained relatively unchanged over the 1980s. In 1980, the three largest markets for Hong Kong's garment-making industry were the United States, West Germany, and Britain, which bought 38.7, 15.4, and 12.7 percent respectively of Hong Kong's garment exports. In 1990, the rank order of these three markets remained the same. Nevertheless, Hong Kong's dependence on the American market increased during the 1980s, so that 46.8 percent of all garment exports were destined for the United States in the early 1990s (CSD 1992a:99). On the whole, however, the garment-making industry does not seem to have changed its marketing strategies dramatically.

Although both the garment-making and textile industries have experienced considerable downsizing in employment, the pattern of restructuring in the two industries has differed. Garment-making has continued to rely on its flexibility and international commercial networks, as well as on expanding its use of subcontracting and outworkers, to compete and survive on a smaller scale, while textiles have revitalized by investing heavily in more advanced machinery and reducing considerably the labor content of its production.

We can gauge the contrasting performance of the two industries by comparing their labor productivity. Both industries improved their productivity considerably in the 1980s, but textiles outperformed garments by increasing output per worker by 3.3 times versus 2.3 times in garment-making between 1980 and 1989 (calculated from CSD 1992a:55). As a result of this restructuring, the textile firms improved their bottom lines significantly. The ratio of profits (value added minus compensation of employees) to sales increased from an estimated 6 to 7 percent in the 1978–80 period to about 10 percent in the late 1980s. By contrast, the garment-making industry saw its profits to sales ratio fall from a peak of 8 percent in 1982–83 to about 6 to 7 percent in subsequent years (CSD 1985:47; CSD 1992a:55).

Impact of Restructuring on Wages and Working Conditions

How has the process of restructuring affected workers' welfare in the two industries? As in other countries, although restructuring processes in work organization "may provide 'flexibility' for management, they tend to bring with them increased instability and insecurity for employees" (Harrison and Bluestone 1988:13). One immediate effect of the reduction in the scale of production or reorganization of production from closing existing plants was job losses. Between 1981 and 1982, more than ten thousand workers were forced to leave the textile industry. Member mills of the Spinners Association shed nearly half their work force between 1979 and 1982. Garment-making had fifty thousand fewer workers in 1990 than in 1984. In a few cases, decisions by spinning firms to close their mills so that the factory site could be used for redevelopment resulted in thousands of retrenchments. Even textile workers in the early 1980s and garment workers in the late 1980s who retained their jobs undoubtedly experienced a heightened sense of job insecurity.

Accompanying the restructuring process was a jump in the number of bankruptcies and liquidations. When employers defaulted, workers not only lost their jobs but sometimes back wages and severance pay as well. This was particularly true in the garment industry. There was a smaller number of bankruptcies and liquidations among textile firms, since most in the weaving and dyeing branches occurred in the first half of the 1980s. The garment-making industry experienced a much higher number of bankruptcies and liquidations after 1981, reaching a record 102 cases in 1990.[13] The rate of bankruptcies and liquidations per thousand establishments in garment-making also showed a rising trend in the 1980s and was generally higher than textiles, as shown in figure 7.1.

The bankrupt firms left behind sizable liabilities, including wages and

Figure 7.1. Rates of Bankruptcies and Liquidations per Thousand Establishments in Hong Kong's Garment-Making and Textile Industries, 1976—80

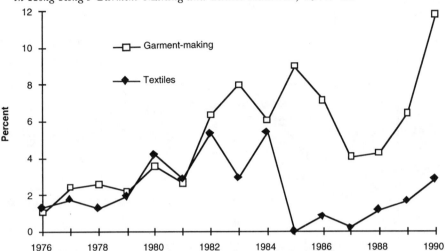

Sources: Bankruptcies and liquidation figures, from Registrar General, various years; number of establishments, from Census and Statistics Department, *Annual Digest of Statistics,* various years.

severance payments that were in arrears. As the Working Group on Problems Experienced by Workers of Companies in Receivership (1983:11) points out: "Sudden insolvency of employers creates serious distress and financial hardship to employees and their families. Even if dividends are available for distribution, they often come many months later and besides, do not necessarily result in full payments of their entitlements." Between 1981 and 1990, bankrupt textile and garment firms accumulated total liabilities of H.K.$288 million and H.K.$1,526 million respectively, an average of H.K.$2.6 million and H.K.$2.5 million per bankrupt firm (Registrar General, various years).[14]

For those workers who remained employed, wage changes served as another indicator of the effects of restructuring on their welfare. Although nominal wages continued to rise in both textiles and garment-making during the 1980s, the picture changes once nominal wage increases are discounted by the inflation rate. We have plotted the real wage indexes of the garment-making and cotton-spinning industry by constructing two separate wage indexes, one for crafts workers and operatives and the other for middle-level (supervisory, clerical, and technical) employees.[15] In the case of crafts workers and operatives, trends for real wages for the two industries show a contrasting pattern. This is shown in figure 7.2.

Workers in cotton spinning and weaving saw little improvement in their real incomes in the 1979-84 period (and suffered a temporary drop in real income in 1983-84 as a result of the slump in business) but experienced

Figure 7.2. Daily Real Wages in H.K.$s in Hong Kong's Garment-Making and Textile Industries (March 1982 = 100)

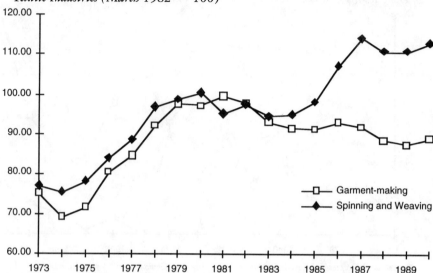

Sources: Census and Statistics Department, *Hong Kong Annual Digest of Statistics,* various years. The indexes are created by linking two wage indexes compiled by the Census and Statistics Department. For the differences between the new and old indexes, see Census and Statistics Department 1982.

considerable improvement in subsequent years. Garment workers fared worse as their real incomes deteriorated over the 1980s. This perhaps reflects the different restructuring strategies of these industries in the light of their different market situations. The spinning industry modernized its plants and machinery, while garment firms continued their labor-intensive methods of production. Facing severe international competition and declining profit margins, garment firms could not afford to pay their workers above the inflation rate.

Another trend in the wage movements of the two industries in the 1980s was that internal stratification among employees became accentuated. There were two manifestations of this trend. First, there was a widening gap between mid-level and lower-level employees. This pattern was clearest in the garment-making industry. While lower-level workers saw their wages being eroded by inflation (down by 9.1 percent from 1982 to 1990), their mid-level co-workers still received substantial increases in real wages (up by 19.5 percent), as shown in figure 7.3.

Although the disparity in real wage increases can be observed in both textiles and garment-making, the gap is more visible among workers in the latter industry. Restructuring in the two industries has thus further stratified the labor market by rewarding mid-level employees more than production workers. It can be inferred, therefore, that restructuring has

Figure 7.3. Real Wage Indexes of Operatives and Mid-Level Employees in Hong Kong's Garment-Making and Textile Industries (March 1982 = 100)

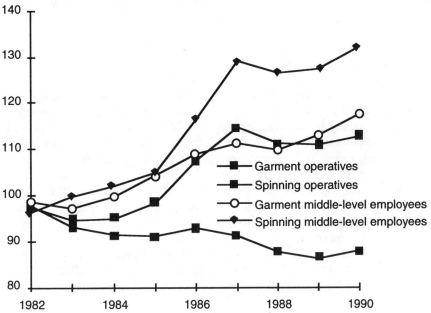

Source: Census and Statistics Department 1992a:45.
"Operatives" includes craft workers. Mid-level employees include supervisory, technical, and clerical employees. Wage index for operatives refers to average daily wages, while that for mid-level employees refers to monthly salaries.

made supervisory, clerical, and technical employees more important in the firms' operations.[16] Since flexibility in garment manufacturing depends on obtaining as much market information as possible and relying on international commercial networks in order to react swiftly to market changes, clerical and nonproduction workers have become more important. Similarly, when textile manufacturing became more automated and capital-intensive, the value of technical personnel increased.

Second, restructuring has also exacerbated the pay inequalities between the sexes. In 1979, for example, the average daily wage of females (excluding fringe benefits) was 92 percent that of males (H.K.$26.7 versus H.K.$29). In 1990, the figure had fallen to 84 percent (H.K.$158 versus H.K.$188) (Commissioner for Labour 1980, 1991). Over the decade, basic daily wages for male workers increased by 6.5 times versus only 5.9 times for female workers. Furthermore, these two sources of inequality (gender and occupation) reinforce each other, since most of the operatives in the garment industry (82 percent in 1981 and 1991) are female, while most of the mid-level employees are male (cf. Levin 1991).

One might expect that another possible indicator of the effects of industrial restructuring on labor welfare would be the figures for industrial accidents in the two industries. One hypothesis would be that under pressure to restructure, employer power would be used to increase the pace and intensity of work, in which case we would expect to find a rise in the number of industrial accidents in both industries (Harrod 1987:211; Nichols 1989). This hypothesis is not supported by the available data, however. The rate of industrial accidents per thousand workers in Hong Kong's textile and garment-making industries dropped during their respective periods of restructuring; that is, in textiles in the early 1980s and in garment-making in the late 1980s.[17]

Our hypothesis is that this trend reflects the particular forms that restructuring took in the two industries. Rather than intensifying the labor process, the textile industry modernized by reducing the labor content of production. In garment-making, especially toward the late 1980s, the main problem facing workers was underemployment, not overwork. The more extensive use of outworking and subcontracting would also tend to result in lower official accident figures, since outworkers and small subcontractors are probably less likely to report their injuries. That most garment manufacturing firms now rely on a core of highly skilled workers to produce high-end fashion may also contribute to lowering the industrial accident rates.

Industrial Disputes and Trade Unions

The retrenchments, layoffs, and plant closings, not surprisingly, spurred industrial disputes in the two industries. During the period from 1980 to 1982, when the restructuring activities in textile firms peaked, the industry experienced a major increase in industrial disputes over previous years. This is apparent in figure 7.4.

Disputes arose even when firms, most in spinning, announced their intentions to relocate within Hong Kong (see Chiu and Levin 1993:41–43 for details of one case). Since restructuring decisions usually were made without consulting with workers, they would become highly apprehensive when such decisions were suddenly disclosed. Demands for severance payments would immediately be made because the workers believed that the announcement of the relocation was a prelude to their company going bankrupt, in which case the workers would not be able to obtain any compensation. Such beliefs were not irrational, since cases of companies going bankrupt and leaving workers high and dry were well known to the employees. In the case of textile firms that decided to redevelop existing sites and relocate operations elsewhere within Hong Kong, workers felt it was legitimate to claim compensation beyond their legal entitlement on

Figure 7.4. Industrial Disputes in Hong Kong's Garment-Making and Textile Industries, 1976–89

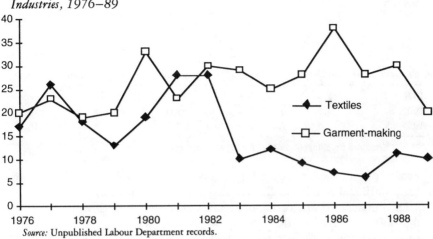

Source: Unpublished Labour Department records.
Industrial disputes include both strikes and disputes that did not result in work stoppages.

the grounds that their employers were making massive profits by selling their factory sites.[18]

The trend is similar in garment-making, but the increase in industrial disputes occurred in the 1980s rather than in the second half of the 1970s. The figures for the two industries diverge from 1982 onward, however, indicating that the period of restructuring and consolidation has been longer in garment-making than in textiles, where restructuring was concentrated in the first three years of the 1980s. A breakdown of industrial disputes from 1976 onward by the issues involved—shown in table 7.2—indicates that the majority of the disputes were caused by insolvencies; this accounted for 62 percent of all disputes in the 1980–84 period and for 72.3 percent in the 1985–89 period. This pattern testifies to the instability within the industry as it restructured to adapt to the new business environment.

The increase in industrial disputes under restructuring is related to the nature of industrial relations in the two industries. As in most other industries in Hong Kong, there was no formal collective bargaining in garment-making or textiles. As mentioned above, management unilaterally made all decisions regarding restructuring, even when they led to major retrenchments or plant closings. Under such circumstances, it is not surprising that workers reacted strongly to restructuring. In garment-making, the small size of most of the firms also contributed to the high failure rate and hence was another source of the disputes.

Unions were also affected by the restructuring. The combined union membership in textiles, wearing apparel, and leather products was 12.6

Table 7.2. Issues Causing Industrial Disputes in Hong Kong's Garment-Making Industry (in percent)

Period	Redundancy and retrenchment	Dismissal	Insolvency and cessation of business	Wage arrears	Other
1976–79	21.5	10.8	32.3	10.8	24.6
1980–84	9.1	5.0	62.0	5.8	18.1
1985–89	3.5	2.1	72.3	5.7	16.4

Source: Compiled from unpublished Labour Department records.

percent of the total membership in unions in 1977.[19] After 1977, the share continued to fall, until it reached 6.5 percent in 1990.

The impact of restructuring on the unions in the two industries differed. The unions in the textile industry were numerically stronger and were better established. Of the six trade unions in the textile industry as of 1980, all except one were established before 1955. Four were affiliated with the pro-China Hong Kong Federation of Trade Unions (FTU), while two were affiliated with the pro-Taiwan Hong Kong and Kowloon Trades Union Council (TUC). Of these unions, the FTU-affiliated SWDGU and the TUC-affiliated CIGU, which targeted the larger spinning firms, were the largest and most influential. The fortunes of these two unions were adversely affected by the restructuring in the industry.

The SWDGU lost 8,520, or 43 percent, of its members between 1978 and 1981 and another 1,144 between 1981 and 1985. The CIGU, whose membership was only about one-fifth that of the SWDGU, had 22.3 percent fewer members in 1981 than in 1978 (Registrar of Trade Unions 1979, 1982). The decline was thus apparently related to the contraction of the textile industry, especially in spinning, from the late 1970s to the early 1980s. As a result of the membership decline, union density in the industry plunged from 20 percent in 1978 to a low of 11.4 percent in 1987.[20]

Following restructuring, unions were involved in some of the large-scale industrial disputes in the textile sector. The SWDGU, in particular, often acted as an adviser to workers. The Hong Kong Christian Industrial Committee, an independent labor organization formed in the late 1960s, also intervened in disputes on workers' behalf. On the whole, however, only a small fraction of the disputes involved the presence of unions.[21] Most disputes were resolved either directly between workers and their employers or through mediation by the Labour Department. Given the weakness of workplace union organization and the absence of a shop steward system, union involvement was largely passive; unions typically intervened only after workers approached them for assistance.

In garment-making, where unions were not as well established as in textiles, the impact of restructuring on the unions was different. In 1980, there were three unions in garment manufacturing. The Hong Kong Garment Industry Free Workers General Union, affiliated with the TUC, had only eighty-nine declared members in that year. The two FTU affiliates, the Hong Kong and Kowloon Machine-Sewing and Garment-Making Trade Workers' General Union and the Hong Kong and Kowloon Machine-Sewing Workers' Union, had memberships of 4,523 and 1,468 respectively.[22]

The outstanding feature of the union situation in the 1980s, however, was not the decline in membership but the formation of new unions.[23] In 1983, five FTU affiliates in the wearing apparel industry (including three tailoring unions) formed a joint office to coordinate their efforts.[24] In 1986, they formed the Wearing Apparel Industry Employees General Union. At the same time, the Clothing Industry Workers' General Union (CIWGU), an independent union, has been actively assisting garment workers involved in disputes arising from restructuring since its formation in 1986.[25] The CIWGU has also led a campaign to keep knitwear production in Hong Kong by urging the government to enforce more strongly country-of-origin rules governing local knitwear exports.

The CIWGU's intervention was also a response to another problem arising from industrial restructuring. When firms planned to relocate or reduce or close down their production but were unwilling to bear the costs of paying severance payments to workers, they often laid off workers for a lengthy period of time to induce them to resign voluntarily. The CIWGU therefore consistently pressed the government to clarify and modify legislation governing the conditions under which workers could receive severance payments.[26]

The union density rate in the garment-making industry has been persistently low. In 1978, only 3.4 percent of the workers in the industry were union members. Union density declined to 2.1 percent in the mid-1980s, but it climbed back slowly after 1985 to 4.1 percent in 1990.[27] This follows given the discussion above of the formation of new unions amid the restructuring of the industry. It seems that unions gained more support by mobilizing workers around the issues arising from the restructuring process.

The increase in union presence in garment-making is also reflected in the figures for industrial disputes. The proportion of disputes involving unions was 3.1 percent and 5.8 percent in 1976–79 and 1980–84 respectively. In the 1985–89 period, however, unions were involved in some 16.3 percent of the industrial disputes in the industry. The CIWGU, in particular, accounted for the bulk of the unions' direct involvement in disputes (calculated from unpublished Labour Department records).

Interpreting the Restructuring Process

This chapter has interpreted the patterns of industrial restructuring and
its impact on labor and industrial relations in Hong Kong's textile and
garment-making industries from a sectoral organization perspective. This
approach has been used as a means of integrating international, national,
and subnational levels of analysis. As predicted by this framework,
similarities in the international environment of the two sectors are likely
to result in some basic similarities in the restructuring process.

Indeed, the "triggers" of restructuring in the two industries are broadly
similar. The decline in Hong Kong's comparative advantage was one of
the main causes of the restructuring in both industries. On the one hand,
the rise in wages increased the cost of production, while, on the other
hand, the rise of low-cost producers in other less developed countries
further eroded the competitiveness of the two industries. These dual
pressures forced local firms to adjust their scale and methods of production
in order to survive.

The international organization of the two sectors also shaped the pattern
of restructuring. The creation of a quota system for exports produced by
developing countries restricted the growth of local textile and garment-
making industries. Yet, during the period of restructuring, the quota
system also slowed down the contraction of the two industries because of
country-of-origin rules, which tied the production of textiles and garment
products for export to Hong Kong. Restructuring by relocation is thus
only a limited option. In this respect, the institutional rules associated
with international regimes governing trade in textiles conditioned significantly the pattern of industrial restructuring in Hong Kong.

World economic forces do not predetermine the course of restructuring
in any locality. The interface between firms and the state in a national
economy is also a significant force. Thus, features of Hong Kong's political
economy contributed to the outcomes. For example, the role of the
noninterventionist state was important. Although the colonial government's influence on the economy has increased during the past two decades
as a result of Hong Kong's larger public sector and the expanded provision
of social and infrastructural services, the government has consistently
remained uninterested in pursuing an industrial policy. There has been no
policy, for example, to engineer a "soft landing" for various "sunset"
industries. Consequently, under direct market pressures, the industries
that lost their comparative advantage contracted rapidly in a short period
of time. The textile industry completed its consolidation in a period of five
years, from 1977 to 1981.

Garment-making, by contrast, faced an abrupt downsizing in employment after 1986, especially in 1990. Firms responded directly and swiftly

to market signals, free of any "external" and noneconomic influences. Workers had no job protection, although they were entitled to severance payments.[28] An underlying feature suggested by our conceptual model is that the interaction between public policies and firms should produce similar results if the role of the state in the organization of the two sectors does not differ radically.[29]

Another component of the institutional environment of local firms was the minimal role played by unions and workers in the restructuring process. Unions in Hong Kong have been numerically weak, organizationally fragmented, and lacking in shop-floor linkages throughout much of the postwar period (Levin and Chiu 1993). For these reasons, as well as the absence of collective bargaining between employers and unions, neither unions nor workers had any input into corporate decision-making processes. They were neither consulted nor informed about restructuring decisions until the final moment. This added to the "flexibility" of local firms in reacting to market changes, but one consequence was an intensification of conflicts during restructuring. Workers became apprehensive about management's intentions and plans as a result of the lack of communication, and union mediation inevitably sparked disputes. Furthermore, as the case of textiles shows, unions were often the biggest casualties under restructuring, when contraction in employment and changes in the composition of employees undermined the unions' existing membership strongholds.

Nevertheless, as we pointed out in our discussion, the patterns and impact of restructuring also differed in the two industries. One difference was in the use of technological upgrading. We have described how textile firms modernized their production by investing heavily in facilities and machinery, whereas garment-making firms generally continued to rely on well-tried, labor-intensive production methods. As a result, the growth in productivity in textiles was much greater than in garments, which, in turn, contributed to the former's rebound in profitability toward the latter half of the 1980s. Textile workers who remained in the industry enjoyed substantial growth in their real incomes, while garment workers experienced a stagnation in the purchasing power of their wages.

A second difference is in the handling of worker dismissals. In the case of the textile industry, the firms involved in closings and retrenchments (especially the spinners) compensated their workers above the statutory minimum standards, while the garment-making firms often simply folded up, leaving their debts and wage arrears behind.

It is our contention that subnational differences in sectoral organization, arising from a combination of historical contingencies, differences in technology, and institutional factors, best explain the contrasting pattern of restructuring in these two industries. Hong Kong's textile industry was not the result of a slow process of evolution but was created in a brief span of time by a migratory group of Shanghainese entrepreneurs who were already experienced in the financial, marketing, and managerial aspects of running large spinning companies. From the start, the textile industry was more capital-intensive and had a larger scale of production, on average, than garment-making, which had a background as a domestic cottage industry. As a result, labor costs accounted for a smaller proportion of total costs in textiles than in garment-making.[30] Once restructuring occurred, it is not surprising, given their greatly trimmed labor force and higher productivity, that textile firms could afford to reward their workers more adequately than their counterparts in the garment sector.

The early location of the spinning mills also influenced decisions concerning restructuring, as well as the outcomes. Because of their scale and relatively capital-intensive production, the spinning mills required large factory sites that were available only in the then-outlying areas of Hong Kong. The rising value of their land as Hong Kong developed and urbanization spread enabled the spinning firms to diversify into real estate by selling off or redeveloping their land. The handsome returns they reaped from land deals made it possible for them to pay higher wages and to invest in more modern machinery. The garment firms, by contrast, were, on average, smaller and had weaker financial capabilities. Under severe competitive pressures from overseas lower-cost producers, they could neither invest heavily in capital equipment nor increase their workers' wages above the rate of inflation. Some crumbled in the face of competition and high production costs and simply closed their plants, while others moved parts of their production to China or elsewhere.

The different strategies of restructuring were also influenced by the repertoire of technological choices available. Technological breakthroughs (open-end spinning machines, shuttleless looms, computer-operated knitting machines), fostered by textile machinery manufacturers (notably in Germany, Switzerland, and Japan) in the early 1970s, enabled Hong Kong's textile firms to increase their productivity substantially (Cline 1987:84–85). The spinners were quick to take advantage of these new technologies. Their commitment to technological modernization was not new but is evident from the earliest stages of the industry in Hong Kong (Wong 1988:46–49).

By contrast, the technological possibilities for major increases in productivity in the apparel industry have been much more limited. Technological advances have occurred in the preassembly phases through the use of computerized machines and laser-beam methods in cutting, but sewing has remained difficult to mechanize. Cline (1987:86) says: "Faster machines have helped only marginally, as the bulk of a machine operator's time is spent loading and unloading fabric. Separating a single ply of fabric and guiding it through the sewing machine remains almost strictly manual because of the difficulty of mechanization." In this respect, garment manufacturers faced technological constraints that closed off the kinds of options available to textile manufacturers.

The role of sectoral organization in the process of restructuring was not confined to the economic and technological factors specific to each industry. There were also sectoral differences in the institutional rules and norms governing the behavior of employers that played a role in influencing their strategies in dealing with labor under the impact of restructuring. In the postwar decades, different managerial styles and employment relations evolved in textiles and garments. Textile entrepreneurs (notably in the spinning branch) developed a more paternalistic system of labor management, comparable in some respects to R. Dore's (1973) concept of an "organization-oriented" employment system. These entrepreneurs offered their workers a higher wage, better benefits, company dormitories, and more stable employment than the garment-makers, although these advantages were combined with strict discipline (Wong 1988:72). In restructuring their industries, these entrepreneurs seem to have felt under some obligation to compensate their workers above what was legally required.

Although their financial capabilities clearly made possible their permissive condition, other institutional factors, historical in origin, were probably also significant. First, the Shanghainese textile entrepreneurs were strongly concerned about their public image (Wong 1988:72), which may have been related to their relatively small numbers, their cohesiveness, and their minority status in Hong Kong. Besides, since many textile firms are listed in the stock exchange, protracted industrial disputes would probably have depressed their share prices and antagonized their shareholders.

Second, the larger scale of the textile operations increased the "visibility" of their actions in dealing with their employees, so that the manner in which they dealt with their workers was more likely to be publicized in the press. Given their concern about their public image, employers in the spinning sector may have been encouraged to give redundant workers special allowances above the statutory requirement (see SWDGU 1978, 1979, 1980, and 1983).

Third, the behavior of Shanghainese textile manufacturers toward their workers during restructuring may have been influenced by their historically close relations with the government on such matters that affected the industry as cotton imports, textile quotas, and labor standards.[31] As important members of the business community who had benefited from government actions on their behalf, the entrepreneurs may have felt under some obligation to be seen as acting responsibly toward their work force. The size, small number, and visibility of the textile mills also prompted the government to pay closer attention to industrial disputes within the sector.

Fourth, and finally, even though the Shanghainese entrepreneurs held negative views of Hong Kong trade unions and were reluctant to negotiate with them, they nevertheless could not ignore them entirely if they wished to maintain stable industrial relations (cf. Wong 1988:95).

The typically much smaller garment-making firms, by contrast, had evolved so-called Cantonese-style employment relations (England and Rear 1981:83–91). The owner-managers exercised a highly personalized control over their enterprises. They compensated their workers according to market pressures and were not known as model employers (cf. Harrod 1987, chap. 5). They lacked the cohesiveness of the Shanghainese spinning entrepreneurs, and their labor practices lacked the same degree of visibility (cf. Aggarwal 1985:69–70).

In restructuring their companies, the garment-making employers were usually willing to pay their workers only the statutory minimum. The state, however, found it difficult to intervene in industrial disputes tandem to the restructuring process, given the sheer numbers and typical small size of the garment manufacturers, so that the actions of individual firms were almost invisible to the state. For example, the state found there was not much it could do in cases in which employers simply disappeared and fled following a plant closing. For these reasons, we have argued that institutional factors were relatively stronger in influencing the behavior of the textile entrepreneurs toward labor under industrial restructuring than they were in influencing the behavior of the garment manufacturers.

Conclusion

We have tried to show that the technoeconomic and institutional features of the sectoral organization of the textile and garment-making industries in Hong Kong have been important in shaping their restructuring strategies and outcomes.[32] Two further implications derive from our analysis. The first is that the technoeconomic and institutional aspects of sectoral organization are often inseparable empirically, since an existing form of sectoral organization is invariably a mixture of both technoeconomic and institutional aspects (cf. Whitley 1992:8–9). Technical and economic rationality are socially constructed and in turn constrain the range of institutional forms an industrial sector can take. In the case of textiles, the transplantation of Shanghainese capital and managerial and technical skills enabled the sector to match the international norm of the industry in terms of capital intensity and method of production. The size and capital intensity of the textile mills, in turn, enabled the managers to develop a more organization-oriented employment system.

The national and international institutional environments also produced similarities that cut across the sectoral differences. The international forces impinging on the two industries have not been simply economic ones, such as market demand and comparative advantage, but institutional ones, such as the regime of managed trade. International trade has rarely been so perfectly competitive that the economic theory of international trade can be applied in a straightforward manner.

The second implication of our analysis is that industrial development is clearly path-dependent (cf. North 1990). The historical trajectory an industry travels often constrains and shapes current choices. Once certain choices are made that generate distinctive features of sectoral organization, other choices become closed off, while still other possibilities open up. This squares with A. Stinchcombe's (1965) argument that firms will tend to retain those organizational forms they adopted when their industry first developed. The sectoral organization of Hong Kong's textile and garment industries that emerged in the early postwar years has thus had, we argue, a significant impact on the subsequent patterns of restructuring.

What does the future hold for the survival of these two sectors in Hong Kong? B. Toyne and his colleagues (1984:20–21) suggest that "textile complexes" follow a life cycle ranging from embryonic to declining. In their terms, Hong Kong's textile and clothing industries have passed through the "golden age" and are reaching the "full-maturity" stage of this cycle (cf. also Khanna 1991:137–38). At this stage, overall employment declines, though total output may still be increasing. Product and process sophistication reach very high levels, and capital intensity increases significantly. This was the stage Japan, the United States, and Italy reached about a decade ago. Beyond full maturity is the final stage of "significant decline," when both employment and the number of firms decrease significantly and substantial trade deficits appear. The international diffusion of textile production and changing comparative advantages are held to be largely responsible for the transition among stages in individual countries.

Will Hong Kong be able to avoid significant decline? Both the number of firms and employment in garment-making and textiles declined further between 1990 and 1991. The decline in garment-making employment (13.5 percent) was almost double that in textiles (6.3 percent) (CSD 1992b:33). Yet domestic exports of clothing and textile fabrics rose in 1991 compared with the previous year by 3.5 and 2.3 percent respectively (CSD 1992b:99). Does this signify that Hong Kong's textile and garment-making industries are moving into a stage of significant decline? Or have the two industries reached their equilibrium level of downward adjustment? The answer appears to depend on three factors: the international trade regime, automation, and the Hong Kong–China connection.

Whether or not Hong Kong's two industries contract even further hinges critically on changes in the institutional rules governing world trade in textiles and clothing. The conclusion of the Uruguay round of world trade talks has signaled the demise of the quota system and the birth of a more liberal international trade regime. Quotas on garment and textile exports will be phased out in ten years. Without the quotas, manufacturers in both industries will find even less reason to continue to produce locally and the market share of Hong Kong's textile exports will probably be eroded by low-cost competitors. Thus, the long-term prospects seem to be clear for Hong Kong's clothing industry. Either they will have to relocate to lower-cost countries—this means basically China—or they will need to shed their manufacturing operations and turn themselves (if they remain in the textile and garment business at all) into sourcing and trading agents for overseas buyers or relocated firms.

Some garment manufacturers will remain in Hong Kong, to be sure, serving local fashion outlets and overseas high-fashion markets. Most firms might still hire a few workers to produce samples at short notice. Nevertheless, the days will be gone when Hong Kong's factories produced clothing for a large portion of the Western mass consumption markets and yarns and fabrics for the garment industry. In the end, with Hong Kong's increasing integration with South China, it will be hard to distinguish Hong Kong's textile and garment-making industry from that of China.

A second factor that will shape the fortunes of the two industries is the application and speed of diffusion of microelectronics in textiles and garment production and the development of automated production methods. There are those who claim that the potential for further labor-saving automation in both industries is vast as a result of the advent of microelectronics (Mody and Wheeler 1991).

Automated production represents an opportunity as well as a threat to Hong Kong producers. If firms can master the technology embodied in state-of-the-art capital equipment, their competitive disadvantage vis-à-vis countries with cheaper labor could be offset, at least temporarily, as in Japan. Although the labor component in production would drop, there would probably be a growing demand for technologists and technicians. The quality of products would increase, thus enabling Hong Kong to remain competitive.

At the same time, the advent of microelectronics and automation in garment and textile production also creates the threat of "a vanishing middle" in the international textile and garment industry (Mody and Wheeler 1987; Hoffman 1985). The late-comers have a cost advantage in industries that use more stable and manual technologies, while the advanced industrial countries are in a better position to adopt the cutting-edge technology of automated production. Thus, manufacturers in Hong Kong and other newly industrialized countries could be squeezed out of the market if they cannot muster the necessary capital to buy automated equipment, which is expensive and rising (cf. Gibbs 1988).

The third and perhaps the most important variable shaping the future of Hong Kong's garment-making and textile industries is the developing economic nexus between Hong Kong and China. With its one-billion-strong population, China is both a potent base of production and a market. On the one hand, the Hong Kong textile industry, with its proximity to the burgeoning clothing industry in China, should be able to capitalize on the increasing demand for higher-quality fabrics, which in terms of quality and quantity the Chinese textile industry has not been able to supply thus far. The increase in the exports of fabrics to China in the 1980s seems to bear this out. On the other hand, Hong Kong textile firms have also been relocating their production to China (and elsewhere).

For the garment-making industry, the potential of the "China connection" is twofold. First, the Chinese demand for high-quality consumer products offers ample opportunities for Hong Kong manufacturers to cater to the growing niche for higher-quality fashions. Second, Hong Kong can team up with China to produce for export markets. As Mody and Wheeler (1991) demonstrate, a high-cost country with advanced technology can gain by cooperating with a low-cost country in garment production. In the case of Hong Kong and China, Hong Kong's expertise in marketing, design, and production should make such a "joint venture" very competitive in the world market (cf. Mytelka 1991). If this scenario materializes, the story of Hong Kong labor under industrial restructuring could be rather different at the beginning of the twenty-first century than it has been during the past decade.

Part III

Changing Labor Relations at the Workplace Level

8

Workplace Relations in the Global Corporation: A Comparative Analysis of Subsidiaries in Malaysia and Taiwan

Stephen Frenkel

After being at the margin of social research for nearly a decade, the workplace has now become a focal point for analysis and prescription. Slow economic growth and increasing competitiveness have placed a premium on improving workplace performance. Further, new demands are being made as a result of information technology and developments in management techniques aimed at improving productivity, quality, and service standards (Dertouzos et al. 1989; Gunn 1992; Harmon 1992). Managers and employees are thus under more pressure to improve workplace performance. But in the era of global competition, workplaces do not exist in isolation. They are often part of global production chains, many of which are organized as vertically integrated multinational corporations that are responsible for an increasing amount of direct investment in overseas countries; hence the interest in and concern about Japanese companies in the United States, and, conversely, the "hollowing out" of U.S. manufacturing as American corporations increase their investments in overseas subsidiaries (Harrison and Bluestone 1988:26–38).

The analysis in this chapter follows A. Kalleberg's (1990:154–55) call for more comparative research on employment relations and shares T. Kochan, R. Batt, and L. Dyer's concern (1992:329–31) about the international transfer of human resource practices. The analysis here takes seriously the simultaneity and relevance of both global and local factors and the interdependence of the whole (corporation) and part (subsidiary) in shaping contemporary workplace relations.

This study is part of a wider project comparing patterns of manual

Thanks to Teresa Poon for research assistance and to PH managers and employees for their cooperation and comments on a previous draft. Useful comments were also provided by Jeffrey Harrod, Sandy Jacoby, Paul Marginson, and George Strauss. The usual disclaimer applies.

workplace relations in five subsidiaries of an American multinational pharmaceutical company (hereafter PH). The affiliates are located in Malaysia, Taiwan, Australia, South Africa, and the United Kingdom. The reasons for choosing the Malaysian and Taiwanese affiliates for comparison are threefold: first, because of the growing importance of East Asia as a site for foreign direct investment (Australian Bureau of Industry Economics [BIE] 1991:52); second, because this study illuminates a previously little-researched area, namely, the way workplace relations are conducted in countries where strong growth-oriented states might be expected to play a significant role in shaping workplace relations (Deyo 1989; Frenkel, Hong, and Lee 1993; Kuruvilla 1992); and third, because the Malaysian and Taiwanese workplaces are broadly similar in size and product mix.

Differences in political and institutional factors and in management and work force characteristics in Malaysia and Taiwan led me to expect that patterns of workplace relations would differ considerably in the two subsidiaries. This view was reinforced by their apparent autonomy from corporate headquarters: both subsidiaries were established to serve their respective local markets, and each is small relative to other affiliates and hence not critical to the growth of the corporation (Hamill 1984; Garnier 1982). As will become evident, however, the similarities in workplace relations are more striking than the differences. I argue that workplace relations in both subsidiaries approximate the neo-Taylorist ideal type; however, the Taiwanese affiliate shows signs of a tendency toward lean production.

The first section of the chapter defines the concept of workplace relations and distinguishes between neo-Taylorist and lean production, including factors that might account for the persistence of neo-Taylorism as well as differences between the two affiliates. The second section looks at PH specifically—its changing business strategy, structure, and guiding values—and the main features of the two affiliates. These include their relationships with headquarters and details of their respective political, institutional, and economic settings. In the third section, the patterns of workplace relations are compared on the dimensions that comprise the ideal types outlined earlier. The fourth section uses the variables introduced earlier to explain the findings. The fifth and concluding section summarizes the argument and considers future workplace relations patterns in the two affiliates in light of Dore's (1989) convergence thesis. This section also identifies several conditions that are likely to undermine neo-Taylorism and support alternative forms of workplace relations.

Workplace Relations: Elements of a Theory

In this chapter, the term "workplace relations" is used to describe five key sociological features of production derived from comparative studies

Table 8.1. Characteristics of Neo-Taylorism and Lean Production

Variables	Neo-Taylorism	Lean production
Job characteristics		
Task range	Narrow	Narrow
Job flexibility	Low	High
Emphasis on learning	Selective, limited	Very high, continuous
Work organization		
Management style	Directive	Consultative/facilitative
Employee involvement	Low	High, e.g., QCs
Teamwork	Low	High, group pressure
Functional integration	Low	High
Reward system		
Main basis of payment	Job, working conditions, union	Person/position company performance
Labor market	External/internal	Internal
Employee representation		
Plant level	Nonunion	Union, joint consultation
Union structure	Not relevant	Enterprise
Management-employee relations		
Main form of regulation	Bureaucratic	Normative
Basis of relationship	Contractual, uncertain	Integrative, more certain
Status distinctions, management versus workers	Marked differences	Limited differences

examined and explicated in previous work (Frenkel 1986, 1994). These features are job characteristics; work organization; reward systems; forms of employee representation; and management-employee relations, including the dominant forms of employee regulation. These variables cohere to form ideal types of workplace relations patterns, thereby providing a benchmark against which empirical research findings can be compared. For the purposes of the present analysis, neo-Taylorist and lean production workplace regimes are seen as the most relevant.[1] These regimes are outlined in table 8.1.

Although the stylized patterns listed in table 8.1 derive from research in the American, Japanese, and, to a lesser extent, British and French auto and engineering industries (Womack, Jones, and Roos 1990; Lane 1989), distinctions in workplace patterns are becoming part of a wider discourse on the future of manufacturing (Dertouzos et al. 1989). Moreover, the multinational scope of many large manufacturing companies makes it possible to transfer all or part of these patterns to foreign countries. Nevertheless, caution is needed in applying these concepts to pharmaceutical plants, especially those outside the above-mentioned countries. Neo-Taylorism is frequently associated with the production of high-volume standardized goods in the United States or other industrialized countries. This implies that the plants involved are large and that there are labor unions present.

Since the focus of this chapter is on relatively small workplaces, a more suitable ideal type is the low-volume, nonunion variant summarized in table 8.1. Unlike neo-Taylorism, the lean production ideal type needs no modification since it is a flexible form of manufacturing geared to high-product-variety workplaces that are producing at high and lower volumes. As we shall see, lean production is also favored, albeit in a modified form, by PH's corporate management.

Neo-Taylorism

Workplaces of the neo-Taylorist type are operated on the assumption that managers are the repositories of technical knowledge and that managers manage and workers obey. This clear distinction between managers and workers, in turn, underpins the contractual, rather than the integrative, nature of management-employee relations. Manual jobs are closely defined, involve short cycle times, and permit employees little autonomy, although workers are required to be more flexible than in large plants, where there tends to be more job specialization. Learning is selective in two senses: only younger workers destined for skilled jobs receive intensive training to perform current functions, and training tends to be period-specific. In other words, training is aimed at ensuring adequate production standards, not at investing in continuous improvement.

The management style is directive, concerned mainly with target attainment. Management may be centralized or decentralized and may be supplemented by human resource techniques that promote employee participation—for example, briefing groups and regular meetings between supervisors and employees—but these do not alter the strong hierarchical structure of authority. Focused on minding single machines and assembly-line production, the work is mainly machine-paced and tends to isolate workers from their colleagues. Officially sanctioned teamwork is confined to indirect (nonproduction) employees and to the limited group initiatives mentioned above. Departments tend to be distinct and infrequently exchange personnel. Joint projects are also uncommon, so that functional integration tends to be low.

Manual workers are paid according to the job performed and extant working conditions. Wage increases, employment security, and job progression are dependent on external labor market comparisons and the profitability of the enterprise. Recruitment is not restricted to internal applicants. Although employment rules are formalized, thereby protecting employees against arbitrary treatment, there is no union representation. Management-employee relations are contractual, based mainly on specific rather than diffuse obligations and rights (Fox 1974). Consequently, relations may be cooperative or adversarial, depending on perceptions of fairness and the distribution of power between management and the employees. Uncertainty tends to be high because plant survival is problematic in a rapidly changing environment where MNCs pursue strategies aimed at rationalizing production (Mueller and Purcell 1992). Symbolically, for example, in their dress codes and access to workplace facilities, management and manual workers differ noticeably. This dual-status system is consistent with the separation of conception from execution, the basic principle underpinning neo-Taylorist workplace relations.

Lean Production

Lean production is characterized by short-cycle jobs that are restricted to a relatively few tasks. Extensive job rotation keeps the monotony to a minimum and enables workers to become acquainted with a broad range of jobs. Management encourages continuous learning from entry age, typically after high school. This is based on the assumption that employees are capable of contributing significantly to workplace performance. This attitude is supported by a philosophy of continuous improvement, embodied in the just-in-time manufacturing system and institutionalized in the detailed documentation of all improvements in work processes and tasks (Adler and Cole 1993). This attitude is also encouraged by payment systems that reward individual and group achievement. Management is consultative in style; supervisors facilitate and coordinate the endless search for higher productivity and quality. Teamwork is founded on members undertaking similar work and being responsible for internal customers (colleagues) further up the production chain. Quality circle work, aimed at improving product quality and productivity, is a team activity.

Several of the characteristics of lean production mentioned above encourage a high level of interdepartmental integration and knowledge of the manufacturing process. These include job rotation; broad-based learning; strong interdependence (and peer pressure), encouraged by just-in-time manufacturing; and fostering of organizational commitment by management.

Pay is based on several criteria, including age—implying that employees are rewarded for higher skill and experience; assessments of their personal ability by supervisors; position or grade; and wage and bonus increases arising from union negotiations. Rewards are distributed to some extent in accordance with individual ability. Employees may also be given needs-based supplements, such as transportation allowances. Promotion is typically from within the enterprise and provides additional pay to core employees who have employment security and who tend to remain with the same company for most of their working lives. In essence, the reward system is person-oriented rather than position-oriented.

Employees in lean production firms are typically represented by an enterprise union that includes blue- and white-collar employees. This reduces differentials in employment and working conditions, thereby narrowing status differences and thus contributing to social cohesion. Because the unions are enterprise-based, workers' interests are more easily coordinated with those of management. The involvement of union officials in workplace decision making with management supports the tendency toward integration promoted by the broader corporate governance norms and structures (see Dore 1987:108–68). Although formalized rules exist for handling disputes, discipline, and personal problems, management-employee relations are based mainly on values and norms that are directed toward satisfying the joint interests of management and employees. Greater employment security and a career in the company for core employees contribute to a relatively high level of workplace social integration.

Factors Influencing Patterns of Workplace Relations

After careful consideration, six broadly defined variables—two extraorganizational and four intraorganizational—appear to have significant influence on the pattern of workplace relations.[2] The two environmental variables are the product and labor markets and the political-institutional arrangements regulating these markets. The four firm-related variables are the nationality of the corporate owners, including senior managers; management's ideology, strategy, and style; the extent of product homogeneity and intersubsidiary dependence; corporate-subsidiary relations; and the technological setting. Note that the intraorganizational variables may have an effect at the corporate and/or workplace level and that the two affiliates have some attributes in common.

Product markets can be distinguished according to the extent and basis of competition. Thus, highly competitive, price-responsive markets place a premium on management strategies that emphasize cost cutting, tight labor control, and numerical flexibility, often resulting in adversarial management-employee relations. By contrast, limited competition, based on the delivery of high-quality products and reliability, may encourage a value-adding management strategy, characterized by expanded job roles and career prospects, employee involvement, in-house training, performance-related pay, and mutual commitment by management and employees (Cappelli and McKersie 1987; Walton 1985; Kochan and McKersie 1992). A tight external labor market will encourage management to take employees' requirements more into account, because the employees are represented by a union and/or there are proactive human resource policies designed to retain competent employees (Kochan and Chalykoff 1987).

Laws and local institutions can also affect whether firms cooperate on strategic issues and use advanced technology (Piore and Sabel 1984; Streeck 1991). There is strong evidence that laws and institutions regulating the labor market, which are in turn products of history, have a significant impact on workplace relations (see Frenkel 1986; Turner 1991; Shire 1994).[3] In essence, these factors may encourage managers to treat employees as valuable human resources or, alternatively, as dispensable commodities.

Turning to the intraorganizational variables, foreign-owned companies have been shown to structure and manage their labor relations differently from local companies (Hamill 1984). This is strikingly illustrated in the case of Japanese auto transplants in the United States and United Kingdom (Florida and Kenney 1991; Oliver and Wilkinson 1989), although, as R. Milkman (1991) indicates, this is not inevitable, particularly where labor is plentiful and employed in routinized jobs managed by local managers. Nevertheless, differences between foreign companies according to nationality have also been found in Asian countries (Lawler, Zaidi, and Atmiyanandana 1989; Redding and Whitley 1990), suggesting that the nationality of the corporate owners—which usually influences senior management's behavior—is potentially significant in shaping workplace relations.

Although the various factors alluded to above affect management choice, the pattern of workplace relations depends on what is actually decided and how these decisions are implemented. Corporate managers tend to make strategic business decisions that have significant implications for resource allocation and subsidiary policies, including labor relations (Banaji and Hensman 1990; Kochan, Katz, and McKersie 1986). Interpreting and applying higher-level rules and norms, and exercising discretion within certain parameters, are matters for the management of the subsidiary. How this is achieved depends mainly on the ideology, strategy, and style of the local line management (Storey 1992). Managers may share a variant of the unitary or pluralist ideology (Fox 1974; Purcell and Sisson 1983:112–20), they may emphasize a cost-cutting or value-adding strategy, or they may differ in style, tending toward conservatism or innovation and being directive or consultative.

The amount of decision-making discretion given to subsidiaries also varies. This depends on corporate characteristics and the role assumed by the subsidiaries. Company affiliates that produce relatively homogeneous products that are confined to a single industry and/or whose business units are highly interdependent (in terms of materials' supply, production, and distribution) tend to have less autonomy (Marginson et al. 1988, chap. 7; Hamill 1984). This suggests that workplace relations in subsidiaries with these characteristics are more likely to resemble one another than are conglomerate enterprises where there is little contact between affiliates.

Subsidiaries tend to be allocated varying roles and therefore to have different relationships with headquarters (Bartlett and Goshal 1989; Goshal and Nohria 1993; Gupta and Govindarajan 1991). Some subsidiaries may be given the necessary resources and encouraged to innovate, while others may be required to conform to established policy. Drawing largely on C. Bartlett and S. Goshal (1989), a two-dimensional typology ascribing strategic importance to the corporation (suggested by proximity to large or otherwise profitable markets) and according to quality of resources and competencies (substantial/minimal) yields four types of subsidiaries. The *strategic leader* is high on both dimensions; the *nascent leader* is high on strategic importance but low on resources and/or competencies; the *implementer* is low on both dimensions; and the *local innovator* is low on strategic importance but has considerable resources and competencies. Arguably, to stay ahead of the competition, strategic leaders particularly, but also local innovators, are likely to have quite different patterns of workplace relations than nascent leaders and implementers.

The impact of technology on work has been of long-standing interest to industrial sociologists (see Francis 1986). Traditional, semiautomatic, machine-minding settings are well suited to neo-Taylorism (Blauner 1964). Flexible, computerized manufacturing technology enables a greater variety of high-quality items to be produced at relatively low cost. Effective use of this technology requires higher-skilled employees working on more flexible, team-based job assignments (Dean and Sussman 1989; MacDuffie and Krafcik 1992). Under particular institutional conditions, management may abandon neo-Taylorism and, preferring lean production, adopt a more human-centered approach to workplace relations (Kern and Schumann 1992; Roth 1992).

I shall discuss the characteristics of the two affiliates in terms of the five elements of workplace relations noted earlier. I shall then explain how the six factors mentioned above contribute to explaining the persistence of neo-Taylorism in both the Malaysian and Taiwanese affiliates and why Taiwan shows a tendency toward lean production. An important qualification to this discussion is that, common to all comparative studies in which the number of variables is large relative to the number of cases, it is impossible to determine the exact impact of each variable and its interaction with other variables (see Collier 1991; Ragin 1987).

PH Corporation: Strategy, Structure, and Culture

PH is among the fifteen largest and most profitable MNCs in the pharmaceutical industry. In 1992, the company's annual turnover exceeded

U.S.$5 billion, and it employed nearly thirty-five thousand employees in more than forty countries. PH developed mainly by a series of acquisitions and mergers of companies specializing in prescription and over-the-counter (OTC) health-care and related consumer products. In 1992, nearly 60 percent of PH's revenue came from the sale of nonprescription products. PH is best described as a diversified pharmaceutical company.

Beginning in the early 1980s, corporate management initiated a strategy aimed at rapidly increasing profitability. This was based on two approaches: restructuring and revitalization. Several earlier acquisitions and unprofitable businesses worth more than U.S.$35 million were divested to focus on profitable, core product lines. This resulted in a 25 percent reduction in corporatewide employment between 1984 and 1986. Cost-reducing measures, particularly in the form of head-count reductions, and rationalization of manufacturing units, especially in Europe, are continuing.

Revitalization entailed changes in organizational structure and culture. A relatively uncoordinated federation of merged and diverse businesses was slowly brought together by a strong, centralized management. The company was divided into a U.S. and an international section, and the latter was further subdivided into geographical regions. Corporate managers who had previously been acquainted with a section of the business now had to take responsibility for a wider range of products. The new structure represented an integrated company with many different product lines being sold in geographically distinct markets.

Based on the assumption that people were the most critical resource in achieving competitive success, corporate management announced a new approach to human resources. A managing statement and corporate culture (credo) document were introduced. These emphasized particular values that were incorporated into the performance appraisal process for most white-collar employees. Key values included the provision of a satisfying environment involving creative, challenging work; opportunities for employee participation in job-related decisions; and openness in management-employee relations. Corporatewide programs covering management training, performance appraisal, and salary determination for supervisory and higher-level personnel were also implemented.

In 1982, corporate headquarters began fostering a version of the just-in-time manufacturing system. This is continuing under the title of TCS, or total customer satisfaction. TCS emphasizes the paramount importance of quality and the satisfaction of internal and external customer expectations and the need to reduce inventory levels and, relatedly, to forge dependable, efficient relationships with suppliers. To ensure improvements in quality and productivity, TCS encourages the establishment of voluntary quality improvement teams trained in problem-solving and simple statistical methods. The teams—made up of five to seven people from various departments—are ultimately responsible to a steering committee that includes senior plant-level representatives.

TCS supports the emphasis in the corporate credo on innovation and employee involvement. Fostered by a group within the technical section at corporate headquarters, the program is a means of "constructively channeling a restless discontent with the status quo." In the words of a senior member of the group: "We coached rather than directed. We provided information and encouraged affiliates, arranged seminars and helped set up teams."

TCS initiatives were attempted at a number of subsidiaries, including the one in Taiwan, where nine teams of forty-one members were operating in 1989. Despite an initial positive assessment, only half these teams were operating a year later, and by 1991 all the teams had disappeared. In Malaysia, TCS teams were confined to the quality control department, where several successful projects were accomplished.

More generally, manufacturing excellence was part of the revitalization strategy of the 1980s. Annual awards were introduced to reward plants with superior performance. Assessment was based on corporate headquarters' (technical section) analysis of voluntary submissions made by subsidiaries in response to a detailed standardized questionnaire that requested data in a variety of performance areas.[4] In contrast to the affiliate in Taiwan, which did not win any awards between 1987 and 1992, the affiliate in Malaysia won awards for manufacturing excellence in 1988 and 1989.

By the end of the decade, the restructuring and revitalization strategy had resulted in significant improvements in PH's performance. Nominal sales per employee had increased by two-thirds in the period 1985–90, and the cost of goods as a percentage of sales (a measure of economic efficiency) had been reduced from 37 percent in 1987 to 32 percent in 1990. PH was also more profitable, having improved its ranking in the U.S. pharmaceutical industry's league table of firms. Better performance was not enough to sustain the company over the longer term, however. To understand why, it is necessary to look at three interrelated difficulties faced by corporate management.

First, although R&D expenditure increased at an average of 15 percent a year between 1987 and 1992, the rate of innovation in new prescription products has been declining.[5] This is a serious problem since new prescription products are potentially the most profitable part of PH's business.[6] The company faces strong competition from larger firms investing more funds in R&D, and there is increasing pressure from producers of generic prescriptions, since some of PH's major products are no longer protected by patents. Further, growth in health-care and related consumer goods has been adversely affected by the U.S. recession, so that strong profitability has been achieved largely by effective cost-reducing strategies, including head-count reductions, and by charging higher than average prices for prescription products in the United States. These strategies have become difficult to sustain, so that senior management has given priority to boosting sales growth. This is seen as imperative if senior management wishes to avoid a takeover.[7]

Globalization became the new watchword in PH's 1990 corporate strategy. This should be seen against the backdrop of the relatively strong growth in the Asian market and the significant potential in the European Union. Globalization entailed organizational restructuring, reflecting management's responsibility to product groups—prescription drugs and consumer products respectively—rather than to regions. This strategy presupposed an emphasis on global strategic planning but not on further centralization of decision making. Global marketing was expected to provide economies of scale, while global monitoring of product performance would enable opportunities for growth to be more easily detected than in the recent past, when regional managers concentrated mainly on the largest-selling products. There has not been a total switch, however. Globalization is being actively pursued in the large markets of North America, Japan, and Europe. The remaining areas of the world—characterized by complex differences in national product market regulations—are grouped together under a president, to whom the East Asian regional office (composed of only four managers) and the general managers of the Asian subsidiaries report.

In 1991, globalization was supplemented by a new concept in corporate-subsidiary relations reflected in policies affecting organizational structure and corporate culture. Corporate headquarters' new role is deemed to be one of "strategic leadership," rather than "coordination and control." Championed by the new chief executive officer, this has involved three major changes: streamlining, empowering, and fostering new value priorities. As a result of the streamlining, corporate headquarters has little effective operational control over the subsidiaries. Consequently, the subsidiaries no longer need to provide corporate headquarters with such large volumes of data. The staff at headquarters has also been reduced substantially. Finally, through the introduction of electronic mail, communication between managers in different locations has improved.

As a result of the emphasis on empowerment, the managers of the subsidiaries are expected to adopt a more proactive role in pursuing new initiatives, such as developing local strategic alliances and purchasing new products that can be reformulated, branded, and marketed locally. Managers of the subsidiaries are being given greater autonomy to make decisions, although how far this will go is not yet clear. More discretion means more sharing of responsibility between corporate headquarters and the subsidiaries. It is symbolized by the substitution of the term "colleague" for "employee" in all documents from corporate headquarters and by the introduction of a share-ownership scheme available to 40 percent of PH's employees; of those who are excluded, most are lower-level and unionized workers.[8]

To promote desirable management behavior, corporate management is deemphasizing programs that are designed and "rolled out" from headquarters. The emerging emphasis is on forging a new corporate culture based on five values that will be reinforced by a revised management appraisal and reward system that was piloted in selected subsidiaries. The five values are open and candid communication (between "colleagues" at various levels); creativity (management support for risk-taking and tolerance if projects fail); swift action (for example, short decision-making cycles and rapid movement from idea stage to product introduction); focusing activities (resources to be directed at priorities); and rewards for success (providing more rewards and career opportunities for high-performing employees).[9]

Impact of Changing Corporate Strategy on Subsidiaries

As noted above, the new strategies have supplemented rather than replaced earlier initiatives, and the pace of change has quickened in recent years. The subsidiaries have been under pressure, first, to meet annual financial performance targets in light of uncertainty about their future in a globalized environment where rationalization of manufacturing continues to be a major means of cost reduction; second, to achieve cost reductions to offset difficulties in achieving sales growth with mature products; and, third, to retain the most productive employees and improve morale under tight financial conditions.

The subsidiaries also share six common problems. The first is that there is a limited number of new products coming through the development pipeline. Moreover, when new products are introduced, they tend to be complex chemical entities that are produced with advanced technology in the larger plants in Europe or in Puerto Rico, where tax incentives have been attractive. Consequently, the subsidiaries cannot easily boost their sales by manufacturing products domestically.

The second problem is that engaging in local initiatives—such as switching prescription products to over-the-counter status, acquiring, developing, and registering local products with the relevant government authorities, and entering into joint ventures—is constrained by corporate headquarters. The main limitations are the lack of resources and limited devolution of authority, although both these limitations vary according to the role of various subsidiaries. Nevertheless, the two problems noted above encourage the affiliates to manage current products more efficiently, rather than to introduce new products and processes. This strategy entails cost containment as the most viable means of meeting profit and other financial targets.

The third common problem is that corporate headquarters requires that the subsidiaries market as many of the corporation's products as possible. Although general managers now have discretion to discontinue the manufacture of very low-volume products, the basic policy of producing a wide range of products leads to a lack of scale economies, a large number of machine changeovers, and idle capacity, partly resulting from the use of dedicated machinery.[10] This is exacerbated by the fourth problem: the limited technology available to minimize planning and scheduling problems. Until 1991, when a regional initiative resulted in a common approach to information technology (currently being installed in Malaysia and Taiwan), each affiliate attempted to develop its own information system. In most cases these systems had serious deficiencies.

The fifth problem has to do with estimating future sales. For various reasons, the subsidiaries' marketing departments are not able to do this very precisely. The resulting fluctuations in product demand adversely affect manufacturing costs. In addition, because they are frequently called upon to meet unplanned orders, the directors of manufacturing are likely to manage by reaction rather than by planned intervention.

The sixth and final problem is that there are increasingly stringent government good manufacturing practice (GMP) requirements. Products may be banned from being distributed if they are not produced according to specified and rigorously enforced standards. In sum, the directors of manufacturing work under a series of constraints that typically influence manufacturing performance and therefore overshadow workplace relations.

From the standpoint of the shop-floor workers, the imperatives and problems referred to above are transmitted mainly via manufacturing and human resource management. Product quality and costs are monitored regularly, and improvements are introduced gradually. Apart from headcount reductions or "containment," which was a requirement of corporate headquarters, the management of the affiliates does not see a reduction in unit labor costs in manufacturing as a major goal. Cutting unit labor costs by reducing machine changeover times or introducing preventive maintenance, for example, rarely is seen as a key issue. A large part of the reason for this view lies in the limited significance of manufacturing labor costs as a proportion of total pharmaceutical costs. Labor typically represents less than 15 percent of manufacturing costs, and manufacturing accounts for about a third of the total pharmaceutical costs of the affiliates.[11] In effect, savings on labor costs are not likely to have much impact, particularly in an industry where changes in marketing strategy can be of far greater consequence. Manufacturing labor costs therefore do not usually attract much attention.

Higher productivity through technological upgrading is an alternative

Table 8.2. Sales and Employment Data for PH's Affiliates in Malaysia and Taiwan

	Malaysia	Taiwan
Sales in U.S.$ (in millions), 1992		
All products	12.8	24.8
Ethical and health care only	9.1	12.4
Number of employees		
Total	129	186
Manufacturing	63	58
Annual average growth (in percent)		
Sales, 1988–92	13.0	13.0
Sales per employee, 1988–89	29.5	20.3
Sales per employee, 1990–92	13.8	14.7

Source: Company data.

route to cost reduction. But as the Malaysian manufacturing director explained: "Apart from a new machine here and there, we don't have the volume to justify such investment. So we go for incremental improvements." This route is difficult, however, because, besides manufacturing labor costs being a small proportion of total costs, general managers do not have a background in manufacturing and so tend not to investigate ways to improve performance. Other constraints include the employment of underqualified managers, particularly in production control and process engineering. Further limitations on introducing TCS, particularly inventory reduction, are imposed by the dependence on imported raw and semiprocessed materials, which account for more than two-thirds of the affiliates' manufacturing costs. Small affiliates, such as those in Malaysia and Taiwan, also find it difficult to control the price, quality, and timeliness of local suppliers' products (bottles, labels, boxes, and so on).

Malaysian and Taiwanese Affiliates and Their Respective Contexts

The way more general pressures and opportunities influence the management of the subsidiaries depends on the characteristics and recent history of these business units. Table 8.2 provides relevant data on the affiliates in Malaysia and Taiwan.

Both subsidiaries were established more than twenty years ago as part of a process of staking out territory in foreign markets. Sales continue to be directed toward the local market. For the Malaysian affiliate, this includes Singapore. Compared with Malaysia, Taiwan derives relatively less of its sales from locally produced pharmaceutical (ethical and health-care) goods and more from personal consumer goods and confectionery, imported from affiliates in Hong Kong and Thailand respectively. In Malaysia, comparable products, representing slightly more than a third of total sales, are also imported from these affiliates.

Manufacturing employees account for less than half of PH's total work force in Malaysia and less than a third in Taiwan. The marketing departments dominate, especially in Taiwan, where the sales force is more widely distributed throughout the country than in Malaysia. Eighty percent of the managers in the Malaysian subsidiary are Chinese, but among the shop-floor workers, the two major Malaysian ethnic groups are nearly equally represented: 47 percent are Malaysian, and 47 percent are Chinese; Indians account for most of the remaining 6 percent. By contrast, in Taiwan, all the employees are Chinese. Women make up nearly two-thirds of the manufacturing employees in both workplaces and are employed mainly in semiskilled positions. A small number of managers, including executive directors, are women.

Sales of locally produced pharmaceuticals in U.S. dollars per manufacturing employee (not shown in table 8.2) are nearly 50 percent higher in Taiwan than in Malaysia. Without physical output data, it is impossible to know how much this reflects a higher rate of productivity, differences in the sales product mix, prices, or exchange rates in the two countries. Nevertheless, in terms of nominal sales growth, in the period 1988–92, the affiliates appear to be on a par. This is not a true picture, however, because a significant proportion of Taiwan's sales in the period 1986–89 were returned as goods unsold. These goods represent additional costs not shown in table 8.2. Consequently, the figures belie the relative weakness of the Taiwan affiliate in these years and, by implication, highlight the affiliate's subsequent recovery, which includes rectification of the unsold goods.

According to the data on nominal growth in sales per employee, Taiwan's performance slowed less markedly than that of Malaysia in the period 1990–92, signifying better performance relative to previous years compared with its Malaysian counterpart. Finally, over the past five years, both affiliates have maintained, rather than increased, their market shares in most segments.

There are some important differences in the recent history of the two affiliates that are pertinent to understanding their workplace relations. Corporate management has regarded the Malaysian affiliate as a training ground, mainly for upwardly mobile expatriates, most of whom have been assigned to the general manager's (GM's) position for two years. Turnover in this most senior position in the subsidiary has been high—five in the period 1987–91—whereas other members of the senior management team (the local executive directors) have had an average tenure of approximately seven years. Accordingly, corporate management has looked to the management team to provide support to incoming general managers. The high turnover in general managers has brought several problems, including the adoption of short-term policies ("GMs want to see quick results"), changes in priorities ("GMs want to be seen to make a difference"), different methods of working ("Some GMs like formal reporting; others are more informal"), inconsistencies in the handling of problems ("Some GMs are firm but fair; others are weaker"), and delays in decision making ("There's always quite a long period between the announcement of a resignation and the taking up of the position by a new GM").

From the standpoint of shop-floor relations, these management characteristics have had two noteworthy consequences. First, over the years, the manufacturing director (MfgD) has developed an understanding with fellow senior managers of the role and capacity of manufacturing. In spite of criticism from some quarters, GMs have, until now, been content with performance in this area. Second, in the field of labor policy, the human resources director, with the financial director's support, has argued strongly in favor of following existing procedures. This has been necessary since manufacturing management, sometimes with the GM's support, has been tempted to step outside the affiliates' policy to satisfy employee expectations.

A central feature of the Taiwanese subsidiary has been the change in GMs and most other directors in early 1990 against a background of financial crisis. The previous GM resigned in mid-1989 after "irregularities" were discovered. Other members of the senior management team subsequently resigned in search of more lucrative positions in a booming economy. The new GM, who is Chinese, had worked at regional headquarters in Hong Kong before being appointed as the GM in Malaysia, where he worked for eighteen months. The new senior managers were recruited locally. From the start, the GM emphasized participation, open communications, teamwork among senior management, and a sharpened focus on key issues. His strategy was to move the affiliate upstream by concentrating on higher-technology products more appropriate to a high-cost economy.

The GM in Taiwan saw the human resources director as a key figure in building the new management team and in fostering a high-commitment climate in the affiliate. The human resources director argued that procedures, policies, and leadership by example had to replace the alleged informality, laxity, and arbitrariness of the previous management regime. Accordingly, there was an urgent emphasis on clarifying management's expectations and on instilling discipline in the affiliate, which was described as being in "utter confusion" and a place in which a "nobody cares" attitude prevailed. Following this early phase, and aimed at changing employee expectations, the human resources director began to support employees in obtaining improvements in wages and working conditions.

He met with them regularly, a process that helped promote social cohesion and convey management expectations.

Between 1990 and 1992, the Taiwanese affiliate recovered from a loss-making position to one in which profit after tax as a proportion of sales exceeded 10 percent. Corporate headquarters recognized this improvement by granting the affiliate investment funds to upgrade the buildings and purchase some new machinery. This was facilitated by the tax incentives on new capital investment mentioned earlier.

Improving performance has been painful, however. The previous MfgD was discharged for poor management skills, and the confectionery plant, which had employed forty-five persons, was closed because of the relaxation of import duties and its high labor costs relative to manufacturing in Thailand. Thirty-three workers were made redundant, and the remainder were transferred to the pharmaceutical division. Not surprisingly, manual employees have been concerned about job security, although, as noted below, morale has improved under the new management's leadership. Senior managers are optimistic, particularly in view of new initiatives being taken in China by the company's regional directors.

As described above, improving performance in the Taiwan subsidiary was a matter of survival. The most recently, albeit experienced, GM was given the opportunity to choose a new senior management team. Nonetheless, many problems remained, some of which required personnel in manufacturing to make changes in their behavior, including establishing a better liaison with the marketing department; demanding more consistent quality and timing from suppliers; introducing a more effective planning and scheduling system; and achieving higher quality and productivity standards.

Unlike most of his counterparts, the GM was attentive to manufacturing, thereby providing a further spur to improvement. Finally, the new MfgD—who had been the human resources director for his initial fifteen months with the company—regarded manufacturing as a challenge. As we shall see, his leadership skills contributed to the improved performance of manufacturing in the most recent period.

Product and Labor Market Contexts of the Subsidiaries

Some important features of the local product and labor markets for the subsidiaries merit comment. Beginning with the product market, governments in both countries regulate the definition, registration, manufacture, and distribution of pharmaceuticals, but there are no price controls or levies on imported drugs in Malaysia. There are, however, import limitations on drugs if five or more manufacturers produce a specific drug locally.

In Taiwan, the pharmaceutical industry is included within the government's definition of an advanced technology sector, thereby permitting generous tax deductions for new capital investment. Although there are many firms competing in both countries, the Taiwanese product market is more difficult for MNCs, including PH, than the product market in Malaysia. This is because locally owned firms in Taiwan have some additional competitive advantages. These arise for the following four reasons. First, import duties are applied at a rate of 5 to 12 percent (down from 20 to 30 percent a decade ago); second, restrictions exist on the import of some products and materials; third, foreign patent registration laws are apparently not enforced; and fourth, labeling requirements are inadequate, so that hospitals—the largest purchasers of drugs—tend to opt for locally produced generic products rather than higher-quality, brand items.

Strong economic growth has resulted in rapidly rising wages and high rates of interfirm labor mobility in both countries, but especially in Taiwan, where the level of economic development is much higher than in Malaysia.[12] Thus, in the period 1987–91, the earnings of manufacturing workers increased by an estimated 6 percent a year in Malaysia and by 12 percent in Taiwan (Council of Labor Affairs [CLA] 1992:186). The annual average labor separation rate (an indicator of labor mobility) over the same period was about 40 percent in Taiwan (CLA 1992:56), compared with an estimated 10 percent in Malaysia. In the latter country, workers were attracted mainly from the primary sector (which accounted for 26.8 percent of the total work force in 1992 compared with only 12.2 percent in Taiwan). The Taiwanese government has attempted to alleviate supply bottlenecks by encouraging education and training, but this seems to have been almost exclusively for workers in technical and professional occupations.[13]

The governments of both countries have successfully restricted the power of independent trade unions. In Malaysia, this has been achieved by ensuring that unions remain small. These so-called peanut unions represent an estimated 10 percent of the work force. Unions are also restricted in the issues over which they can bargain, and industrial action is heavily circumscribed (Ayadurai 1993; Ponniah and Littler 1993).

In Taiwan, union recognition is a legal right if it is requested by workers in workplaces where there are more than thirty adult employees, but most employers, including MNCs, discourage unionization. Where workers have been organized, the government has made sure that the union leaders were incorporated into the ruling Kuomintang party or failed to win reelection. Not surprisingly, industrial action has been, and continues to be, tightly circumscribed by law. Autonomous unions have nevertheless emerged since the beginning of democratization, in 1987, but these organizations remain weak (Frenkel, Hong, and Lee 1993). Union density in Taiwan is estimated to be about 33 percent, but this includes independent contractors and other persons joining unions for social insurance purposes. Only about 9 percent of Taiwan's manufacturing workers are covered by collective contracts (Frenkel, Hong, and Lee 1993:179). In both countries the state provides mechanisms for resolving industrial disputes.

Individual workers in Malaysia and Taiwan are formally protected by various laws that stipulate the standard hours in a workweek, holidays, and other entitlements, such as pensions and compensation for industrial accidents. There are also laws regulating employee dismissals. Employees in both subsidiaries are entitled to compensation by the state for injury or sickness, but there are no specific unemployment benefits in either country. Although there are regulations pertaining to the manufacture of pharmaceuticals, law enforcement is weak concerning factory employment and working conditions, particularly in Taiwan.

The laws in Taiwan, unlike those in Malaysia, require that employers establish consultative councils and welfare fund committees (Frenkel, Hong, and Lee 1993). The consultative councils are expected to provide information and facilitate discussions on ways to improve employees' welfare and the performance of the enterprise. The welfare fund committees are supposed to be run by employees or labor unions and to expend income, in legally prescribed proportions from employers and employees, on employee welfare activities.

A final point concerns the characteristics of the labor force in the two societies. In Malaysia, workers are drawn mainly from three ethnic groups: the Malays (60 percent of the population), the Chinese (31 percent), and the Indians (8 percent). Although the public sector consists largely of Malay employees, Malays are also employed in less skilled, private sector jobs. The Chinese and Indians work mainly in the private sector, and the former group is strongly represented in managerial and professional positions. In Taiwan, by contrast, the population is almost entirely Chinese. Differences between mainlanders and indigenous Taiwanese have become blurred through intermarriage and common experience since the Kuomintang seized power in Taiwan nearly forty years ago.

In summary, the Taiwanese affiliate has faced a more quality- and price-competitive market. Since quality standards enforced by corporate management and governments cannot easily be compromised, competition is based mainly on marketing. The tight labor market and the need to produce high-quality products mean that employees are paid and treated reasonably well. The stronger competition in Taiwan, together with the tax incentives to invest in new technology, and legislation encouraging employee consultation can be expected to foster more change based on a different pattern of workplace relations than in Malaysia. These factors are unlikely to be sufficiently powerful, however, to overcome the basic cost-cutting approach encouraged by PH's corporate management. One can thus assume that traditional patterns of workplace relations patterns will be reinforced at both subsidiaries, although less in Taiwan, where contrary influences are stronger.

From a corporate standpoint, neither subsidiary is strategically significant: both are small in scale and serve relatively limited, albeit rapidly expanding, domestic markets. The subsidiary in Taiwan is nonetheless more important strategically than the one in Malaysia. This is because of Taiwan's improved trading status with China, whose huge pharmaceutical market has only recently been opened to foreign investment and the possibility this provides to import drugs from Taiwan. Neither subsidiary has been profitable enough to justify *major* investment. Nor has either of these affiliates exhibited clearly superior competencies in recent years, compared with other PH business units. In short, the evidence suggests that both affiliates most resemble the *implementer* type (characterized by low strategic significance and limited resources and competencies) noted earlier. The greater strategic importance of the subsidiary in Taiwan, however, coupled with the competence of its key senior managers, suggests a tendency toward the *strategic leader* type. Accordingly, with regard to workplace relations, the status quo is likely to predominate at both affiliates, although signs of a more innovative pattern appear to be evident in Taiwan.

Patterns of Manual Workplace Relations in the Subsidiaries

The focus of this section is on the five elements referred to earlier that distinguish the two ideal types of workplace relations patterns. In this section, I compare the subsidiaries with the ideal types. In the course of undertaking fieldwork research, data were collected by various means.[14] Table 8.3 summarizes relevant information on workplace relations in the two affiliates. This is elaborated in the subsequent discussion.

Job Characteristics

Manual work at the two affiliates is similar: jobs are relatively specialized and repetitive. Operators tend machines or work on short assembly lines; packers pack and unpack materials and finished products. A few storepeople check incoming and outgoing goods, and there are one or two skilled maintenance workers. Operators are expected to follow GMP procedures and to clean and perform simple maintenance on machines. The new MfgD in Taiwan has provided precise written details of management's expectations to avoid unnecessary ambiguity and uncertainty. In addition, a job-transfer system is being introduced: packers may apply to work as operators and vice versa. In Malaysia, there is some job rotation on an

Table 8.3. Summary of Workplace Relations in the Malaysian and Taiwanese Subsidiaries of the PH Corporation, 1992

Variables	Malaysia	Taiwan
Job characteristics		
Task range	Narrow	Narrow
Job flexibility	Limited, some job rotation	Limited, some job rotation
Emphasis on learning	Limited, only GMP	Limited, mainly GMP
Work organization		
Management style	Delegate	Direct and support
Hierarchy index	3	2
Management as percentage of total manufacturing employees	25.4	15.5
Teamwork	None	Some, project related
Functional integration	Low	Higher
Reward system		
Basis of pay	Collective bargain and bonus	Management determined and bonus
Labor market	External	External
Employee representation		
Affiliate level	Weak industrial union	Consultative committee
Management-employee relations		
Main form of regulation	Bureaucratic	Bureaucratic
Climate	Fairly good	Improving
Absenteeism[a]	4.9	7.6
Labor turnover	0.9	18.6
Collective action	None	None

[a]Absenteeism and labor turnover rates are annual averages covering the period 1990–92. Labor turnover includes voluntary and involuntary quits as a percentage of average employment over the year. Separate figures for these two categories are not available.

annual basis, and workers are given an opportunity to work on the small number of new machines that have been commissioned in recent years.

In both plants there is little emphasis on learning beyond essential GMP procedures. Thus, over the 1990–92 period, only about 6 percent and 4 percent of the manufacturing employees in the Malaysian and Taiwanese subsidiaries respectively received formal training in maintenance and statistical process control skills. In Taiwan, there is some group problem-solving activity, but in both affiliates on-the-job training by supervisors is the main way workers learn. Managers in Malaysia have a pessimistic view of the manual workers' abilities. A production manager commented: "I can't involve them in a lot more responsibility as they do not have much education [on average about three years secondary schooling], and most cannot read English [the medium of business and pharmaceutical documentation]."

In Taiwan, where most of the manual workers are high school graduates, unsatisfactory work behavior has been attributed mainly to inadequate management. The MfgD explained: "It is a matter of the managers setting a good example. I arrive early, I share information. I thank people for doing overtime. I have no fear that employees would betray the company. I am confident that they will improve. If you support them, they will support you." In addition, the MfgD is aware that lack of management attention to worker education and career opportunities has led to employee frustration and higher labor turnover than at the Malaysian affiliate. The new training programs and job rotation are helping to resolve these problems.

Work Organization

In line with the requirements of corporate headquarters, management has reduced the number of employees, mainly by contracting out unskilled manual jobs, particularly those associated with packaging nonprescription items.[15] At the Malaysian subsidiary, redundancies contributed to the 25 percent decline in the number of manufacturing employees between 1987 and 1992, most of which occurred in the 1987–89 period. In Taiwan, there was a 12.7 percent reduction over the same period, or 18.8 percent if contract workers are excluded. Most of this reduction was in the confectionery plant, which was closed down in 1991. Its goods are now imported from the corporation's Thai affiliate. The management style in the two subsidiaries differs in several respects. In Malaysia, the high turnover of GMs coupled with the relative stability of the affiliate's other executive directors has encouraged the latter to defend their interests against the changing priorities of the new GMs and indeed major change more generally. The MfgD relies a great deal on delegation. He establishes broad goals, typically derived from the affiliate's annual targets, meets regularly with key suppliers and the other directors, and monitors progress. He also resolves more intractable interdepartmental problems, in consultation with other senior managers and his immediate subordinates. The remaining work is delegated to the heads of the various departments within manufacturing.

Application of the management appraisal and reward system, which emphasizes the achievement of individual targets, has made managers risk-averse, so that managing has become mainly a reactive rather than a proactive activity. Management is also slow to act, given the presence of an extended chain of delegation and a relatively high management to employees ratio, as indicated in table 8.2. Delegation depends on lower-level managers encouraging teamwork.

As noted earlier, problem-solving teams exist among employees in the quality control department, but the limited conceptual and English-speaking skills of the manual workers were seen as barriers to implementing effective quality circles on the shop floor. Longer lines of authority, limited "hands-on" leadership, and a production manager who is burdened with a wide range of responsibilities and is relatively new to the position have contributed to a lower level of functional integration than at the Taiwanese subsidiary.

In Taiwan, the change in senior personnel led to a significant change in management style. Clarity of vision, the communication of clear principles, and formalized rules have been hallmarks of the new GM, who is committed to staff involvement. This style contrasts with that of the previous GM and the then-incumbent MfgD. The latter manager had been in the position for more than five years. He acceded to pressure from corporate headquarters to reduce gradually the number of employees. Like his Malaysian counterpart, he preferred to delegate responsibility while at the same time trying to meet unplanned requirements by the marketing department. These characteristics placed a substantial burden on the shoulders of his subordinates, who, together with other manufacturing employees, claimed to be underpaid and overworked.

Following the MfgD's replacement by the human resources director in early 1991, the GM's preferred "firm but fair" style was introduced. This included improvements in pay and working conditions against the back-drop of redundancies and employee transfers arising from the closure of the confectionery goods plant. Most noticeable was the new MfgD's "hands-on" approach, which encourages managers and workers to communicate regularly and to contribute their ideas for improving planning, scheduling, and supply systems. This style was compatible with the TCS initiative that had been encouraged by corporate headquarters in 1988, and this approach contributed to eliminating barriers that had developed between departments within manufacturing. In addition, the expectations of the marketing managers were redefined, after they were advised about what could reasonably be expected from manufacturing regarding meeting unplanned demand.

Reward System

Rewards at both affiliates fall into two categories: monetary compensation and nonmonetary benefits. The former includes the following elements: base rate, allowances, bonus, service and merit pay, and awards. Nonmonetary rewards include accident, health, and retirement support and various benefits such as food subsidies, the provision of uniforms, and discounted prices on nonprescription items. These improve on existing statutory provisions or provide a wider range of support.

In both affiliates, the job descriptions are similar to those used by other firms. Pay rankings accord with differences in skill and the responsibility attached to various positions, but relative differences vary considerably. Thus, although a mechanic at both subsidiaries receives about 75 percent more pay than a packer, the differential between manual workers and the MfgD in the Taiwanese affiliate is greater than in Malaysia. Thus, the packer to MfgD pay ratio in 1992 was 1:10 in Taiwan compared with 1:8.6 in Malaysia. This reflects various factors, one of which is the presence of a union.[16] Before noting further such effects, a few brief remarks on other monetary rewards are in order.

Bonuses at the two affiliates are calculated based on employees' monthly pay and may be adjusted upward if a firm performs exceptionally well or, more likely in Taiwan, if other firms raise their level of bonus payments. Subject to satisfactory performance over the previous year, bonuses are equivalent to two months' pay, which is similar to the rate at comparable firms in both countries. In Taiwan, a few high-performing workers receive slightly larger bonuses.

Merit pay increases, based on individual appraisals by superordinates, constitute less than 5 percent of the total wage in both plants; merit pay was only recently introduced in Taiwan. The most important award at the plants is the GM's Excellence Award, which in Malaysia amounts to about U.S.$365 and includes a trophy and certificate. It is presented annually to the most deserving employee (below director level) from the marketing/sales area and from the rest of the company respectively.[17]

The human resources department in Malaysia introduced two additional awards: the innovation program, which rewards shop-floor and white-collar workers for their suggestions of ways to improve quality or productivity, and the attendance award, which provides a free restaurant meal to the individual and the work group whose annual rate of absenteeism is below a stipulated figure determined by management each year.

Finally, workers at both establishments receive service raises at five-year intervals until retirement in Malaysia and up to twenty-five years' service in Taiwan. Together with the relatively generous medical and retirement benefits and favorable working conditions, these benefits contribute to an average tenure for manual employees of about seven years. There is no systematic training and career advancement, however, as is characteristic of internal labor markets.

The union at the Malaysian subsidiary appears to have gained various concessions not available to its Taiwanese counterpart. These include annual service raises, which account for approximately 8 percent of total pay, and two allowances, termed call-out (working after hours) and acting assignment (temporary transfer) allowances respectively. In addition, whereas pay at the Malaysian plant is similar to that in other pharmaceutical MNCs, in Taiwan the wages have been below average in recent years. In 1992, management attempted to tackle this problem by increasing manual employees' pay by more than it had in previous years.

Taiwan's legal requirement to maintain a welfare committee and support its activities has led to greater expenditures on social and recreational items than in Malaysia. These include an annual picnic or dinner, family outings on selected festival days, and gifts to workers on special occasions, for example, upon their marriage, the birth of a child, and the death of kin. Additional expenditures, including small education subsidies for a number of employees' children, are paid through the company's miscellaneous benefits fund according to specific procedures. About 5 percent of workers' basic wages are in the form of subsidies and gifts, nearly double the estimated proportion expended at the Malaysian affiliate.

Employee Representation

Although there is no closed-shop agreement or checkoff provision for PH employees, almost all the manual workers in the Malaysian subsidiary are members of the Chemical Workers' Union, an organization whose total membership is a little more than three thousand. Dues are approximately 1 percent of workers' wages. No other employees at the affiliate are unionized, although in the past the union covered salespeople. The contracting out of health-care and confectionery sales to a third party gave management the opportunity to secure an informal agreement with the union committee limiting the union's jurisdiction to shop-floor workers.[18]

Every three years, immediately after the collective agreement has been signed, a union committee of five people is elected. The committee has irregular meetings with management; its main function is to represent workers in the triennial negotiations. The workplace union secretary is the shop steward, but very few grievances are raised with the union. In interviews I conducted with him, he claimed to deal with only two or three grievances a year, mainly from individuals who sought clarification of their rights under the contract or who alleged mistreatment by their manager. Workers who were interviewed nevertheless saw the union as a positive force; they claimed it influenced management to grant concessions in negotiations and that it was a useful shield against harsh treatment in redundancy or similar situations.

Management did not see the union as a threat to company interests; on the contrary, the MfgD believed it fulfilled a useful function by providing the workers with psychological security. Although the union's representatives (who usually included the union's general secretary) were treated respectfully in the triennial contract negotiations, the shop steward was critical that management did not regularly consult with the union and did not disclose information on the affiliate's performance and prospects.

Corporate policy is to continue to maintain union-free status at affiliates that are not unionized and to ensure cordial relations in plants that are unionized. Taiwan's human resources director emphasized that management provides communication and representation channels for workers so that unionization is unnecessary and undesirable. In his own words: "Unions are another bureaucracy that are bound up in politics and are a challenge to management. They aren't necessary if management does its job properly—this means keeping communication channels open and dealing with problems as soon as they occur." New employees are informed of management's expectation that the status quo will remain undisturbed.

PH has fulfilled its local legal obligations by establishing two committees, whose six employee representatives (one representative each from direct and indirect factory staff and four representatives from sales and office staff) are elected for three years. The consultative committee includes an equal number of senior managers, thereby conforming to the Labor Standards Law of 1984. A welfare committee, composed of the employee representatives and the human resources director, who is elected and acts as chairperson, functions in line with the Employee Welfare Fund Law of 1943 (Frenkel, Hong, and Lee 1993:165).

In practice, these committees, which meet on a monthly or sometimes bimonthly basis, operate as a single body. Decisions regarding expenditures of the welfare fund are left to the employee representatives, while other decisions are made jointly, or more frequently by management, in response to requests by employee representatives. Items most frequently raised at committee meetings include enterprise community activities, gifts and subsidies (for a marriage, the birth of a child, and the like), and pay in its various forms. Other employee relations issues, for example, working conditions and management-employee relations, are also discussed.[19] In effect, the committee acts as a device for eliciting employee commitment through the provision of welfare services and as a forum for worker representation.

Employee representatives are expected to report back to their constituents, but this is a haphazard process. Minutes posted on notice boards keep workers informed. Occasionally, employee representatives are asked about particular items of interest to employees. Workers also sometimes request that certain issues be raised at committee meetings. In effect, the representatives act as worker delegates, similar to populist-type shop stewards (Batstone, Boraston, and Frenkel 1977:34–40).

The effectiveness of the labor-management committee is difficult to gauge. Both management and employees stated that it was useful but had several shortcomings. Workers argued that by having fewer factory than white-collar representatives, the committee tended to be biased against manual workers' interests. Workers also accused management of being unresponsive to manual employees' requests. The GM believed that the committee discussed too many trivial issues. By contrast, the human resources director emphasized the usefulness of the committee as a means of communicating with employees. Arguably, worker representatives have been disadvantaged by the structure of the committee meetings, which are designed to foster communication between individuals rather than to facilitate negotiations between groups. Although management often appeared to speak with one voice at the meetings, employee representatives seemed divided in their views.

Management-Employee Relations

Workplace relations in both plants are based mainly on formal rules. Some of these reflect existing labor law, for example, disputes procedures in the Malaysian affiliate and welfare and consultation procedures in Taiwan. In Malaysia, adjustments are also made in light of union demands. In both affiliates, rules relating to the work process derive from GMP regulations. The remaining rules reflect local management policies, which are required to be within parameters established by corporate headquarters. For example, managers of the subsidiaries must consult with regional management and corporate headquarters on prospective increases in labor costs (as part of the annual strategic planning exercise) and on any departures from existing arrangements that might significantly increase the affiliates' costs. Also, all policies have to be consistent with the values espoused in PH's credo and managing statements.

Malaysia differs from Taiwan in that many matters that are management's prerogative in the latter affiliate are covered by collective agreement in Malaysia. Examples include pay, leave, and retrenchment beyond legal minima. Both affiliates provide new employees with handbooks in the local language that clearly and concisely explain employee rights and obligations. In Taiwan, both new and longer-serving manual workers get pay adjustments every six months, but increases in the base rate are dependent on the subsidiary's capacity to pay and market rates. In Malaysia, raises are provided annually, although contract negotiations take place triennially. These are conducted by the MfgD and the human resources director following an analysis of a pay survey of competing firms, discussion with the GM, and a mandate agreed to with corporate headquarters. Larger raises cannot be given without reference back to the regional vice president of human resources. Negotiations include ritualistic displays of give and take, invariably followed by an amicable settlement. This is transmitted to, and subsequently endorsed by, the Industrial Court, and so becomes an award of the court under the restrictive Industrial Relations Act of 1967.

The Malaysian handbook of employment provides a detailed description of discipline and disputes procedures that include provision for union involvement and ultimately conciliation and arbitration by the relevant government bodies, as provided in the Industrial Relations Act of 1967. In Taiwan, the new management's concern for creating and maintaining order led to a revision of the employee handbook, which now outlines four punishments—reprimand, record of misdemeanor, record of serious misdemeanor, and dismissal—and five awards—commendation, formal record of achievement, formal record of significant achievement, prize money, and promotion. Attached to each form of punishment is a list of unacceptable practices, totaling seventy-eight infringements. There is a disputes procedure that employees can use to appeal a decision.[20]

Recorded misdemeanors are very rare at both affiliates, and no grievances were lodged under the Malaysian disputes procedure. This harmony was more apparent than real, however: shop-floor workers did raise problems with their immediate supervisors, and in Taiwan, requests for better pay and conditions were put to the consultative committee. Responses to occasional surveys administered by management also indicated discontent. The surveys, however, were not made available to me.[21]

Managers at both subsidiaries indicated that they were not content with employees merely conforming to the rules. Senior management emphasized the importance of particular values and norms to improve employee commitment. Examples included attempts by the human resources department at the Malaysian affiliate to raise awareness of the company's new credo document and the establishment of project teams to find practical ways of pursuing the values outlined therein. In Taiwan, the MfgD was directly inculcating the values of discipline, diligence, teamwork, and innovation. These were in effect normative overlays on a primarily bureaucratic basis of integration.[22]

Various indicators can be used to assess the quality of management-employee relations at PH's Malaysian and Taiwanese subsidiaries. Interviews with managers and employee representatives revealed that in Malaysia the relationship between manual workers and management was viewed as "fairly good," while in Taiwan it had been "fair" but was rapidly improving. In Malaysia, management enjoyed good relations with union representatives, who acknowledged that most employees valued their jobs at the firm. Indeed, several manufacturing managers claimed that labor turnover had been too low, resulting in an aging, undereducated work force with little enthusiasm for change.

In both establishments, workers were concerned about job security, since redundancies had occurred on three occasions in the Malaysian affiliate during the second half of the 1980s and in 1991 in Taiwan. Interviews revealed, however, that the Taiwanese workers were more enthusiastic about the company's future than their Malaysian counterparts. The new MfgD's style, including management's support for better pay and working conditions, probably had significantly influenced this attitude. The Taiwanese employees could also see the fruits of success: improvements in buildings and the introduction of new technology, albeit on a limited scale. Reductions in absenteeism and labor turnover reveal an improvement in morale since the 1989 crisis period.[23] Finally, there had been no collective action at either workplace over the past decade.

These data confirm that management-employee relations tend to be harmonious at both affiliates. Although Malaysia has a superior record, Taiwan has shown strong signs of improvement over the most recent period.

Summary of Workplace Relations

On the one hand, the striking similarities in workplace relations in the two affiliates suggest a tendency toward the neo-Taylorist pattern outlined earlier. On the other hand, some noteworthy differences indicate a tendency toward lean production, particularly in Taiwan.

The similarities include the low-discretion manual work roles, the restricted opportunities for learning, the centralized management style, and the limited opportunity for employee involvement and teamwork. The reward systems are based on payment according to relative pay in the external labor market, the affiliate's capacity to pay, and performance. Both subsidiaries provide benefits beyond statutory requirements, a practice that promotes management-employee cooperation. Employment relations decisions are made by management of the subsidiary within broader parameters set by corporate headquarters and the law. Employee rights and obligations are formalized in handbooks, although they differ in content, for example, regarding discipline and disputes. Employee compliance is based largely on bureaucratic control and is seemingly effective despite the uncertainty inherent in labor contracts of this kind. According to management, absenteeism and labor turnover have been lower than in comparable firms in either country, and, as noted above, collective action has not occurred in the recent past. At the same time, a norm of conflict avoidance, common in Asian societies, may have been operating to discourage manifestations of open discontent.[24]

One noteworthy deviation from the neo-Taylorist model at both workplaces is that there are performance-based elements in the payment systems. Bonuses tend to be inflexible, however, and individual merit payments are relatively small. Also noteworthy in that it deviates from the ideal type is the presence of the union at the Malaysian affiliate. As noted earlier, union representation has provided benefits to workers, but it has had no impact on the other aspects of workplace relations discussed above.

Evidence of a tendency toward lean production in the Taiwan affiliate includes the following: the changes in job characteristics, toward a greater

emphasis on meeting management's high expectations regarding commitment and cooperation; the introduction of a job-transfer system; and the
introduction of a system to provide better training. The relatively new
management instituted changes in work organization along TCS lines.
These included improvements to the planning, scheduling, and supply
systems, aimed at enabling the subsidiary to compete more effectively in
the production of higher value-added pharmaceutical products. A flatter
hierarchy and improved communication between departments have led to a
relatively high level of functional integration. Management has established
norms regarding employee discipline, diligence, and involvement in problem solving; there has also been more communication and consultation
with employees. Together with the improvements in rewards, these
changes have contributed to the better employee morale and the more
cooperative management-employee relations. Although there is no union,
the operation of the consultative/welfare committee, together with the
supervisory role of the human resources department, has meant that
employee representation is similar to that in an enterprise union system.
In sum, although these developments are in their infancy, they suggest
that the Taiwan subsidiary is less bound by a neo-Taylorist tradition.

Explaining the Workplace Relations Patterns

Each of the factors mentioned in the second section of the chapter
contributes to explaining the workplace relations patterns at the Malaysian
and Taiwanese affiliates. The local product markets are competitive in
quality and price, particularly in Taiwan, for reasons noted earlier. In both
affiliates, high standards of quality are achieved, in classical, neo-Taylorist
fashion, by employees who follow detailed instructions and as a result of
the employment of quality-control specialists in manufacturing.

As in the affiliate in Malaysia, the workplace relations in the Taiwanese
affiliate are essentially neo-Taylorist; however, the introduction of new
technology and the specialization in higher value-added products provided
an incentive to adopt some elements of TCS. Management also supplemented the predominantly bureaucratic approach to employee relations by
emphasizing particular values and norms. But, although there have been
changes in the direction of lean production in Taiwan, market and
government incentives have not led to comprehensive technological and
organizational change. In short, the traditional neo-Taylorist workplace
pattern continues to prevail.

Although quite different in detail, the labor market regulations in
both countries essentially result in workers being treated as commodities
requiring protection from accidents and ill health and from arbitrary and
unreasonable treatment by employers. Over and above this floor of rights,

management has considerable discretion in organizing workplace relations. Indeed, the main constraint on total management autonomy is not the law, which, as mentioned earlier, is often poorly enforced, but corporate values and the need to retain efficient workers under tight labor market conditions.[25] Apart from changing GMP requirements, which necessitate providing employees with limited training, the law and public policy in both countries do little to foster continuous skill enhancement and employee involvement in job-level decision making as, for example, in Singapore (Begin chap. 4). In essence, extant labor market institutions support the continuation of neo-Taylorist job designs and work organizations. In addition, the inadequate state social welfare provisions in societies where paternalism is a feature of the social organization more generally encourages workers to expect their employers to supplement existing benefits. This is the case in Malaysia and Taiwan, where management provides a wider range and a higher level of benefits than are legally required (see Deyo 1989:159–60).[26]

Labor laws and institutions also influence employee representation. The law and government policy in Malaysia have fostered small unions. This is illustrated by the presence of the Chemical Workers' Union at the Malaysian affiliate, which nevertheless won some concessions from management. In Taiwan, management has successfully avoided unionization but has followed the law by establishing a composite consultative/welfare committee that functions to represent employee interests and promote management-labor cooperation.

In summary, the institutional arrangements explain some of the differences in workplace relations in the two affiliates. It is their similarity, however, in regarding labor as a tradable commodity subject to limited protective rights, rather than as a resource necessitating continuous investment, that reinforces management's traditional view of labor.[27] Thus, management has used its considerable discretion to reinforce traditional neo-Taylorist workplace relations patterns, a proposition that assumes neo-Taylorism to be the traditional pattern. This requires explanation.

A close look at the impact of the four intraorganizational factors mentioned in the second section above provides an answer to the question of why this pattern has emerged. That PH is an American company is important, for U.S. manufacturing industry is the source of neo-Taylorist ideas and bureaucratic organization (Edwards 1979, chap. 8). There is no reason to suppose that pharmaceutical production would be any different from manufacturing more generally. The ownership nationality hypothesis also points to Malaysia as being a more receptive environment for institutionalizing neo-Taylorism, as evidenced by the control exercised over the affiliate by the successive expatriate GMs dispatched by corporate headquarters. By contrast, over the past decade, the Taiwanese subsidiary has been managed mainly by Chinese managers, who might be expected to have diluted some American norms and practices.

A response to this argument is that, since the various GMs assigned by corporate headquarters to manage the Malaysian affiliate paid little attention to manufacturing, their association with headquarters would not really have affected workplace relations. This confuses the GMs' inattention to the details of manufacturing costs with their concern with procedures and practices. In fact, the GMs insisted that management adhere to manufacturing standards and protocols acceptable to corporate headquarters, and the costs of noncompliance—in lost sales and company reputation, not to mention career opportunities—would probably have been substantial. By conforming, the continuity of neo-Taylorism was assured.

A second and at first sight more plausible counterargument is that by the end of the 1980s corporate headquarters had discarded neo-Taylorism in favor of a modified form of lean production. If this were true, and we follow the logic of the corporate ownership argument, Malaysia is less, not more, likely to have maintained a neo-Taylorist workplace relations pattern. The assumption that corporate headquarters abandoned neo-Taylorism in favor of lean production is, however, incorrect. Although it is true that the technical section at headquarters promoted a form of JIT, referred to as TCS, the influence of this section at the subsidiary level was limited and was further diminished in 1991 when the staff at headquarters was severely cut back and reorganized.

In the words of a senior technical section manager: "Previously we were a catalyst in trying to encourage plants to learn from each other. There were meetings of manufacturing managers from our plants, and we used successful managers in our work at different facilities. But as far as I know, these meetings are going to be discontinued on cost grounds. . . . It is going to be more difficult for us to maintain worldwide process and product standards to ensure high quality." In sum, although a section of headquarters favored a modified form of lean production, neo-Taylorism continued to be the conventional form for organizing workplace relations on the shop floor.

The above discussion only touched on the role of management ideology and strategy. This can be taken further by noting that, in conjunction with stronger market pressure, corporate management was pressing local management in Taiwan to improve performance, something the new GM and MfgD pursued vigorously. It is not necessary to repeat the guiding values of these managers, except to note that their values were fully consistent with the new change-oriented, participative culture management in headquarters was promoting. Two other related aspects of this argument are noteworthy, however, one favoring a tendency toward lean production, the other impeding it.

On the one hand, the institutional legacy of employee participation associated with the introduction of TCS in 1988 was helpful in laying the foundation for employee involvement as an element of a broader system. On the other hand, although the MfgD regularly communicated manufacturing targets to employees (productivity, quality, inventory control, and so on), he did not articulate a manufacturing strategy. In short, there was no overarching grand plan that included steps to realize the targets. Thus, management in Taiwan pursued improvements in worker morale and management-employee relations more vigorously than did their Malaysian counterparts. These innovations could be interpreted as part of a wider value-adding strategy, but, in fact, they were not part of a systematic attempt to introduce lean production. Management's ideology was attuned to short-term goals aimed mainly at improving the financial position of the affiliate. In manufacturing, enhanced performance largely reflected the determined efforts of new senior managers to secure a positive response from subordinates and ordinary employees.

The Malaysian subsidiary did not have a manufacturing strategy either, but this reflected the MfgD's satisfaction with, and the other directors' accommodation to, the current manufacturing system, which had been gradually upgraded over the years. Consequently, less sustained pressure from corporate headquarters and successive GMs to improve performance had resulted in the adoption of a conservative approach by senior management. This was facilitated by a less competitive product market than in Taiwan. The net result was an extended hierarchy, management by delegation, and the neo-Taylorist workplace relations pattern described earlier.

The future in Malaysia may be different. The opinion survey and accompanying strategies to align the affiliate's values with those favored by corporate management have placed change firmly on the agenda. Much will depend on the new GM's strategy and the support he receives from the management team.

The above analysis highlights two important points. First, the common denominators under which the affiliates operate account for the limited moves that have been made in both affiliates to improve performance by transcending neo-Taylorism. One powerful factor is the pressure the subsidiaries have been under to meet their profit and sales targets. But given corporate management's emphasis on R&D and marketing, and corporate headquarters' interest in rationalizing manufacturing, particularly in Europe, improving productivity in plants serving relatively small markets has been a secondary concern. Consequently, limited resources have been directed toward hiring highly qualified staff and introducing new manufacturing systems. Other factors militating against major change in the two affiliates include problems associated with low-volume, nonstandardized production, the need to import bulk chemicals from overseas subsidiaries, and the limited bargaining power with local suppliers of inputs, all of which make it difficult to introduce lean production. And, as noted above, there is little incentive for management to use manual labor more creatively.

Second, despite the many common systems devised and administered by corporate management, pressures vary depending on the financial position of the subsidiaries and senior managers' interpretations of their roles. In Taiwan, there was both more pressure to improve performance and a GM and a MfgD who saw themselves as bearers of a new order. In Malaysia, the internal environment and the attitudes of relevant senior managers worked against large-scale change. It was the human resources director, supported by the financial director, who was most keen to take up the challenge of change. Thus, common factors need to be examined carefully for their variable impact on workplace relations.

Insofar as PH's main activity is the production of pharmaceuticals and the two affiliates are integrated into a corporate network that provides materials, advanced technology products, and marketing strategies, discretion on the part of the affiliates is likely to be limited. In addition, as noted earlier, the strategic importance and resources available to the affiliates suggest a tendency toward the role of implementer. This is less true in the case of the Taiwan subsidiary, whose strategic significance and management competence suggest a tendency toward the role of strategic leader. Hence, in Taiwan, there is more workplace innovation, reflected in a tendency to introduce aspects of lean production. Nevertheless, even in Taiwan, there is insufficient support from corporate headquarters and regional headquarters to improve workplace relations.

Last but not least, technology has played an important role in maintaining existing workplace relations patterns at both affiliates. The estimated average age of the machinery is eighteen years in Malaysia and thirteen years in Taiwan. Plant layout and operational procedures were derived from corporate headquarters, which, in turn, based its decisions on neo-Taylorist principles. In Malaysia, the plant buildings have been gradually renovated, but, as noted earlier, there has been little change technologically.

New management information technology is being introduced in both subsidiaries, but this is unlikely to affect manual workers dramatically. The technology in Taiwan is similar to that in Malaysia except that the machinery is more varied, reflecting the wider product range, and the equipment that has been introduced very recently. This is a consequence of, and a further incentive to maintain, management's commitment to high-performance standards and employee consultation and support. Nevertheless, technological change has not yet been on a large enough scale to warrant any major change in job redesign and work organization.

In sum, a combination of factors account for the patterns of workplace relations identified in this chapter. These factors have, by and large, reinforced the status quo. In Taiwan, however, where there has been a tendency toward lean production, the six factors have been slightly more conducive to change. Arguably, the ideology, strategy, and style of management at the subsidiaries are the most critical set of variables, for the other factors constrain or facilitate choice and behavior; finally, it is management discretion that most distinguishes the two affiliates and their patterns of workplace relations.

Conclusion

This chapter has examined workplace relations in two comparable subsidiaries of a large, American-owned, diversified pharmaceutical corporation. The subsidiaries are located in Malaysia and Taiwan, two leading East Asian industrializing countries. The focus of the research has been on manual workers, whose employment is less regulated by corporatewide human resource procedures than that of their technical, professional, and managerial counterparts. The study is more than a snapshot of workplace relations, however, for it attempts to analyze the relationship between corporate and workplace dynamics over a four-year period (1988–92).

Workplace relations were defined in relation to five variables: job characteristics, work organization, reward systems, employee representation, and management-employee relations, including the dominant forms of employee regulation. Based on these variables, I identified two ideal patterns of workplace relations, labeled neo-Taylorism and lean production. These alternative patterns provided a framework for comparing workplace relations in the two affiliates. Contrary to a simple institutional argument—that is, that because product and labor market institutions in the two countries differ in detail, workplace relations patterns will vary accordingly—the research showed that the patterns in workplace relations were similar and most closely resembled the neo-Taylorist ideal type. There were some differences, however, indicating that the affiliate in Taiwan is moving toward a pattern of lean production. Thus, compared with the managers in Malaysia, those in Taiwan were more directive yet participative; there was less hierarchy and a stronger emphasis on teamwork. The affiliate in Taiwan had achieved a higher level of functional integration, and management encouraged employee commitment by promoting key values and norms underpinned by support for improving workers' pay and welfare.

Six variables were discussed to explain the research findings. The broad similarity in market characteristics (competitive on the basis of quality and price), institutional arrangements (labor as a commodity requiring protection), nationality of the corporate owner (American), corporate management strategy (emphasis on quality and cost reduction; productivity improvement), corporate-subsidiary relations (both were implementer-type subsidiaries), and the fact that there was very limited technological change, accounted for the persistence of workplace relations patterns that resembled the neo-Taylorist ideal type. Differences in the intensity of intra- and extra-organizational pressures, which in turn contributed to differences in management behavior, accounted for variations in workplace relations. Thus, having been recruited at a time of financial crisis and been charged with significantly improving the affiliate's performance, the management in Taiwan introduced changes that appeared to presage a longer-term move toward lean production.

Two important implications of the foregoing analysis relate to future trends in the two affiliates and the conditions under which alternatives to neo-Taylorist workplace relations patterns are likely to flourish. R. Dore (1989) has argued that the world is converging on the Japanese "organization-oriented system" (1989:427–29). This form of organization—which is virtu-ally the same as lean production—is supposed to be most apparent in the "late-late" developing countries, since these societies have had an opportunity to establish modern institutions geared to industrialization rather than having to reform already entrenched structures.

Although Dore's categories are slightly different from those used in this chapter, the research findings reported above do not support his argu-ment.[28] Thus, in regard to Malaysia, there is no evidence of the lean production pattern of workplace relations, although the new GM may be more sympathetic to change in this direction. In regard to Taiwan, several points can be made. First, there is no lifetime employment; indeed, job security is precarious, given the possibility of MNCs rationalizing manufacturing, as they are currently doing in the European Union. Second, although an element of merit-based pay has recently been introduced, the pay system is based largely on the market rate for the job and is not governed by an internal labor market. Third, the affiliate provides very little training. Management relies mainly on employees having the neces-sary skills. Fourth, and finally, there is no enterprise union or collective bargaining at the affiliate level. We did observe some tendencies toward lean production, but these have not been formulated in a strategic plan and depend crucially on the stability of the current management team and continuing institutional and corporate incentives to maintain momentum.

As explained in more detail above, several characteristics of the drug industry militate against changes in workplace relations patterns. Corpo-rate priorities are R&D and marketing. Margins are relatively high, and manufacturing costs represent a small proportion of total costs. In addition, the combination of low-volume, high-product-variety manufacturing and the emphasis on product quality discourages major changes in affiliates that serve relatively small markets. In particular, without substantial investment in automated technology, qualitative change is unlikely. Thus, one of the variables that Dore claims is critical in promoting the Japanese pattern of employment relations—technological change—is of little consequence in my account.

Two further variables that form part of Dore's explanation of convergence are absent from the above analysis. These are the emergence of the welfare state and of strong trade unions. As noted in the chapter, the state in Malaysia and Taiwan has up until now provided limited social welfare benefits for the labor force and has actively constrained the power of autonomous unions. Other than improvements in the public health system in Taiwan, there is no evidence that this is changing.

Despite the generally negative industry effect noted above, certain circumstances are likely to encourage the adoption of alternative forms of workplace relations. These conditions are more typical of Japan and of the countries of Western Europe than of the societies of East Asia. The requisite combination of factors appears to be as follows: quality-based competitive markets; tight labor markets where there is a surplus of highly skilled employees; institutions that encourage continuous investment in human resources, or at least discourage the treatment of labor as a commodity; corporate owners whose tradition is not rooted in neo-Taylorist principles; a management whose goals are continuous quality, productivity, and human resource enhancement rather than cost reduction; a strategic leader-type enterprise; and corporate commitment to technological upgrading. The future research challenge is to identify which of these factors are the most powerful levers of change.

9

Human Resource Management for Production Workers in Large Korean Manufacturing Enterprises

Taigi Kim

orean industrial relations has undergone dramatic changes since the summer of 1987. Between that time and the first half of 1989, the industrial relations situation was seriously unstable. Labor union membership increased sharply, and almost all the large manufacturing firms became unionized and were struck. The militancy of the unions was reflected in an explosive increase in the number of labor disputes. Despite this trend, in the second half of 1989, it appeared that industrial peace had been restored. Union militancy diminished, and the number of labor disputes and the membership growth of unions decreased sharply. But in spite of these changes, there has been a continuing fast rise in wages, and union leadership at the enterprise level has remained unstable.

To understand the recent changes in Korea, it is important to have some background. From the summer of 1987 to the first half of 1989, the growth in the labor movement was closely related to democratization. The labor movement had been a conspicuous target, compared with other social movements, for oppression under authoritarian regimes. Essentially, the fast growth of the economy provided the potential for rapid development of the labor movement, triggered by the process of democratization. The Korean economy in 1987 was enjoying special boom conditions that it had never before experienced. The balance of trade was positive, and the demand for labor exceeded the supply. In addition, the money supply had risen with increases in government spending. Under these conditions, the costs of unstable industrial relations were relatively easily absorbed by the general health of the economy.

I would like to thank Stephen Frenkel and Jeffrey Harrod for their editorial assistance with this chapter.

Table 9.1. Large Industrial Groups' Share in Manufacturing Sales and Employment in Korea, 1977–89

Industrial Group	Sales					Employment				
	1977	1981	1985	1987	1989	1977	1981	1985	1987	1989
Top 10	21.1	28.4	30.2	27.9	27.0	12.5	12.1	11.7	11.6	11.8
Top 30	32.0	39.7	40.2	36.8	35.2	20.5	19.8	17.6	17.6	16.6

Source: Yoo 1992.

Since 1989, there has been growing concern about social instability and possible economic difficulties. Within the framework of rapid democratization, the student movement, which had been supportive of the labor movement, has become more oriented toward socialism and violence, and the Korean economy has not sustained its previous growth levels. The inflation rate has increased, the price of real estate has soared, and Korean products have lost some of their competitiveness in the export market.

In the early 1990s, a consensus developed on the nature of the difficulties facing the Korean economy. The government has thus actively sought to stabilize industrial relations and wages. It has moved to counter militancy in the labor movement, on the one hand, and to pursue wage stabilization, on the other. Supportive public opinion has helped make the first policy a success, but because of labor shortages, wage stabilization has not been effective.

The Korean economy developed within the framework of an active government industrial policy biased toward the promotion of the heavy-manufacturing and chemical industries. These industries were supported by providing preferential access to credit and other incentives. The result was a concentration of large heavy-manufacturing enterprises in the hands of a small number of owners. Further, Korea has become a country in which industrial groups, the so-called *Chaebols*, play an unusually large role in most sectors of the economy (see table 9.1). In the 1980s, the Korean government promoted small and medium-sized manufacturing enterprises so as to avoid an excessive tilt of the industrial structure in favor of the large enterprises.

The purpose of this chapter is to examine the features and problems of human resource management (HRM) policy for production workers in large Korean manufacturing firms and to suggest a direction for improvements in HRM policy. In particular, this chapter seeks to explain how the HRM policy has evolved in response to changes in the domestic and foreign environments of the enterprises and how HRM policy is related to the government's economic policy and to three mechanisms elaborated below. The chapter highlights the main characteristics of current HRM policy and explores changes that are necessary in view of developments in the domestic and foreign environment. Obstacles to change are also noted.

The empirical evidence cited in this chapter comes from a study conducted in late 1990 of HRM policy among large Korean manufacturing firms (Kim and Park 1992). One large firm was selected from each of seven major manufacturing industries: garments, pharmaceuticals, food, steel, automobiles, electronics, and shipbuilding. The seven firms have an average employment of forty thousand employees, and all are unionized, although only two were unionized before 1987. The researchers interviewed an average of thirty employees per firm. These included general production workers, labor union officials, supervisors, and managers in personnel and production departments.[1]

Since the history of large Korean manufacturing firms has been short, their management ideology and HR strategy have not been very well identified. Clearly, industry characteristics and owner characteristics are important. The pervasiveness of export-oriented, capital-intensive, and owner-concentrated firms demonstrates a management ideology and style that are dynamic in response to changes in external conditions and offensive in relation to employees. The typical example is found in the case of shipbuilding.

The large Korean manufacturing firms began to be prosperous in the 1970s through their role as the locomotive for industrialization. They held "more and faster production" as a top management goal. In that context, they had a management ideology but did not articulate it. Under the influence of an authoritarian regime, their management style was paternalistic to employees. As they have been faced with rising competition, the emergence of a labor movement, and democratization, they have been seriously reconsidering their management ideology. They now emphasize the achievement of consumer satisfaction and human resource development as the basis for their management ideology and at the same time are developing concrete strategies to achieve these goals.

If we compare the management ideology and approach to HRM of large Korean manufacturing firms with that of their counterparts in other countries, the Korean firms appear to combine the management styles of firms in both the United States and Japan. In American firms, management power and information are concentrated at the top, while production workers are not taken seriously and investments in human resource development are small. In Japanese firms, seniority is an important factor for promotion and wage determination. Labor unions are organized in individual firms. Large Korean manufacturing firms differ from their American and Japanese counterparts in that they are quicker than their counterparts to make strategic decisions and to reshape the organization.

Research on HRM policy related to production workers in large Korean manufacturing firms is fragmentary, and most such studies have been oriented toward nonproduction workers. The goal of this chapter is to explain systematically and for the first time the features of HRM policy affecting Korean production workers. Although there may be shortcomings in this attempt, as a result of the limited sample and the relatively small number of interviewees, it nevertheless provides a starting point for further studies in this area. In the past, management studies of Korea usually were used to analyze HRM policy and to explain its practices. This has meant that the background and rationale of the policy were not examined with sufficient thoroughness. To reform HRM policy, the background and rationale must first be thoroughly understood.

The structure of this chapter is as follows. The first section considers the characteristics of large Korean manufacturing firms and the theoretical approach adopted so as to examine HRM policy in relation to productivity and enterprise organization. The second section examines the work execution mechanism, focusing on the features and problems associated with the selection of and skill formation systems for production workers. The third section explores the impact of payment and promotion systems on employee motivation. It also explains how the work system has changed in recent years as a result of the active labor movement. The fourth section examines the decision-making mechanism by focusing on the organization of the firm and communication at the workplace level. The fifth and final section considers how the HRM policy for production workers might be improved in response to changes in business and production strategies.

Characteristics of Chaebols

Although the market share of *Chaebols* in manufacturing sales and employment has been diminishing since the mid-1980s, it still remains high. This is evident from data in table 9.1. Consequently, large manufacturing enterprises, most of which belong to major industrial groups, have been very important in Korean industrial relations. The unionization rate is strongly correlated with firm size. Thus, in 1990, firms with fewer than 100 employees had a 5 percent unionization rate, firms with 100 to 299 employees had a rate of 41 percent, firms with 300 to 499 employees had a rate of 54 percent, and firms with more than 500 employees had a rate of 82 percent.

Differences in the rate of strikes have been substantial and are also correlated with enterprise size. In 1989, firms with fewer than 99 employees experienced only 0.4 percent of the total strikes; firms with 100 to 299 employees, 6.9 percent; firms with 300 to 499 employees, 11.4 percent; firms with 500 to 999 employees, 16.7 percent; and firms with more than 1,000 employees, 36.5 percent.

The unions based in the large manufacturing firms have played a leading role in both the union movement and wage bargaining, and the stability of wage bargaining in other firms has been affected by the outcome of wage bargaining in the large firms. Since the large firms have a "rent" from their oligopolistic power in the product market, their labor unions have been able to secure a relatively fast rate of wage growth. More recently, however, the oligopolistic rent of these enterprises has become eroded by increasing competition and the rising cost of their labor has threatened their competitiveness. Given that the macro-level performance of the Korean economy has also been heavily dependent on that of large manufacturing firms, the government has actively intervened in wage bargaining in such firms with the objective of stabilizing wages.

Theoretical Approach to HRM, Productivity, and Enterprise Organization

The productivity of a firm can be maximized by optimally combining hardware and software; machines and equipment are the "hardware" of production, whereas their operation and management capability are the "software."[2] The combination of hardware and software usually depends on the prices of the machines and equipment and their importance to the firm. Government economic policies, along with market conditions, have enabled Korean firms to pursue a management policy that emphasizes hardware rather than software. During the past thirty years, the Korean government has actively provided finance and tax advantages for Korean firms to invigorate their investment in hardware. The government has also driven export-promotion policy forward by focusing on low- and medium-priced products through various subsidies. This policy has had considerable success, although it has undoubtedly been helped by a favorable export market for Korean products. Moreover, the government has been strongly involved in measures to stabilize wages and industrial relations.

A firm can be characterized as an organization created and designed to achieve a certain goal within a hierarchical structure. The HRM policy of a firm stems from its corporate goals and strategies; it can be understood as a combination of the work execution mechanism, the motivation endowment mechanism, and the decision-making mechanism.[3] Corporate goals and strategies are formulated through a decision-making process, and once a decision to achieve a goal or a strategy is made, it is executed by workers. Moreover, the efficiency of work execution depends on the workers' level of motivation. In this sense, the decision-making, work execution, and motivation endowment mechanisms are interrelated with HRM policy. Optimal HRM policy requires the best combination of these three mechanisms, which, in turn, requires that each individual mechanism be operating at optimal efficiency.

The work execution mechanism is related to three conditions: how workers are assigned a job, the characteristics of the job, and how the job is undertaken. The work execution mechanism directly depends on a firm's production technology, its production scale, the quality of its products, and the skill level and experience of the workers. The motivation endowment mechanism is related to two conditions: how workers' performance and efforts are rewarded and how workers' suggestions are elicited. This mechanism directly depends on the quality and size of the work force and the type of job the workers are performing. Finally, the decision-making mechanism depends on three conditions: how work goals are determined; the role of workers in the production process; and the administration system. All of these mechanisms are directly related to the organizational structure, management goals, and strategy of the firm.

Features and Problems of the Work Execution System

Intermittent hiring and personally based recruitment are features of the Korean *Chaebols*. When the supply of labor was abundant and the union movement inactive, firms were able to hire workers when they needed them. Thus, they hired production workers in response to the business environment, when demand and production conditions were favorable. As labor-management relations have become more unstable and as wages have risen explosively in recent years, firms paying high wages have refrained from hiring any new production workers, even though the business environment is improving. This downsizing policy has encouraged the intermittent hiring of production workers. At the same time, firms paying low wages have had a severe labor shortage and production workers are choosing to enter firms selectively. There are three reasons firms hire workers intermittently: changing the size of their labor forces has enabled the firms to adjust to the fluctuations in business; only a short period of time is required for a production worker to reach the skill level needed; and the turnover rate for production workers has been high in any case.

Korean firms recruit new production workers mainly through the personal connections of incumbent workers, supervisors, and so on. These connections are usually regionally or school-based. This practice has been reinforced recently as labor-management relations have become more unstable. There are three reasons to hire new workers with personal connections to the existing enterprise work force: it helps reduce turnover; it decreases the chances that the new workers will participate in militant labor disputes; and it costs less than to recruit and select new workers in open competition, especially since the costs to use the latter approach are high given the level of skills required in production.

In general, Korean firms had high turnover rates among production workers before labor-management relations became unstable. This situation has changed in accordance with the firms' ability to pay; thus, firms that pay relatively high wages now have much lower turnover rates and may even have waiting lists of workers. Low-wage firms, in contrast, continue to have high turnover, and their relatively small core work force is largely the result of their failure to secure new workers. As a consequence, they have been actively exploring the possibility of introducing part-time employment practices.

In Korea, the right to make workers redundant is very strictly regulated by labor law. Further, large manufacturing firms are not inclined to resort to layoffs out of a social concern for their employees. They prefer to stop hiring employees, to reduce their operating hours, or to transfer workers to other plants. Although many high-paying firms have small work forces because of these policies, some still have redundant workers. The relocation of these workers has become an important problem as the business environment has deteriorated and labor-saving production methods have been actively introduced.

When labor was abundant, most production workers had only a middle or elementary school education. After they entered the company, they went to an in-firm training center or entered a firm-affiliated high school. This training played a role in equalizing workers' commitment to their firms. Since the very recent past, most production workers have had a high school or even a technical junior college education. Hence, the in-firm training centers and firm-affiliated high schools are not operating to capacity. Because skill requirements for workers in production have not risen, there is now a gap between workers' expectations and the reality of their jobs. Further, as educational levels among production workers have risen, workers have had a greater desire to advance their careers. At the same time, their concerns about the personnel and management policies of their firms have increased. These workers' frustrations have been reflected in their demands for higher wages.

As the educational level of production workers has improved, the period spent learning after being hired has been shortened and workers reassess their relationship with the firm earlier. The time needed to reach the peak point in their learning curve naturally depends on the features of the job assigned to them and their attitudes, but it usually takes from six months to three years. After reaching the peak point, workers tend to feel bored doing the same work. As a result, many workers consider changing occupations or diminish their level of involvement in, and commitment to, the firm. After overcoming this "crisis," they have less desire to change jobs. This does not necessarily mean that the level of their job satisfaction has risen. Rather, it means that the cost of changing jobs has increased and they have chosen to stay with the firm.

Skill Acquisition

Production workers in large Korean manufacturing firms acquire their skills essentially by performing simple tasks repetitively. All that the firms usually require is that they have the simple skills of fabrication or assembly. The job-rotation system inherent in HRM has not been widely used for three reasons: firms usually produce a narrow range of products in large quantities; even though the quality of some products has been low, low prices and a favorable market have sustained a high sales volume; and the turnover rate among production workers has been high. Korean firms have not been prepared to risk the drop in productivity required to bear the costs of education and training associated with the operation of a job-rotation system. That is, they have had a short-term vision of HRM policy for production workers and have not considered the long-term benefits.

Insofar as production workers are required to do only simple jobs in repetitive ways, they have little or no incentive to learn new skills. Further, although the amount or intensity of labor needed differs significantly among job assignments, this difference is not properly reflected in wages or allowances. Hence, the first job to which production workers are assigned upon entering a company assumes crucial importance vis-à-vis their wages and allowances during their whole period of employment with the firm. Given that hiring practices are casual and often based on personal connections, many production workers see a good first job assignment as the result of "luck."

Rather than using a job-rotation system, Korean firms have sought to combat labor shortages and increasing labor costs through a diversified skill-formation system. This system has been implemented in a random yet simple manner whereby an incumbent production worker is required to take the place of another production worker when he or she leaves. Thus, diversified skill formation occurs but not through any planned system. Workers thus feel that the skill intensity of their jobs increases but that it is not reflected in compensation schedules.

Most production employees work in a continuous-process operation. To understand the total nature of their work, three levels of understanding are required. These include the content of the work, the features of the equipment and machines being used, and the general features of the manufacturing process.[4] Although the basic requirements are that production workers have the first two levels of understanding, higher efficiency requires that the workers understand their role in the work process, as well as the manufacturing process more generally.

On average, it takes from three to six months for newly hired Korean production workers to understand the content of their work. This period tends to be shorter as the educational levels of the workers increase. In a continuous-process operation, the levels of skills that are required are simple: fabrication, assembly, packing, and so on. Production workers educated in a technical high school tend to be required to have lower-level skills than they acquired at school. Indeed, firms have a tendency to prefer production workers who graduated from nontechnical schools since there is almost no difference in the productivity of these employees and those who have more advanced education. Moreover, management saves on the allowances paid to employees with better qualifications.

After entering a company, the production workers learn from senior workers. Beyond a certain level, however, the on-the-job learning becomes monotonous for two reasons. First, the skills required of production workers are limited in depth and scope, so that the senior workers do not increase their skills as they work; and second, there is insufficient incentive for the senior workers to impart skills to the junior workers.

Production workers do not usually develop an understanding of the machines and equipment they use beyond their operation and maintenance. They rarely have the chance to learn the features of the machines and equipment, yet, because of their experience, it is possible that they could very well learn the basics of the machines and be capable of undertaking repairs if the problems were not too serious. Repairs are usually made by mechanical engineers, however, which means that it is difficult for operators to accumulate mechanical knowledge. This work structure also makes it difficult for the equipment to be used to optimal efficiency.

Further, production workers generally have a very limited understanding of the manufacturing process. Before working on the production line, employees have only a short time to become acquainted with the flow of operations. In addition, they have very little opportunity to obtain further education or training after they are assigned to work on the line. To make matters worse, the content of any training that is offered is general rather than job-related. And in the rare case when a job-rotation system is introduced, workers' understanding of the manufacturing process does not improve in accordance with their length of service with the firm. This lack of understanding is an obstacle to cooperation among workers in different sections and departments and also makes workers reluctant to suggest ideas for improvement or to point out defects in the manufacturing process.

Motivational Features and Problems

Seniority-based pay is the most common form of remuneration for blue-collar workers in large Korean manufacturing firms. The wage level of a production worker is directly and almost exclusively related to years of service. The skill and performance of a worker, and the difficulty and intensity of the job, have not been adequately reflected in wages for several reasons: first, the simple and repetitive tasks on which production is based have not made it necessary to differentiate wages on the basis of skill, performance, difficulty, intensity, and so on; and second, even when wage differentiation has become necessary, it has been difficult to create objective criteria for differentiating wages without a reliable job analysis and merit system.

Since the union movement has become active, the seniority-based payment scheme has been strengthened and wages have tended to be increased on a fixed-sum basis regardless of the differences between workers. This has weakened the value of the payment scheme as a motivational device. Recently, as the environment of industrial relations has changed in favor of giving firms greater flexibility, efforts have been made to correct the seniority bias in the wage structure by strengthening the merit system and by introducing new payment schemes, such as performance-based pay.

In recent years, large Korean manufacturing firms have increasingly begun to introduce a serial pay-step system, usually for clerical and administrative workers, which is based mainly on the workers' length of service and occupational grade. Merit has rarely had any effect on determining wages. To reap the advantages of a merit system, some firms have introduced a "special advancement system," which ties increases in pay to merit points. Since the labor movement has become active, however, this practice has been resisted by labor unions, which believe that the merit system is not just and could be used as a mechanism of control rather than reward.

Normally, basic pay has been proportionately low relative to the total wages of production workers and overtime pay proportionately high. Since the labor union movement has become active, new allowances have been introduced, or the amount received as allowances has increased. Basic pay as a proportion of total pay has thus been further reduced.

Firms and unions recognize that the wage structure is unfair: first, the basic pay does not properly reflect differences in jobs or workers' characteristics; second, unions have resorted to allowances to compensate minority groups, such as senior workers, who receive less benefit from across-the-board increases; and third, labor and management have both felt that the wage structure was necessary to counter the government's wage stabilization policy, which can penalize firms for violating wage guidelines.

The wage curve of production workers in large Korean manufacturing firms is shown in figure 9.1. As the service period becomes longer, wages increase more slowly. This reflects the fast rise in productivity at the beginning of service and the period of stagnation later in the worker's tenure. The relationship between pay and productivity is a serious problem.

This problem has now become more serious as the labor unions have become more active. Union activity has shifted the wage curve to the left as higher wages have been secured, but the productivity curve has not shifted at all. In addition, the period of service has lengthened as the labor turnover rate has declined. For the firm, this means that optimal retirement

Figure 9.1. Wage Curve for Production Workers in Large Korean Manufacturing Firms

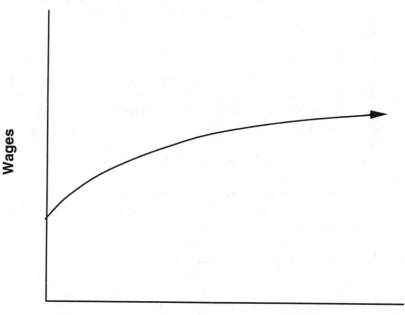

time has been shortened at the same time that period of service has been lengthened. This results in considerable losses for the firm.

Promotion to Supervisory Positions

It is possible for production workers in large Korean manufacturing firms to be promoted to supervisory jobs. Upon promotion, the production worker's concern is more administration and monitoring than developing workers' skills. This orientation occurs for several reasons: the firm's production strategy is to achieve a cost advantage rather than a quality advantage; production technology has required the employment of large numbers of workers rather than fewer, more skilled workers; the emphasis has been on control, the rate of the work, and the production process, which has had to vary because of the heavy dependence on the fluctuating export market; and finally, workers have had limited discretion in their work roles.

The promotion ladder for production workers in large manufacturing firms may have between three and five steps (e.g., Cho-Jang, Ban-Jang, Jik-Jang, and Ki-Jang-Ki-Won). The Cho-Jang, for example, is the head of a Cho, which is the basic work unit and which in combination can comprise a Ban. The ladder is usually extended to accommodate the tendency for management to offer additional promotions. The number of workers in a unit of Cho and of Ban differs even within a company, and the time frame for production workers to be promoted to Cho-Jang and from Cho-Jang to Ban-Jang and from Ban-Jang to Jik-Jang has been three, four, and five years respectively. Despite this structure, there has to be a vacancy for a worker to be promoted and these occur randomly. The more recent reduction in the hiring of production workers has caused the pattern of manpower distribution to change from a pyramid-type shape to a diamond-type shape, centered around workers with four to five years' service. This has made the pattern of promotion for production workers even more uncertain.

There are differences in the promotion systems for production workers and for clerical and administrative workers. First, the power and authority of production workers do not increase as they are promoted to higher supervisory positions as much as they do for clerical and administrative workers. The highest position a production worker can achieve is equivalent to a section chief (Gua-Jang) of clerical and administrative workers. Second, the division of duties among the Jo-Jang, Ban-Jang, and Jik-Jang is less well defined. The supervisors of production workers are under the control of the Gua-Jang of a section or the Bu-Jang of a department. There have occasionally been conflicts between administrative officials of sections. Third, promotion opportunities for production workers are more limited than for clerical and administrative workers, although production workers are formally permitted to move to clerical or administrative jobs.

In determining whether to promote a production worker to a supervisory position, management places more emphasis on the worker's leadership abilities than on the results of the merit rating system. Merit ratings are carried out by both the supervisor above the worker being evaluated and by the supervisor just above the evaluator. Even when a decision to promote a production worker has finally been made by the head of the department, the opinion of the immediate supervisor is essential.

The wages of production workers are calculated on an hourly or daily basis but they are paid monthly; when production workers are promoted to supervisory positions, however, their wages are determined on a monthly basis. Before the labor movement became active, supervisory workers had virtually absolute power over production workers. Supervisory workers now have much less authority, although they still monitor attendance and conduct merit ratings for production workers. Also, wage differences between production workers and supervisory workers used to be substantial; hence, production workers had a strong desire to be promoted to the supervisory grades.

As the labor movement has become more active, the desire of production workers to be promoted to supervisory positions has decreased significantly:

first, the power of supervisory workers has become limited because of the rise of labor union power; as the management style has become less authoritarian, production workers have become less concerned about infringements on their rights; and the wages of supervisory workers have increased relatively less than those of production workers.

Features and Problems of the Decision-Making Structure

Large Korean manufacturing firms tend to centralize decision making and are characterized by their many levels of hierarchy and limited formal functional integration. That the top manager tends also to be the owner has a centralizing effect on decision making. It leaves middle managers with little power in the decision-making process. Indeed, middle managers are so insecure in relation to top management that they dilute their accountability when exercising power by an overwillingness to seek joint action with colleagues in related departments. Thus, often a job that could have been carried out by one person, or by one section, is done by two people, or two sections. Because of the centralized and duplicative nature of these organizations, the decision-making process is often lengthy and complicated and communication ineffective. The lack of functional focus also makes cooperation between sections inefficient.

After the labor movement became active, the role of middle managers was further constrained. Previously, the orders they gave to production workers were carried out, even if they tended to be "unreasonable." Currently, production workers express resistance when they think that orders are not "reasonable." With these changes, the vertical channels of communication between the top and the bottom of the organization have developed bottlenecks. This problem is illustrated in figure 9.2. Communication within circles at the top and bottom has been relatively more open than communication between the top and the bottom.

The horizontal communication among workers has not been as intense as the vertical communication because decision making in a firm takes the following route: an important issue is initiated at the top; a decision is made at the top without fully exchanging opinions with middle managers; middle managers are required to implement and monitor the decision. Since middle managers have neither participated in initiating the decision or had a chance to express their opinions, they feel less need to communicate with related persons or departments. Hence, information within the department is not delivered fully to other departments, causing bottlenecks even in the horizontal structure of the firm's organization, as illustrated in figure 9.3.

To correct these problems, large Korean manufacturing firms have been actively trying to delegate decision-making power and shorten the decision-

Figure 9.2. Communication Bottlenecks in the Vertical Structure of Large Korean Manufacturing Firms

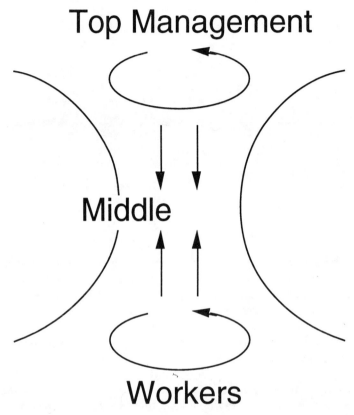

Top Management

Middle

Workers

making process. They have also attempted to improve organizational flexibility by merging sections into larger divisions. In addition, firms have been reducing the number of administrative workers by limiting the number of new administrative employees who are hired or by transferring workers to other companies.

A Work Organization for Monitoring Purposes

The communication problems at the workplace level have been even more serious, despite the active communication between workers who happen to have close personal relationships. Most of the interest in stimulating communication has focused on clerical and administrative workers for several reasons: production workers are not well acquainted with their co-workers because the firms in which they work are so large; many production workers are casual employees; these workers' contacts are

Figure 9.3. Communication Bottlenecks in the Horizontal Structure of Large Korean Manufacturing Firms

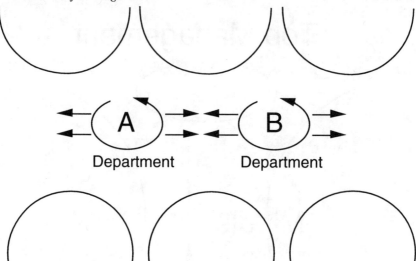

limited because they have not been rotated from one job to another; and the work unit is organized to make monitoring easy, which is not necessarily conducive to communication. The lack of communication among production workers has made them reluctant to point out problems or to suggest ways to improve the work process.

Large Korean manufacturing firms have not taken seriously the possibility of redesigning their work processes or organizations. Machines and equipment have not been introduced systematically or positioned conveniently for production workers. These oversights have made the flow of the work process uneven. For example, one line in the work process may be assembling 450 units a day while the next line is assembling only 400 units. This problem was especially evident when automation was introduced.

To overcome the problem of unevenness in output, computer-integrated manufacturing systems have been introduced. The parts and raw materials needed by production workers are supplied daily in a manner designed to enhance the efficiency of administration and monitoring. Daily work goals are set by the chief of the production department with the aid of the production workers' supervisors, and these goals are usually met.

Quality circles appear to be active in large Korean manufacturing firms, but they are usually so formal in style that they do not stimulate communication among production workers. Part of the reason for the apparently active QCs is that the government has encouraged them. There are several reasons for their limited effectiveness: First, the firms have not attached great importance to the QCs. They do not expect them to suggest major improvements, since production workers carry out simple jobs in repetitive ways. Second, production workers have had limited interest in the QCs, since the workers are not accustomed to providing productive ideas to their co-workers or supervisors. Workers tend to believe that they are supposed to carry out only the work their supervisors have ordered. Third, the scope of QC activities has usually been limited to reducing the amounts of defective products. Because QC activities do not help solve employees' problems, workers do not strongly identify with this form of participation.

Other programs to improve productivity have been pursued in large firms through various campaigns. They have usually set certain goals, such as a "30 percent cost decrease." Production workers have not been very sympathetic to such programs. Although productivity improvement movements are intrinsically related to corporate goals, production workers have not been very conscious of them. One reason is that they have rarely participated in setting these goals. Rather, the goals are decided by the top managers. Further, production workers have been skeptical because they are afraid productivity improvement programs will lead to increased labor intensity without proper compensation for the rise in productivity. Finally, most of the productivity programs have not been carefully prepared and communicated. They have been based on the existing work system.

As large Korean manufacturing firms have experienced severely unstable labor-management relations, they have actively tried to inform workers of the results of business performance or developments in the business environment, either directly or indirectly. At the same time, they have introduced an "open-door policy," which enables production workers to meet directly with the heads of their departments or companies and regular meetings to be held between low-level employees, including production workers, and top managers.

These measures would seem to indicate progress toward stimulating communication among production workers. Workers tend, however, to be suspicious of information, such as business performance records, that are given to them by their employers. Korean workers are not very familiar with talking to top managers directly.

Future HRM Policy for Production Workers

Changes in the domestic and foreign environments have encouraged the reform of HRM policies in Korean firms along several lines. First, foreign demand for low- and medium-priced products is being met by the so-called late developing countries, such as Thailand and Mexico. Second, major export destinations for Korean products, such as the United States and the countries in the European Community, have resisted aspects of the

Table 9.2. Old and New Paradigms in HRM Policy for Production Workers in Korea

Economic environment	Management strategy	HRM policy
OLD PARADIGM		
Quantitative growth	*Large-volume production*	*Repetition of simple jobs*
Government subsidy	Heavy reliance on the	Occasional and personally
Favorable export market	capacity of machinery	connected hiring
Low wages	Large-scale employment	Sluggish education and
Abundant labor	Research and development	training
Restrained union activity	Concentration of decision-	Seniority-based pay scheme
	making power with the	Career development toward
	owner of the firm	supervisory and
		administrative jobs
		Monitoring-purpose work
		organization
NEW PARADIGM		
		Diversified and specialized
Qualitative economic growth	*High value-added production*	*qualification*
High wages	Many items, small lots	Pay scheme reflecting the
Labor shortage	High quality and	differences in work
Active labor movement	technology	Promotion scheme to
Increasing competition in	Business specialization	develop ability
domestic and foreign	Separation of management	Emphasis on education and
markets	from ownership	training
Reduced government		Introduction of job rotation
subsidies		

Korean government's industrial policy, such as its export subsidies. Third, the cost of introducing new machines, facilities, and technology has risen as a result of the increasing reluctance of technologically advanced countries to transfer technology. Fourth, financial support as the main means of stimulating a firm to make investments needs to be reconsidered and the support reduced because of the rapid increase in wages and the structural shortage of labor.

The direction of change in HRM policy will be determined by changes in the conditions that led to the past policies. Table 9.2 outlines the old and new paradigms in HRM policy, including their respective backgrounds and features.

These features indicate that a new policy will have to reflect changes in the economic environment and be in accordance with the general management strategy of Korea's large manufacturing firms. Clearly, firms will have to involve production workers more in decision making and develop specific management policies toward labor unions. The environmental conditions have changed so drastically that it is unlikely that a partial reform of HRM policy for production workers will correct such structural contradictions as the discrepancy between workers' educational levels and the content of their jobs.

The Korean government is still powerful enough to induce reform in HRM policies. The government should try to ensure that these policies are aligned to the broad goal of ensuring economic growth based on qualitative change that depends on the use of advanced technology and higher skills. The government has, indeed, already recognized the changes in the economic environment and has recently been placing more emphasis on qualitative growth of the economy by improving its relations with firms and workers. The government's basic policy, however, is still oriented toward quantitative growth, thus creating confusion for both firms and workers. The government should pursue a consistent policy that encourages firms and workers to improve productivity.

Research has shown that firms have focused mainly on HRM policies for production workers at the level of the motivation endowment mechanism and have tended to neglect the work execution and decision-making mechanisms. A more comprehensive policy is now unavoidable; and if the firms are to succeed in their stated objectives of overcoming their increasing labor costs, reducing the instability of labor-management relations, and raising competitiveness, the work execution mechanism should be revised to develop workers' skills. Also, if workers are to become more involved in decision making, then the decision-making mechanism and motivation endowment mechanism will have to become the foci for reform.

The current work execution mechanism does not easily enable production workers to adapt to changes in HRM policy. The resultant mentality has tended to be that "we provide labor, firms just pay." For this attitude to change, skill enhancement and more intense communication within the organization must be a recognized part of the work.

Employee Selection, Skill Formation, Promotion, and Payment Systems

Firms in Korea that pay relatively low wages are being pushed to hire casual production workers and to recruit workers through personal procedures. At the same time, firms that pay relatively high wages need to hire workers regularly rather than casually. Since many production workers are ready to work, an open selection method could be adopted, enabling greater emphasis to be placed on recruiting qualified workers and on developing a rational plan for labor utilization.

Any reform of HRM has to entail more emphasis on or the introduction of on-the-job training, the development of diversified skills, and the introduction of a job-rotation system, especially at firms that pay relatively high wages and that have low turnover. For on-the-job training to be effective, there must be incentives for senior workers to work with trainees; a diversified skill-formation system requires that firms balance the characteristics of jobs and those of workers; and implementation of a job-rotation system means that firms need to plan educational and training programs for production workers.

The promotion of production workers under any HRM reform system would have to occur concomitant with skill development; production workers with a talent for administration and production workers with a talent in a skill need to climb different career development ladders. Members of the first group should be promoted as their administrative talents improve, and members of the latter group should be promoted as their production skills widen and deepen.

Likewise a new payment structure for production workers is essential. Such a structure would have three stages to ensure that there are both wage and productivity raises as the service period lengthens. The old payment scheme has only one stage of skill and productivity development. The result is that before service ends, wages continue to rise while the rate of productivity growth stagnates. Under the three-stage system, a new skill/productivity path is started *before* the peak of productivity and wages is reached (the point at which a rising wage rate crosses a flattening productivity curve). As this process is repeated at least three times in a career, wage growth is below productivity growth at the end of service. This tends to optimize the wage/productivity relationship, but it also accommodates the tendency for job duration to lengthen.

Decision-Making Structures and the Role of Government

As the decision-making structures of firms under a new HRM policy came under pressure, the following changes could be envisaged: decentralization of decision-making power; streamlining of the organization; intensification of both vertical and horizontal communication among workers; introduction of a systematic job analysis and reinforcement of the merit rating system; and restructuring of production processes and reorganizing of work units. In addition, the consultation system with unions should be strengthened. Finally, the work unit could emerge as a place to learn skills and self-regulation, in contrast to its role in strict supervision in the past.

Any government that is serious about adapting to change has to pursue a policy based on a recognition of the need to provide support for the country's firms, using profitability of production rather than the amount of sales as a criterion. The government also has to consider the need to increase business and separate ownership from management. Labor laws have to be changed to increase the utilization of workers on the demand side and to facilitate in-firm education and training on the supply side. Many of these requirements lead to the conclusion that there should be a positive recognition of workers' rights to organize and, at the same time, that unions should be encouraged to cooperate with management in shaping HRM policy for production workers.

10

Overseas Japanese Plants under Global Strategies: TV Transplants in Asia

Atsushi Hiramoto

During the worldwide recession in the first half of the 1980s, Japanese economic growth was considerable relative to other advanced countries, and Japanese corporations were very competitive in the world market. This competitive strength was attributed to several factors, the most important of which seemed to be Japan's unique style of management. Since the early 1980s, so-called Japanese management has attracted growing interest overseas. Indeed, much to the surprise of many Japanese managers, companies in the United States and Europe have attempted to introduce a "Japanese style" into their management practices. The emerging consensus is that this is both possible and desirable (Lincoln and Kalleberg 1990; Womack, Jones, and Roos 1990). I argue that there are constraints that limit the transfer of particular elements of Japanese-style management. Moreover, it is unclear whether a complete transfer would be desirable from an economic efficiency perspective.

To explore these issues, I focus on Japanese multinationals whose top managers, including those responsible for overseas subsidiaries, typically manage according to the Japanese style, this being especially true in Japanese subsidiaries in East Asia. Thus, by comparing the Japanese parent company plants and their transplants in other countries, it is possible to identify those features that are, and are not, transferable overseas. Factors impeding transferability can also be identified.

At the outset, it is worth noting two factors that are likely to limit the transfer of some Japanese management practices. The first such factor is the strategy and structure of the transplants, which are strongly conditioned by the parent company's global strategy. The parent company's global strategy

I wish to thank Tokunaga, Shigeyoshi, and Nomura, Masami, for their cooperation, and Stephen Frenkel and Jeffrey Harrod for their helpful comments. Errors, if any, are mine.

affects management practice, thereby making transplants different from their domestic counterparts, as discussed below. The second factor is the local hiring practices. Such practices make it difficult for a company to transfer management practices that are unfamiliar to, or indeed not likely to be favored by, local managers. Personnel managers in Japanese transplants are often hired locally, thereby limiting the extent to which labor relations are conducted along Japanese lines.

This chapter draws on recent empirical research, specifically the results of a survey of Japanese television (TV) transplants located in Asia and Europe. This survey was conducted in two large electronics companies (referred to as company A and company B) in 1989–90. All of the transplants in Asia and Europe that produce TVs were studied, including two plants in Taiwan, one in China, one in Singapore, two in Malaysia, two in the United Kingdom, and two video cassette recorder (VCR) plants in Germany. The parent plants were surveyed before researching the transplants.[1]

This chapter is limited to a comparison of two of the transplants: one in Taiwan and one in Malaysia. These were chosen because both were export-oriented and had between five hundred and one thousand employees. These establishments are cited as transplant TB and transplant MA respectively. T and M represent the two countries, and A and B represent the two companies. The scope of the discussion is restricted to the survey results on corporate strategy and structure and on labor-management relations. The performance of the PCB assembly shops will also be mentioned.[2]

The plan of the chapter is as follows. The global strategies of the two TV MNCs will be sketched briefly, including the constraints imposed on the transplants because of global corporate strategies. The results of the survey of the transplants in Taiwan and Malaysia are then summarized. Included is a discussion of such items as the strategy and organization of the plants, recruitment methods, promotion systems, wage systems, labor-management relations arrangements, and the manufacturing process of PCB assembly. Such items are useful in uncovering differences between parent plants and transplants and in indicating similarities and differences between transplants. These, together with the factors accounting for such differences and some of the more important implications, are discussed in the concluding section of the chapter.

Global Strategies of Japanese Electronics Companies

The Japanese electrical and electronics industry accounts for the largest share of accumulated direct foreign investment of Japan's manufacturing industries. This amounted to 22 percent in 1990. Within this segment, TVs are one of the dominant products; thus, 60 percent of the total production of Japanese TV manufacturers was produced in foreign countries in 1990. This figure is much larger than that of the automobile industry (13.3 percent in 1990), another prominent industry in overseas production.

History of Overseas Production

Japanese consumer electronics companies started overseas production in the early 1960s, primarily in Southeast Asia. Sanyo Electric Co. Ltd. established a radio manufacturing plant in Hong Kong in 1961, and Matsushita Electric Industrial Co. Ltd. began producing household electrical appliances in Thailand in 1961 and in Taiwan in 1962. The aim was to secure the local market and thus avoid import restrictions imposed by the governments of these countries.

The early transplants had to diversify production in order to grow in small markets. Most of the transplants began the process of diversification through the manufacture of radios and TVs; they then progressed to the manufacture of household electrical appliances, such as electric fans, rice cookers, refrigerators, and washing machines. These items were produced in small quantities.

TVs were one of the most important products and the key household appliance marketed locally. It was comparatively easy to set up TV production: there was no need for heavy investments or skilled workers. TV parts, including tubes, could be imported from suppliers or the parent plant in Japan. The value of a TV was relatively high compared with the resources needed to produce it. In contrast, the production of refrigerators, for example, needed heavy investments, skilled workers, and in-house production of particular parts. Not surprisingly, TVs became the leading product of overseas Japanese electrical machinery companies.

From the early 1970s, Japanese electrical machinery companies began to establish transplants in advanced countries. The Sony Corporation started TV production in the United States in 1972 and in the United Kingdom in 1974. Matsushita acquired the TV business of the Motorola Company (a U.S. firm) in 1974 and started TV production in the United Kingdom in the same year. Sanyo acquired Warwick Electronics' TV manufacturing operations in the United States in 1976. The trade frictions that developed between the advanced countries and Japan centered mainly around the voluntary restrictions on TV exports, which promoted further direct investment by Japanese companies. Other large electrical machinery companies established transplants in the United States and in the United Kingdom beginning in the late 1970s and early 1980s.

In contrast to the earlier transplants in the Asian countries, the transplants in the advanced countries were much larger, reflecting the larger size of the local market. They also concentrated on TV production.

Large plants with a narrow product range intended for export to a third market were also established in Taiwan, Singapore, and Malaysia from the late 1960s. These plants took advantage of the low wages in these countries and were integrated into an emerging network of global production. Consequently, the early transplants in the Asian countries were partially reorganized. Some transplants were required to export some special products; for example, Matsushita required its Malaysian plant to export electric irons, vacuum cleaners, and washing machines and required its Taiwanese plant to export headphones and radio recorders. Both plants, however, remained multiproduct companies that supplied the local market.

The volume of TV set production by all the Japanese transplants increased substantially in the 1970s and 1980s. By the end of the 1970s, it exceeded exports from Japan, and by the end of the 1980s, production in Japan.

Global Network of Production

Japanese consumer electronics companies built up their global networks of production in the late 1980s. By and large, they operate these networks today as follows. The subsidiary companies in the United States and Europe are strongly oriented toward local markets, and this orientation affects the function and the organization of the subsidiaries. Thus, they tend to connect local sales activities and marketing done by affiliated sales companies directly with their manufacturing process. For example, company A established the North America TV Division, the aim of which was to integrate manufacturing and sales activities. Company B combined its sales company in the United States with its TV manufacturing company.

These subsidiaries possess the authority to plan their production volume and schedules. Furthermore, the subsidiaries are trying to introduce development and design functions into their local businesses. The transfer of R&D functions from the Japanese parent companies to the subsidiaries is becoming a controversial issue as the basic design tends to be undertaken by the parent company while product modifications are made by the subsidiaries.

The subsidiaries in Asian countries function differently. The early multiproduct transplants are also oriented to the local market, and their production is connected directly to the local sales activities of affiliated sales companies, but their products tend to be developed and designed by the parent company in Japan. In the case of TV production, basic design is undertaken in Japan.

In the case of the mass-product TV plants that were established later, their production volume and schedules are planned and ordered by the parent division in Japan, since their export markets are composed of heterogeneous countries in which local sales companies carry out sales activities. These transplants export to the surrounding countries of Asia, including Japan and Oceania. Market information is gathered by the parent company in Japan and is used in planning the production schedule of the transplant. Simply put, the organization of these transplants tends to center around the production function. At the same time, the parent plant or division in Japan develops new technology and products and functions as supplier to the domestic market and as exporter to other Asian countries, including China. The division also plans the global strategies for the transplants.

In the case of company A, the company developed its global plan for TV production in 1988. According to the plan, the world TV market is divided into four groups, namely, America, Europe, Asia, and Japan, each having a main production base. The transplant in the United States was assigned the role of supplying the full range of TV products to North America, Central America, and South America. The transplant in the United Kingdom was in charge of supplying the whole range of TV products, other than larger (thirty-seven-plus-inch) TVs and liquid crystal TVs, to Europe. In Asia, transplant MA was newly established and given the role of supplying popular TV models (from fourteen-inch to twenty-one-inch) to Southeast Asia, China, Oceania, the Middle and Near East, and Japan. This transplant was also designated the international procurement center for parts. The parent division in Japan assumed responsibility for supplying the full range of products to the domestic market, large-screen TVs to other markets, and R&D for high-technology products. According to a company document, by establishing a division of responsibilities, the company aimed at "supplying the most suitable goods to the most suitable market from the most suitable plant" and thus at retaining its share of the world market.

Effects of Global Strategies on Transplants

A parent company's global strategy not only determines the products, markets, and organization of its transplants, it also requires that the transplants remain flexible. Although each transplant has its own problems, the global strategy imposes an important problem common to all the transplants.

Generally speaking, to compete successfully in international markets, a company must be able to adapt its global operations to changing external conditions. Companies must adjust rapidly to changes in government policies, the relative cost of factors of production, and exchange rates. To adjust to such changes, they must alter their product mix by, for example, introducing new products or new models or by transferring products from one transplant or the parent plant to a different plant.

This organizational flexibility is important for Japanese MNCs because Japanese corporations place importance on the long-term accumulation of business resources, rather than on achieving high profit through the short-term mobility of resources, including frequent acquisition and withdrawal from specific markets (Kagono et al. 1983:31). If overseas production for a Japanese corporation requires the transfer of management style, the costs to establish a new plant and to close down an existing plant are relatively high, because the transfer process is both lengthy and expensive. In fact, there is evidence that Japanese MNCs are more reluctant than their foreign counterparts to withdraw transplants from countries that have become less attractive.[3] To stay in a country where wage rates are rising rapidly, it is necessary to introduce high-value-added products or models, in addition to rationalization measures that reduce costs. This means that the transplants must be prepared to make changes in products, or to add new products or models, more frequently than local independent companies of the same size.

Japan's transplants have been able to remain flexible in part because they are supported in making product changes by their parent companies' large development capacity, a capacity local companies typically do not possess. For example, at transplant TB in Taiwan, product changes have been carried out as follows. Established in 1969, transplant TB concentrated on the production of radios and monochrome TVs for export to the United States. The plant has specialized in exports ever since. Because of the high demand in the U.S. market, transplant TB started to produce color TVs (CTVs) in 1970, tape recorders in 1972, and stereo sets in 1976. It began to supply CTV chassis to the United States instead of finished products in 1979, because of the introduction of export quotas on Taiwanese-made TVs. It also started to produce radio cassette recorders in 1979.

In 1984, production for export of all radio cassette recorders was transferred to the transplant. It also began to produce monochrome character displays in 1984, color character displays in 1986, compact disc players in 1986, and projection TV chassis in 1987. It discontinued production of monochrome TVs in 1982 and recently transferred the production of TV parts and CTV chassis to two transplants in Malaysia, because wage increases and rising exchange rates had eroded the competitiveness of Taiwanese products.

In the latter half of the 1980s, the export of CTVs, including CTV chassis, decreased sharply. The proportion of CTV sales to total sales fell from 79 percent in 1983 to 37 percent in 1989 because of deteriorating competitiveness. An increase, mainly in the number of stereo sets exported to Europe, compensated to keep total sales relatively stable.

The need to change the product mix to cope with shifting market conditions is more pressing for export-oriented transplants than it is for transplants that produce for domestic markets. Those that produce for domestic markets have another problem in a developing country, however. As mentioned above, they must produce a variety of products to expand in the small local market. For example, at transplant TA in Taiwan, product change has been carried out as follows: transplant TA began producing radios, record-players, and loud speakers in 1962. It added rice cookers and monochrome TVs in 1963, toasters and refrigerators in 1965, electric fans and washing machines in 1967, air-conditioners and CTVs in 1969, cassette radios and recorders in 1973, sewing machines in 1979, automated machinery in 1983, VCRs and computer monitors in 1984, and microwave ovens and vacuum cleaners in 1987.

These examples demonstrate that both export-oriented and domestic-oriented Japanese transplants have had to make frequent changes or additions in their product lines. These changes have provided management with a constant challenge: how to reorganize existing resources, including the work force, to produce new items efficiently.

Japanese Staff at the Transplants

Japanese transplants usually have Japanese presidents and managers of accounting departments. As mentioned earlier, the managers of the personnel departments are usually hired locally. The managers of other departments, such as manufacturing, design, purchasing, production control, and quality assurance, may be Japanese or locals depending on circumstance. Besides these managers, most of the Japanese who are dispatched abroad are design, production, or production control engineers.

Since the development of new products and models and their basic design is generally undertaken by the Japanese parent plant or division, the primary function of the engineers who are dispatched from Japan is to assist local engineers in adapting designs to the needs of the local or export markets; the Japanese engineers also assist in producing new items or new models and provide advice regarding production control. Because this is ongoing work, the number of Japanese engineers who are dispatched abroad tends to be consistent over time.

The transplants in Malaysia and Taiwan have become dependent on the Japanese staff for another reason. In their parent plants, there are unique jobs that cross the boundaries of the design and production departments, requiring a broad grasp of the manufacturing function, and they are strategically important to manufacturing. For example, the person assigned to the position of Kojyo-gijutsu (factory engineer) in company A is responsible for reconciling the needs of the design and production departments by modifying designs in accordance with the constraints of the manufacturing process. In company B, the person occupying the position of Kohmu (factory affairs) is in charge of production control. This entails production scheduling by adjusting the activities of the design, production engineering, materials, quality assurance, and business administration departments.

M. Aoki (1988, chaps. 2 and 6) asserts that the ambiguous and fluid demarcation between jobs in the Japanese corporation enables production adjustments to be made more efficiently in response to changes in the market than the hierarchical structure of the Western corporation with its strict job demarcations and limited horizontal communications. The Japanese manager of company B agrees that the development of a liaison job, such as Kohmu, has contributed substantially to the plant's efficiency. As we shall see with regard to PCB assembly in transplant TB, being able to modify designs to meet the needs of manufacturing has had a positive effect on the efficiency of production. The development of liaison jobs is one reason Japanese consumer electronics companies excel at mass production.

Since neither of these jobs can easily be done by engineers from the host country, the parent companies often dispatch Japanese staff to the transplants. This is another reason the number of Japanese staff tends to remain constant over time.

That the employment of dispatched staff is not a transient phenomenon can be seen from the following data. In the case of company A, the ratio of dispatched to local staff was 1.7 percent in 1973, 1.5 percent in 1978, 1.8 percent in 1983, and 1.4 percent in 1989. The number of Japanese staff in the transplants would have decreased had the transplants been more successful in recruiting, training, and promoting competent local engineers. This has not occurred, so that the ratio of dispatched staff to total employees remains relatively stable. For example, according to a 1984 survey conducted in Taiwan, the ratio of foreign employees to total employees was 2.4 percent for clerical jobs in Japanese electronics MNCs and 1.9 percent for engineering jobs. In U.S. electronics MNCs, the corresponding figures were 1.8 percent for clerical jobs and 0.5 percent for engineering jobs. The figures for European and other MNCs were 1.4 percent and 1.9 percent respectively (Koryu Kyokai 1987:22).

This dependence on dispatched staff affects the promotion prospects of local staff. The greater the dependence on dispatched staff, the harder it is to recruit competent local staff, who are able to find jobs with better opportunities for promotion elsewhere. A vicious cycle is created. Since internal promotion from employee to manager is one of the most crucial elements of so-called Japanese management (creating a sense of unity within the company), not hiring, or promoting, local engineers and clerical staff obstructs the transfer of authority to local employees. Thus, the firms' global strategies have a contradictory aspect: the frequent change in products and technical expertise required to attain the high levels of efficiency necessitates that the company hire Japanese engineers, which impedes the longer-term effectiveness of the transplants because they are unable to retain some of their most competent local managers. The high ratio of dispatched staff to local staff is characteristic of Japanese multinationals and reflects the global division of business functions and the conditions imposed by the global products strategy on the management of the transplants.

Adjusting to Fluctuations in Exports: Transplant TB

As mentioned earlier, transplant TB was established in 1969. Company B fully owned the plant. The initial goal of the transplant was to export radios and TVs to the United States, taking advantage of the cheap labor in Taiwan. Since its establishment, the plant has specialized in exports to the United States, Europe, and Japan.

In Taiwan, there are three types of TV manufacturers. The largest group is composed of MNC transplants, which concentrate solely on exports. This is a legal obligation of plants located in the special export zone. The production volume of these manufacturers amounted to 70 percent of total TV production in Taiwan in 1984. The second group of TV manufacturers is composed of transplants whose production is directed toward the domestic market, usually in a joint venture with local enterprises. Transplant TA is in this group. The third group is composed of local companies that produce for domestic and export markets, most of which have concluded technical agreements with Japanese MNCs.

TV production in Taiwan is predominantly for export. In 1988, the ratio of exports to total production was 92 percent. Rising wage rates and appreciation of the New Taiwan dollar since the mid-1980s have dampened exports, however, and led to a decline in total TV production.

Transplant TB has experienced product changes, as mentioned above. As shown in table 10.1, among its products, as of 1990, were CTVs, including the chassis, displays, projection TV chassis, compact disc players, stereo sets, and radio cassette recorders.

When transplant TB opened, its Japanese president intended to introduce the parent company's style of production. The plant adopted the parent plant's work methods and relied on Japanese engineers for production engineering and design. With the exception of the personnel department, Japanese staff occupied senior management positions. Five years later, however, management decided that local staff should be assigned to the senior positions in each department; Japanese employees would continue as president and vice presidents.

As of 1990, the plant had seven departments: finance, general affairs, materials, manufacturing, design, quality assurance, and production control. Unlike the parent plant, transplant TB does not have a sales or product development department; this reflects the global division of functions mentioned earlier. Furthermore, the design department concentrates on modifying basic designs, which are developed by the parent plant to meet the needs of the transplant's market and manufacturing abilities.

Table 10.1. Characteristics of Transplant TB (Taiwan) and Transplant MA (Malaysia), 1990

	Transplant TB	*Transplant MA*
Start-up date	May 1969	May 1988
No. of employees	960	635
No. of Japanese staff	9	32
Products	CTVs, stereos, displays, CDs, radio cassette recorders	CTVs
Market	Export	Export
Production volume	80,000 sets and 230,000 chassis	600,000 sets
Recruitment	Regularly: new high school graduates; occasionally: other	Occasional
Labor turnover	35%	72%
Promotion system	Internal	Internal and external
Pay system	Qualification and personal evaluation	Job grade and personal evaluation
Employee representation	In-house union	No union (anticipated recognition of industrial union)

Source: Interviews.

Local staff manage each department, although Japanese nationals have been made the managers of the finance department and the manufacturing department. In the former department, this occurred because the local manager died. In the case of the manufacturing department, the president wished to strengthen the management team by putting a Japanese employee in charge.

In 1989, the transplant employed 1,080 persons. The number of Japanese staff, including the president, was seven in 1970, fifteen in 1974, ten in 1979, ten in 1984, and ten in 1989. Of the total work force, Japanese staff represented 1.7 percent in 1970, 0.9 percent in 1974, 0.7 percent in 1979, 0.8 percent in 1984, and 0.9 percent in 1989. The proportion has therefore remained relatively stable for fifteen years. As of 1990, there were six Japanese engineers, one for quality assurance, one for production engineering, and four for design.

Recruitment and Promotion

In Taiwan, the labor market has been tight and mobility of labor has been high. Wages are set at the company level, but because of the high turnover among workers, wage differentials tend not to increase.

Similar to the parent company, the transplant recruits new high school graduates regularly. Because labor turnover is much higher than at the parent plant, the transplant also recruits workers who have had experience in other companies. The turnover rate for this plant is about 35 percent per year, whereas it is 1 percent for male workers at the parent plant and 4.2 percent for female workers. Regular recruitment of new high school graduates appears to be unique to Taiwan and Japan.

Transplant TB has an arrangement with a high school near the plant whereby management can hire girls from the school, who study and work in rotation, on the condition that management will pay their school expenses. The aim of this program is to secure a loyal work force. About 120 girls from the school work in the plant.

The production volume of the plant is subject to market fluctuations. As noted earlier, the parent company's global strategy leads to frequent changes in products and markets. Seasonal fluctuations in demand are also significant. The production volume in the first quarter of the year is half the peak volume, which occurs in the third quarter of the year, before Christmas sales.

Work force adjustments to meet the fluctuations in demand are made by having employees work overtime, employing temporary workers, encouraging voluntary retirement, and taking advantage of the high turnover. The plant has encouraged voluntary retirement on several occasions when business suddenly slackened. The plant does not recruit workers for specific jobs, and it is not uncommon for workers to be shifted to other jobs as a result of a downturn in demand.

The plant relies on newspaper advertisements and personal connections to recruit engineers. Because companies in Taiwan cannot recruit new graduates—since they are required to enter military service following graduation—management has difficulty recruiting sufficient numbers of engineers.

Internal promotion is the norm at the plant. The managerial hierarchy is as follows: president, vice president, plant superintendent, department manager, section manager, chief of branch, and team leader. All senior positions are, in principle, filled by internal promotion. Furthermore, many department managers and section managers have experienced managers or chiefs or team leaders in departments or sections other than their own as subordinates. This is less true of the finance department and quality assurance section.

Although there are opportunities for advancement, some managers and team leaders still resign. In fact, more than a few managers and leaders have moved to other companies. In the case of chiefs of branches and team leaders, two or three, on average, leave the plant each year.

Education and Training

The plant has had an education program since 1979. Workers undergo training in basic skills, including soldering and screwing. There are four grades based on skill certificate examinations. The first and second grades are approved by management according to national standards and the third and fourth grades according to company standards. Employees who pass an examination are entitled to a skill allowance, which varies according to grade. The accumulated number of successful applicants reached 901 for soldering and 352 for screwing in 1985.

Employees at the chief of branch level undergo a management training program modeled on the system at the parent plant. In addition, each year several employees are sent to the parent plant for training. The accumulated number of such employees reached 111 in 1984. In other words, on average, 7.4 persons were dispatched each year.

Qualification and Wage System

The plant has a qualification system similar to that of the parent company (see Tokunaga, Nomura, and Hiramoto 1991). Courses are divided into clerical and managerial courses and worker and engineer courses. Each course has several qualifications, and qualifications are divided into grades. Qualifications roughly correspond to positions and functions in the managerial hierarchy. For example, in the qualification system reformed in 1979, the section manager is positioned at the qualification known as Fuku-Kanrishi (vice managerial master, according to the Japanese translation of the Chinese script). Some vice section managers are also positioned as Fuku-Kanrishi, but some are positioned as Jori-Kanrishi (junior managerial master). This is a qualification just under the former one. Chiefs of branch are also positioned as Jori-Kanrishi or Kōkyu-Jimuin (senior clerk). The latter is a qualification immediately below Jori-Kanrishi. Team leaders are positioned as Kōkyu-Jimuin.

An employee's treatment, including his pay, is determined by his qualification, not by his position in the managerial hierarchy or the job. Newcomers are positioned in a particular grade with a qualification consistent with their education, their results on the company's entrance examination, and an appraisal based on an interview. A specific proportion of employees are promoted to a higher grade or qualification every year.

Wages are determined primarily by qualification and evaluation of individual performance, based on the following calculation: standard monthly earnings = basic wage + additional wage + various allowances (commutation allowance, housing allowance, nonabsence service allowance, and so on). An individual's basic wage reflects his qualification and an evaluation of his individual performance. The additional wage is 20 percent of the basic wage, although this varies from a minimum of 16 percent to a maximum of 24 percent, according to the individual's evaluation, which is based on monthly performance using criteria such as rate of attendance, product defect rate, and the working to nonworking ratio of the machine for which the person is responsible. The allowances are fixed amounts. In addition to this monthly wage, bonuses, based on an individual's basic wage and a performance evaluation, are paid twice a year.

A person's initial pay and annual increase, in particular, are strongly influenced by the surrounding wage level. Among the transplants surveyed, the wage system used in Taiwan bears the closest resemblance to that of the parent companies, in that it is determined by qualification and personnel evaluation (Nomura 1992).[4] The wage systems in the other transplants tend to be based more on the nature of the jobs.

Using the same system does not necessarily produce the same effects, however. For example, it is common for workers to show the results of their performance evaluations to one another in Taiwan, something that rarely happens in Japan. As a result, supervisors in the Taiwanese transplant are reluctant to reward high-performance workers more than low-performance workers.

Labor-Management Relations

Generally speaking, the Japanese transplants prefer in-house unions. The Taiwan plant recognizes an in-house union, which was established in 1980 under the guidance of the administrative office of the special exporting area. All employees are, in principle, obliged to participate in the union, which consists of seventy to seventy-five groups, corresponding roughly to workshops. The union's fifteen officials—all of whom are paid by management—are elected by representatives of each workshop. These officials do not work for the union full time; rather, they are permitted to engage in union duties at particular times during working hours. Most officials are chiefs of branches or team leaders.

The union's demands focus on higher wages, higher bonuses, and employees' welfare. Management has had good relations with the union. The plant was awarded the prize for good labor-management relationship by the administrative office of the special exporting area in 1981.

Quality circle activities have been conducted since 1980. In 1984, there were sixty-nine circles in which 1,083 people participated. Between 1980 and 1984, circles from the plant won prizes at the national tournament of quality circles seventeen times.

Since 1978, employees have been encouraged to submit suggestions of ways to improve production. The number of suggestions per person increased from 0.3 in 1978 to 2.0 in 1982 and to 12.9 in 1984.

Manufacturing Process and Productivity: PCB Assembly Line

In our investigation of the printed circuit board assembly lines in the transplants and their parent plants, we found significant differences in the manufacturing process. First, compared with the insertion lines in Japan, on which odd-shaped parts are inserted by robots, those in the transplants involve automated insertion of only axial and radial parts. The insertion machines or robots for odd-shaped parts are deemed unprofitable in the transplants, mainly because of the cheap labor in the local market and the small scale of production. Insertion of odd-shaped parts in the transplants is thus done manually. Second, PCB assembly subcontracting, which amounts to about half the total work volume in Japan, is hardly ever done outside that country (Hiramoto 1992).

Organization of the PCB assembly section in transplant TB is similar to that of the parent plant. It consists of three branches: assembly, quality assurance, and machine maintenance. The assembly branch inserts axial parts and radial parts into PCBs, using insertion machines, in a three-shift system. The machine maintenance branch is in charge of maintaining the insertion machines.

There is a skill-formation order among the jobs in the assembly section. The most basic job is that of the operator of the assembly branch, who operates about two automated insertion machines. Her (about 60 percent of the operators are female) job is to supply parts, set up the machines, operate them, cope with simple machine troubles, and do basic machine maintenance. Workers in the quality assurance branch (all female) and in the machine maintenance branch (all male) work as operators for a few years. Team leader and chief of branch positions are filled by internal promotion.

The labor turnover rate in the automated assembly section is the highest in the plant, and particularly high among the operators. The annual average turnover rate in this section is 76 percent. The average length of service in this section is 2.1 years, compared with 12 years for the corresponding section at the parent plant. The reason for the high rate is said to be, first, the disadvantages associated with shift work; second, the low wages; and third, the monotony of the work.

The section manager has devised three countermeasures in response to the dissatisfaction. First, he supplies earplugs to operators to cut down on the noise. Second, he ensures that the plant's pay levels are commensurate with those of other companies. Third, he promotes competition among operators by comparing their records of performance and, at the same time, training employees with good records. The most competent workers can expect to be promoted to the maintenance branch.

The productivity of the section seems low compared with that of the parent plant. Thus, if we take mean time between failures (MTBF) of the

automated machines as an indicator, the MTBF of the insertion machine
for axial parts, on average, is 17 minutes at the transplant compared with
120 minutes for the parent plant; that of the machine for radial parts is 12
minutes compared with 85 to 90 minutes for the parent plant. This means
that the output of the machines at the transplant is much lower than that
of the parent plant and suggests that the number of workers per machine
is considerably higher than at the parent plant. The output per person
therefore appears to be much lower than at the parent plant.

According to an analysis by the manager of the automated assembly
section, there are five reasons for the differences in MTBF between the two
plants. First, and most significant, the machines are maintained differently.
This explains about 50 percent of the difference in MTBF. To raise the
operation ratio of the machines, workers must maintain them. For example, they must change machine parts before they fail. Regularly exchanging
parts, as described in the manual, does not necessarily work well. Experience must be gained in maintenance; this is knowledge that goes beyond
that contained in the manual. The high turnover rate among workers
hinders the accumulation of such know-how.

Second, the insertion machine at the parent plant is improved after
installation to increase its efficiency. Workers in the machine maintenance
branch of the parent plant are so skillful that they can remodel a machine
to achieve efficiency beyond the supplier's specification. Workers in transplant TB are less skilled at making such improvements; this explains about
20 percent of the difference in MTBF.

Third, local parts are of poor quality. For example, the unevenness of
the tape produced by a local supplier produces more insertion errors than
in Japan. This explains about 10 percent of the difference in MTBF.

Fourth, machine adjustment is not done as well by transplant TB's
workers as by the parent plant's workers. Fifth, and finally, the narrower
space between the parts to be inserted in the transplant contributes to the
lower MTBF. The space between parts in the transplant is 4.5 mm, versus
5 mm in the parent plant. The machines at both plants can insert parts at
a distance of 4.5 mm, but the smaller space inevitably causes more errors.
In the parent plant, the insertion section strongly demanded that the space
between the parts should be at least 5 mm.[5]

To sum up, the difference in MTBF, and hence labor productivity, can
be attributed mainly to differences between the transplant and the parent
company in the workers' skills and accumulation of experience and knowledge; these differences are strongly related to the difference in the length
of service of employees in the two plants.

Toward "Best Quality in the World": Transplant MA in Malaysia

Transplant MA was established in 1988 when company A implemented
a global plan; this plan constrains management behavior in the plant. All

items that the transplant produces are exported. Company A has another transplant in Malaysia that was established in the 1960s and that supplies various electric and electronics products, including TVs, to the domestic market and some products for export. Including these two plants, company A and its affiliated company in Japan had eleven transplants in Malaysia in 1990. Transplant MA specializes in exports. This is true of all the other transplants except one established early on to serve the domestic market. Company A's transplants account for an estimated 3 percent of Malaysia's gross national product ("Japanese Access," 1993).

The main aim of transplant MA is to produce highly competitive products, but it has several additional goals: to maintain a profitable business, to promote local business by training local staff, to help transplants producing TVs in the surrounding countries advance their technological base, and to help all plants, including the parent division, procure parts.

The motto of transplant MA is "The Best Quality in the World from Malaysia." The parent company's managers believe that the most important factor determining competitiveness in world markets is product quality. Since products from this plant are intended to substitute for Japanese exports, the plant emphasizes quality. Management attempts to convince employees of the importance of quality by maintaining that better quality means lower cost, a larger profit, increased prosperity for the plant, and, thus, greater national prosperity. This strategy is based on company A's philosophy that supplying products of good quality at cheap prices in large quantities will enhance the prosperity of Malaysian society.

The plant is well endowed with machinery and equipment. One reason is the large volume of items produced; another is that the automated line is necessary to maintain product quality. The plant has introduced the latest machines, including some that the parent plant in Japan has not yet installed. Again, achieving product quality is the goal. Such machines could not have been introduced if the company had taken a narrow economic perspective, because the wage level in Malaysia is approximately one-seventh that in Japan. It is noteworthy that the TV production line of another domestic-oriented transplant in Malaysia is less well equipped and less automated than transplant MA. The latter plant has almost double the equipment investment of the other transplant.

The transplant's strategy is reflected in its organization, illustrated in figure 10.1.

Transplant MA has an R&D center, which develops and designs transplant MA's products, and an international procurement office (IPO). The operation of the IPO is directly related to the company's global strategy. Thus, the IPO buys parts for both the transplant and for TV plants in other countries, thereby purchasing parts more cheaply by buying in large quantities. The IPO also tests and approves new parts that have been imported for use in the transplant.

252 *Atsushi Hiramoto*

Figure 10.1. Organization of Transplant MA, in Malaysia, 1990

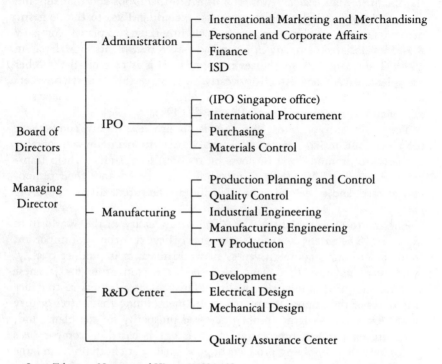

Administration
 ─ International Marketing and Merchandising
 ─ Personnel and Corporate Affairs
 ─ Finance
 ─ ISD

IPO
 ─ (IPO Singapore office)
 ─ International Procurement
 ─ Purchasing
 ─ Materials Control

Board of Directors
 |
Managing Director

Manufacturing
 ─ Production Planning and Control
 ─ Quality Control
 ─ Industrial Engineering
 ─ Manufacturing Engineering
 ─ TV Production

R&D Center
 ─ Development
 ─ Electrical Design
 ─ Mechanical Design

Quality Assurance Center

Source: Tokunaga, Nomura, and Hiramoto 1991:158.

Figure 10.1 also shows that Japanese staff occupy most management positions in the transplant's sections and departments. Local staff occupy only the positions of manager of the personnel and corporate affairs section and of the production planning and control section. This is partly because this plant has not had enough time to train competent local staff. In addition, the management in Japan has been reluctant to entrust the plant to local staff given the emphasis on product quality. In contrast, at another Malaysian transplant owned by the same company, local staff have been assigned as managers of each department, except for the positions of managing director and executive directors, which are held by Japanese nationals.

Recruitment and Promotion

In Malaysia, the labor market is linked with the educational system. Recruitment, job responsibilities, and rewards are based on a person's school record. Transplant MA follows this practice. The plant divides its employees (in this plant, all employees are called staff) into nonexecutive and executive groups. The nonexecutive category consists of manual and clerical workers and supervisors; the executive category consists of managers. The nonexecutives are divided into seven grades, from A to H, each of which corresponds roughly to job sets. For example, general workers and gardeners are ranked grade H; technician 6, clerk 6, operations staff 6, and production staff 3 are ranked grade F; technician 4, clerk 4, operation staff 4, production staff 1, and electronic data processing staff 4 are ranked grade G; foreman, technician 1, confidential staff 1, and operation staff 1 are ranked grade A. Subcategories, for example, production staff, clerk, operation staff, technician, and data processing staff, are each divided into several steps. Similarly, executives have eight categories.

A person without a lower-school certificate is recruited and ranked as grade H, while an employee with a recognized lower-school certificate is ranked grade G; one with a recognized school certificate is ranked grade F; one with a recognized higher school certificate is ranked grade E; one with a recognized diploma or certificate is ranked grade D or grade C, according to the person's school and qualifications.

Recruitment is usually done through newspaper advertisements. So far, recruitment has not been difficult. The labor turnover rate, however, is considerable. Generally speaking, workers in Malaysia change jobs to obtain higher wages. Of the 200 employees who were recruited in April 1989, when the plant began operating, 144 had left by the end of June 1990. In other words, 72 percent left the company in fifteen months. The reasons given for leaving were "entrance into a school of higher grade" (31 percent), "absence without due notice" (26 percent), "job-hopping" (10 percent), and "other" (33 percent). One hundred and six people (74 percent) of the 144 left the company within the probationary period (in the first six months). At the end of June 1990, there were 635 employees, of whom 476 were direct workers, 127 were indirect workers, and 32 were Japanese staff. The average age of employees is twenty-three years. The ratio of male to female employees is 53 percent to 47 percent.

The Malaysian government asks firms to employ ethnic Malay staff in the same ratio as they are represented in the population. The ratio of ethnic Malay employees in this transplant is 66 percent, slightly higher than the requested level.

It is company policy to promote suitably qualified current staff from within the organization. If, in the opinion of senior plant management, there are no suitably qualified candidates for a vacant position, however, workers are recruited from outside. It is clear that employees prefer internal promotion, but management cannot depend totally on this arrangement given that the plant is still at an early stage in its development.

The terms and conditions of service specify that employees may be transferred within the organization to any other unit of company A in Malaysia. In fact, six skilled workers—a foreman, three assistant foremen, and two line leaders—were transferred from the domestic-oriented trans-plant to this plant when it commenced operations.

Education and Training

As mentioned above, the plant promotes the use of local staff. Their education and training are central to this goal. To operate the heavily equipped and up-to-date line efficiently, employee training, especially for maintenance staff (engineers and technicians), is particularly important. The plant has a program called the Human 21 Campaign, which consists of education and training in technological and managerial skills. Training is based on a five-year module.

Management also promotes a particular corporate culture via a scheme known as GEMS, which stands for "Greeting, Etiquette, Manner, and Smile." Japanese managers think it is important to develop an employee's disposition and to foster a corporate culture that will generate a sense of unity between employer and employees and maintain product quality.

Working Hours

The standard workweek in the plant is forty-four hours. By law, employees may not work more than sixty-four hours of overtime per month. The average total annual overtime per person was sixty-three hours in fiscal year 1989. There are no limits, other than the legal limit, on overtime, since the plant has not yet recognized a union. And even when the plant does recognize a union, it is unlikely that management will make an agreement to limit overtime, given that no such agreement has been made between the domestic-oriented transplant and its recognized union, the Electrical Industry Workers.

Employees cannot refuse an order for overtime without sufficient reason, even when the order is given on the day the overtime work will be executed. The same condition exists in the unionized, domestic-oriented transplant.

Payment System

Wages are determined by grade in the case of nonexecutives and by category in the case of executives; workers also receive individual perform-ance evaluations. Evaluation is done annually for every employee, and items on the evaluation differ according to job. For example, the relevant items for production staff are knowledge and skill, understanding, respon-sibility, speed and correctness, and work attitude and interpersonal skills. According to the total points reached by adding the points for each item together, production staff are assigned a category from A to E.

Each grade has a minimum wage. An employee will receive the minimum wage plus an amount based on the results of his or her performance evaluation. The percentage wage increase for employees in each rank changes from year to year; however, an employee's wage cannot exceed a maximum for his or her grade. In addition, general wage increases are provided annually. If the plant recognizes a union, the wage system will change slightly. In the case of the domestic-oriented transplant, for example, the labor agreement is revised every three years, as is common in Malaysia, so that there is a fixed annual increase for three years. Thereafter, increases based on performance are left to management's discretion.

Pay differentials between employees who have different educational qualifications are larger in the transplant than in the parent company. In 1985, the initial salary of a university graduate was, on average, 1.31 times that of a high school graduate in the parent company. The initial salary of a person who had a university diploma in the plant (grade C) was 1.81 times that of an employee who had a recognized school certificate (grade F) and 1.58 times that of an employee who had a recognized higher school certificate (grade E). Because educational qualifications influence promotion significantly, these pay differentials exist throughout the company.

Bonuses are also paid, but at the sole discretion of plant management. In 1989, everyone received at least double the sum of their December wage. People who received good results on their performance evaluations were paid more. Employees with excellent evaluations could receive a maximum of three times their December wage.

Overtime is paid at the legal rate of 50 percent above normal rates and at more than 100 percent for holiday work.

Wages and working conditions are supposedly rigid in Malaysia. The Malaysian-Japanese Chamber of Commerce and Industry warns Japanese companies considering investing in Malaysia that working conditions, once decided upon, are understood to be rights, whether a company has recognized a union or not, and that it is very difficult to alter working conditions even when business deteriorates.

Labor-Management Relations

Management intends to recognize the Electrical Industry Workers' Union (EIWU) when a planned extension of the plant is complete. The Malaysian government sanctions the presence of industrial unions in the electrical industry but advises companies in the electronics industry not to recognize a union or to recognize an in-house union only. The plant describes itself as belonging to the electrical industry, so that it is certain to recognize the EIWU.

In 1990, the EIWU had a membership of about fifteen thousand, covering some forty-five companies. The employees of Japanese transplants constituted the majority of the members. About ten thousand employees in twelve Japanese transplants belong to the EIWU. The union estimates that union density in the industry is about 50 percent.

The EIWU has a policy of enlisting all employees of a company when the union gains recognition from management. Thus, all employees of the domestic-oriented transplant are union members, although the labor agreement does not include a union shop clause. Management collects union dues on behalf of the union.

Working conditions are not likely to change drastically when transplant MA recognizes the EIWU, because all transplants of company A attempt to maintain equal working conditions. Transplant managers meet regularly to exchange information about labor and management. In addition, transplant MA tries to offer the same conditions to its employees as other Japanese transplants offer.

What is clear, however, is that union recognition will impose a burden on management. Unlike unions in Japan, the EIWU is reputed to make heavy demands in negotiations with companies, regardless of their feasibility. Such conduct is deemed dishonorable in Japan. Consequently, a company that recognizes the EIWU typically spends considerable time—as much as half a year—revising its labor agreement.

To improve understanding between management and the employees, management at transplant MA has introduced several committees. There is the industry hygiene and safety committee, the environment committee, the cafeteria committee, the sports and recreation committee, the suggestion committee, the QC committee, and the big sister society. The big sister society—which is modeled on the same society at the parent company—matches senior female employees, called big sisters, with female newcomers.

QC activities are undertaken every Wednesday after working hours for one hour, and workers who are involved are paid at the normal overtime rate. All direct workers belong to circles organized in each workshop (e.g., maintenance, repair, and so on). One circle consists of seven or eight people. The leader of a circle is usually the line leader, who is the person in the position just under the assistant foreman, or the assistant line leader. Company A transplants organize a presentation meeting of QCs every year.

Manufacturing Process for PCB Assembly

Figure 10.2 shows the organization of the TV production section. Since this plant uses the most up-to-date machines, the auto-insertion ratio (number of auto-inserted parts in relation to all parts) in the automated insertion section of PCB assembly is almost the same as that of the parent plant. Automated insertion is done in three shifts. A, B, and C in figure

Figure 10.2. Organization of the TV Production Section at Transplant MA, in Malaysia, 1990

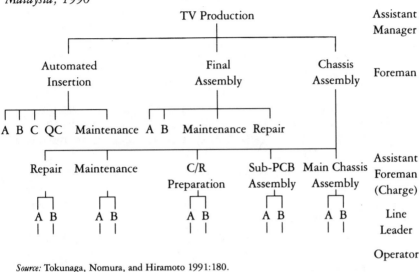

10.2 represent the operating groups that are in charge of each shift. One operator is in charge of, on average, five machines. The maintenance group is in charge of machine maintenance, and the QC group is in charge of making numerical control tape, quality control, and material control. These two groups work in two shifts.

The plant emphasizes maintenance activity in an effort to operate the heavily equipped lines as effectively as possible. Five technicians, including assistant technicians, are posted at automated insertion and five at final assembly. In addition, skilled workers inspect for quality and repair and are posted at each shop. As noted earlier, the most competent production workers are selected and trained as maintenance and repair staff. Japanese nationals are in charge of their education and training. Four production staff were trained at the parent plant for three months.

The plant recommends the development of an exhaustive manual, and technical and production staff are asked to create the manual themselves. For example, there is a manual for coping with machine problems. This is written in a flow chart style so that a worker can repair a problem by answering "yes" or "no" questions. When mechanical trouble occurs that is not described in the manual, the maintenance worker who repairs it must make an entry in the manual. This is not confined to skilled workers. Even at the manual insertion shop, each production employee is required to record any problems in daily work and how they were resolved. The aim of creating the manual is to transfer the know-how of competent workers to other workers, so that if the competent workers leave the organization, the know-how will remain in the plant. The system also is a means of coping with job-hopping, which is especially prevalent in Malaysia.

An education corner has been established showing the overall flow of production, the work content of each shop, and the operation rate and defect rate of each process. This serves to clarify each position in the plant and its influence on succeeding positions and processes. The education corner encourages information sharing between employees.

Thorough inspections of parts and products are undertaken to maintain quality. The plant does incoming inspections of parts by sampling, an exercise no longer done in the parent plant, because the defect rate for parts made in Japan is low compared with the rate in transplants in Southeast Asia. After incoming inspections, all assembled PCBs are subjected to further inspection, as are all assembled chassis. Finally, finished products are inspected by sampling.

The belief that rigorous parts and products inspections are necessary to sustain quality prevailed in the parent plant thirty years ago. Management of the parent plant now believes that quality must be maintained within the line. Management at transplant MA looks forward to being able to decrease the number of inspections in the future, commensurate with the training and skill enhancement of local staff.

The performance of the PCB assembly line seemed to be a little worse than that of the parent plant. We could not gather exact data, but two points suggest this conclusion. First, the operation rate of the automated insertion machines was 75 to 77 percent, which was lower than that of the parent plant by 3 to 4 percentage points. The Japanese manager at the transplant stated that the difference was mainly due to the inferior maintenance standards. Second, the cumulative process defect rate of 3 percent was double the rate of the parent plant. At the same time, the defect rate for products was almost the same as that of the parent plant. This means that extra work is being done in the transplant to rectify defects in products and thereby keep the quality at the same level as in the parent plant.

Conclusion

It is clear from my research that transplants TB and MA intended to introduce Japanese-style management. This was especially true of transplant TB; in the case of transplant MA, a strong emphasis on the need for high-quality products and the need to operate an automated line—both of which arose from the company's global strategy—have, so far, made the plant deeply dependent on Japanese staff and the Japanese management system.

The following aspects of the Japanese management system have been transferred to the two transplants. In the case of transplant TB, these include regular recruitment of new graduates of high schools; the formation of a job hierarchy and associated qualification requirements; the introduction of an educational and training system; internal promotion of managers and supervisors; ease in making job changes; the development of a performance evaluation system; regular payment of bonuses; small-group activities; and the establishment of an in-house union. The internal promotion system, the ease in making job changes, the educational and training system, the performance evaluation system, the regular payment of bonuses, and small-group activities also exist at transplant MA. In addition, this plant has a strong orientation toward quality, a production line that has the most modern automated machines, an R&D center, a corporate culture based on improving personal habits, and no regulation of overtime, all of which are associated with the Japanese system. Transplant MA, however, does not regularly recruit new high school graduates, and it does not have a qualification-based wage system or an in-house union. These three points represent major differences between the two plants from the standpoint of labor management. In short, with regard to strategy and structure, transplant MA more closely resembles the parent plant than does transplant TB. Regarding labor management, however, transplant TB is more like the parent plant. The labor system of transplant MA is more like that of a Western organization.

Our survey of ten transplants in Asia and Europe shows that all the transplants have a system for internal promotion. Payment of bonuses and small-group activities, with one or two exceptions, are also common. Performance evaluation systems and in-house unionism are substantially affected by the structure of the local labor market and are therefore not so easily installed in transplants. Among the transplants surveyed, one in Singapore and one in the United Kingdom do not use performance evaluation. Regular recruitment of new high school graduates and qualification systems are rare, except in the Taiwanese transplants. Thus, it seems that personnel management in the Taiwanese transplants most closely resembles that in Japan.

The two cases discussed in this chapter suggest that tight local labor markets have a significant limiting effect on the transfer of some aspects of Japanese management to Asian transplants. Thus, in Taiwan, the turnover rates are high, in spite of various measures, such as the internal promotion system, wage increases that correspond to length of service, and welfare facilities, to redress the problem. The high turnover rate is uncharacteristic of the "Japanese system." So-called lifetime employment for core workers and the existence of a segmented internal labor market are assumed to be basic elements of the Japanese system, as J. C. Abegglen (1958, chap. 2) first noted. The high turnover rate does not, however, unduly concern the management of the transplants because production volumes tend to fluctu-

ate so substantially that management is at times obliged to curtail
employment, as in the case of transplant TB. There is no doubt that the
plant would have resorted more often to voluntary retirement without the
high rate of turnover. As noted earlier, the fluctuation in volume stems
from the company's global strategy and the seasonality of the market. The
virtual absence of subcontracting functions as a buffer to such fluctuations
in large companies operating in Japan.

Moreover, a similar system does not necessarily assure a similar result.
This is partly because internal promotion at transplant TB is limited to
relatively few, highly committed employees. Management performance is
apparently weaker at the transplant. For example, the Japanese president
of transplant TB has complained about the limited knowledge and experience of local managers and leaders regarding jobs adjacent to their own. In
his opinion, Japanese managers have wider knowledge and experience.
Thus, in terms of job ability, a Japanese manager or supervisor of a certain
rank is equivalent to a member of the local staff who is one or two ranks
higher. This reflects limitations in the internal training and promotion
systems and in the capacity of local staff.

The performance evaluation system also appears to have a different effect
on workers in transplant TB. It is said that workers in Taiwan place more
importance on relations between themselves than on relations with their
superiors (Wang and Haraguchi 1990:61–62). Competition between workers—fostered in part by the performance evaluation system in Japan—
seems to have less effect on performance in Taiwan.

Small-group activities occur in almost all transplants. In contrast to the
situation in Japan, however, management must pay for the time devoted
to this activity. Furthermore, employees of the transplants seem to devote
less energy to group activities than do Japanese employees. Certainly,
group activities in the East Asian transplants do not have as positive results
for management as in Japan.

In sum, the extent to which Japanese-style management is practiced in
Japanese transplants does not necessarily correlate with plant performance.
We were unable to collect systematic data on performance, but two
examples are worth noting. The first example involves a comparison of the
MTBF rates for the automated insertion machines in three transplants of
company B. The MTBF rates for the insertion machine for axial parts and
for the machine for radial parts were seventeen minutes and twelve minutes
respectively in transplant TB, compared with eighty minutes and forty
minutes in the transplant in Singapore and less than ten minutes in the
United Kingdom.

The management at the Singapore transplant appears to have been less
eager to introduce the Japanese management system than the management
at transplant TB. Accordingly, the system is less in evidence there. The
annual labor turnover rate is very high (from 40 to 74 percent between

1987 and 1990); internal promotion of workers is limited to a particular position; and an employee recruited as a worker can be promoted to supervisor but not to assistant manager. The plant's wage system is very simple, based as it is on an employee's trade and not on a performance evaluation. Nevertheless, its MTBF is superior to that of the other plants.

According to the Japanese president of the plant in Singapore, this good performance mainly reflects the use of comparatively new machines, encouraged by the Singapore government's tax incentives for new capital investment. Another reason is the good maintenance. In the opinion of the Japanese manager of the parent plant, the maintenance performances in Taiwan and Singapore are comparatively good. Which of these two factors is more important is difficult to say, but what is clear is that MTBF rates do not correlate with the extent to which the Japanese management system has been introduced.

The second example involves a comparison between company B's U.K. and German transplants. The transplant in Germany is apparently less eager to introduce the Japanese system. A German manager in charge of personnel affairs in the factory claims that the plant is operated along German lines. The recruitment method, wage system, and joint management council system (*Betriebs rat*) are based on the German system. Nevertheless, some Japanese elements, such as performance evaluation and small-group activities, have been introduced. Direct workers on the production line, for example, receive a blanket 50 points on their performance evaluations, which means the evaluations are not carried out according to Japanese norms; in other words, they are not used as a means of differentiating employees.

In contrast with the German plant, the U.K. transplant has endeavored to gain labor flexibility by removing various restrictive practices and introducing the following Japanese practices: representation by one union for all employees, tightened workplace discipline, and flexibility regarding jobs and duties. This was the only plant in our survey that had a Japanese personnel manager. This suggests that management was more eager to introduce the Japanese system than at the German transplant.

What have been the effects on performance? The transplant in the United Kingdom had a deficit for a long time. Only recently has it shown a small profit. The German plant, which was established in 1982, showed a profit soon after operations commenced. One cannot conclude very much from these findings because profit is affected by many factors other than labor management, but clearly a non-Japanese style of factory operation can contribute to good business results, even in Japanese MNCs. In this regard, it is noteworthy that in both transplants TB and MA the intention was to entrust management to local staff. For several reasons, this has not been fully implemented. First, the transplants have had difficulty securing competent engineers and managers through internal promotion given the tight local labor market, and second, as noted earlier, the global strategy of the parent company has imposed restrictions on internal promotion.

In conclusion, our survey shows that the transfer of the Japanese management system is constrained by factors that lie both within and outside the realm of the company. It thus remains an open question whether total transfer of the Japanese system contributes to high performance in overseas transplants.

Notes

Chapter 1. *Labor, Management, and Industrial Relations*

1. An important early contribution to the literature on MNCs and the relocation of employment from advanced to developing countries is Fröbel, Heinrichs, and Kreye 1980. For a useful critique, see Cohen 1991:125–49.

2. Neo-Taylorist patterns of workplace relations are discussed in chapter 8. Although there are variants on this ideal type, the main features of neo-Taylorism in relation to manual workers employed in large corporations are as follows: a clear hierarchical separation between managers (responsible for planning and directing) and workers (responsible for executing largely routinized tasks); a low level of functional integration; a detailed division of labor, including closely defined, narrow work roles; limited training for the acquisition of job-specific skills; direct forms of employee participation consistent with hierarchical organization; payment systems based largely on job definition rather than performance; and bureaucratic regulation of employment, which may include union representation.

3. The concept of industrialization should be qualified in two ways. First, beyond a certain point, the industrial sector tends to decline relative to services, so that the process of industrialization is more applicable to societies whose secondary sectors are continuing to expand relative to manufacturing. Second, the term "industrialization" is often used synonymously with "economic development," implying that industrialization is a virtuous process. But development can come at great human and environmental cost, and the fruits of economic growth can be very unequally distributed. Thus, the concept of industrialization does not necessarily imply progress.

4. According to G. Gereffi (1990:17), development patterns vary according to the types of industries that are most prominent during various phases of industrialization, the extent to which these industries are oriented toward exports or import substitution, and the major economic agents that implement and sustain development.

5. Kerr argues that "in patterns of work life the jobs and rules governing work are mostly similar from nation to nation and from one type of society to the other. And in the workplace there now seem to be some nearly universal trends toward more emphasis on seniority on the job, more participation in workplace decisions, and more options in such arrangements as work time and the use of fringe benefits" (1983:54–55).

6. This is a controversial thesis. For a critique, see Berggren 1992, chap. 13.

7. This is less true of the entrepôt cities of Hong Kong and Singapore. As

indicated in table 1.1, these economies derive substantial income from services such as banking and transportation. Note too that the value of foreign trade exceeds domestic transactions in these two societies (col. 6, table 1.1).

8. This is elaborated in Joffe, Maller, and Webster's analysis in chapter 5. Maree and Godfrey (chap. 6) point out that the transition to majority rule and the integration of South Africa into the world economy are inextricably connected. Political and economic changes therefore appear to be having a profound impact on economic restructuring and industrial relations in that country.

9. A fourth reason concerns similarities between South Africa and Malaysia that invite detailed comparative analysis, a task that lies beyond the confines of this book. Thus, as indicated in table 1.1, both countries are at similar levels of economic development but remain dependent on exports of primary commodities and hence are sensitive to disruption, including industrial conflict, in key industries. The two countries are ethnically divided between a minority that enjoys considerable economic power and a majority whose interests are advanced through political means. This has taken the form of positive discrimination in Malaysia (the Bumiputra policy). In South Africa, something similar in form though not in content can be anticipated under a majority-rule government. As an aside, there is a direct tie between Malaysia and South Africa. Malay and Indonesian people were transported to the Cape as slaves, political outcasts, and free immigrants in the late seventeenth and eighteenth centuries. In 1991, there were an estimated 157,815 "coloured muslims" living in South Africa (personal communication, J. Maree, based on Midgley 1967 and 1991 population census).

10. It is noteworthy that the levels of education in Thailand have trailed those in Malaysia. One likely consequence has been severe skill shortages (World Bank 1993:43–77; Frenkel 1993a:33).

11. The authors are grateful to Johann Maree for drawing our attention to these differences.

Chapter 3. Industrial Relations Policy in Malaysia

1. Sharma suggests that there will be a political pattern of labor orientation in the least industrialized countries, a repressive pattern in semi-industrialized countries, and an accommodative pattern in newly industrialized countries.

2. Deyo (1989) emphasizes that the suppression of labor by the state was consequent to export-oriented industrialization in East Asia (Hong Kong, Singapore, Taiwan, and South Korea). He addresses the complex nexus between state authoritarianism, development policy, and union weakness.

3. European firms owned 83 percent of the land being cultivated, and British companies owned 60 percent of the mining firms, engaged in 60 to 70 percent of the external trade, and controlled 75 percent of the banking sector.

4. Foreigners continued to own 61.5 percent of corporate assets, although the Chinese and Indians' share increased to 23.7 percent.

5. There were many doubts about the viability of these big projects; in particular, critics argued that they would increase budget deficits. Clearly, there was some truth to these criticisms, insofar as the PROTON project had a capacity

of only 40 percent of the 200,000 units a year deemed necessary for economic viability in the auto industry (Bowie 1991).

6. Hourly compensation costs, calculated in 1989, suggest the following: (all figures are in U.S. dollars): United States, $8.32; Singapore, $1.58; Hong Kong, $1.33; South Korea, $1.19; Malaysia, $.84; Philippines, $.63; Thailand, $.43; and Indonesia, $.35.

7. The AFL-CIO has made two petitions to the U.S. government to revoke Malaysia's GSP status. The second petition, in 1990, was rejected by the U.S. Department of Trade, on the grounds that the petition did not contain substantially new information compared with the previous petition. It is likely that U.S. corporations operating in Malaysia successfully lobbied the government to retain Malaysia's GSP status (Grace 1990).

8. In contrast, workers in the electrical and consumer products industries (televisions, stereos) are allowed to affiliate with national unions, such as the Electrical Industry Workers' Union (EIWU). Support from the national union, which has established and experienced leaders, is critical to the growth of unions in the electronics sector, which is characterized by unskilled, mostly female labor with little trade union experience.

9. Mahathir Mohammed articulated his "Look East" policy in conjunction with the HIP. The essential aim of the policy was to emulate the industrial practices of Japan and Korea. The policy called for the introduction of Japanese institutions (such as enterprise unions) but also exhorted Malays to be more disciplined and productive, like their East Asian counterparts. See Bowie 1991 or Arudsothy and Littler 1993 for a description of the policy.

Chapter 4. Singapore's Industrial Relations System

1. From 1960 to 1987, Singapore's GNP increased at a compound rate of 8.3 percent per year, more than any member of the Organization for Economic Cooperation and Development (OECD). The GNP per capita increased at an annual compound growth rate of 6.5 percent, to a level that is the highest in Asia except for Japan (Porter 1990:22). Wages are also higher than in other Asian countries except for Japan. Singapore's quality-of-life indicators rank high in many categories in international comparison (Ministry of Trade and Industry 1991:24, 25). The rate of home ownership, for example, is the highest of any country, and the infrastructure of roads, subways, housing, hospitals, schools, and airport is well planned, modern, and clean.

2. These categories are commonly used to group IR policies (e.g., see Beer et al. 1984 and Dyer 1984).

3. Much of the survey data available did not break down the results by business sector, but the interviews, the limited data that were available by business sector, the overrepresentation of manufacturing organizations in the samples, and the fact that most manufacturing organizations are not large suggest that the overall results are generally true for manufacturing.

4. During 1989, workers, in fact, worked an average of 9.1 hours per week beyond their normal workweek (forty-four hours for many full-time workers) (Ministry of Labour 1989:89).

5. Amendments to the Employment Act have made it easier to adopt flexible work patterns, including multiple shifts.

6. For example, to expand the labor supply, employers are encouraged to use part-time employees, particularly to attract women into the labor market (the female labor force participation rate [LFPR] is about 50 percent, low in comparison with developed countries). A set of guidelines was developed to establish minimum conditions of employment for part-time employees (Ministry of Labour 1990). And policies covering such things as maternity leave and child-care arrangements were intended to improve the female LFPR. In international comparison, however, part-time workers comprise a much smaller proportion of the work force (3 percent compared with 12 percent for Japan, 17 percent for the United States, and 24 percent for Sweden) (National Wages Council [NWC] 1990). The NWC has recommended that the use of part-time employees be increased (1990).

The LFPR of older workers is also low based on international comparisons, in part because the retirement age is fifty-five: the LFPR for those between fifty-five and sixty-four years is only 36 percent, compared with 63 percent in Japan, 55 percent in the United States, and 70 percent in Sweden (NWC 1990). Again, to enhance the nation's labor supply, the government has extended its retirement age to sixty, and the NWC has recommended that private employers do the same (1989). Contributions to the Central Provident Fund for workers over fifty-five have been reduced to encourage employers to raise the retirement age (NWC 1988).

Foreign guest workers also may be used to expand the labor supply. They make up 12 percent of the labor force, mainly in low-skill service, textile, electronics, ship-repairing, and construction firms (Wilkinson and Leggett 1985:11). The government's desire to phase out the use of foreign guest workers has been hedged in the face of the tight labor market, and the requirements for employing foreign guest workers have been relaxed.

7. The institutions of higher education are the National University of Singapore (NUS), Nanyang Technological Institute, Singapore Polytechnic, the Institute of Education, and the College of Physical Education. The private, nonprofit Singapore Institute of Management (SIM) also offers degree programs for working adults through universities from the United Kingdom, Australia, and the United States.

8. The Ministry of Education in Singapore is enhancing the opportunities for higher education by expanding the enrollment at NUS, adding a fourth polytechnic, and starting an open university administered by SIM in which the courses will be accredited by the United Kingdom's Open University (Davie 1992; Ministry of Trade and Industry 1991).

9. Nondegree vocational or professional skills training is conducted by the Vocational and Industrial Training Board (which conducts about fifty full-time training courses at fifteen training institutes), the Economic Development Board (which operates five training centers or institutes that train technicians and skilled crafts workers), the Construction Industry Development Board (which operates the Construction Industry Training Center), the National Productivity Board (which offers consulting and training services), the Institute of Systems Science (which operates education and R&D programs), and the private, nonprofit SIM and SIPM, both of which offer degree and nondegree professional management programs. The 1990 enrollments in public vocational programs totaled 29,102,

compared with 88,992 for all preuniversity and university programs (*Yearbook of Statistics* 1990:286).

10. A large proportion (81 percent) of Singaporean firms have formal training programs, but on-the-job training is still the most common training given to new rank-and-file employees (Singapore Institute of Personnel Management [SIPM] 1991:25, 27). The SIPM survey indicated that, on average, about a quarter of each company's employees attended formal training in a year (26). To help remedy the little training given by organizations and to help workers prepare for more high-technology jobs, in 1979 the government created the Skills Development Fund to subsidize training, but skill development in organizations has still not taken hold, partly because of the high rate of turnover in Singaporean organizations (Hilowitz 1987; chap. 3 also discusses the Skills Development Fund).

11. As an example of the government's efforts to improve the work ethic, in 1977 the NWC recommended that wage increases be tied to low rates of absenteeism, low rates of tardiness, satisfactory performance, and longevity; however, the tight labor market and implementation difficulties produced a very low adoption rate (Anantaraman 1990).

12. During the first ten years of its operations, the NWC made its recommendations uniformly to all organizations without allowance for variable economic contexts across firms, and the conservative nature of the recommendations was useful "in creating for Singapore a comparative advantage in labour-intensive manufacturing exports" (Pang Eng Fong 1988a:229). In the 1980s, to encourage the reallocation of investments to more productive uses, the NWC recommended large salary increases over a three-year period, from 1979 to 1981. From 1981 on, industry- and company-specific conditions were reflected in NWC recommendations, thus strengthening the role of market forces. Pang Eng Fong (1988a:229) concludes that "these interventionist policies achieved some of their objectives, e.g., slowing employment growth through high wage increases, encouraging capital spending, and promoting the establishment of new high-value-added industries. But they also greatly raised labour costs, eroding Singapore's competitive edge and increasing the severity of the recession when it appeared in 1985."

13. The government, through amendments to the Employment Act, also attempted to improve productivity and efficiency and reduce turnover by making entitlement to fringe benefits contingent on disciplined behavior. The changes were never popular with employers, however, and were never fully implemented.

14. In the early 1980s, the NWC recommended a two-tier wage structure in which only the meritorious would receive second-tier increases. The poorly implemented performance appraisal systems undermined the pay-for-performance system, however, and the two-tier structure was dropped. Nonetheless, the government encouraged the development of effective performance appraisal systems, and by the early 1990s they were in widespread use; currently, more than three-quarters of Singapore's companies conduct formal appraisals for managers, supervisors, and rank-and-file workers at least once each year (SIPM 1991:31).

15. In 1987, an NWC subcommittee detailed its principles of flexible wage systems. It recommended that wages be composed of the basic wage, an annual wage supplement of one month's basic wage, and a variable component of about two months' basic wage (NWC 1987).

16. Benefits are applied uniformly without regard to the specific needs of

employees (SNEF 1990b); only 21 percent of the SIPM survey firms listed flexi-benefit programs as part of their QWL efforts (1991:42).

17. In 1981, the Committee on Productivity, appointed by the National Productivity Board (NPB), recommended that company identification be rein-forced through the development of better welfare and benefit programs for workers; a portion of a company's CPF contribution was retained for financing such programs. By the mid-1980s, only a few companies had initiated such programs (Lee 1985:151), and the recent Strategic Economic Plan reported that only four of the twenty companies in the pilot program were still active (Ministry of Trade and Industry 1991:105). The plan called for renewed efforts to reexamine this or alternative plans for improving employee-employer cohesiveness.

18. Because of a problem with strikes over grievances, the final level of appeal is the Ministry of Labor rather than any form of arbitration.

19. A recent SIPM survey covering 408 firms is insightful in evaluating the state of participation systems. The most common were employee communication meetings (51 percent) and suggestion schemes (52 percent). QCCs were used by only 21 percent of the firms (1991:36). Performance/production issues were the most common topics on which employees were consulted; these were discussed at 46 percent of the firms. Salary and benefit issues and training issues were discussed with employees in a much smaller number of organizations. The least used devices for communicating with employees were more sophisticated: slides and tape/slides (14 percent), film/videos (18 percent), union representatives (23 percent), conferences/seminars (26 percent), newsletters (26 percent), and employee hand-books (37 percent). Only 11 percent of the surveyed firms offered stock ownership as a form of participation (39). Putti and Toh (1990:271) also concluded that participation plans were not widely discussed in Singapore as a means of building worker commitment to organizations. The Task Force on Job-Hopping, for example, did not discuss it as a mechanism for building organizational loyalty.

20. Another possible indication of workers' commitment to their employing organizations and to society is the extent to which they emigrate to other countries. It is difficult to find statistical information on emigration from Singa-pore, but in August 1989, Prime Minister Lee Quan Yew showed concern when he disclosed that in 1988, 4,707 families—19,000 individuals—emigrated ("The Phantom of the Opera" 1989). Australia, Canada, and the United States were the favorite destinations. Although this is not a large outflow, the fact that many of these emigrants were highly skilled (Lee indicated that 25 percent came from the top of Singapore's society) is of some concern for a country seeking to develop more advanced technologies.

Work-related reasons did not dominate the explanations for leaving, although unfulfilled career goals were one reason given. More typically, emigrants left Singapore because of dissatisfaction with the restrained rights of individuals, the education system, and the high cost of living, particularly the high cost of private housing and automobiles. Singapore's human rights rating by one organization was 59 percent, the same as for South Korea, but it is lower than that for Hong Kong (83 percent), Japan (88 percent), the United States (90 percent), the United Kingdom (94 percent), and Germany (97 percent) (Humana 1986).

Chapter 5. South Africa's Industrialization

1. The research reported on in this chapter forms part of a wider project, based in the Sociology of Work Unit at the University of the Witwatersrand, that focuses on the restructuring of work, industrial strategy, and its implications for industrial relations in South Africa.

2. See Gelb (1990), who adapts Lipietz's (1987) term "peripheral Fordism" and develops the notion of "racial Fordism."

3. Recent statistics indicate, however, that whites' share of total income is dropping, while that of other racial groups is rising (South African Institute of Race Relations 1992:411).

4. No reliable Gini coefficient has been computed for South Africa in the 1990s.

5. The *World Development Report* (World Bank 1992) lists the per capita income for South Africa as U.S.$2,470 in 1989, placing the country in the upper-middle-income bracket, between Venezuela and Brazil.

6. An International Monetary Fund survey projected a decline in metal and mineral prices by the mid-1990s. A calculation from the mid-1980s revealed that for every 1 percent increase in domestic expenditures, the value of imported manufactured commodities increased by 2.16 percent (see Lewis 1992).

7. The Labour Relations Act excludes farmworkers, domestic workers, and large sectors of the public service.

8. There are several other federations. The National Council of Trade Unions (NACTU), whose roots lie in the black consciousness movement, is aligned with the Pan African Congress and has approximately 250,000 members. The Federation of South African Labour Unions represents members who belong mainly to white-collar unions, while the United Workers' Union of South Africa (UWUSA), the labor arm of the Zulu-based Inkatha Freedom party, has a very small membership, estimated at less than 30,000. The South African Confederation of Labour Association (SACLA), the oldest federation, limits its membership of 30,000 exclusively to whites and is aligned with the right-wing Conservative party. Finally, there is the recently formed Federation of Independent Trade Unions, which claims to speak on behalf of 217,000 members, many of whom are drawn from the old craft unions (International Labour Office 1992).

9. COSATU withdrew from the National Manpower Commission shortly after joining it, claiming that its conditions for participation were not being met, namely, proportional representation and the extension of trade union rights to farm and domestic workers. The withdrawal was a tactical decision, and COSATU has recently reentered the commission, in its restructured form.

10. A survey designed to investigate the nature of restructuring in the metal industry examined firms affiliated with the Steel and Engineering Industries Federation of South Africa, an association of employers from the iron and steel, fabricated products, machinery, electrical, and automotive sectors. These sectors are strategically located in the manufacturing industry as a result of their production of capital and consumer goods, their significance as an employer, their relatively high rate of unionization, their potential for growth, and preliminary indications of restructuring. The sample for the survey was a stratified random

group of 700 companies (out of a total of 3,419) affiliated with the federation. The sample was also stratified by region and sector. In addition, a 100 percent sample of three hundred companies affiliated with the Motor Industries Federation and the National Association of Automotive Component and Allied Manufacturers was used. A 40 percent response rate was obtained. The careful design of the sample and the relatively high response rate suggest that the results of the survey may safely be generalized for the manufacturing industry as a whole.

11. Parts of this sections are drawn from Webster and von Holdt 1992.

12. The Chemical Workers Industrial Union, the Transport and General Workers Union, and the South African Commercial and Catering Workers Union are examples of affiliates that question what they see as an attempt to "manage capitalism."

13. The Inkatha Freedom party has a presence in the labor movement through the creation of the UWUSA in 1986. The party opposed COSATU and its support for the ANC's international campaign of sanctions and disinvestment against the South African government. The UWUSA remains small (see n6); it is a party to only a handful of recognition agreements and hence has little influence on workplace bargaining (Bendix 1992:371).

14. At the end of 1990, there were 237 registered employer associations in South Africa, including several unregistered bodies, such as the Chamber of Mines, that engaged in collective bargaining on behalf of their members (Bendix 1992). This fragmentation is exacerbated by the trend among large employers to pursue enterprise bargaining rather than industry-level bargaining. In the future, particular segments of business are likely to pursue initiatives that clash with labor's objectives, although it is desirable for strong bargaining partners to emerge if a corporatist system of industrial governance is to work effectively. It may be possible to avoid the situation that occurred in Australia, where the Business Council of Australia has not been party to successive accords between the Australian Council of Trade Unions and the various Labor governments in recent years and yet has succeeded in setting an enterprise bargaining agenda. This could possibly be avoided in South Africa if the new state drew business and labor into an accord at an early stage in the period of reconstruction.

Chapter 6. Mesocorporatism in the South African Textile Industry

1. An industrial council is a permanent body for centralized collective bargaining, formed voluntarily by one or more registered employers' associations and by one or more registered trade unions, and is itself registered under the terms of the Labour Relations Act. An equal number of representatives of the two sides forming the council negotiate collective agreements on a regular basis. These agreements may be made legally binding on all employers and employees (including nonmembers) within the registered jurisdiction (i.e., the industrial scope and area) of the council if the minister of labor deems this to be expedient and if the parties to the council are sufficiently representative. Thereafter, the permanent staff of the council administers and polices the agreements.

2. Because of a loophole in the act, the exclusion of African workers from the definition of "employee" did not apply to African women. This did not have a great deal of relevance in the first half of the century because of the insignificant number of African women in the industrial work force. The loophole was closed in 1953, by which time increasing numbers of African women were entering industry.

3. By 1944, it was found that for every U.S.$100 worth of goods imported by the manufacturing sector (exclusive of imports of machinery and equipment), only U.S.$7.60 of manufactured goods were exported (Houghton 1973:132).

4. Some of the information in this section was obtained in an interview with Norman Daniels, the ex-general secretary of TWIU, on 12 March 1990.

5. The highest rate, which is also the highest in the manufacturing sector as a whole, applies to only one product: woven polyester fabrics, which contain less than 85 percent by mass of such fibers, mixed mainly or solely with cotton, of a mass between 300 and 350 grams per square meter (Belli, Finger, and Ballivian 1993:12).

6. The thirteen textile product groups are classified according to the chapters of the Harmonized System. These chapters are as follows: 50—silk; 51—wool and other animal hair; 52—cotton and cotton-related products; 53—other vegetable textile fibers; 54—chemical filaments; 55—chemical staple fibers; 56—wadding, felt, ropes, and cables; 57—carpets and other floor coverings; 58—special woven fabrics; 59—industrial textiles; 60—knitted fabrics; 61—knitted clothing; 62—clothing not knitted; and 63—other textiles and worn clothing (IDC 1992b).

7. The internationally acceptable term "chemical" is used in preference to the term "man-made" because of the latter term's gender bias and insensitivity.

8. A local textile manufacturer calculated that a clothing company could obtain duty-free imports that were 2.7 times the value of its exports once it exported 2.5 percent of its output.

9. For the details of the company case studies, see Maree 1993.

10. See Bessant 1991, chaps. 6-9, for an outline of such techniques.

11. Although the NUTW was only one of a number of unions that formed part of SACTWU, its organizational principles and style of unionism dominated in the new union.

12. The exodus of employers from the Industrial Council for the Cotton Textile Industry (Cape) after the NUTW had gained membership eventually led to the disbandment of the council.

13. According to E. Patel, the assistant secretary general of SACTWU, the union has a density of about 78 percent and 93 percent in the textile and clothing industries respectively.

14. The elites were the large and prestigious textile and clothing firms that had historically lobbied government over the issue of protection.

Chapter 7. Hong Kong's Textile and Garment-Making Industries

1. Between 1970 and 1976, output grew faster (7.8 percent a year) than employment (2.9 percent a year) or the number of spindles (3.9 percent a year),

largely because of the increasing use of open-end spindles (ACD 1979:42–43). There was a brief growth spurt in spinning in the mid-1970s caused by a boom in the production of denim. Hong Kong was able to take advantage of the boom because it held sizable quotas of cotton, which had been built up under earlier textile restraint agreements.

2. Between 1960 and 1978, the growth in textile exports in current prices was 9.3 percent per year. Major markets included the United States, the United Kingdom, and Australia. The percentage of textile exports going to these three markets was 55 percent in 1960, falling to just less than 45 percent in 1978 (ACD 1979:45). Exports are not an adequate indicator of the economic performance of the textile industry since a significant proportion of its total output came to be used by the Hong Kong clothing industry.

3. More than 60 percent of the total value of exports between 1968 and 1978 was accounted for by the United States, the Federal Republic of Germany, and the United Kingdom (ACD 1979:46–48).

4. See Wong 1988:88 for a discussion of the economic rationality of these practices. For a study contrasting the authoritarian style of small-scale Shanghainese entrepreneurs with the "human relations" style of small-scale Cantonese entrepreneurs, see King and Leung 1975.

5. The two largest unions in garment-making (excluding tailoring) in 1956 were the Hong Kong and Kowloon Underwear Workers' General Union (later renamed the Hong Kong and Kowloon Machine-Sewing and Garment-Making Trade Workers' General Union) and the Hong Kong and Kowloon Machine-Sewing Workers' Union, with 1,962 and 1,155 members respectively.

6. The Shanghai industrialists had begun to reequip their mills in China by importing machinery from abroad. When Shanghai fell to the Communists in 1949, much of this new machinery was still in Hong Kong warehouses waiting to be shipped. "Many of the industrialists decided to move to Hong Kong where, using the new equipment, they laid the foundations of the Colony's textile industry" (Commerce and Industry Department 1965:9).

7. Spinning and weaving represented 18.5 percent and 23.2 percent respectively of total textile employment in 1978. By 1989, their shares had dropped to 7.5 percent and 12.1 percent respectively. The share of knitting and finishing, by contrast, increased from 33.7 percent and 15.1 percent in 1978 to 45 percent and 25.5 percent in 1989 (CSD 1981, vol. 2, pt. 2; 1991b).

8. How much of the total output in weaving was for export and how this figure changed over time is not known, but two pieces of information can serve as references. About 18 percent of total sales in weaving is estimated to have been due to exports in 1990 (CSD 1991c:4). It is also estimated that between 50 and 60 percent of the textile industry's total output is consumed by the local clothing industry (Industry Department 1991). No information is given on the basis for these estimates, and there are no reliable production statistics to work with, but no matter which estimates we take as the benchmark, the rising importance of exports in the 1980s is unmistakable.

9. Cline (1987:84) attributes the pervasiveness of small firms in the apparel industry to market and technological factors: "Economies of scale are much more limited than in textiles, and technological change has been relatively scale-neutral. While cutting is subject to greater efficiency at larger volume, sewing apparently

is not. The need to gear production closely to fashion tends to limit production runs, and flexibility in production tends to be more important than cost reduction through larger volume operations. Because of the lesser scale requirements and lower barriers to entry, the apparel sector has remained less concentrated than that of textiles."

10. The automation survey claimed that three factors served as strong disincentives to pursue automation in Hong Kong: the lack of an "automation culture," the lack of automation manpower, and the lack of infrastructural support (Industry Department 1992:11–12). Two of these supposed cultural barriers to automation ("lack of appreciation of the value-added nature of operational matters in industry" and "lack of a common and broad perception of the nature and benefits of industrial automation") appear to be less applicable to textiles than to garment-making.

11. Only 15.4 percent of the textile establishments surveyed (25 out of 162) reported having production facilities outside Hong Kong, and most of these were in China. Of the 41 out of 186 clothing establishments that reported having such facilities, 35 reported that they were located in China (of which 30 were in Guangdong province) (Industry Department 1990:35). Subsequent surveys on investments by Hong Kong manufacturers in southern China show that much higher proportions of firms invested in this region, though this may reflect the particular sampling frames used (Tan 1992).

12. In 1978, payment for outwork as a percentage of total labor costs was 3.9 percent and 4 percent for firms hiring one to nine workers and ten to nineteen workers respectively. In 1988, the corresponding figures were 22.8 percent and 12 percent. The use of outwork in firms in other size categories showed a slight decrease. The 1978 figures are compiled from CSD 1981, vol. 2, pt. 2, 70. The 1988 figures are from unpublished cross-tabulations by the CSD. We are grateful to Lui Tai-lok for providing us with this information. On subcontracting arrangements of smaller firms in wearing apparel, see Sit, Wong, and Kiang 1979:339–46 and Sit and Wong 1989:178–98. See Peck 1991 on the growth in outworking in the Australian clothing industry.

13. Out of a total of 4,723 cases of liquidations and bankruptcies between 1981–82 and 1990–91, 12.5 percent were garment-making firms and 2.5 percent were textile firms (Registrar General, various years). There are problems, however, in comparing the data over time since the Registrar General has not used a consistent industrial classification scheme.

14. It is difficult to gauge how much of this amount is wage arrears and other obligations to employees. In the *Report of the Working Group on Problems Experienced by Workers of Companies in Receivership* (1983), it states that out of 519 cases of liquidations and bankruptcies in 1980–82, a total of H.K.$77.9 million in wages and other claims of employees was recorded. The total liabilities incurred by all bankruptcy and liquidation cases from 1980–81 to 1982–83, in turn, was H.K.$2,004 million. The share of workers' claims to total liabilities was thus about 4 percent. This is a very rough estimate, however, since the above report uses the calendar year as the unit of accounting, while the Registrar General uses the financial year.

15. We emphasize again that spinning is not the only branch within textiles and that there are variations within the industry. The wage movements for workers

in knitting (not reported here to simplify discussion) are more similar to those for workers in garments than to those in spinning.

16. V. F. S. Sit and S. L. Wong (1989:229) note that "out-processing facilities in China enable large scale expansion of total business for the Hong Kong firm involved, which however now concentrates more on marketing, product design, quality control, purchase of raw materials, inventory control, management and technical supervision, and financial arrangements and control." Our argument, however, is contrary to the claim of H. A. Turner, P. Fosh, and S. H. Ng (1991:31–32) that there had been a leveling of pay differentials between white and blue-collar workers in Hong Kong's textile and garment-making industries between 1976 and 1985.

17. Between 1981 and 1985, there were an average of 31 industrial accidents per year per thousand workers in textiles, versus 37.5 per year for the 1980–91 period. In garment-making, the rate of industrial accidents fluctuated between sixteen and seventeen per thousand workers per year between 1980 and 1987, but it began to drop after 1986 and was 14.5 in 1990 and 12.5 in 1991 (CSD 1985:30; 1992a:36; Commissioner for Labour, various years).

18. Even workers who were offered jobs at new sites sometimes turned them down because the sites were inconvenient to get to. Women workers, in particular, face major difficulties when factories move since they are able to combine work and family duties only if their workplace is close to home. This often becomes impossible when a factory relocates.

19. The Registrar of Trade Unions provided membership figures only for the three industries combined. Leather manufacturing and craft unions (such as tailoring and embroidery) had about 10 percent of the combined membership in 1980.

20. Union density is estimated by first distinguishing textile unions from the official category of "textiles, wearing apparel and leather products" industries and then dividing the union membership thus obtained by the number of workers engaged in textile establishments.

21. Between 1980 and 1989, only 22 percent of the 128 industrial disputes in the textile industry involved the presence of unions (calculated from unpublished Labour Department records).

22. Since both unions had almost identical names and belonged to the same federation, it is probable that their membership overlapped substantially.

23. The formation of new unions was not necessarily related to the restructuring since there was a political inducement to create them. The election of five labor representatives to the government's Labour Advisory Board and from 1985 of two representatives from the labor functional constituency (composed of all registered trade unions) to the Legislative Council were based on the one-union, one-vote principle. That is perhaps the reason the TUC in particular kept its minuscule unions on the trade union registry and the FTU formed a new wearing apparel union when it already had two unions representing garment workers. There is little incentive for the federations to merge their existing unions into larger ones since amalgamation would reduce their number of votes in elections.

24. To avoid losing votes in elections, the new federation registered itself as a separate union. The five member unions were also kept on the union registry.

25. Most of the disputes involved firms that owed large arrears of wages after

they closed. In one well-publicized case, union officials had to accompany workers on a trip to mainland China to locate the fleeing owner of an insolvent garment firm and reclaim their defaulted wages.

26. In several cases, the CIWGU helped workers take their cases all the way to the Supreme Court in order to establish a precedent for the interpretation of the legal statutes surrounding severance and layoff. The FTU-affiliated Wearing Apparel Industry Employees General Union, formed in 1986, has also demanded that the government amend the Employment Ordinance's provisions on layoff to favor workers. It has also lobbied unsuccessfully for the amendment of the Employment Ordinance to extend its coverage to internal contractors, who hire ambulatory workers to work for firms such as garment factories to do specific functions such as ironing and packaging. In cases of insolvency or closure, these internal contractors, who are practically employees of the firms in some cases, often find themselves unable to meet their obligations to the ambulatory workers. Unions have demanded the extension of the Employment Ordinance to cover these contractors and workers, whose use has been increasing (see "Legislation Protecting Subcontractors Should Be Installed" 1988).

27. We again excluded tailoring unions in the calculation of union density. This may result in an underestimation of union density since we use the total number of workers engaged in wearing apparel establishments, which includes tailoring shops, as the denominator. Nevertheless, because garment-manufacturing and tailoring have such different markets, production methods, and labor force characteristics, we felt that the two must be distinguished from each other. Since the Wearing Apparel Industry Employees General Union is really a federation of five member unions but also admits individual members, we eliminated union members who were counted twice in calculating the density rate. Before the adjustment for double counting, the total declared membership was 5.6 percent of all workers engaged.

28. According to the Employment Ordinance, an employee with twenty-four or more months of continuous service who is dismissed by reason of redundancy or laid off is entitled to a severance payment calculated at the rate of eighteen days' wages or two-thirds of a month's pay, subject to a maximum of two-thirds of H.K.$15,000, for every year of service. The maximum severance payment cannot exceed the total amount of wages earned during the twelve months immediately prior to the dismissal or layoff, or H.K.$180,000, whichever is less (Commissioner for Labour 1992:15).

29. Short of a sectoral industrial policy, one response of the government to the problems associated with restructuring was that it provide some basic legal protection. Following the wave of bankruptcies and liquidations in the first half of the 1980s and in recognition of the potentially explosive problems, the government enacted the Protection of Wage on Insolvency Ordinance in 1985. See Chiu and Levin 1993 for details of the provisions of this ordinance.

30. From 1978 to 1989, compensation to employees accounted for 16.4 to 19.6 percent of total costs in textiles, while the corresponding proportion in garments varied from 25 to 30.5 percent (CSD 1985:47, 1992a:55).

31. Wong (1988:25) notes that the colonial government "adopted a flexible and responsive attitude to the needs of the incoming [Shanghainese textile] industrialists" in the late 1940s. One example was the concessions on labor

standards. Although women and children were not permitted to work night shifts under the Factory and Workshops Ordinance, "Apparently at the request of the textile industrialists, the government relaxed this prohibition in 1948 to permit women and children to work between the hours of 6 A.M. and 10 P.M."

32. The institutional environment for restructuring in textiles and garment-making in Hong Kong appears radically different from the institutional environments for restructuring in Japan or the "Third Italy" (Best 1990; Dore 1986: 153–243). In organizational terms, restructuring in Japan and Italy seems to have taken place within a framework of relatively tightly coupled interorganizational networks within and cutting across sectors, whereas in Hong Kong it has taken place within a framework of much more loosely coupled and unstable organizational networks. The comparative international experience of restructuring remains to be explored. M. H. Best's comment, however, that the institutional frameworks for industrial restructuring in the NICs resemble those found in Japan and Italy is wide of the mark so far as Hong Kong is concerned.

Chapter 8. Subsidiaries in Malaysia and Taiwan

1. There are other ideal-type workplace relations patterns, including the large-scale, unionized, neo-Taylorist variant and the artisanal or craft production type. An emerging alternative to lean production is human-centered production, which is characterized by job and work design oriented to the craft ideal of long cycle times and intrinsically satisfying tasks based on teamwork, extensive learning, and relatively high levels of employee participation in decision making (Adler and Cole 1993; Berggren 1992; Jürgens 1991; Roth 1992). Human-centered production presupposes a tight labor market and strategically powerful employees, who are usually organized by a strong industrial union. Since these conditions are absent in Malaysia and Taiwan, this type is not relevant to this chapter.

2. Several other factors were considered, including the size of the workplace and the gender and ethnicity of the workers. These factors did not appear to have explanatory value, although an analysis of more cases and ethnographic research might lead to a different conclusion.

3. Capital and materials supply markets, which at first sight appear to be economic phenomena, are in reality politically constructed. These potentially important variables require further research. The supply market is thus a potentially important variable that requires substantial further research.

4. These included manufacturing innovation, quality, delivery of goods, productivity, safety, environmental management and energy conservation, training and development of people, maintenance management, and conservation of working capital.

5. This is true of the industry generally (Ballance, Pogány, and Forstner 1992:98). The costs of introducing a new drug probably quadrupled between 1976 and 1990, averaging $230 million in the United States in 1990. Nevertheless, the search for new drugs has intensified since potential profits are enormous (see n6) in some therapeutic areas.

6. The largest pharmaceutical company, Merck, reaped nearly 39 percent of its total pharmaceutical sales from its two best-selling heart treatment drugs, Vasotec

and Mevacor. Forty-four percent of the revenue earned by the second largest pharmaceutical company, Glaxo, came from the ulcer drug Zantac ("Blurred Vision" 1993:70; James Capel & Co. 1993:18).

7. The late 1980s witnessed feverish merger activity in pharmaceuticals that has continued at a slower pace. Between 1985 and 1989, there were eight major mergers involving firms with an estimated combined sales of U.S.$17.4 billion (at 1988 prices), or nearly 17 percent of worldwide pharmaceutical sales (Chetley 1990:38; "Drug Company Mergers" 1989:61).

8. The scheme was ostensibly introduced to give employees an ownership stake in the corporation. This was expected to enhance employee identification with the company and hence lead to improved work performance. This official view is not the full story. The timing of the introduction of the scheme suggests that senior management viewed it as a way to counter a possible takeover threat. The intention is to extend the benefit to nonunionized personnel in countries where there is no threat of nationalization. Unionized personnel may be excluded because unions cannot be relied upon to support the incumbent management.

9. Some of these values were in the company credo and underpinned by the performance management system currently in use, but they were not emphasized so strongly.

10. The Malaysian and Taiwanese affiliates produce more than thirty different products, including liquids and dry items (tablets and capsules), in a large number of volume (e.g., bottle size) and pack sizes (e.g., tablet boxes). The Taiwanese affiliate also produces a small volume of ointments and sterile products. In recent years the number of packs has been reduced, but the number of products manufactured at the two plants is only slightly lower than it was five years ago. Because most of the machinery is dedicated to a particular product area, there is usually considerable idle capacity. Very low-volume products are often highly profitable because the marginal costs associated with their production is low and prices for these products tend to be high. Manufacturing managers therefore prefer to produce these items in-house rather than import them from other affiliates.

11. Compare these data with those for a representative U.K. mechanical engineering firm, where labor represents about 30 percent of manufacturing costs (Williams, Williams, and Haslam 1989:284).

12. Over the period 1987–91, GDP increased at an annual average rate of 8.3 percent in Malaysia and 7.9 percent in Taiwan (*Far Eastern Economic Review* [FEER] 1993:7). Inflation has averaged less than 5 percent in both countries over the same period (Asian Development Bank [ADB] 1992). The average annual exchange rate of the Malaysian dollar against the U.S. dollar worsened slightly between 1987 and 1992. In 1987, it was 2.58:1; it fell to 2.75:1 in 1991 and recovered to 2.55:1 in 1992. By contrast, the new Taiwanese dollar strengthened from 31.85:1 in 1987 to 26.80 in 1991 (International Monetary Fund [IMF] 1993:344; Economist Intelligence Unit [EIU] 1992:3). Taiwan's per capita income in 1991 was U.S.$8,083, compared with U.S.$5,529 in 1987 (FEER 1993:7).

13. In 1992, education in Taiwan accounted for 14.5 percent of the budget expenditure, versus 3.7 percent in Malaysia (FEER 1993:9). In 1993, the Human Resources Development Act in Malaysia established a Training Fund and Development Council, supported by a levy of 1 percent of the monthly salary bill of manufacturing companies with fifty or more employees.

14. Approximately twenty research days were spent at each site. Interviews of about two hours in duration were conducted with fifteen managers, employees, and union (Malaysia) and welfare committee (Taiwan) representatives at each affiliate. After the data were collected, differences and similarities in the findings for the two subsidiaries were discussed with managers at each subsidiary and were supplemented by interviews with and data from managers at the East Asia regional office and at corporate headquarters. Information was also obtained from published sources, chiefly company and industry reports. The data on local labor market institutions and trends come from government, business, and academic publications.

15. At both affiliates, the sale of health-care items is also contracted out to distributors, mainly because of the highly fragmented retail markets. This has met with limited success because of the lack of control over the contractors, so that product promotion is less vigorous than expected and small in scale, resulting in the affiliates having little bargaining power over the sales organizations; further, there have been labor turnover problems among the employees of the sales organizations, leading to even less effectiveness in promoting the affiliates' products.

16. There are three main reasons for this difference. The first factor is the tighter labor market for managers in Taiwan, which tends to bid up their remuneration. The second factor is the more systematic use of comparative firm wage surveys for benchmarking increases in Malaysia, a process disrupted by the turnover among senior management and the financial difficulties in Taiwan between 1988 and 1991. Together with the third factor—the presence of a union in the Malaysian affiliate—this tends to increase wages and reduce relativities with senior management compared with its nonunion, Taiwanese counterpart.

17. This award was developed by the Taiwan affiliate's GM when he managed the Malaysian subsidiary. He subsequently introduced it to Taiwan.

18. Following a human resource efficiency audit (see Frenkel 1994) in 1988, the regional vice president for human resources advised the director of human resources to try to deunionize the plant. Instead, union representation was restricted to the shop floor. This assuaged corporate concern but did not directly threaten the good relations between management and the union representatives.

19. These observations are based on an analysis of the minutes of twenty-nine consultative/welfare committee meetings in the period 1990–92.

20. An employee is permitted the support of another employee only at the highest level within the enterprise, that is, at a meeting with the GM. There is a provision for third-party arbitration in accordance with the law if the dispute involves a group of employees.

21. Apparently, recent surveys showed evidence of dissatisfaction with management style in Malaysia and pay in Taiwan.

22. As Hofstede (1992:153) has observed, however, workplace socialization has only a limited effect on changing employees' values. It "takes place at a more superficial level of mental programming than family and school socialization."

23. Absenteeism among manufacturing employees averaged 8.6 percent in the period 1988–90 compared with an annual average of 7.4 percent in 1991–92. Labor turnover declined over the corresponding period from close to 25 percent to about 17 percent. More recently, turnover declined from 22.2 percent in 1991 to

11.5 percent in 1992. Direct workers recorded a labor turnover rate of zero in 1992. According to one employee representative, "You feel that management are listening to us and supporting us now."

24. Conflict avoidance and a preference for compromise are characteristic of workers in Chinese cultures (Redding 1990). The human resources manager at the Malaysian affiliate maintained that this was also true of Muslim and Hindu workers in Malaysia.

25. The PH credo implies that there will be strict compliance with the law. The relevant section reads as follows: "We commit ourselves to being responsible corporate citizens, actively initiating and supporting efforts concerning the health of society and stewardship of the environment." The credo ends with the following statement: "Above all, our dealings with these constituencies [customers, colleagues, shareholders, business partners and society] will be conducted with the utmost integrity, adhering to the highest standards of ethical and just conduct."

26. One indication of this is that Malaysian and Taiwanese employees are more keen to engage in workplace-related social activities than their counterparts in PH's Australian, South African, and U.K. subsidiaries.

27. This analysis suggests that the institutional argument is strongest where comparisons are made between labor markets that are markedly different in the *extent* of regulation or, more especially, where they are highly regulated and where the *forms* of regulation are very different (see Clegg 1976, Turner 1991, Lane 1989, and Frenkel 1991).

28. The convergence thesis may apply, however, to workplace relations among the growing number of white-collar employees. This is a matter for further research.

Chapter 9. Human Resource Management in Korean Manufacturing

1. There have been some changes in HRM policy for production workers in these firms since the study was conducted, but these changes have not been followed up. Reform of HRM policy in Korea continues to be oriented mainly toward white-collar workers.

2. This concept was introduced by W. J. Abernathy, K. B. Clark, and A. M. Kantrow (1981).

3. Similar concepts can be found in the literature. See, for example, Sorge and Streeck 1988 and Hall 1991.

4. A similar concept has been used by K. Koike (1988).

Chapter 10. Overseas Japanese Plants under Global Strategies

1. The survey results concerning the printed circuit board (PCB) assembly process in the parent plants and all the transplants are analyzed in Nomura 1992.

The results of the survey, excluding the issue of parts procurement, can be found in Tokunaga, Nomura, and Hiramoto 1991. The survey results for one of the parent plants are published in Tokunaga et al. 1991.

2. The survey also covered parts procurement, which was shown to be one of the most difficult management problems in a transplant. This was mainly because relationships with suppliers differed significantly from the customary Japanese model (see Hiramoto 1992).

3. A number of Japanese companies have closed their overseas plants, but textile companies, which have been among the most advanced manufacturers involved in overseas production, were reluctant to close their transplants in the 1970s, even though external conditions had deteriorated drastically (Okamoto 1989:81–85). In the mid-1970s, Japanese MNCs in Taiwan were also reluctant to reduce employment levels in spite of the business effects created by the oil shock. This is in contrast to U.S. MNCs, which significantly reduced their employment levels in Taiwan (Taiwan Kenkyujo 1979:364). The number of U.S. companies in Taiwan decreased from 445 in 1983 to 351 in 1987, apparently because of the rapid rise in wage rates and the appreciation of the local currency (Taiwan Kenkyujo 1989:529).

4. W. Liao, D. Yang, and Y. Young (1990:96) suggest that the qualification system in East Asia was influenced by Confucianism. The influence of Confucianism is quite different in Japan and China, however (Mizoguchi 1989:187–95), which raises the question of whether there is any strong causal relationship between these two variables.

5. One might wonder why transplant TB did not follow the parent company in requiring that the parts be at least 5 mm in width. Generally speaking, the work methods in the transplants differ from those of the parent plant and other transplants. Furthermore, as this example indicates, the relationship between the design department and the manufacturing department is different in the two plants. In the parent plant, the manufacturing department commonly asks for design improvements when a fault or difficulty is discovered in the design. As a result, a design usually undergoes frequent improvement. The transplants rely more on their design departments, and they find it difficult to match the improved designs developed at the parent plant.

References

Abegglen, J. C. 1958. *The Japanese Factory: Aspects of Its Social Organization.* *U.S.A.* Glencoe, Ill.: Free Press.

Abegglen, J. C., and G. Stalk, Jr. 1985. *Kaisha: The Japanese Corporation.* New York: Basic Books.

Abernathy, W. J., K. B. Clark, and A. M. Kantrow. 1981. "The New Industrial Competition." *Harvard Business Review,* Sept.–Oct., 68–81.

Adler G., J. Maller, and E. C. Webster. 1992. "Unions Direct Action and Transition in South Africa." In *Peace, Politics and Violence in Southern Africa,* edited by N. Etherington, 306–43. London: Hans Zell.

Adler, P., and R. Cole. 1993. "Designed for Learning: A Tale of Two Auto Plants." *Sloan Management Review* 34 (3): 85–93.

Advisory Committee on Diversification. 1979. *Report of the Advisory Committee on Diversification 1979.* Hong Kong: Government Printer.

African National Congress. 1990. "Discussion Document on Economic Policy." Typescript.

———. 1992. "Ready to Govern: ANC Policy Guidelines for a Democratic South Africa." Typescript.

Aggarwal, V. 1985. *Liberal Protectionism: The International Politics of Organized Textile Trade.* Berkeley: University of California Press.

Allie, N., ed. 1991. *Directory of South African Trade Unions.* Johannesburg: University of Cape Town, South African Labour and Development Research Unit.

Amjad, R., and Mritiunjoy Mohanty. 1991. "Industrial Restructuring and Implications for Human Resource Development in ASEAN." Working paper. ILO-UNDP Project, Asian HRD Planning Network.

Amsden, A. 1989. *Asia's Next Giant: South Korea and Late Industrialization.* New York: Oxford University Press.

———. 1990. "Third World Industrialization: 'Global Fordism' or a New Model?" *New Left Review* 182: 5–31.

Anantaraman, V. 1990. *Singapore Industrial Relations System.* Singapore: Singapore Institute of Management and McGraw-Hill.

Anderson, K., ed. 1991. *New Silk Roads: East Asia and World Textile Markets.* Cambridge, U.K.: Cambridge University Press.

Anderson, K., and Y. I. Park. 1991. "Effects of China's Dramatic Reforms on Its Neighbours and on World Markets." In *New Silk Roads: East Asia and World Textile Markets,* edited by K. Anderson, 30–51. Cambridge, U.K.: Cambridge University Press.

Angebrandt, A. M. 1990. "Labour Top Concern for Chip Executives." *Electronic Business Asia,* Nov., 9–10.

281

Aoki, M. 1988. *Information, Incentives, and Bargaining in the Japanese Economy.* New York: Cambridge University Press.

Appelbaum, E., and R. Batt. 1993. *The New American Workplace: Transforming Work Systems in the United States.* Ithaca, N.Y.: ILR Press.

Appelbaum, R. P., and J. Henderson, eds. 1992. *States and Development in the Asian Pacific Rim.* Newbury Park, Calif.: Sage.

Arensman, R. 1990. "Malaysia Heads for a Labour Showdown." *Electronic Business Asia,* Sept., 45–52.

Ariff, M., and H. Hill. 1985. "ASEAN Manufactured Exports: Performance and Revealed Comparative Advantage." *ASEAN Economic Bulletin* 2 (1): 33–55.

Arom Pongpa-ngan Foundation. 1988. "Labour Relations Strategies and Short-Term Employment." Typescript.

———. 1991. *Temporary Employment after the Ministry of Interior Decree No. 11* (in Thai). Bangkok.

Arudsothy, P. 1990. "The State and Industrial Relations in Developing Countries: The Malaysian Situation." *ASEAN Economic Bulletin* 6 (March): 25–45.

Arudsothy, P., and C. Littler. 1993. "State Regulation and Fragmentation in Malaysia." In *Organized Labor in the Asia-Pacific Region: A Comparative Study of Trade Unionism in Nine Countries,* edited by S. Frenkel, 107–32. Ithaca, N.Y.: ILR Press.

Arul, F., B. Saidin, and A. M. Abu. 1987. "The Public Bank Berhad." In *Labour Relations and Productivity at the Enterprise Level: Selected Case Studies from within ASEAN,* 32–49. Geneva: ILO.

Asian Development Bank. 1992. *Asian Development Outlook.* Manila.

Australian Bureau of Industry Economics. 1991. *The Pharmaceutical Industry: Impediments and Opportunities.* Canberra: Australian Government Public Service.

Ayadurai, D. 1990. "Industrial Relations in Malaysia: Issues and Responses." *Malaysian Management Review* 25 (1): 38–50.

———. 1993. "Malaysia." In *Labour Law and Industrial Relations in Asia,* edited by S. Deery and R. Mitchell, 61–95. Melbourne: Longman Cheshire.

Balakrishnan, N. 1989. "Golden Handcuffs." *Far Eastern Economic Review* 144 (21): 32.

Ballance, R., J. Pogány, and H. Forstner. 1992. *The World's Pharmaceutical Industries: An International Perspective on Innovation, Competition and Policy.* Aldershot, U.K.: United Nations Industrial Development Organization.

Bamber, G., and R. Lansbury, eds. 1993. *International and Comparative Industrial Relations.* Sydney: Allen & Unwin.

Banaji, J., and R. Hensman. 1990. *Beyond Multinationalism: Management Policy and Bargaining Relations in International Companies.* New Delhi: Sage.

Barker, H. 1963. "A Comment on Textile Development in South Africa." *South African Journal of Economics* 31: 285–303.

Barnard, A. L. 1992. "Labour Law in Malaysia: A Capitalist Device to Exploit Third World Workers." *Law and Policy in International Business* 23 (2): 415–40.

Bartlett, C. A., and S. Goshal. 1989. *Managing across Borders: The Transnational Solution.* Boston: Harvard Business School Press.

Baskin, J. 1991. *Strike Back: A History of COSATU.* Johannesburg: Ravan Press.

———. 1993. *Corporatism: Some Obstacles Facing the South African Labor Movement.*

CPS Social Contract Series. Research Report no. 30. Johannesburg: Center for Policy Studies.

Batstone, E., I. Boraston, and S. Frenkel. 1977. *Shop Stewards in Action: The Organisation of Workplace Conflict and Accommodation.* Oxford: Blackwell.

Beer, M., et al. 1984. *Managing Human Assets.* New York: Free Press.

Begin, J. P. 1991. *Strategic Employment Policy: An Organizational Systems Perspective.* Englewood Cliffs, N.J.: Prentice-Hall.

———. 1992. "Comparative HRM: A Systems Perspective." *International Journal of Human Resource Management* 3 (3): 379–408.

Behrman, J. R. 1990. *Human Resource Led Development: Review of Issues and Evidence.* Geneva: ILO.

Bell, R. T. 1990. "The Prospects for Industrialization in the New South Africa." Inaugural Lecture, Rhodes University.

Belli, P., M. Finger, and A. Ballivian. 1993. "South Africa: Review of Trade Policy Issues." Informal Discussion Papers on Aspects of the Economy of South Africa. Paper no. 4. Southern Africa Department, World Bank, Washington, D.C.

Bello, W., and S. Rosenfeld. 1990. *Dragons in Distress: Asia's Miracle Economies in Crisis.* San Francisco: Institute for Food and Development Policy.

Bendix, S. 1992. *Industrial Relations in South Africa.* 2d ed. Johannesburg: Juta.

Berger, P. 1986. *The Capitalist Revolution: Fifty Propositions about Prosperity, Equality and Liberty.* New York: Basic Books.

Berggren, C. 1992. *Alternatives to Lean Production: Work Organization in the Swedish Auto Industry.* Ithaca, N.Y.: ILR Press.

Bessant, J. 1991. *Managing Advanced Manufacturing Technology.* London: Hutchinson.

Best, M. H. 1990. *The New Competition: Institutions of Industrial Restructuring.* Oxford: Polity Press.

Bird, A. 1992. "COSATU Unions Take Initiatives in Training." *South African Labour Bulletin* 16 (6): 46–50.

Bjorkman, M., L. Lauridsen, and H. Marcussen. 1988. "Types of Industrialization and Capital-Labour Relations in the Third World." In *Trade Unions and the New Industrialization of the Third World,* edited by R. Southall, 59–80. London: Zed Books.

Black, A. 1991a. "Manufacturing Development and the Economic Crisis: A Reversion to Primary Production?" In *South Africa's Economic Crisis,* edited by S. Gelb, 156–74. Cape Town: David Philip.

———. 1991b. "Current Trends in South African Industrial Policy: Selective Intervention, Trade Orientation and Concessionary Industrial Finance." Paper presented at biannual meeting of Economic Trends Research Group, University of Cape Town.

———. 1992. "Changing Global Trends in Auto Assembly and Component Manufacture: Implications for the Future of the South African Industry." Discussion paper. Industrial Strategy Project, University of Cape Town.

Blauner, R. 1964. *Alienation and Freedom.* Chicago: University of Chicago Press.

"Blurred Vision." 1993. *Economist,* 29 May, 70.

Board of Trade and Industry. South Africa. 1950. *The Textile Manufacturing Industry.* Report no. 323. Pretoria.

————. 1988a. *A Policy and Strategy for the Development and Structural Adjustment of Industry in the Republic of South Africa.* Pretoria.

————. 1988b. *The Development and Structural Adjustment Programme of the Apparel Textile and Clothing Industries.* Pretoria.

Bot, Tengku Omar bin Tengku. 1988. "Voluntary and Compulsory Arbitration of Labour Disputes in Malaysia." In *Voluntary and Compulsory Arbitration of Labour Disputes: A Survey of Current Situation in ASEAN,* 11–32. ILO/UHDP/ASEAN Programme of Industrial Relations for Development. Geneva: ILO.

Bowie, A. 1991. *Crossing the Industrial Divide: State, Society, and the Politics of Economic Transformation in Malaysia.* New York: Columbia University Press.

Boyer, R., ed. 1988. *The Search for Labour Market Flexibility: The European Economies in Transition.* New York: Oxford University Press.

Brown, A., and S. Frenkel. 1993. "Union Unevenness and Insecurity in Thailand." In *Organized Labour in the Asia-Pacific Region: A Comparative Analysis of Trade Unionism in Nine Countries,* edited by S. Frenkel, 82–106. Ithaca, N.Y.: ILR Press.

Brunhes, B. 1989. "Labour Flexibility in Enterprises: A Comparison of Firms in Four European Countries." In *Labour Market Flexibility: Trends in Enterprises,* edited by B. Brunhes, 11–36. Paris: OECD.

Butters, H. R. 1939. *Report by the Labour Officer on Labour and Labour Conditions in Hong Kong.* Hong Kong: Noronha.

Callinicos, L. 1985. *Working Life: Factories, Townships and Popular Culture on the Rand, 1886–1940.* Johannesburg: Ravan Press.

Cappelli, P., and R. B. McKersie. 1987. "Management Strategy and the Redesign of Workrules." *Journal of Management Studies* 24: 441–42.

Castells, M. 1984. "The Shek Kip Mei Syndrome: Public Housing and Economic Development in Hong Kong." Paper presented at seminar, Urban Informal Sector in Center and Periphery, Johns Hopkins University.

Caves, R. E., and R. W. Jones. 1973. *World Trade and Payments.* Boston: Little, Brown.

Cawson, A. 1986. *Corporatism and Political Theory.* Oxford: Blackwell.

Census and Statistics Department. Hong Kong. 1981. *1978 Survey of Industrial Production.* Hong Kong: Government Printer.

————. 1982. *Quarterly Report of Wages, Salaries, and Employee Benefits Statistics.* Hong Kong: Government Printer.

————. 1985. *Hong Kong Annual Digest of Statistics 1984.* Hong Kong: Government Printer.

————. 1991a. *Estimates of Gross Domestic Product.* Hong Kong: Government Printer.

————. 1991b. *1989 Survey of Industrial Production.* Hong Kong: Government Printer.

————. 1991c. *Report on Textile Production Statistics, 4th Quarter 1990.* Hong Kong: Government Printer.

————. 1992a. *Hong Kong Annual Digest of Statistics 1991.* Hong Kong: Government Printer.

————. 1992b. *Hong Kong Annual Digest of Statistics 1992.* Hong Kong: Government Printer.

Central Statistical Service. South Africa. 1992a. *South African Statistics, 1992.* Pretoria: Government Printer.

————. 1992b. "Utilisation of Production Capacity, Manufacturing." News release, Sept.

————. 1993a. "Labor Statistics: Employment and Salaries and Wages: Mining and Quarrying, Manufacturing, Construction and Electricity, December 1992." News release, June.

————. 1993b. "Indices of Physical Volume of Manufacturing Production, December 1992." News release, March.

————. 1993c. "Labor Statistics: Employment and Salaries and Wages: Mining and Quarrying, Manufacturing, Construction and Electricity, October 1992." News release, Feb.

Charsombut, P. 1990. *Provincial Industry Labor Market.* Bangkok: Thailand Development Research Institute Foundation.

Chee, P. L., and Poh Ping Lee. 1983. "Japanese Direct Investment in Malaysia, with Special Reference to Japanese Joint Ventures." In *ASEAN-Japan Relations: Investment, Singapore,* edited by Sueo Sekiguchi, 61–92. Institute for South East Asian Studies.

Cheong, K. C., and K. C. Lim. 1981. "Implications of the Transfer of Technology and Primary-Ancillary Linkages: A Case Study of the Electronics and Electrical Industry in Malaysia." *Ekonomie Malaysia* 3–4: 119–46.

Chetley, A. 1990. *A Healthy Business? World Health and the Pharmaceutical Industry.* London: Zed Books.

Chew, S. B. 1991. *Trade Unionism in Singapore.* Singapore: McGraw-Hill.

Chiu, S. W. K. 1987. "Strikes in Hong Kong: A Sociological Study." Master's thesis, University of Hong Kong.

Chiu, S. W. K., and D. A. Levin. 1993. "Labour under Industrial Restructuring in Hong Kong: A Comparison of Textiles and Garments." Occasional Paper no. 21. Hong Kong Institute of Asia-Pacific Studies, Chinese University of Hong Kong.

Chowdhury, A., I. Islam, and C. Kirkpatrick. 1988. *Structural Adjustment and Human Resource Development in ASEAN.* Geneva: ILO.

Clairmonte, F., and J. Cavanagh. 1981. *The World in Their Web: Dynamics of Textile Multinationals.* London: Zed Books.

Clark, C. 1989. *Taiwan's Development: Implications for Contending Political Economy Paradigms.* Westport, Conn.: Greenwood Press.

Clegg, H. 1976. *Trade Unionism under Collective Bargaining: A Theory Based on Comparisons of Six Countries.* London: Blackwell.

Cline, W. R. 1987. *The Future of World Trade in Textiles and Apparel.* Washington, D.C.: Institute for International Economics.

Cohen, R. 1991. *Contested Domains: Debates in International Labour Studies.* London: Zed Books.

Collier, D. 1991. "The Comparative Method: Two Decades of Change." In *Comparative Political Dynamics: Global Research Perspectives,* edited by D. A. Rustow and K. P. Erickson, 7–31. New York: HarperCollins.

Collier, R. B., and D. Collier. 1991. *Shaping the Political Arena.* Princeton, N.J.: Princeton University Press.

Commerce and Industry Department. Hong Kong. 1965. *Textiles Hong Kong.* Hong Kong: Government Printer.

Commissioner for Labour. Hong Kong. 1989. *Annual Departmental Report.* Hong Kong: Government Printer.

————. 1992. *Annual Departmental Report.* Hong Kong: Government Printer.

Council of Labor Affairs. Taiwan. 1992. *Yearbook of Labor Statistics: Taiwan Area, Republic of China, 1991.* Taiwan.

Cox, R. W. 1987. *Production, Power, and World Order: Social Forces in the Making of History.* New York: Columbia University Press.

Davie, S. 1992. "SIM Takes Up Governmnent Offer to Run Open U Courses." *Straits Times,* June 10.

de la Torre, J. 1984. *Clothing-Industry Adjustment in Developed Countries.* New York: St. Martin's Press.

Dean, J. W., and G. I. Sussman. 1989. "Strategic Responses to Global Competition: Advanced Technology, Organization Design, and Human Resource Practices." In *Strategy, Organization Design, and Human Resource Management,* edited by C. C. Snow, 297–332. Greenwich, Conn.: JAI Press.

Deery, S., and R. Mitchell, eds. 1993. *Australian Industrial Relations in Asia.* Melbourne: Longman Cheshire.

Department of Statistics. Singapore. 1990. *Yearbook of Statistics.*

Dertouzos, M., et al. 1989. *Made in America: Regaining the Productive Edge.* Cambridge: MIT Press.

Development Bank of South Africa. 1991. *Annual Report 1990–1991.* Johannesburg.

Deyo, F. C. 1987. "Introduction." In T*he Political Economy of the New Asian Industrialism,* edited by F. C. Deyo. Ithaca, N.Y.: Cornell University Press.

————. 1989. *Beneath the Miracle: Labor Subordination in the New Asian Industrialism.* Berkeley: University of California Press.

————. Forthcoming. "Competition, Flexibility, and Industrial Ascent: The Thai Auto Industry." In *Global Capital, Local Labor: The World Automobile Industry,* edited by F. Deyo. London: Macmillan.

Deyo, F., ed. 1987. *The Political Economy of the New Asian Industrialism.* Berkeley: University of California Press.

Directorate-General of Budget Accounting and Statistics. Executive Yuan. Republic of China. n.d. "Abstract of Employment and Earnings Statistics in Taiwan Area, Republic of China, 1989."

Doner, R. 1991. *Driving a Bargain: Automobile Industrialization and Japanese Firms in Southeast Asia.* Berkeley: University of California Press.

Dore, R. P. 1973. *British Factory-Japanese Factory: The Origins of National Diversity in Industrial Relations.* London: Allen & Unwin.

————. 1986. *Flexible Rigidities: Industrial Policy and Structural Adjustment in the Japanese Economy 1970–80.* London: Athlone Press.

————. 1987. *Taking Japan Seriously: A Confucian Perspective on Leading Economic Issues.* Stanford, Calif.: Stanford University Press.

————. 1989. "Where Are We Now: Musings of an Evolutionist." *Work, Employment and Society* 3 (4): 425–46.

Drucker, P. 1993. *Post-Capitalist Society.* New York: HarperCollins.

"Drug Company Mergers: Love Potion Number 9." 1989. *Economist,* 5 Aug., 61.

Dunlop, J. 1958. *Industrial Relations Systems.* Carbondale: Southern Illinois University Press.

Duthie, S. 1990. "Electronics Union in Malaysia Stifled by Merging of Firms." *Asian Wall Street Journal Weekly,* 1 Oct., 5–6.

Dyer, L. 1984. "Studying Human Resource Strategy: An Approach and an Agenda." *Industrial Relations* 23 (2): 156–69.

Economist Intelligence Unit. 1992. *Taiwan.* Country Report no. 4. London: Economist.

Edwards, R. C. 1979. *Contested Terrain: The Transformation of the Workplace in the Twentieth Century.* New York: Basic Books.

Ellison, C., and Gereffi, G. 1990. "Explaining Strategies and Patterns of Industrial Development." In *Manufacturing Miracles: Paths of Industrialization in Latin America and East Asia,* edited by G. Gereffi and D. L. Wyman, 368-404. Princeton, N.J.: Princeton University Press.

Enderwick, P. 1985. *Multinational Business and Labour.* London: Croom Helm.

England, J., and J. Rear. 1981. *Industrial Relations and Law in Hong Kong.* Hong Kong: Oxford University Press.

Fajnzylber, F. 1990. "The United States and Japan as Models of Industrialization." In *Manufacturing Miracles: Paths of Industrialization in Latin America and East Asia,* edited by G. Gereffi and D. L. Wyman, 323–53. Princeton, N.J: Princeton University Press.

Fama, E. F., and M. C. Jenes. 1983. "Separation of Ownership and Control." *Journal of Law and Economics* 26 (2): 301–25.

Far Eastern Economic Review. 1993. *Asia 1993 Yearbook.* Hong Kong: Review Publishing.

———. 1994. *Asia 1994 Yearbook.* Hong Kong: Review Publishing.

Fine, A. 1993. "Miners Want Deal on Social Plan." *Business Day,* 18 Feb., 3.

Fine, A., and E. C. Webster. 1989. "Transcending Traditions: Trade Unions and Political Unity." In *South African Review 5,* edited by G. Moss and I. Obery, 256–74. Johannesburg: Ravan Press.

Florida, R., and M. Kenney. 1991. "Transplanted Organizations: The Transfer of Japanese Industrial Organization to the U.S." *American Sociological Review* 56: 381–98.

Foo, C., C. Chan, and D. Ong. 1991. *A Primer on Collective Bargaining.* Singapore: McGraw-Hill.

"The Fortune 500." 1992. *Fortune,* 20 April.

Fox, A. 1974. *A Sociology of Industry.* London: Collier Macmillan.

Francis, A. 1986. *New Technology at Work.* Oxford: Clarendon Press.

Frank, A. G. 1967. *Capitalism and Underdevelopment in Latin America.* New York: Monthly Review Press.

Frenkel, S. 1986. "Industrial Sociology and Workplace Relations in Advanced Capitalist Societies." *International Journal of Comparative Sociology* 27 (1-2): 69–86.

———. 1991. "State Policies and Workplace Relations: A Comparison between Thatcherism and Accordism." In *The Future of Industrial Relations: Proceedings of the Second Bargaining Group Conference,* edited by H. C. Katz, 47–72. Ithaca, N.Y.: ILR Press.

———. 1993a. "Theoretical Frameworks and Empirical Contexts of Trade

Unionism." In *Organized Labor in the Asia-Pacific Region: A Comparative Study of Trade Unionism in Nine Countries,* edited by S. Frenkel, 3–58. Ithaca, N.Y.: ILR Press.

———. 1993b. "Variations in Patterns of Trade Unionism: A Synthesis." In *Organized Labor in the Asia-Pacific Region: A Comparative Study of Trade Unionism in Nine Countries,* edited by S. Frenkel, 309–46. Ithaca, N.Y.: ILR Press.

———. 1994. "Patterns of Workplace Relations in the Global Corporation: Toward Convergence?" In *Workplace Regimes in International Perspective,* edited by J. Bélanger, P. K. Edwards, and L. Haiven. Ithaca, N.Y.: ILR Press.

Frenkel, S., ed. 1993. *Organized Labor in the Asia-Pacific Region: A Comparative Study of Trade Unionism in Nine Countries.* Ithaca, N.Y.: ILR Press.

Frenkel, S., J. C. Hong, and B. L. Lee. 1993. "Trade Union Resurgence and Fragility in Taiwan." In *Organized Labor in the Asia-Pacific Region: A Comparative Study of Trade Unionism in Nine Countries,* edited by S. Frenkel, 162–86. Ithaca, N.Y.: ILR Press.

Friedman, M., and R. Friedman. 1980. *Free to Choose.* Harmondsworth, U.K.: Penguin Books.

Friedman, S. 1987. *Building Tomorrow Today.* Johannesburg: Ravan Press.

Friman, H. R. 1990. *Patchwork Protectionism: Textile Trade Policy in the United States, Japan, and West Germany.* Ithaca, N.Y.: Cornell University Press.

Fröbel, F., J. Heinrichs, and O. Kreye. 1980. *The New International Division of Labour: Structural Unemployment in Industrialised Countries and Industrialisation in Developing Countries.* Cambridge, U.K.: Cambridge University Press.

Galbraith, J. 1989. *Japanese Transplants.* CEO Publication C 9020. Los Angeles: University of Southern California.

Gallie, D. 1978. *In Search of the New Working Class: Automation and Social Integration within the Capitalist Enterprise.* Cambridge, U.K.: Cambridge University Press.

"Garments Hold Up." 1982. *Textile Asia,* April, 69–70.

Garnier, G. H. 1982. "Context and Decision Making Autonomy in the Foreign Affiliates of U.S. Multinational Corporations." *Academy of Management Journal* 25 (4): 893–908.

Gelb, S. 1990. "Introduction." In *South Africa's Economic Crisis,* edited by S. Gelb, 1–32. Cape Town: David Philip.

———. 1991. "Capitalism: There Is No Alternative . . . for Now." *Work in Progress* 76.

General Agreement on Tariffs and Trade. 1990a. *International Trade 89–90.* Vol. 1. Geneva.

———. 1990b. *International Trade 89–90.* Vol. 2. Geneva.

"The General Agreement on Tariffs and Trade (GATT)." 1993. *Global Trade* 1 (3): 2–5.

Gereffi, G. 1983. *The Pharmaceutical Industry and Dependency in the Third World.* Princeton, N.J.: Princeton University Press.

———. 1990. "Paths of Industrialization: An Overview." In *Manufacturing Miracles: Paths of Industrialization in Latin America and East Asia,* edited by G. Gereffi and D. L. Wyman, 3–31. Princeton, N.J.: Princeton University Press.

Gibbs, D. C. 1988. "Restructuring in the Manchester Clothing Industry: Technical Change and Interrelationships between Manufacturers and Retailers." *Environment and Planning A* 20: 1219–33.

Giles, A. 1989. "Industrial Relations Theory, the State, and Politics." In *Theories and Concepts in Comparative Industrial Relations*, edited by J. Barbash and K. Barbash, 123–54. Columbia: University of South Carolina Press.

Godfrey, S. 1992. *Industrial Council Digest.* Cape Town: Industrial Relations Project.

Gold, T. 1986. *State and Society in the Taiwan Miracle.* Armonk, N.Y.: M. E. Sharpe.

Goldthorpe, J. 1984. "Introduction." In *Order and Conflict in Contemporary Capitalism*, edited by J. Goldthorpe, 1–14. Oxford: Clarendon Press.

Goodstadt, L. F. 1969. "Profits in Pawn." *Far Eastern Economic Review*, 17 April, 224–26.

Gordon, D. M., R. Edwards, and M. Reich. 1982. *Segmented Work, Divided Workers: The Historical on Transformations of Labor in the United States.* Cambridge, U.K.: Cambridge University Press.

Goshal, S., and N. Nohria. 1993. "Horses for Courses: Organizational Forms for Multinational Corporations." *Sloan Management Review* 34 (2): 23–35.

Grace, E. 1990. *Short Circuiting Labour: Unionizing Electronic Workers in Malaysia.* Kuala Lumpur: Insan.

Grant, W. 1985. "Introduction." In *The Political Economy of Corporatism*, edited by W. Grant, 1–31. London: Macmillan.

Gunn, T. G. 1992. *Twenty-First Century Manufacturing: Creating Winning Business Performance.* New York: Harper Business.

Gupta, A. K., and V. Govindarajan. 1991. "Knowledge Flows and the Structure of Control within Multinational Corporations." *Academy of Management Review* 16 (4): 768–92.

Haggard, S. 1989. "Introduction: The International Politics of Industrial Change." In *Pacific Dynamics: The International Politics of Industrial Change*, edited by S. Haggard and C. I. Moon, 1-22. Boulder, Colo.: Westview.

———. 1990. *Pathways from the Periphery: The Politics of Growth in the Newly Industrializing Countries.* Ithaca, N.Y.: Cornell University Press.

Haggard, S., and C. I. Moon, eds. 1989. *Pacific Dynamics: The International Politics of Industrial Change.* Boulder, Colo.: Westview Press.

Hall, D. T. 1991. "Business Restructuring and Strategic Human Resource Development." In *Turbulence in the American Workplace*, edited by P. B. Doeringer, 179-200. New York: Oxford University Press.

Hamill, J. 1984. "Labour Relations Decision-Making within Multinational Corporations." *Industrial Relations Journal* 15 (2): 30–34.

Harmon, R. L. 1992. *Reinventing the Factory II: Managing the World Class Factory.* New York: Free Press.

Harris, L. 1992. "South Africa's Economic and Social Transformation: From 'No Middle Road' to 'No Alternative.'" Paper presented at conference, Rethinking Marxism, University of Massachusetts, Nov.

Harrison, B., and B. Bluestone. 1988. *The Great U-Turn: Corporate Restructuring and the Polarizing of America.* New York: Basic Books.

Harrod, J. 1987. *Power, Production, and the Unprotected Worker.* New York: Columbia University Press.

———. 1992. *Labour and Third World Debt.* Brussels: ICEF.

Hattie, P. 1991. Technology and Reconstruction Colloquium, University of Cape Town, 3–5 May.

Henderson, J. 1989. *The Globalisation of High Technology Production: Society, Space and Semiconductors in the Restructuring of the Modern World.* London: Routledge.

Henley, J. 1983. "Corporate Strategy and Employment Relations in Multinational Corporations: Some Evidence from Kenya and Malaysia." In *Industrial Relations and Management Strategy,* edited by K. Thurley and S. Wood, 111–30. New York: Cambridge University Press.

Herzenberg, S., J. F. Perez-Lopez, and S. K. Tucker. 1990. "Labor Standards and Development in the Global Economy." In *Labor Standards and Development in the Global Economy,* edited by S. Herzenberg and J. Perez-Lopez, 1–16. Washington, D.C.: Department of Labor.

Higgins, W. 1987. "Unions as Bearers of Industrial Regeneration: Reflections on the Australian Case." *Economic and Industrial Democracy* 8: 213–36.

Hill, H. 1993. "Employment and National Enterprises in Indonesia." In *Multinationals and Employment: The Global Economy in the 1990s,* edited by P. Bailey, A. Parisotto, and G. Renshaw, 189–214. Geneva: ILO.

Hilowitz, J. 1987. "Education and Training Policies and Programmes to Support Industrial Restructuring in the Republic of Korea, Japan, Singapore and the United States." Discussion Paper no. 18. Training Policies Branch, ILO, Geneva.

Hiramoto, A. 1992. "Subcontracting Strategies of Japanese Companies in Europe and Asia: A Case Study of the Electronics Industry." In *New Impacts on Industrial Relations: Internationalization and Changing Production Strategies,* edited by S. Tokunaga, N. Altmann, and H. Demes, 225–42. Munich: Iudiciun Verlag.

Hirsch, A. 1979. "An Introduction to Textile Worker Organisation in Natal." *South African Labor Bulletin* 4 (8): 3–42.

Hirsh, B. W., and P. Ellis. 1974. *An Introduction to Textile Economics.* Manchester: Textile Trade Press.

Hirst, P., and J. Zeitlin. 1991. "Flexible Specialization vs. Post-Fordism: Theory, Evidence, and Policy Implications." *Economy and Society* 20 (Feb.): 1–56.

Hoffman, K. 1985. "Clothing, Chips and Competitive Advantage: The Impact of Microelectronics on Trade and Production in the Garment Industry." *World Development* 13 (3): 371–92.

Hoffman, K., and R. Kaplinsky. 1988. *Driving Force: The Global Restructuring of Technology, Labour, and Investment in the Automobile and Components Industries.* Boulder, Colo.: Westview Press.

Hofstede, G. 1980. *Culture's Consequences: International Differences in Work-related Values.* Beverly Hills, Calif.: Sage.

Holman, R. "Singapore's Production Allure." 1993. *Wall Street Journal,* 3 Feb., A10.

Hong Kong Cotton Spinners Association. 1988. *Forty Years of the Hong Kong Cotton Spinning Industry.* Hong Kong.

Houghton, D. 1973. *The South African Economy.* 3d ed. Cape Town: Oxford University Press.

Humana, C. 1986. *World Human Rights Guide.* London: Hodder and Stoughton.

Industrial Development Corporation. 1992a. *Key Facts: IDC and RSA.* Johannesburg.

————. 1992b. *Sectoral Data Series: Manufacturing.* Sandton.

————. 1992c. *Trade Data for Clothing and Textile Industry.* Vol. 2. Sandton.

————. 1993. *Import and Export Statistics.* Sandton.

Industry Department. Hong Kong. 1990. *Survey of Hong Kong's Manufacturing Industries.* Hong Kong: Government Printer.

————. 1991. *Hong Kong's Manufacturing Industries 1990.* Hong Kong: Government Printer.

————. 1992. *Report on Industrial Automation Study.* Hong Kong: Government Printer.

Innes, D. 1983. "Monopoly Capitalism in South Africa." In *South African Review 1*, edited by the Southern African Research Service, 171–83. Johannesburg: Ravan Press.

Institute for Industrial Education. 1974. *The Durban Strikes 1973.* Durban: Institute for Industrial Education and Ravan Press.

International Institute for Management Development. 1993. *The World Competitiveness Report 1993.* Geneva: Institute for Management Development/World Economic Forum.

International Labour Office. 1992. *Report of the Fact-Finding and Conciliation Commission on Freedom of Association concerning the Republic of South Africa.* Geneva.

International Monetary Fund. 1992. News release, no. 9.1-2, 9 April.

————. 1993. *International Financial Statistics.* New York.

Islam, I. 1987. "Manpower and Educational Planning in Singapore." In *Human Resource Planning: The Asian Experience*, edited by R. Amjad, 114–50. Geneva: ILO.

————. 1989. "Industrial Restructuring and Industrial Relations in ASEAN—A Firm-Level Chronicle." In *Restructuring, Employment and Industrial Relations*, edited by G. Edgren, 81–151. Geneva: ILO.

Jain, H. C., H. C. Jain, and C. S. Venkata Ratnam. 1992. "Human Resource Management Practices of Japanese and Other Foreign Companies in Developing Countries." In *Proceedings of the Forty-Fourth Annual Meeting of the Industrial Relations Research Association*, 359–84. Madison, Wisc.: Industrial Relations Research Association.

James Capel & Co. 1993. *Global Pharmaceutical Review.* London.

"Japanese Access" (in Japanese). 1993. *Nihon Keizai Shinbun*, 27 Jan., 1.

Joffe, A. 1991. "COSATU Economic Policy Conference." *South African Labour Bulletin* 15 (8): 41–44.

Joffe, A., and D. Lewis. 1992. "A Strategy for South African Manufacturing." *South African Labour Bulletin* 16 (4): 24–31.

Joffe, A., et al. 1993. "Meeting the Global Challenge: A Framework for Industrial Revival in South Africa." Paper presented at conference, South Africa's International Economic Relations in the Nineties, Institute for Democratic Alternatives in South Africa, Johannesburg.

Jourdan, P. 1992. "Mineral Beneficiation Industries." Paper presented at workshop, Industrial Strategy Project, University of Cape Town, July.

Jürgens, U. 1991. "Departures from Taylorism and Fordism: New Forms of Work in the Automobile Industry." In *The Politics of Flexibility: Restructuring State and Industry in Britain, Germany and Scandinavia*, edited by B. Jessop et al., 233–47. Aldershot, U.K.: Edward Elgar.

Jürgens, U., T. Malsch, and K. Dohse. 1993. *Breaking from Taylorism: Changing Forms of Work in the Automobile Industry.* Cambridge, U.K.: Cambridge University Press.

Kagono, T., et al. 1983. *Comparison of Management between Japan and the United States* (in Japanese). Tokyo: Nihonkeizai Shinbunsha.

Kahn, B. 1992. "Exchange Rate Policy and Industrial Restructuring." In *South African Review 6: From Red Friday to Codesa*, edited by G. Moss and I. Obery, 493–508. Johannesburg: Ravan Press.

Kalleberg, A. 1990. "The Comparative Study of Business Organizations and Their Employees." In *Comparative Social Research: A Research Annual, Business Institutions*, edited by C. Calhoun, 153-75. Greenwich, Conn.: JAI Press.

Kaplan, D. 1991. "Targeting Technology in South Africa: An Examination of Our Current Technological Capabilities and Some Suggestion for Reform." Paper presented at Technology and Reconstruction Colloquium, University of Cape Town, 3–5 May.

Kaplinsky, R. 1992. "South African Industrial Performance and Structure in a Comparative Context." Industrial Strategy Project, University of Cape Town. Typescript.

Katz, H., S. Kuruvilla, and L. Turner. Forthcoming. "Trade Unions and Collective Bargaining 1992." In *Impediments to Competitive Labour Markets: An Overview of Policy and Research Issues*. Washington, D.C.: World Bank, Personnel and Human Resources, Education and Employment Division.

Katzenstein, P. 1985. *Small States in World Markets.* Ithaca, N.Y.: Cornell University Press.

Keet, D. 1992. "Shop Stewards and Worker Control." *South African Labour Bulletin* 16 (5): 29–39.

Kenney, M., and R. Florida. 1993. *Beyond Mass Production: The Japanese System and Its Transfer to the United States.* New York: Oxford University Press.

Kern, H., and M. Schumann. 1992. "New Concepts of Production and the Emergence of the Systems Controller." In *Technology and the Future of Work*, ed. P. Adler, 151–70. New York: Oxford University Press.

Kerr, C. 1983. *The Future of Industrial Societies: Convergence or Continuing Diversity?* Cambridge: Harvard University Press.

Kerr, C., et al. 1960. *Industrialism and Industrial Man.* Cambridge: Harvard University Press.

Khan, M. 1989. *Labour Administration: Profile on Malaysia.* Bangkok: ILO and ARPLA.

Khanna, S. R. 1991. *International Trade in Textiles: MFA Quotas and a Developing Exporting Country.* New Delhi: Sage.

Kim, H. J. 1993. "The Korean Union Movement in Transition." In *Organized Labor in the Asia-Pacific Region*, edited by S. Frenkel, 133–61. Ithaca, N.Y.: ILR Press.

Kim, T., and J.-S. Park. 1992. *Case Studies in Labor-Management Relations I: Large Korean Manufacturing Firms* (in Korean). Seoul: Korea Labor Institute.

King, A. Y. C., and D. H. K. Leung. 1975. *The Chinese Touch in Small Industrial Organizations.* Hong Kong: Chinese University of Hong Kong, Social Research Centre.

Kirkbride, P. S., and S. F. Y. Tang. 1992. "From Kyoto to Kowloon: Cultural

Barriers to the Transference of Quality Circles from Japan to Hong Kong." In *Proceedings of the Third Conference on International Personnel and Human Resource Management,* edited by P. S. Kirkbride, K. Rowland, and J. B. Fisher. Berkhamsted, U.K.: Ashridge Management Center.

Kochan, T. A., R. Batt, and L. Dyer. 1992. "International Human Resource Studies: A Framework for Future Research." In *Research Frontiers in Industrial Relations and Human Resources,* edited by D. Lewin, O. S. Mitchell, and P. D. Sherer, 309–37. Madison, Wisc.: Industrial Relations Research Association.

Kochan, T. A., and J. B. Chalykoff. 1987. "Human Resource Management and Business Life Cycles: Some Preliminary Propositions." In *Human Resource Management in High Technology Firms,* edited by A. Kleingartner and C. S. Anderson, 183-200. Lexington, Mass.: Lexington Books.

Kochan, T. A., and H. C. Katz. 1988. *Collective Bargaining and Industrial Relations: From Theory to Practice.* Homewood, Ill.: Irwin.

Kochan, T. A., H. Katz, and R. McKersie. 1986. *The Transformation of American Industrial Relations.* New York: Basic Books. Reprint, Ithaca, N.Y.: ILR Press, 1994.

Kochan, T. A., and R. B. McKersie. 1992. "Human Resources, Organizational Governance, and Public Policy: Lessons from a Decade of Experimentation." In *Transforming Organizations,* edited by T. A. Kochan and M. Useem, 169–87. New York: Oxford University Press.

Koike, K. 1988. *Understanding Industrial Relations in Modern Japan.* London: Macmillan.

Korpi, W. 1978. *The Working Class in Welfare Capitalism: Work, Unions and Politics in Sweden.* London. Routledge and Kegan Paul.

Koryu Kyokai. 1987. *The Labor Problem in Taiwan* (in Japanese). Tokyo.

Kuo, E. C. Y., L. Low, and M.-H. Toh. 1989. "The Singapore Telecommunications Sector and Issues Affecting Its Competitive Position in the Pacific Region." *Columbia Journal of World Business* 24 (1): 59–71.

Kurt Salmon Associates. 1987. "Final Report on Techno-Economic and Marketing Research Study on the Textiles and Clothing Industry for Hong Kong Government Industry Department." Typescript.

Kuruvilla, S. 1992. "Industrialization Strategy and Industrial Relations Policy in Malaysia." Working paper. School of Industrial and Labor Relations, Cornell University.

———. 1994. "Industrialization Strategies and Industrial Relations Policies in Malaysia and the Philippines." In *Proceedings of the 1994 Annual Meeting of the Industrial Relations Research Association.* Madison, Wisc.: Industrial Relations Research Association.

———. 1995. "Industrialization Strategies, National Industrial Relations Policies and Workplace Industrial Relations Practices." In *The Comparative Political Economy of Industrial Relations,* edited by L. Turner and K. Wever. Madison, Wisc.: Industrial Relations Research Association.

Labour Department. Thailand. 1991. *Yearbook of Labour Statistics, 1990.* Bangkok.

Lane, C. 1989. *Management and Labour in Europe.* Hampshire, U.K.: Edward Elgar.

Laothamatas, A. 1992. "The Politics of Structural Adjustment in Thailand: A Political Explanation of Economic Success." In *The Dynamics of Economic Policy*

Reform in Southeast Asia and the Southwest Pacific, edited by A. MacIntyre and K. Jayasuriya. Singapore: Oxford University Press.

Lawler, E. 1992. *The Ultimate Advantage: Creating the High-Involvement Organization*. San Francisco: Jossey-Bass.

Lawler, J. J., M. A. Zaidi, and V. Atmiyanandana. 1989. "Human Resource Strategies in Southeast Asia: The Case of Thailand." In *Research in Personnel and Human Resource Management*, Suppl. 1, 201–21. Greenwich, Conn.: JAI Press.

Lazear, E. P. 1979. "Why Is There Mandatory Retirement?" *Journal of Political Economy* 87: 1261–84.

Lee Boon Hiok. 1985. "Innovative Approaches in Industrial Relations: Consensus Building in the Singapore Context." In *Innovative Approaches to Industrial Relations in ASEAN*, 133–67. Geneva: ILO.

Leger, J. P., and M. Nicol. 1993. "Gold Mining in South Africa: Priorities for Restructuring." *Transformation* 20: 17–35.

Leggett, C. 1993. "Corporatist Trade Unionism in Singapore." In *Organized Labor in the Asia-Pacific Region: A Comparative Study of Trade Unionism in Nine Countries*, edited by S. Frenkel, 223–48. Ithaca, N.Y.: ILR Press.

"Legislation Protecting Subcontractors Should Be Installed" (in Chinese). 1988. *Wen Wei Po*, 14 May.

Levin, D. A. 1991. "Women and the Industrial Labor Market in Hong Kong: Participation and Perceptions." In *Status Influences in Third World Labor Markets: Caste, Gender, and Custom*, edited by J. G. Scoville, 183–214. New York: de Gruyter.

Levin, D. A., and S. Chiu. 1991. "Enforcing Workplace Safety Legislation." In *Crime and Justice in Hong Kong*, edited by H. Traver and J. Vagg, 153-71. Hong Kong: Oxford University Press.

———. 1993. "Dependent Capitalism, a Colonial State, and Marginal Unions: The Case of Hong Kong." In *Organized Labor in the Asia-Pacific Region: A Comparative Study of Trade Unionism in Nine Countries*, edited by S. Frenkel, 187–222. Ithaca, N.Y.: ILR Press.

Levy, Andrew, and Associates. 1992. *Annual Report*. Johannesburg.

Lewis, D. 1991a. "The Character and Consequences of Conglomeration in the South African Economy." *Transformation* 16: 32–35.

———. 1991b. "State Intervention the Key to Korea's Economic Miracle." *Business Day*, 4 Oct, 8.

———. 1992. "The Debate on Economic Development Policy in South Africa." Paper presented at seminar, South Africa's Socio-Economic Problems: Future Role of the United Nations System in Helping Address Them, Windhoek, 22–24 May.

Lewis, J. 1984. *Industrialisation and Trade Union Organisation in South Africa, 1924-1955: The Rise and Fall of the South African Trades and Labour Council*. Cambridge, U.K.: Cambridge University Press.

Liao, W. C., D. Yang, and Y. D. Young. 1990. "Social Structure of the Workplace" (in Japanese). *Rokkodai Ronshu* 36 (4): 94–109.

Lim, D. 1984. "Industrial Restructuring in Singapore." Asian Employment Programme Working Papers. ILO, Geneva.

Lim, L. 1978. "Multinational Firms, and Manufacturing for Export in Less

Developed Countries: The Case of the Electronics Industry in Singapore and Malaysia." Ph.D. diss., University of Michigan.

———. 1990. "Singapore." In *Labor Standards and Development in the Global Economy*, edited by S. Herzenberg and J. Perez-Lopez, 73–93. Washington, D.C.: Department of Labor.

Lim, L., and Pang Eng Fong. 1986. *Trade, Employment, and Industrialisation in Singapore*. Geneva: ILO.

———. 1991. *Foreign Direct Investment and Industrialisation in Malaysia, Singapore, Taiwan and Thailand*. Paris: Organisation for Economic Co-operation and Development.

Lincoln, J., and Kalleberg, A. 1990. *Culture, Control, and Commitment: A Study of Work Organization and Work Attitudes in the United States and Japan*. Cambridge, U.K.: Cambridge University Press.

Lipietz, A. 1987. *Mirages and Miracles: The Crisis of Global Fordism*. London: Verso.

Lipton, M. 1986. *Capitalism and Apartheid, South Africa, 1910-1986*. Aldershot, U.K.: Wildwood House.

Lui, T. L., and S. Chiu. 1992. "A Tale of Two Industries." Paper presented at workshop, Industrial Restructuring and Regional Adjustment in the Asian NIEs, Centre for Advanced Studies, National University of Singapore, 25–27 March.

———. 1993. "Industrial Restructuring and Labour Market Adjustment under Positive Non-Interventionism." *Environment and Planning A* 25: 63–80.

Lynn, M. 1991. *The Billion Dollar Battle: Merck v. Glaxo*. London: Mandarin.

Mabry, B. 1987. "The Labour Market and the Practice of Professional Management in Thailand." *Journal of Southeast Asian Studies* 18 (2).

McCord, W. 1991. "The Asian Renaissance." *Society* 28 (6): 49–61.

MacDuffie, J. P., and J. F. Krafcik. 1992. "Integrating Technology and Human Resources for High-Performance Manufacturing: Evidence from the Internal Auto Industry." In *Transforming Organizations*, edited by T. A. Kochan and M. Useem, 209–26. New York: Oxford University Press.

McGrath, M. D. 1984. "Inequality in the Size Distribution of Income in South Africa." Development Studies Paper no. 2. Centre for Applied Social Studies, University of Natal, Durban.

Maller, J. 1992. *Conflict and Co-operation: Case Studies in Worker Participation*. Johannesburg: Ravan Press.

Maree, J. 1986. "An Analysis of the Independent Trade Unions in South Africa in the 1970s." Ph.D. diss., University of Cape Town.

———. 1993. "An Industrial Strategy for the South African Textile Industry." Industrial Strategy Project, Development Policy Research Unit, University of Cape Town. Typescript.

Marginson, P. M., et al. 1988. *Beyond the Workplace: Managing Industrial Relations in the Multinational Enterprise*. New York: Blackwell.

Mathews, J. 1989. *Tools of Change: New Technology and the Democratization of Work Organization*. Sydney: Pluto Press.

Midgley, J. 1967. "Conformity and Social Control in the Cape Malay Community." Master's thesis, University of Capetown.

Milgrom, P., and J. Roberts. 1990. "The Economics of Modern Manufacturing:

Technology, Strategy, and Organization." *American Economic Review* (June): 511–28.

Milkman, R. 1991. *Japan's California Factories: Labor Relations and Economic Globalization.* Los Angeles: Institute of Industrial Relations, University of California.

Mills, C. P. 1984. *Industrial Disputes Law in Malaysia.* Kuala Lumpur: Malayan Law Journal.

"Miners Want Deal on Social Plan." 1993. *Business Day.*

Ministry of Labour. Singapore. 1989. *Yearbook of Labour Statistics.* Singapore.

———. 1990. *Guidelines on Part-Time Employment.* Singapore.

Ministry of Trade and Industry. Singapore. 1991. *The Strategic Economic Plan.* Singapore.

Mintzberg, H. 1983. *Structure in Fives: Designing Effective Organizations.* Englewood Cliffs, N.J.: Prentice-Hall.

Mizoguchi, Y. 1989. *China as a Method* (in Japanese). Tokyo: Tokyo Daigaku Shuppankai.

Mody, A., and D. Wheeler. 1987. "Towards a Vanishing Middle: Competition in the World Garment Industry." *World Development* 15 (10–11): 367–82.

———. 1991. *Automation and World Competition.* New York: St. Martin's Press.

Moll, T. 1990. "From Booster to Brake? Apartheid and Economic Growth in Comparative Perspective." In *The Political Economy of South Africa,* edited by N. Nattrass and E. Ardington, 73-87. Cape Town: Oxford University Press.

Mueller, F., and J. Purcell. 1992. "The Europeanization and Decentralization of Bargaining: Multinational Management Strategies in the European Automobile Industry." *International Journal of Human Resource Management* 3 (1): 15–34.

Munck, R. 1988. *The New International Labour Studies: An Introduction.* London: Zed Books.

———. 1989. *Third World Workers and the New International Labour Studies.* London: Zed Books.

Mytelka, L. K. 1991. "Technological Change and the Global Relocation of Production in Textiles and Clothing." *Studies in Political Economy* 36: 109–43.

National Clothing Federation. 1992. *The South African Clothing Industry: Annual Report.* Bedfordview.

———. 1993. *The South African Clothing Industry: 1993 Executive Handbook/ Diary.* Bedfordview.

National Productivity Board. 1988. *Report of the Task Force on Job-Hopping.* Singapore.

National Trade Union Congress. 1990. *May Day Annual '90.* Singapore.

National Union of Metalworkers of South Africa. 1992. "Industrial Policy in the Metal Sector." Typescript.

National Union of Textile Workers. 1982. "Industrial Councils—New Dimensions to the Struggle in the Textile Industry." *South African Labor Bulletin* 7 (4–5): 94–101.

National Wages Council. 1988. Singapore.

"Neither Bleak Nor Broad." 1979. *Textile Asia,* Sept., 280.

Ngoasheng, M. 1991. "Restructuring the Manufacturing Sector in a Post-Apartheid South Africa." Paper presented at Conference on South Africa, Copenhagen, Feb.

Nichols, T. 1989. "The Business Cycle and Industrial Injuries in British Manufacturing over a Quarter of a Century: Continuities in Industrial Injury Research." *Sociological Review* 37: 538–50.

Nihei, Y., D. Levin, and M. Ohtsu. 1982. "Industrialization and Employment Practices in Asia: A Comparative Study of Ten Spinning Factories in Five Asian Countries." *Economic Development and Cultural Change* 31 (1): 145–71.

Nomura, M. 1992. "Japanese Personnel Management Transferred: Transplants of the Electronics Industry in Asia and Europe." In *New Impacts on Industrial Relations: Internationalization and Changing Production Strategies*, edited by S. Tokunaga, N. Altmann, and H. Demes, 117–32. Munich: Iudiciun Verlag.

North, D. C. 1990. *Institutions, Institutional Change and Economic Performance.* Cambridge, U.K.: Cambridge University Press.

Ntshangase, W., and A. Solomons. 1993. "Worker Participative Schemes: A Trade Union Response." *South African Labour Bulletin* 17 (4): 31–35.

Ogden, M. 1992. "The Future of Unionism in Australia." Australian Council of Trade Unions. Typescript.

Ogle, G. 1993. *South Korea: Dissent within the Economic Miracle.* London: Zed Books.

Okamoto, Y. 1989. "Multinational Enterprise and the Multinationalization of Japanese Business Enterprise 2" (in Japanese). *Keizaigaku Ronshu* 54 (3): 67–92.

Oliver, N., and B. Wilkinson. 1989. "Japanese Manufacturing Techniques and Personnel and Industrial Relations Practices in Britain: Evidence and Implications." *British Journal of Industrial Relations* 27 (1): 73–91.

Onn, F. C. 1989. "Wages and Labour Welfare in the Malaysian Electronics Industry." *Labour and Society* 14: 81–102.

Ooi, S. 1987. "A Wage for Bad Times and Good." *Straits Times*, 9 Feb., 15.

Osaka Prefectural Institute for Advanced Industry Development and Osaka Chamber of Commerce and Industry. 1989. *Survey on Management Trends and Parts Procurement of Japanese Overseas Companies* (in Japanese). Osaka.

Pack, H. 1987. *Productivity, Technology and Industrial Development: A Case Study of Textiles.* New York: Oxford University Press.

Panel and Task Group for the Textile and Clothing Industries. 1994. *Long-Term Strategic Plan for the Textile and Clothing Industries in South Africa.* Pretoria: Department of Trade and Industry.

Pang Eng Fong. 1982. *Education, Manpower, and Development in Singapore.* Singapore: National University of Singapore Press.

———. 1988a. "Development Strategies and Labour Market Changes in Singapore." In *Labour Market Developments and Structural Change*, edited by Pang Eng Fong, 195–242. Singapore: Singapore University.

———. 1988b. "Structural Change and Labour Market Developments: The Comparative Experiences of Five ASEAN Countries and Australia." In *Labour Market Developments and Structural Change*, edited by Pang Eng Fong, 1–12. Singapore: Singapore University.

———. 1990. "Emerging Issues of Labor Markets and Industrial Relations in Singapore." Typescript.

Pang Eng Fong, and L. Cheng. 1978. "Changing Patterns of Industrial Relations in Singapore." In *The Role of Trade Unions in Developing Societies*, edited by E. M.

Kassalow and U. G. Damachi, 31–50. Geneva: International Institute for Labour Studies.

Park, Y. I., and K. Anderson. 1991. "The Experience of Japan in Historical and International Perspective." In *New Silk Roads: East Asia and World Textile Markets,* edited by K. Anderson, 15–29. Cambridge, U.K.: Cambridge University Press.

Peck, J. A. 1991. "Outwork and Restructuring Processes in the Australian Clothing Industry." *Labour and Industry* 3 (2–3): 302–29.

Pehie, M., B. L. Mansour, and V. S. Chen. 1988. "The Problem of Union Recognition in Malaysia." In *The Problem of Union Recognition: A Survey of the Current Situation in ASEAN,* 13–35. Geneva: ILO.

Penn, R., A. Martin, and H. Scattergood. 1991. "Gender Relations, Technology and Employment Change in the Contemporary Textile Industry." *Sociology* 25: 569–87.

"The Phantom of the Opera." 1989. *Economist,* 11 Nov., 40–41.

Phizacklea, A. 1987. "Minority Women and Economic Restructuring: The Case of Britain and the Federal Republic of Germany." *Work, Employment and Society* 1 (3): 309–25.

Pi'i, A. B., and K. Kumaraguru. 1989. "Labour Relations and Development in Malaysia: A Brief Overview." In *Labour Relations and Development: Summary and Working Papers of the Third ASEAN Tripartite Course on Labour Relations and Development, 14–21 April,* 53–60. Phuket.

Ping, L. L., and M. A. K. Haji. 1987. "Malaysian Airlines Systems Berhad." In *Labour Relations and Productivity at the Enterprise Level: Selected Case Studies from within ASEAN,* 50–72. Geneva: ILO.

Piore, M., and C. Sabel. 1984. *The Second Industrial Divide: Possibilities for Prosperity.* New York: Basic Books.

Piriyarangsan, S., and K. Poonpanich. 1992. "Labour Institutions in an Export-Oriented Country: A Case Study of Thailand." Paper presented at the International Workshop on Labour Institutions and Economic Development in Asia, Bali, 4–6 Feb.

Pityana, S., and M. Orkin, eds. 1992. *Beyond the Factory Floor.* Johannesburg: Ravan Press.

"Pleasing Result." 1982. *Textile Asia,* April, 69–70.

Ponniah, A., and C. Littler. 1993. "State Regulation and Union Fragmentation in Malaysia." In *Organised Labour in the Asian Pacific Region: A Comparative Study of Trade Unionism in Nine Countries,* edited by S. Frenkel, 107–32. Ithaca, N.Y.: ILR Press.

Pontusson, J. 1987. "Radicalisation and Retreat in Swedish Social Democracy." *New Left Review* 165: 1–33.

Poole, M. 1986. *Industrial Relations: Origins and Patterns in National Diversity.* London: Routledge.

Porter, M. 1990. *The Competitive Advantage of Nations.* New York: Free Press.

"Productivity by OE." 1979. *Textile Asia,* April, 74.

Purcell, J., and K. Sisson. 1983. "Strategies and Practice in the Management of Industrial Relations." In *Industrial Relations in Britain,* edited by G. S. Bain, 95–120. Oxford: Blackwell.

Putti, J. M., and Toh Thian Ser. 1990. *Cases in Human Resource Management.* Singapore: Singapore Institute of Management and Times Academic Press.

Quinn, J. B. 1992. *The Intelligent Enterprise.* New York: Free Press.

Ragin, C. C. 1987. *The Comparative Method: Moving beyond Qualitative and Quantitative Strategies.* Berkeley: University of California Press.

Rasiah, R. 1988. "Production in Transition within the Semi-conductor Industry and Its Impact on Penang." *Journal of Malaysian Studies* 6 (June): 85–111.

———. 1992. "The Semiconductor Industry in Penang: Implications for the New International Division of Labour Theories." *Journal of Contemporary Asia* 18 (1): 24–46.

———. 1994. "Flexible Production Systems and Local Machine Tool Subcontracting: The Case of Electronics Components Transnationals in Malaysia." *Cambridge Journal of Economics* 18 (3): 279–98.

Redding, S. G. 1990. *The Spirit of Chinese Capitalism.* Berlin: de Gruyter.

Redding, S. G., and R. D. Whitley. 1990. "Beyond Bureaucracy: Towards a Comparative Analysis of Forms of Economic Resource Co-ordination and Control." In *Capitalism in Contrasting Cultures,* edited by S. R. Clegg, S. G. Redding, and M. Cartner, 79–104. Berlin: de Gruyter.

Registrar General. Hong Kong. Various years. *Annual Departmental Report.* Hong Kong: Government Printer.

Registrar of Trade Unions. Hong Kong. Various years. *Annual Departmental Report.* Hong Kong: Government Printer.

Reich, R. B. 1991. *The Work of Nations: Preparing Ourselves for the Twenty-First Century.* New York: Knopf.

Renshaw, G. 1993. "Overview and Conclusions." In *Multinationals and Employment: The Global Economy in the 1990s,* edited by P. Bailey, A. Parisotto, and G. Renshaw. Geneva: ILO.

Rodan, G. 1989. *The Political Economy of Singapore's Industrialization: National, State and International Capital.* London: Macmillan.

Rodgers, R. Forthcoming. "Industrial Relations in the Korean Auto Industry." In *Global Capital, Local Labor: The World Automobile Industry,* edited by F. Deyo. London: Macmillan.

Roth, S. 1992. *Japanization, or Going Our Own Way? Internationalization and Interest Representation.* Dusseldorf: Hans-Böckler-Stiftung.

"SA's GDP Takes 5.1% Tumble." 1993. *Cape Times,* 12 Feb., 13.

Salih, K. 1988. "The Changing Face of Electronics in the Periphery: The Case of Malaysia." *International Journal of Urban and Regional Research* 14: 375–402.

Samakkhitham, S. 1990. *Economic Life of Low-Level Workers* (in Thai). Bangkok: Arom Pongpa-ngan Foundation.

Satitniramai, A. 1992. "The Formation of Labor Movements in the Textile Industry." Master's thesis, Thammasat University.

Schmitter, P. 1979. "Still the Century of Corporatism?" In *Trends toward Corporatist Intermediation,* edited by P. Schmitter and G. Lehmbruch, 7–52. London: Sage.

———. 1982. "Reflections on Where the Theory of Neo-Corporatism Has Gone and Where the Praxis of Neo-Corporatism May Be Going." In *Patterns of Corporatist Policy-Making,* edited by P. Schmitter and G. Lehmbruch, 259–79. London: Sage.

————. 1990. "Sectors in Modern Capitalism: Modes of Governance and Variations in Performance." In *Labor Relations and Economic Performance*, edited by R.
Brunetta and C. Dell'Aringa, 3–39. London: Macmillan.

Scott, A. 1992. "The Roepke Lecture in Economic Geography. The Collective
Order of Flexible Production Agglomerations: Lessons for Local Economic
Development Policy and Strategic Choice." *Economic Geography* 68 (July):
219–33.

Seidman, G. W. 1990a. "Labour Movements in Newly Industrialised Countries:
South Africa and Brazil, 1960–1985." Ph.D. diss., University of California,
Berkeley.

————. 1990b. "The Emergence of Political Unionism in Brazil and South
Africa." *South African Sociological Review* 3 (1): 35–38.

————. 1993. "Facing the New International Context of Development." In
Global Vision, edited by J. Brecher, 179-89. Boston: South End Press.

Seng, T. K., and A. N. Hashim. 1987. "Company M." In *Labour Relations and
Productivity at the Enterprise Level: Selected Case Studies from within ASEAN,* 3–31.
Geneva: ILO.

Shaiken, H. 1991. "The Universal Motors Assembly and Stamping Plant:
Transferring High-Tech Production to Mexico." *Columbia Journal of World
Business* 26 (Summer): 124–37.

Shalev, M. 1981. "Theoretical Dilemmas and Value Analysis in Comparative
Industrial Relations." In *Management under Differing Value Systems*, edited by W.
Dlugos, 241–63. New York: de Gruyter.

Sharma, B. 1985. *Aspects of Industrial Relations in ASEAN*. Singapore: Institute
For Asian Studies.

————. 1991. "Industrialisation and Strategy Shifts in Industrial Relations." In
International Comparisons in Human Resource Management, edited by C. Brewster
and S. Tyson, 92–109. London: Pitman.

Shaw, J. B., et al. 1992. "Human Resource Practices in Hong Kong and
Singapore: A Comparative Analysis." In *Proceedings of the Third Conference on
International Personnel and Human Resource Management*, edited by P. S. Kirk-
bride, K. Rowland, and J. B. Fisher, Section 26. Berkhamsted, U.K.: Ashridge
Management Center.

Shire, K. 1994. "Bargaining Regimes and the Social Reorganization of Produc-
tion: The Case of General Motors in Austria and Germany." In *Workplace
Industrial Relations and the Global Challenge,* edited by J. Bélanger, P. K.
Edwards, and L. Haiven, 137–56. Ithaca, N.Y.: ILR Press.

Siengthai, S. 1988. "Thai-Hino Industry Co., Ltd." In *Case Studies in Labour-
Management Cooperation for Productivity Improvement*, 265–308. Bangkok: ILO.

Simon, H. 1957. *Adminstrative Behavior*. 2d ed. New York: Macmillan. Singapore
Institute of Personnel Management. 1991. *1990 Survey on Human Resource
Management Practices in Singapore*. Singapore.

Singapore Institute of Personnel Management. 1991. *1990 Survey on Human
Resource Management Practices in Singapore*. Singapore.

Singapore National Employers Federation. 1990a. *Report of Sub-Committee on
Contracting Out Work, Multi-tasking and Job Restructuring*. Singapore.

————. 1990b. *Report of Sub-Committee on Fringe Benefits*. Singapore.

————. 1990c. *Report of Sub-Committee on Part-Time Employment*. Singapore.

————. 1990d. *Report of Sub-Committee on Wage Reform and Consequential Wage Adjustments*. Singapore.

Singh, A. 1992. "The Lost Decade: The Economic Crisis of the Third World in the 1980s: How the North Caused the South's Crisis." *Contention: Debates in Society, Culture, and Science* 103 (Spring): 136–68.

Sit, V. F. S., and S. L. Wong. 1989. *Small and Medium Industries in an Export-Oriented Economy: The Case of Hong Kong*. Hong Kong: University of Hong Kong, Centre of Asian Studies.

Sit, V. F. S., S. L. Wong, and T. S. Kiang. 1979. *Small-Scale Industry in a Laissez Faire Economy*. Hong Kong: University of Hong Kong, Centre of Asian Studies.

Sitas, A. 1983. "African Worker Responses on the East Rand to Changes in the Metal Industry, 1960–1989." Ph.D. diss., University of the Witwatersrand.

Sivagnanam, S. 1988. "The Administration and Enforcement of Collective Agreements in Malaysia." In *The Administration and Enforcement of Collective Agreements: A Survey of the Current Situation in ASEAN*, 15–28. Geneva: ILO.

So, A. Y. 1986. "The Economic Success of Hong Kong: Insights from a World-System Perspective." *Sociological Perspectives* 29: 241–58.

————. 1990. *Social Change and Development: Modernization, Dependency, and World-System Theories*. Newbury Park, Calif.: Sage.

Sorge, A., and W. Streeck. 1988. "Industrial Relations and Technical Change: The Case for an Extended Perspective." In *New Technology and Industrial Relations*, edited by R. Hyman and W. Streeck, 19–47. Oxford: Blackwell.

South African Chamber of Business. 1990. "Economic Options for South Africa." Johannesburg.

————. 1991. "A Concept for the Development of a New Industrial Policy for South Africa." Johannesburg.

South African Institute of Race Relations. 1992. *Race Relations Survey, 1991–1992*. Johannesburg.

South African Reserve Bank. 1988. *Quarterly Reports*. March. Pretoria.

————. 1991. *Quarterly Reports*. March. Pretoria.

————. 1992. *Quarterly Bulletin*. Pretoria.

Southall, R. 1988. "Introduction." In *Trade Unions and the New Industrialisation of the Third World*, edited by R. Southall, 1–34. London: Zed Books.

Spinanger, D. 1986. *Industrialization Policies and Regional Economic Development in Malaysia*. Singapore: Oxford University Press.

Spinning, Weaving and Dyeing Trade Workers' General Union. 1978. *Spinning, Weaving and Dyeing Worker* (in Chinese). Hong Kong.

————. 1979. *Spinning, Weaving and Dyeing Worker* (in Chinese). Hong Kong.

————. 1980. *Spinning, Weaving and Dyeing Worker* (in Chinese). Hong Kong.

————. 1983. *Spinning, Weaving and Dyeing Worker* (in Chinese). Hong Kong.

Standing, G. 1989. "The Growth of External Labour Flexibility in a Nascent NIC: Malaysian Labour Flexibility Survey (MLFS)." World Employment Programme Research Working Paper no. 35. Geneva: ILO.

Steenkamp Report. 1983. *The Policy of Protection in regard to Textiles and Clothing*. Pretoria: Government Printer.

Stinchcombe, A. 1965. "Social Structure and Organizations." In *Handbook of Organizations*, edited by J. G. March, 142–69. Chicago: Rand McNally.

Storey, J. 1992. *Developments in the Management of Human Resources: An Analytical Review.* Oxford: Blackwell.

Streeck, W. 1991. "On the Institutional Conditions of Diversified Quality Production." In *Beyond Keynesianism: The Socio-Economics of Production and Full Employment*, edited by E. Matzner and W. Streeck, 21–61. Aldershot, U.K.: Edward Elgar.

Strolz, H. 1991. "Global Excesses in Primary Textiles." *Textile Month*, Jan., 33–39.

"Summit on the Mining Conference." 1991. *South African Labour Bulletin* 15 (8), June.

Sung, Y. W. 1991. *The China-Hong Kong Connection: The Key to China's Open-Door Policy.* Cambridge, U.K.: Cambridge University Press.

Sussangkarn, C. 1990. *Labour Markets in an Era of Adjustment: A Study of Thailand.* Bangkok: Thailand Development Research Institute Foundation.

Taiwan Kenkyujo. 1979. *The General Survey of Taiwan in 1979* (in Japanese). Tokyo.

———. 1989. *The General Survey of Taiwan in 1989* (in Japanese). Tokyo.

Tan, C. 1992. "Growth Triangles from Several Angles: A NIE Perspective Based upon Hong Kong–Guangdong Industrialization." Mimeo.

"13,000 Jobs Lost But Exports Help." 1993. *Argus*, 15 July, 1.

Tokunaga, S., M. Nomura, and A. Hiramoto. 1991. *Japanese Corporation/Global Strategy and Its Implementation* (in Japanese). Tokyo: Dōbunkan.

Tokunaga, S., et al. 1991. *Japanisches Personalmanagement—ein anderer Weg?* Frankfurt: Campus Verlag.

Toyne, B., et al. 1984. *The Global Textile Industry.* London: Allen and Unwin.

Trade Monitor. 1993. Trade Monitoring Project, University of Cape Town. Feb.

Tsao Yuan. 1982. "Growth and Productivity in Singapore: A Supply Side Analysis." Ph.D. diss., Harvard University.

Turner, H. A., P. Fosh, and S. H. Ng. 1991. *Between Two Societies: Hong Kong Labour in Transition.* Hong Kong: University of Hong Kong, Centre of Asian Studies.

Turner, L. 1991. *Democracy at Work: Changing World Markets and the Future of Labor Unions.* Ithaca, N.Y.: Cornell University Press.

Tyers, R., P. Phillips, and C. Findlay. 1987. "ASEAN and China Exports of Labour Intensive Manufactures: Performance and Prospects." *ASEAN Economic Bulletin* 3 (March): 339–66.

Tyson, L., and J. Zysman. 1983. "American Industry in International Competition." In *American Industry in International Competition*, edited by L. Tyson and J. Zysman, 15–59. Ithaca, N.Y.: Cornell University Press.

"Underemployment in Garment-Making: Large Scale Industrial Disputes Expected to Rise This Year." 1990. *Oriental Daily News*, 26 Oct.

United Nations Centre on Transnational Corporations. 1987. *Transnational Corporations and the Electronics Industries of ASEAN Economies.* UNCTC Current Studies Series A, no. 5. New York: United Nations.

United Nations Conference on Trade and Development. 1990. *Handbook on International Trade and Development Statistics 1989.* New York: United Nations.

United Nations Industrial Development Organization. 1990. "C. Textile Machinery. 1. Recent Trends and Technological Developments." Industry and Development Global Report 1990–91. Vienna.

U.S. Department of Labor. Bureau of International Affairs. 1990. *Foreign Labor Trends: Singapore*. Washington, D.C.

van Coller, J. 1992. "Short Term Outlook for Textiles." *Textile Topics* 4 (4): 4–5.

van Liemt, G. 1988. *Bridging the Gap: Four Newly Industrialising Countries and the Changing International Division of Labor*. Geneva: ILO.

Vogel, E. F. 1991. *The Four Little Dragons: The Spread of Industrialization in East Asia*. Cambridge: Harvard University Press.

Von Holdt, K. 1991a. "Productivity—Participating to Achieve Control." *South African Labour Bulletin* 16 (2): 18–24.

———. 1991b. "Summit on the Mining Conference." *South African Labour Bulletin* 15 (8): 45–47.

———. 1993. "Democratisation or Demobilisation? Trade Unions and Transition to Democracy in South Africa, 1985–1994." Master's thesis, University of the Witwatersrand.

Wade, R. 1990. *Governing the Market: Economic Theory and the Role of Government in East Asian Industrialization*. Princeton, N.J.: Princeton University Press.

Wallerstein, I. 1979. *The Capitalist World Economy*. Cambridge, U.K.: Cambridge University Press.

Walton, R. E. 1985. "From Control to Commitment in the Workplace." *Harvard Business Review* 52: 77–84.

Wan, D. T. W., et al. 1989. "Human Resource Management in Singapore: An Overview." *Asia Pacific HRM* 27 (2): 71–86.

Wang, M., and T. Haraguchi. 1990. "An Empirical Study of Employees' Work Motivation in Taiwanese Companies and Japanese Companies in Taiwan" (in Japanese). *Kagoshima Keidai Ronshu* 31 (1): 29–83.

Webster, E. C. 1984. "New Force on the Shop Floor." In *South African Review 2*, edited by G. Moss and I. Obery, 26–190. Johannesburg: Ravan Press.

———. 1985. *Cast in a Racial Mould*. Johannesburg: Ravan Press.

———. 1991. "Taking Labour Seriously." *South African Sociological Review* 4 (1): 61–72.

Webster, E. C., and K. Von Holdt. 1992. "From Resistance to Reconstruction in the South African Labour Movement." Paper presented at the Ruth First Memorial Colloquium, University of the Western Cape, Cape Town.

Weick, K. 1969. *The Social Psychology of Organizing*. Reading, Mass.: Addison-Wesley.

Whalley, J. 1991. "The Multi-fibre Arrangement and China's Growth Prospects." In *New Silk Roads: East Asia and World Textile Markets*, edited by K. Anderson, 78-88. Cambridge, U.K.: Cambridge University Press.

Whitley, R. 1992. *Business Systems in East Asia: Firms, Markets and Societies*. London: Sage.

Wilkinson, B. 1988. "A Comparative Analysis." In *Technological Change, Work Organizations and Pay: Lessons from Asia*, 201–18. Geneva: ILO.

Wilkinson, B., and C. Leggett. 1985. "Human and Industrial Relations in Singapore: The Management of Compliance." *EuroAsia Business Review* 4 (3): 9–15.

304   *References*

Williams, K., J. Williams, and C. Haslam. 1989. "Do Labour Costs Really Matter?" *Work, Employment and Society* 3: 281–305.
Williamson, O. E. 1990. *Organization Theory.* Oxford: Oxford University Press.
Womack, J. P., D. T. Jones, and D. Roos. 1990. *The Machine That Changed the World.* New York: Rawson Associates.
Wong, S. L. 1988. *Emigrant Entrepreneurs: Shanghai Industrialists in Hong Kong.* Hong Kong: Oxford University Press.
———. 1991. "Chinese Entrepreneurs and Business Trust." In *Business Networks and Economic Development in East and Southeast Asia*, edited by G. Hamilton, 13–29. Hong Kong: University of Hong Kong, Centre of Asian Studies.
Working Group on Problems Experienced by Workers of Companies in Receivership. 1983. "Report of the Working Group on Problems Experienced by Workers of Companies in Receivership." Mimeo.
World Bank. 1991. *The Challenge of Development.* Oxford: Oxford University Press.
———. 1992. *World Development Report.* Oxford: Oxford University Press.
———. 1993. *Global Economic Prospects and the Developing Countries.* Washington, D.C.
"World Textiles." 1991. *Financial Times* survey. 3 Oct.
Yellen, J. 1984. "Efficiency Wage Models of Unemployment." *American Economic Association, Papers and Proceedings* 74: 200–205.
Yoffie, D. B. 1983. *Power and Protectionism: Strategies of the Newly Industrializing Countries.* New York: Columbia University Press.
Yong, S. Y. 1987. "Employment Effects of Multinational Enterprises in Malaysia." Working Paper no. 53. ILO Multinational Enterprises Program, Geneva.
Yoo, S. M. 1992. "The Ownership Structure of Korea's Big Business Conglomerates and Its Policy Implications" (in Korean). *Korea Development Institute* 14 (1): 200–19.
Yosamornsunton, A. 1986. "Wages and Working Conditions in the Garment Industry." Master's thesis, Thammasat University.
Zuesongham, S., and V. Charoenloet. 1993. "Fragmentation of the Trade Unions: Inevitably or Not?" Paper presented at conference organized by the Friedrich-Ebert-Stiftung foundation, NICs in Asia: A Challenge to Trade Unions, Singapore, 30 March–1 April.

Contributors

James P. Begin is a professor of industrial relations and human resources at the School of Management and Labor Relations at Rutgers University. The former director of the school, he teaches regularly in Rutgers' master's program in Singapore and has made a significant contribution to the integration of theoretical perspectives on human resources and industrial relations. He has a Ph.D. in industrial relations from Purdue University.

Stephen Chiu is a lecturer in sociology at the Chinese University of Hong Kong. He has a Ph.D. from Princeton University and with David Levin has coauthored several important papers on industrial change and various aspects of labor relations in Hong Kong.

Frederic C. Deyo is a professor of sociology at the State University of New York, Brockport. He has a Ph.D. in sociology from the University of California, Berkeley, and is the editor and author of several well-known publications on East Asia, including *The Political Economy of the New Asian Industrialism* (1987) and *Beneath the Miracle: Labor Subordination in the Asian NICs* (1989).

Stephen Frenkel is a professor at the Centre for Corporate Change in the Australian Graduate School of Management at the University of New South Wales. He has a Ph.D. in economics and politics from Cambridge University. He is the coauthor, with E. Batstone and I. Boraston, of *Shop Stewards in Action* (1975) and, with A. Coolican, of *Unions against Capitalism?* (1984) and is the editor and a contributor to *Organized Labor in the Asia-Pacific Region: A Comparative Study of Trade Unionism in Nine Countries* (1993).

Shane Godfrey is a research associate for the Industrial Relations Project in the Department of Sociology at the University of Cape Town. His research focuses on industrial relations and structural adjustment in South Africa.

Jeffrey Harrod is a professor of international and comparative labor studies at the Institute of Social Studies in The Hague, where he was deputy rector. He has a Ph.D. in political science from the University of Geneva, Switzerland. His major publications include *Trade Union Foreign Policy* (1972), *Power and Production and the Unprotected Worker* (1987), and *Labour and Third World Debt* (1992).

Atsushi Hiramoto is a professor of economics at Tohoku University in Japan. He is a member of a research team that has published extensively in Japanese and German. Among his major recent publications are *Japanisches Personalmanagement—ein anderer Weg?* (1991), coauthored with S. Tokunaga, N. Altmann, and M. Nomura.

Avril Joffe is a lecturer in the Department of Sociology at the University of Witwatersrand in South Africa, where she is completing a Ph.D. and is a member of the Sociology of Work Unit. She codirects the Industrial Strategy Project, a COSATU-commissioned study of the manufacturing sector.

Taigi Kim is a research fellow at the Korea Labor Institute in Seoul. He has a Ph.D. in economics and labor relations from the University of Iowa. He is a leading scholar conducting research and providing advice on Korea's labor market problems and strategy.

Sarosh Kuruvilla is an assistant professor in the School of Industrial and Labor Relations at Cornell University. A specialist in Asian industrial relations, he has a Ph.D. in organizational behavior and industrial relations from the University of Iowa. His work has been published in leading journals.

David A. Levin is a senior lecturer and head of the Department of Sociology at the University of Hong Kong. He has a master's degree in labor and industrial relations from the University of Illinois. Levin is a coeditor (with Y. C. Jao, S. H. Ng, and E. Sinn) of *Labour Movement in a Changing Society* (1988) and the coauthor (with S. Chiu) of "Dependent Capitalism, a Colonial State, and Marginal Unions: The Case of Hong Kong," in *Organized Labor in the Asia-Pacific Region: A Comparative Study of Trade Unionism in Nine Countries* (1993).

Judy Maller was the deputy director of the Sociology of Work Unit in the Department of Sociology at the University of Witwatersrand. She is the author of *Conflict and Cooperation* (1992) and is completing a Ph.D. in industrial sociology. She recently settled in New Zealand, where she continues to work in the industrial relations field.

Johann Maree is an associate professor of sociology and coordinator of the industrial relations project at the University of Cape Town. He has a

Ph.D. in industrial sociology from the University of Cape Town and has written extensively on South African trade unionism. His current research focuses on issues of structural adjustment.

Eddie Webster is a professor of sociology and director of the Sociology of Work Unit at the University of Witwatersrand. He is a prominent figure in debates on South African labor issues and the author of several major publications, including *Cast in a Racial Mould* (1985).

Index

Kalleberg, A., 179
Kampuchea, 3, 13
Kaplinsky, R., 24
Katzenstein, P., 114, 140
Kentucky Fried Chicken, as workers' incentive in Malaysia, 59
Kerr, C.: and convergence theory, 7, 8, 66; and independent nation theory, 5; and perpetuation of elites, 7; and role of elites, 88; and role of labor, 88, 90
Ki-Jang-Ki-Won workers (South Korea), 227
Kim, Taigi, 13, 17, 19–20
Kirkbride, P. S., 86
Knowledge workers, 4
Kochan, T., 179
Kohmu workers (Japan), 242–43
Kojyo-gijutsu workers (Japan), 242
Kōkyu-Jimuin workers (Japan), 247
Korea. *See* South Korea
Kreye, O., 154
Kuomintang party (Taiwan), 196, 197
Kuruvilla, Sarosh, 8, 11, 17

Labor, as a tradable commodity, 19
Labor disputes. *See* Strikes
Laboria Minute (South Africa), 99
Labor relations systems, 5
Labor Standards Law of 1984 (Taiwan), 204
Labor subjugation, 5
Labor weakness, 12
Labour Advisory Board (Hong Kong), 274n. 23
Labour Relations Act of 1981 (South Africa), 95, 99
Labour Relations Amendment (LRA) of 1988 (South Africa), 98, 99
Late developing countries, 232
Latin America: critical historical junctures in, 13, 39; industrialization of, 6–7
Lauridsen, L., 37
Layoffs: in Hong Kong textile industry, 160, 169; in Malaysia, 197; in Taiwan, 197
Lean production systems, 9, 10, 19, 180–84, 207–8, 210, 212, 213–14
Legislative Council (Hong Kong), 153, 274n. 23
Levin, David A., 7, 11, 17, 19
Littler, C., 58
Local innovators, 186
Long Term Arrangement (LTA) regarding International Trade in Cotton Textiles (1962), 152, 153

"Look East" policy (Malaysia), 54
LRA. *See* Labour Relations Amendment (LRA) of 1988 (South Africa)
LTA. *See* Long Term Arrangement (LTA) regarding International Trade in Cotton Textiles (1962)
Lui, T., 158

Mabry, B., 29
MAEI. *See* Malaysian American Electronics Industry (MAEI) trade group
Mahathir Mohammed, 44, 54
Malaysia: compared to South Africa, 264n. 9; convergence in, 8; cost-cutting strategies in, 33; discrimination in, 264n. 9; economic development strategies in, 17–18, 40–47; economic growth of, 3, 40, 42, 196; electronics industry in, 44, 46–47, 49, 59–60; ethnic divisions in, 39, 40–41, 42–43, 44, 193, 197, 253; export-oriented industrialization (EOI) in, 17–18, 39, 44–47, 48–51, 53, 56, 61, 62; flexible production in, 36; foreign debt of, 44, 45; foreign investment in, 12, 40, 42, 44, 45–46, 48, 49, 62; human resource management (HRM) in, 59–61; import-substitution industrialization (ISI) in, 17, 39, 41–44, 47–48, 53, 62; influence of MNCs in, 11, 18; infrastructure of, 40; MNC subsidiaries in, 11, 19, 20, 50–51, 56, 180, 188, 192–215, 237, 238–39, 242, 250–58, 259; plantations in, 56, 62; political turmoil in, 42; privatization of industries in, 45; restricted pluralism in, 47–48, 62; social progress in, 3; standard of living in, 12; state intervention in development in, 43–45, 47–56; textile industry in, 44, 127, 154; trade unions in, 17–18, 37, 40, 44, 47–48, 50–51, 52–60, 62, 196–97, 202, 203, 209, 254, 255–56
Malaysian Airlines (MAS), 51, 60
Malaysian American Electronics Industry (MAEI) trade group, 50–51
Malaysian Industrial Development Finance Corporation, 42
Malaysian-Japanese Chamber of Commerce and Industry, 255
Malaysian Labour Organization (MLO), 55, 57

Nationalism: in Malaysia, 43, 44; rise of, 3; in South Africa, 119

National Labor Relations Act (U.S.), 63

National Labour Court (Thailand), 28

National Manpower Commission (South Africa), 99, 105

National Productivity Board (NPB) (Singapore), 74, 77, 266–67n. 9, 268n. 17; Task Force on Job-Hopping, 77–78, 81–82, 268n. 19

National Trade Union Congress (NTUC) (Singapore), 64–65, 73

National Training Board (South Africa), 105

National Union of Garment Workers (South Africa), 132

National Union of Metalworkers of South Africa, 103, 106

National Union of Mineworkers (NUM) (South Africa), 97–98, 103–6

National Union of Newspaper Workers (Malaysia), 55

National Union of Textile Workers (NUTW) (South Africa), 120, 131–32

National University of Singapore (NUS), 266n. 7

National Wages Council (NWC) (Singapore), 65, 72, 73, 77–78, 80

Nation-states, fragmentation of, 14

NCF. *See* National Clothing Federation (NCF) (South Africa)

NEF. *See* National Economic Forum (NEF) (South Africa)

Neoclassical economics, 83

Neo-Confucianism, 143

Neo-Taylorism, 4, 10, 19, 180–83, 186, 207, 208–11, 213–14

NEP. *See* New economic policy (NEP), Malaysian

"Network of rules" framework, 66–67

New economic policy (NEP), Malaysian, 42–45, 51

New international division of labor (NIDL) theory, 38

Newly industrialized countries (NICs): achieving status of, 35; dependency of, 145; economic growth of, 14, 23–24; economic success of, 3; egalitarian nature of industrialization in, 6; examples of, 4; labor costs in, 14, 16; manufacturing in, 10; standard of living in, 14

NICs. *See* Newly industrialized countries (NICs)

NICTEX. *See* National Industrial Council for the Textile Industry (NICTEX) (South Africa)

NIDL. *See* New international division of labor (NIDL) theory

Nigeria, 13

NPB. *See* National Productivity Board (NPB) (Singapore)

NTUC. *See* National Trade Union Congress (NTUC) (Singapore)

NUM. *See* National Union of Mineworkers (NUM) (South Africa)

Numerical flexibility (internal and external), in Singapore, 67, 81

NUTW. *See* National Union of Textile Workers (NUTW) (South Africa)

NWC. *See* National Wages Council (NWC) (Singapore)

OECD. *See* Organization for Economic Cooperation and Development (OECD)

Organization for Economic Cooperation and Development (OECD), 154, 265n. 1

Organization for European Economic Cooperation, 152

Organization-oriented enterprise, 8

Pakistan, 28

Pan African Congress (South Africa), 98

Pang Eng Fong, 64

PAP. *See* People's Action Party (PAP) (Singapore)

Patel, E., 134–39, 271n. 13

Patriarchy, 12

Patrimonialism, 12

Peak federations, in Malaysia, 47

Peanut unions, 196

People's Action Party (PAP) (Singapore), 64

Peripheral (underdeveloped) countries, 6, 10, 38

Peripheral fordism, 10

Petroleum Development Act of 1976 (Malaysia), 43

Pharmaceutical industry, MNC subsidiaries in, 186–90

Philippines: as competitor with other Asian NICs, 61; industrial restructuring in, 39; textile industry in, 127, 154